IDEOLOGIES OF CONSERVATISM

Ideologies of Conservatism

Conservative Political Ideas in the Twentieth Century

E. H. H. GREEN

OXFORD

UNIVERSITY PRESS

OXFORD

UNIVERSITY PRESS

Great Clarendon Street, Oxford OX2 6DP

Oxford University Press is a department of the University of Oxford.
It furthers the University's objective of excellence in research, scholarship,
and education by publishing worldwide in

Oxford New York

Athens Auckland Bangkok Bogotá Buenos Aires Cape Town
Chennai Dar es Salaam Delhi Florence Hong Kong Istanbul   Karachi
Kolkata Kuala Lumpur Madrid Melbourne Mexico City Mumbai Nairobi
Paris São Paulo Shanghai Singapore Taipei Tokyo Toronto Warsaw

and associated companies in Berlin Ibadan

Oxford is a registered trade mark of Oxford University Press
in the UK and in certain other countries

Published in the United States
by Oxford University Press Inc., New York

British Library Cataloguing in Publication Data

Data available

Library of Congress Cataloging in Publication Data
Green, E.H.H., 1958–
Ideologies of conservatism/E.H.H. Green.
p. cm.
Includes bibliographical references and index.
1. Conservatism—Great Britain—History. I. Title.
JC573.2.G7 G74 2002   320.52'0941—dc21   2001036388
ISBN 0-19-820593-7

1 3 5 7 9 10 8 6 4 2

Typeset in Sabon by
Cambrian Typesetters, Frimley, Surrey
Printed in Great Britain
on acid-free paper by
T.J. International Ltd,
Padstow, Cornwall

TO CLARE

Acknowledgements

THE FINAL ADJUSTMENTS to this book were made shortly after my partner and I returned from Thanksgiving in Atlanta. This was a fitting coincidence, because my main desire on completing this study is to give thanks. My first are to a number of institutions, without whose assistance this book would not have been attempted let alone completed. The President and Fellows of Magdalen College and the Modern History Faculty at Oxford University granted me leave to complete the research and undertake the writing of this book. The Arts and Humanities Research Board funded leave to match that provided by my institutions, for which I am very grateful. In the Fall Semester of 1997 the Minda de Gunzberg Center for European Studies at Harvard University elected me to a Visiting Fellowship, during which time the first chapters were written, and I shall always look back on the time that I spent there with both nostalgia and gratitude. I have benefited from the assistance of the librarians at the Widener Library at Harvard, the Bodleian Library at Oxford, Magdalen College, and the archivists at King's College, London. I would like to express particular thanks to the staff of Room 132 at the Bodleian, especially Colin Harris and Nicky Kennan, and to the archivist of the Conservative party, Jill Davidson Spellman, who all made my research much easier to carry out. Last, but by no means least, I am grateful to the Neurology Department of the Radcliffe Infirmary, and especially to my Consultant Richard Greenhall. Without their assistance it would not have been physically possible for me to undertake this project, and I owe them a great debt.

Many fellow historians have offered assistance to this project, both during its progress and following its completion. Peter Clarke has, as always, been generous with his time, advice, and support, and his comments on the manuscript both in progress and when complete were particularly helpful. My colleagues at Magdalen—Laurence Brockliss, John Nightingale, Nick Stargardt, and Peter Grieder—offered both intellectual and practical support which was well beyond the 'call of duty' during the time that this book was being constructed, and I shall always be grateful for their demonstrations that 'collegiality' is not merely a formal expression. Other colleagues, both within my own institution and in others, have given great support to the project. Jose Harris, Ross Mckibbin, and Peter Ghosh in Oxford, Dave Jarvis in Cambridge, John Ramsden in London, Peter Weiler and Jim Cronin in Boston, Jon Schneer in Atlanta, and Stephen Brooke at York (Ontario) have all contributed greatly to this book through sharing their time, ideas, and research with generosity and warmth. What I owe to other historians will, I hope, be clear from the book's 'scholarly apparatus'. Of course the book's final form is down to OUP, and I am grateful to the staff there, especially my editor Ruth Parr and her assistant Anne Gelling, and my copy-editor Jeff New, who have been both supportive of the project, and very responsive to my requests with regard to the book's structure and appearance.

Other friends, both inside and outside the academic world, have made major contributions to the book, both in terms of stimulating helpful ideas and providing an atmosphere condusive to its writing. Alex Thompson, Sarah Spiller, Rob Hughes, Zoe Penn, Laura Frader, Maria Tippett, Stewart Wood, Camilla Bustani, Tom Kuhn, Myfanwy Lloyd, Cecile Fabre, Gordon Milne, Jo Denton, Amy Black, Sarah Fitzpatrick, Grev Healey, Sophia Parker, Kate Bell, Rachel Smith, Hester Barron, Meredith Nelson, Bob Dewey, Illimar Ploom and Gooding have all assisted me hugely. If they should feel that for me to list them in this way is to make them seem like 'third man at lunch counter' I hope they will forgive me, and that they will know that the reference to a medium we all adore is very much intended as a compliment. Lastly I must say a sad thank you to my 'best friend' Sheba, who joined us from the Blue Cross as I began planning the book and who died two months after it was completed. Her companionship and her warm, amusing presence made a great contribution to both work and to essential distractions. Readers familiar with the similar section of my first book will be reassured to hear that, like her predecessor, she talked more sense than the Education Minister.

Finally, I would like to extend my heartfelt thanks to my family—my mother, Simon and Rachel Green, and Colin and Jean, Chris, Sarah, Katharine, and Julia Brant—all of whom have provided invaluable practical and emotional support during the times when my illness has been in a progressive phase and in the quieter times when they have helped take my mind off the travails that are to come. The kindness of the Brants has, not for the first time, reminded me how lucky I am to share my life and work with Clare Brant. The simplest, fullest statement I can make about what I owe to her is the book's dedication.

Oxford
March 2001

Contents

Introduction   1

1. 'No Settled Convictions'? Arthur Balfour, Political
   Economy, and Tariff Reform: A Reconsideration   18

2. English Idealism, Conservatism, and Collectivism,
   1880–1914   42

3. An Intellectual in Conservative Politics:
   The Case of Arthur Steel-Maitland   72

4. Conservatism, Anti-Socialism, and the End of the
   Lloyd George Coalition   114

5. The Battle of the Books: Book Clubs and Conservatism
   in the 1930s   135

6. Searching for the Middle Way: The Political Economy
   of Harold Macmillan   157

7. The Treasury Resignations of 1958: A Reconsideration   192

8. Thatcherism: A Historical Perspective   214

9. Conservatism, the State, and Civil Society in the
   Twentieth Century   240

10. Conclusion   280

BIBLIOGRAPHY   291

INDEX   305

Introduction

THE CONSERVATIVE party's success in the twentieth century was remarkable. Between 1900 and 2000 the Conservatives were in office, either alone or in coalition governments which they dominated, for sixty-eight years. This tenure of power was a reflection of the party's electoral strength. In fourteen of the twenty-six general elections held over the century the Conservatives secured handsome majorities, and in a further eight they remained either the largest parliamentary party or restricted their main opponents to narrow majorities. On only four occasions—1906, 1945, 1966, and 1997—did the Conservatives experience severe electoral defeats. This electoral success reflected the party's popular appeal. Throughout the century the Conservatives consistently won at least 40 per cent of the popular vote, generally gained a considerably higher share, and their vote only fell below this level on three occasions. Small wonder that in political terms the twentieth century has been labelled 'the Conservative century'.[1]

Until the last decade of the century the Conservatives' success was an under-studied phenomenon. Prior to the 1990s there were relatively few major surveys of the twentieth-century party, even for those periods where the thirty-year rule on access to government records was not an inhibiting factor and where other sources were plentiful. In the 1990s, however, study of the party burgeoned. The completion of the semi-official, multi-volume history of the party from its nineteenth-century origins to 1975 was an important historiographical landmark, but a steady stream of other studies flowed from the presses.[2] Whether scholars used

[1] A. Seldon and S. Ball (eds.), *Conservative Century: The Conservative Party Since 1900* (Oxford, 1994).

[2] Additions to the semi-official history were R. Shannon, *The Age of Disraeli, 1868–81* (1992); id., *The Age of Salisbury, 1882–1902* (1995); J. Ramsden, *The Age of Churchill and Eden, 1940–57* (1995); id., *Winds of Change: From Macmillan to Heath, 1957–75* (1996). (Place of publication is London unless otherwise shown.) A selection of other works published includes E. H. H. Green, *The Crisis of Conservatism: The Politics, Economics and Ideology of the British Conservative Party, 1880–1914*; M. Fforde, *Conservatism and Collectivism, 1880–1914* (Edinburgh, 1990); F. Coetzee, *For Party or Country: Nationalism and the Dilemmas of Popular Conservatism in Edwardian England* (Oxford, 1990); N. McCrillis, *The British Conservative Party in the Age of Universal Suffrage: Popular Conservatism, 1918–29* (Columbus, Ohio, 1998); M. Francis and I. Zweiniger-Bargielowska (eds.), *The Conservatives and British Society, 1880–1990* (Cardiff, 1996); R. Lamb, *The Macmillan Years: The Emerging Truth* (Basingstoke, 1997); P. Murphy, *Party Politics and Decolonization: The Conservative Party and British Colonial Policy in Tropical Africa, 1951–1964* (Oxford, 1995); N. J. Crowson, *Facing Fascism: The Conservative Party and the European Dictators, 1935–40*

the traditional sources of the archival historian or deployed the more diverse tools of the contemporary historian, the result was that no period in the twentieth-century, party's history, from the end of the Salisburyian era to the fall of John Major's administration, remained historical *terra incognita*.

But if the history of the Conservative party as a political *institution* attracted a lot of attention as the 'Conservative century' drew to a close, the same thing could not be said about Conservative *ideas*. This is not to say that Conservative thought in Britain has been completely over-looked. A number of political scientists and political philosophers have produced studies which have addressed British Conservatism as a system of ideas, but important as this work has been it has not, in some important respects, compensated for the relative neglect of Conservative thought.[3] To begin with, the volume of work devoted to British Conservatism is far outweighed by that which has dealt with British Liberalism and Socialism. Furthermore, these studies have been over-whelmingly concerned with the *formal*, doctrinal aspects of Conservative thought rather than with the historical presentation and reception of Conservative ideas. To use the terminology deployed by the political scientist Martin Seliger, it is the 'fundamental' rather than the 'operative' aspects of Conservative thought that have been the focus for political science and political philosophy.[4] With very few exceptions, *historians* of the Conservatives have devoted little time to the party's ideas, and thus whilst the *logic* of Conservative ideology has been explored the *logic of the situation* that Conservatives faced at different times, and how this influenced and was in turn influenced by Conservative thought, has received scant attention.

One reason for this relative neglect was the puzzlingly long-lived notion that, somehow, the Conservative party was 'non-ideological'. J. S. Mill famously described the Conservative party as 'the stupidest party', and although he was being abusive there was a serious point which underlay his remark, namely that the Conservatives were not interested in deep reflection on the meaning of politics and, unlike Mill's own party, were not concerned with articulating a set of principles to

---

(1997); A. Seldon (ed.), *How Tory Governments Fall* (1996); J. Ramsden, *An Appetitite For Power* (1998); A. Clark, *The Tories: Conservatives and the Nation State, 1922–1997* (1998); P. Williamson, *National Crisis and National Government: British Politics, the Economy and Empire, 1926–32* (Cambridge, 1992); id., *Stanley Baldwin* (Cambridge, 1999). The literature on the Thatcher and Major years is too extensive to summarize.

[3] N. O'Sullivan, *Conservatism* (1976); A. Quinton, *The Politics of Imperfection* (1978); W. H. Greenleaf, *The British Political Tradition*, 3 vols. (1981–3), vol. 2, *The Ideological Heritage*; R. Scruton, *The Meaning of Conservatism* (1980); T. Honderich, *Conservatism* (1990); M. Freeden, *Ideologies and Political Theory* (Oxford, 1996).

[4] M. Seliger, *Ideology and Politics* (1976).

explain or legitimate their political behaviour. For Mill, who was able to gaze across the Commons at the ruddy-faced, 'booby' squires who swelled the benches of the mid-Victorian Conservative party, such a view was perhaps understandable, but his view of the Conservatives as a party essentially uninterested in ideas was to be oft-repeated by subsequent commentators, not least by many Conservatives. For example, in the 1920s the Conservative politician Walter Elliot noted that Conservatism was based on 'an observation of life and not *a priori* reasoning',[5] and the Conservative writer John Buchan stated that Conservatism was 'above all things a spirit not an abstract doctrine'.[6] In the later twentieth century Sir Ian (later Lord) Gilmour declared that whatever else it was Conservatism was 'not an ideology or a doctrine',[7] and one of the authors of the party's semi-official history wrote that '*A History of the Conservative Party* . . . does not owe much to the work of philosophers'.[8] Nor was it only Conservatives and Conservative sympathizers who took this view, for one Marxisant scholar of Conservatism contended that 'the Tory tradition is not best understood as a tradition of ideas'.[9]

This conception of Conservatism as a form of 'non ideology' was strange. To begin with it assumed that in some way the Conservative party was fundamentally different in its basic structure to the Liberals, Labour, or indeed any other political party in Britain or elsewhere, a position that is very difficult to sustain. Furthermore, there is the point that a distrust of an 'intellectual' approach to politics, or a definition of oneself as 'non-ideological', are important ideological statements which express a distinctive Conservative view about the nature of and proper approach to politics. Equally important, however, is the fact that although Conservatives may have largely (but not entirely) eschewed *formal* statements of political belief, such statements are not the be-all and end-all of political ideas. Beyond the territory of formal statements lies a hinterland of rhetoric, values, and received ideas, which may be expressed in day-to-day political argument, speeches, correspondence, and legislative acts. 'Great thinkers and their texts' may not be as frequently referred to by Conservatives as by their political opponents, but Conservatives do possess, indeed *must* possess, an ideological map of the world which enables them to identify objects of approval and disapproval, friend and foe. If politics is essentially about defining and finding solutions to a set of problems, then Conservative politicians

[5] W. Elliot, *Toryism and the Twentieth Century* (1927), 4.
[6] J. Buchan, Preface to A. Bryant, *The Spirit of Conservatism* (1929), p. vii.
[7] I. Gilmour, *Inside Right* (1980 edn.), 121.
[8] J. Ramsden, *The Age of Balfour and Baldwin* (1978), p. ix.
[9] A. Gamble, *The Conservative Nation* (1974), 2.

have to find ways of exploring and solving problems in a way that is
recognizably Conservative to an audience of adherents and potential
adherents, and it is difficult to achieve this unless there exists a frame of
reference which identifies what the term Conservative means.

This lacuna in the history of the Conservative party with regard to
Conservative ideology was thrown into relief by the advent and devel-
opment of Thatcherism. During the leadership of Margaret Thatcher
the Conservative party became self-professedly 'ideological'. Margaret
Thatcher herself remarked that as the Labour party had an ideology the
Conservatives needed one too, and a number of groups and 'think
tanks' sought to provide the Conservatives under Thatcher with just
such an ideological cutting edge, notably the Institute for Economic
Affairs, the Centre for Policy Studies, the Adam Smith Institute, and the
Conservative Philosophy Group.[10] On issues as diverse as monetarist
and liberal market economics, the position of trade unions, the provi-
sion of welfare, health and education, and the nature of the family,
Conservative writers and thinkers, both individually and collectively,
engaged self-consciously in a 'battle of ideas'. A central issue in this
battle was the nature of Conservatism itself. Sir Keith (later Lord)
Joseph, a leading Thatcherite, remarked in 1975 that: 'It was only in
April 1974 that I was converted to Conservatism. I had thought that I
was a Conservative but I now see that I was not one at all.'[11] Given that
Joseph had been active in Conservative politics for many years, this was
in some respects an extraordinary statement, for it implied that the
party he had long been a member of, and the policies of the
Conservative governments he had supported as a voter and a backbench
MP, had not been truly Conservative. For Joseph, and other
Thatcherites, the post-1975 Conservative party had discovered, or
rediscovered, the true meaning of Conservatism. Precisely the opposite
view was articulated by Conservative critics of Thatcherism, with Sir
Ian Gilmour providing perhaps the most fluent and sustained statement
of the case that it was the Thatcherites who were not true
Conservatives.[12] Gilmour's position is particularly interesting, given his
comment (cited above) that Conservatism was 'not an ideology or a
doctrine', for if in his view Thatcherism was *not* Conservatism then he
also had to have a view about what was Conservatism, in which case a
Conservative doctrine or ideology had to have existed from which
Thatcherism had departed. Gilmour's objection to Thatcherism could

---

[10] For the think-tanks see R. Cockett, *Thinking the Unthinkable* (1994).
[11] K. Joseph, *Reversing the Trend* (1975), in M. Halcrow, *Keith Joseph: A Single Mind*
(1989), 56.
[12] For Gilmour's position see I. Gilmour, *Britain Can Work* (Oxford, 1982); id., *Dancing
With Dogma* (1992).

have been that its self-consciously 'ideological' approach to politics was *in itself* what made it un-Conservative, but his critique was targeted at the *kind* of ideology Thatcherism embodied in its social, economic, and political actions rather than simply at its willingness to be ideological. For students of Conservatism as well as Conservative politicians, Thatcherism posed important problems. If Thatcherism was to be properly situated then one did indeed need to know what Conservatism had been, and this required serious consideration of the history of Conservative ideas.

Study of Conservative intra-party debate throughout the party's history, and especially over the course of the 'Conservative century', reveals that the controversy over Conservative ideas in the last quarter of the twentieth century was not unique in terms of either its nature or intensity. In the decade before the Great War the Conservative party engaged in prolonged internal debate over, most obviously, the question of tariff reform. But tariff reform encompassed several issues, notably social reform, imperial relations, land reform, industrial and agricultural performance, and the Irish question, all of which had clear implications for the nature and meaning of Conservatism.[13] The range and depth of the Conservatives' internal debate was not surprising, for the party faced major challenges to its identity. As the party of property it had to confront the challenge of Socialism as embodied in the newly emerged Labour party and the fiscal strategy of the New Liberalism. As the party of Empire it had to deal with the fact that Britain faced the growing external challenge of rival powers to Britain's hegemony, and also the internal pressure of the rise of national aspirations in the self-governing Colonies. As the party of the land it was faced with disaffection in rural areas that stemmed from the ongoing fall in agricultural prices, especially in arable districts. As the main party of business it had to contend with concern in a number of industries over the growth of foreign competition and import penetration, trends which led some to talk in terms of British economic decline. Furthermore, as the party of anything the Conservatives had to win elections, and this proved to be the Edwardian party's most intractable problem.[14]

Conservatives at all levels in the party articulated their ideas on how best to respond to these issues in a variety of ways. The period 1900–14 saw a host of books and pamphlets published that engaged with the whole gamut of questions the party faced. Arthur Balfour, the

---

[13] See Green, *Crisis*, *passim*, and Fforde, *Conservatism*, *passim*, for studies of the period which, albeit from very different perspectives, see the party's internal debate in terms of Conservative ideas.
[14] See Green, *Crisis*, *passim*.

Conservative leader from 1902 to 1911, and Prime Minister from 1902 to 1906, produced his own *Economic Notes on Insular Free Trade* in 1904, and in both public and private debate in the ensuing years developed a distinctive position on the tariff question and its meaning for Conservative economic philosophy.[15] Other members of the Conservative hierarchy, although they did not share Balfour's predilection for intellectual debate, also developed clear positions on the tariff question,[16] unavoidably inasmuch as it was impossible for an Edwardian Conservative to avoid taking a stance on tariff reform. Nor was this trend confined to the party leadership, for some members of the lower ranks of the parliamentary party were moved to publish their ideas on the question, with Arthur Fell producing *The Failure of Free Trade* in 1903, *Fallacies of Free Trade* in 1905, and *The Profit and Loss Account of England's Foreign Trade* in 1907, Alfred Bigland publishing *England's Future Under Tariff Reform* in 1907, and George Tryon his *Tariff Reform* in 1908.[17] If one adds the writings of Conservative economists, journalists, and other publicists to the written and spoken views of Conservative politicians, the tariff issue probably saw the largest outpouring of Conservative opinion ever expressed on any subject in the party's history. But, as noted above, tariff reform was inextricably linked to a gamut of other questions which also generated a considerable flow of Conservative thought. Within the parliamentary party one group of MPs produced an 'Unauthorised Programme' of policy proposals in 1908, published in the *Morning Post*, which sought to define the Conservative position and principles on a range of economic and social questions.[18] The same year saw the publication of *The New Order*, a collection of essays on various policy issues written by members of the secret internal party pressure group, the Confederacy. After 1912 the Unionist Social Reform Committee (USRC) engaged in lengthy and detailed discussions on questions of social policy, produced publications on *Poor Law Reform* and *Industrial Unrest*, and was engaged in an in-depth study of the provision of health care at the time of the outbreak of war in 1914. Indeed, the USRC's activities saw the earliest, detailed discussion of Conservative principles concerning the role of the State in the provision of social welfare. Outside the official party, the Compatriots Club, founded in 1904 and made up of a membership of Conservative MPs, academics, journalists, and writers, functioned as a

[15] See Ch. 1.

[16] Principally in their speeches.

[17] Fell was MP for Great Yarmouth, Bigland for Birkenhead, and Tryon for Brighton. Of the three only Tryon was to gain junior office in the inter-war years.

[18] The title of the programme was simply 'Unionism'. For its genesis and contents see Green, *Crisis*, 148–9, 255–60.

a form of 'think tank' to generate Conservative ideas on the economy, imperial relations, defence, and other issues.[19] At the same time a 'legion of leagues' on the fringes of the party—the Anti-Socialist Union, the Tariff Reform League, the British Constitutional Association, the Navy League, the Imperial Maritime League, the National Service League, the Middle Class Defence League—all generated both discussion and publication of Conservative ideas on their subject interests.[20] Particular issues, even fads, were a focus for a number of Conservatives, but there was also a sense within the party of the connection between many of the issues at stake. Books like Lord Hugh Cecil's *Conservatism* (1912), F. E. Smith's *Unionist Policy and Other Essays* (1912), Leo Amery's *Union and Strength* (1912), Alfred Milner's *The Nation and the Empire* (1914), and Keith Feiling's *Tory Democracy* (1914) all traversed the full range of questions confronting the party and viewed them in terms of their implications for the meaning of Conservatism. But although there may have been a shared sense of the 'holistic' nature of the overall issue at stake, this by no means meant that there was a shared 'holistic' conclusion as to what represented 'true' Conservatism, a point that was made very clear by Lord Hugh Cecil in a memorandum to his brother in January 1915. 'There is nothing very serious', Lord Hugh stated,

which divides us from them [Andrew Bonar Law and Austen Chamberlain] except the almost decayed barrier of Tariff Reform. But there is a section of their supporters with whom I do not think it would be ever possible for me to work, and past experience shows that the section has had great influence with both Bonar and Austen and may still exercise a dangerous power over them. This is the section represented by the Morning Post and by Leo [Maxse] in the National Review. The particular point about which we have disagreed in the past is Tariff Reform, but it is not a single issue but the whole attitude they adopt towards politics which is intolerable. I cannot read either the National Review or the Morning Post without being driven into violent antagonism. Even when I agree with the conclusion, the reasons and method of argument are such as to make me hate my own opinions. And upon two great issues which must arise in the future in many political controversies, I disagree vehemently with the principles advocated in the M. P. and the N. R. Briefly I hate Nationalism and I value personal liberty. Over the whole sphere of foreign politics, national defence and social reform, these two principles would bring me into strong controversy with the type of Imperialist to which I am referring.[21]

---

[19] For the Compatriots see ibid. 161–2, 177, 182, 225, 250, 282, and id., (ed.), *Compatriots Club Lectures* (1905, 1998 edn.).

[20] See Coetzee, *Party or Country, passim.*

[21] Lord Hugh Cecil, Memorandum to Lord Robert Cecil, 10 Jan. 1915, Cecil of Chelwood papers, BL Add. MSS, 51157.

Written as it was at a point when, of course, all political differences had been set aside for the sake of wartime unity, Hugh Cecil's memorandum indicated that the battle of ideas within the Edwardian Conservative party was neither forgotten nor over. Particular and immediate differences may have subsided, but underlying tensions remained, and just as wartime did not bring peace within the party, peacetime opened the way to the revival of old and the emergence of new conflicts.

The inter-war years seem at first glance to be an unpromising era for the study of Conservative thought, insofar as the party's apparently almost seamless political and electoral dominance of the period might lead one to think that there was little need or even incentive for Conservatives to engage in self-examination. But in spite of their ascendancy, inter-war Conservatives by no means felt secure about their ability to sustain their position in a new electoral structure in which they were faced by new political enemies and fluid and increasingly difficult economic and diplomatic circumstances. The emergence of Labour as the main political force on the Left meant Conservatives had to consider how to confront Socialism in a new, more threatening guise. The onset of economic recession after 1921, the difficulties faced by Britain's staple industries, the attendant social and economic consequences of long-term mass unemployment and industrial unrest, and finally the Slump were economic problems of a nature and scale previously unknown. At the same time as they wrestled with these domestic challeges Conservatives had to cope with the question of how to govern Britain's vast Empire and then deal with the rise of Fascist aggression in Europe and Japanese imperialism in the Pacific. All of these problems excited concern amongst, and demanded consideration by, Conservative leaders and led and—equally important—prompted an ongoing and often intense dialogue between the two as to what constituted the best, and most recognizably Conservative, response. Conservative ideas in this context were, as before the Great War, expressed sometimes in pamphlets and books, but also in discussions within the party's policy-making apparatus, in the speeches and correspondence of party leaders, at party conferences, and doubtless in conversations at the countless whist drives held by local Conservative associations.

As in the pre-war decade, the inter-war years saw the publication of a screed of Conservative texts that generated much discussion within the party at the time and in subsequent years, notably Noel Skelton's *Constructive Conservatism* (1924), Robert Boothby, Harold Macmillan, John Loder, and Oliver Stanley's *Industry and the State* (1927), Walter Elliot's *Toryism and the Twentieth Century* (1927), Arthur Bryant's *The Spirit of Conservatism* (1929), and Harold Macmillan's *The Middle Way* (1938). But such formal statements of Conservative ideas by no means represented the inter-war party's only engagement in intellectual activity. The Conservative Research Department (CRD) was founded in 1929 to play a key role in the Conservatives' policy-making machinery. As such it was part of the party bureaucracy, but it would be a mistake to define its activities narrowly in such terms. The CRD sought to construct policy ideas in response to issues and problems that were distinctively and recognizably Conservative. A case in point was the CRD Committee on 'Future Relations Between the State and Industry', which was instructed by Neville Chamberlain to examine this question and define an approach 'in keeping with Conservative tradition'.[22] Outside the formal party machinery, the Conservatives established the Bonar Law Memorial College at Ashridge in 1928 as a centre of political education where party activists and members, and also a broader public audience, could attend lectures and take part in discussions on political questions given and led by Conservative speakers and publicists. Ashridge was designed as a Conservative answer to the Labour party's educational activities and the Liberal summer schools, and its activities were described by its main educational director as performing the same role as the Fabian Society had for Socialism.[23] In the same vein two Conservative book clubs, the Right Book Club (RBC) and the National Book Association (NBA), were brought into being in 1937–8, both regarded by their organizers as a means of countering the influence of Victor Gollancz's Left Book Club (LBC).

One of the main instigators of the NBA was Stanley Baldwin, who also became the club's honorary president in 1938. Baldwin's actions here offer some interesting insights into the milieu of Conservative ideas in the inter-war period. Throughout his career Baldwin worked hard to present himself as a simple, straightforward man who was non- or even anti-intellectual. Yet one of the reasons the main organizer of the NBA, the historian and Ashridge lecturer Arthur Bryant, approached Baldwin to become the club's president was because Baldwin had indicated his wish to dedicate his retirement years to political education,[24] a strange desire on the part of someone uninterested in ideas. A further illustration of this 'contradiction' appeared in one Conservative's reminiscences of Baldwin in the mid-1950s. Henry Paul, writing to Walter Monckton, recalled the former editor of *The Times*, Geoffrey Dawson, telling him that what Baldwin had liked most was 'sitting down with Edward Wood on one side of him and Steel-Maitland on the other and having a good

---

[22] Draft Report of Sub Committee 'A' to Conservative Central Committee, 28 Nov. 1934, CPA, CRD 1/65/2.
[23] A. Bryant, Memorandum, 13 June 1928, ABP, C13.
[24] See pp. 146–8.

talk about the future of the Conservative party. Not that Baldwin sa[id] much. He ma[de] the other two talk, From time to time he [took] his pipe out of his mouth and sa[id] "Damn Joynson-Hicks".'[25] This appears to confirm Baldwin's representation of himself, and the unsympathetic post-war view of him, as somewhat of a 'duffer' who was not the equal of 'clever' members of his own or any other party. Yet, again, if he was so uninterested or unable to engage in the exchange of ideas, why was this one of the things he most liked to do? Baldwin's seemingly contradictory behaviour was in fact no such thing. He was, as a recent study has shown, a well-read, thoughtful politician with a deep interest in ideas,[26] but had a suspicion of 'bookish', abstract intellectualism. Nor was Baldwin the only member of the Conservative leadership to hold this prejudice. One of his predecessors as leader, who also served as Foreign Secretary in Baldwin's second administration, Austen Chamberlain, declared in a speech in the Commons in 1924:

I profoundly distrust logic when applied to politics, and all English history justifies me . . . It is because instinct and experience alike teach us that human nature is not logical, that it is unwise to treat political institutions as instruments of logic [and] that it is in wisely refraining from pressing conclusions to their logical end that the path of peaceful development and true reform is really found.[27]

For Chamberlain, like Baldwin, politics not only demanded that Conservatives think through their particular responses to particular questions, but also that they consider how to think politically at all, and thereby construct and articulate a distinctive mode of Conservative thought.

The 1940s, and the turmoil of war, electoral defeat, and post-war reconstruction, saw the Conservative party engage in an extensive, self-conscious examination of the basis of Conservatism. During the war itself Conservatives were forced, most obviously by the emergence of post-war reconstruction plans such as the Beveridge Report, the 1944 White Paper on Employment, the Uthwatt Report, and the Education Act of 1944, to consider the Conservative position on the governance of the economy, social policy, and the balance between individual liberty, civic groups, and State authority. The Conservatives did not produce a unified response to these questions, but spoke in a babel of often conflicting voices, ranging from the libertarian stance espoused by the wartime party Chairman Ralph Assheton, to the interventionist stance

---

[25] H. Paul to W. Monckton, 26 Sept. 1955, Monckton papers, Bodleian Library, Oxford, Dep. Monckton 5, fo. 202.
[26] See Williamson, *Baldwin*.
[27] Quoted in C. Petrie, *The Chamberlain Tradition* (1938), 76–7.

adopted by members of the Tory Reform Committee.[28] In the wake of the 1945 general election defeat the party, at all levels, reconsidered its position on many specific legislative questions, but also engaged in a general re-examination of Conservative thought. As in the pre-1914 and inter-war years, some notable individual texts were produced, such as Leo Amery's *The Conservative Future* (1946), David Clarke's *The Conservative Faith in a Modern Age* (1947), and Quentin Hogg's *The Case For Conservatism* (1947), but, again as in the earlier periods, it was the broader scope of Conservative activity that was more significant. R. A. Butler was appointed head of the CRD in November 1945, and immediately set in train a series of policy studies which were to produce *The Industrial Charter* (1947), *The Agricultural Charter* (1948), and *The Right Road For Britain* (1949). Butler himself described his vision of the CRD's activities in this period in terms of its being a 'thinking machine', charged with the task of formulating a clear and cogent set of responses to the Attlee government's reforms. But this was not the only initiative the Conservatives took. In December 1945 the Conservatives also established the Conservative Political Centre (CPC), with Cuthbert Alport as its first Director. The CPC's task was to bring together Conservative thinkers and to make their ideas available in published form to party members and activists and to the general public. According to Butler, the purpose of CPC 'was not merely to develop political education methods and to influence public opinion indirectly by reasoned instruction within the party, but to create a kind of Conservative Fabian Society which would act as a mouthpiece for our best modern thought and attract that section of the postwar generation who required an intellectual basis for their political faith.'[29] In this context CPC was to help provide the Conservative party with, in Alport's words, 'the equipment needed to wrest the initiative of the *battle of ideas* from the Socialists'.[30] Moreover, this was not regarded as purely a battle between Conservative and Socialist intellectual elites. At a meeting of the NUCA Central Council in November 1945, the future Conservative Cabinet Minister Henry Brooke argued that: 'A vigorous effort is immediately necessary to associate members of the party throughout every parliamentary constituency in the country with the formation of ideas as a basis for policy, and with spreading political

[28] See K. Jefferys, *The Churchill Coalition and Wartime Politics, 1940–45* (Manchester, 1991), 112–205; H. O. Jones, 'The Conservative Party and the Welfare State, 1942–55', unpublished London University Ph.D thesis, 1992.

[29] R. A. Butler, *The Art of the Possible* (1982), 136–7.

[30] C. J. M. Alport, *Objective* (Jan. 1949), 3, in J. D. Hoffman, *The Conservative Party in Opposition, 1945–51* (1964), 73 (my emphasis).

education.'[31] The CPC was the pivot of what was referred to as 'The Two Way Movement of Ideas', which CCO sought to bring about in order to foster 'a continuing partnership between the party leaders and its rank and file in the formation of party policy on political issues'.[32] This entailed CPC providing materials, such as pamphlets and bibliographies, to local party discussion groups in order to facilitate the process whereby CCO could ask local Conservatives *What Do You Think?* and then correlate findings to inform the party as to *What We Think*.[33] The CPC was relatively effective as an exercise in the 'democratic' transmission of ideas within the party, for in its first two years it produced fifty publications which had achieved a total circulation of 750,000.[34] It is true that by the early 1950s its bookshops were closing, but in 1959 it was also noted that it had been responsible for creating 600 discussion groups countrywide and had 'collected and brought to the attention of the party leadership' the opinions of those groups.[35] But in some respects this is beside the point. The very fact that the Conservative party saw it as essential to engage actively in 'the battle of ideas' is itself an indication of a perceived need within the party to take ideas seriously and to recast Conservatism in a form appropriate to the new political environment.

The Conservative electoral recovery in 1950–1 did not bring an end to intra-party debate as to the direction and meaning of Conservatism. Through the 1950s there were ongoing, and often bitter, arguments as to whether the Conservatives should accept the Attlee government's reforms as a *fait accompli* or seek to remove some, or even all, of the 'Socialist detritus'. In the Conservative grass roots antagonism to nationalization, the Welfare State, 'over-full' employment and enhanced trade-union strength, inflation, and the level of personal taxation led to constant calls for a change of direction in economic policy. Party conferences, especially those of 1955–7, caused some discomfort to the leadership, and the emergence of fringe pressure groups such as the Middle Class Alliance and the People's League for the Defence of Freedom further articulated calls for a shift in the Conservative governments' philosophy and strategy. The so-called 'middle-class revolt' of 1955–8, as embodied in a series of poor by-election results for the Conservatives,

[31] H. Brook at NUCA Central Council Meeting, 28 Nov. 1945, Central Council Minute Book II (Mar. 1946), 1–2, in Hoffman, *Conservative Party in Opposition*, 70.

[32] NUCA Conference Report, 1947, in M. Garnett, *Alport: A Study in Loyalty* (Teddington 1999), 74. For the 'Two-Way Movement' see Hoffman, *Conservative Party*, 158–61, 176–8, 195–8, 203–4.

[33] *What Do You Think?* and *What We Think* were the titles of pamphlets that CPC circularized.

[34] Garnett, *Alport*, 74.

[35] CPC Press Release, 24 Mar. 1959, CPA, CCO 150/4/2/5.

expressed not only resentment at various aspects of government policy but a plea for a wholesale change of approach.[36] This was recognized by the party hierarchy, which was why, from the mid-1950s in particular, a number of wide-ranging policy committees were established on, for example, the future of the nationalized industries, the social services, and taxation. Moreover, it was these concerns which generated the discussions in the party which led to the construction of the idea of the 'Opportunity State', which was at the pivot of Conservative thinking on the economy and welfare in the late 1950s and early 1960s.[37] At the same time, the work of the One Nation group provided a further example of Conservative determination to construct a distinctive approach to social and economic questions in particular. Alongside One Nation's major publications—*One Nation* (1950), *The Social Services: Needs and Means* (1952), *Change is Our Ally* (1954), *The Responsible Society* (1959)—the group was instrumental in organizing 'summer schools' to discuss and define Conservative policy ideas.[38] In parallel with these activities, and as a complement to them, the setting up of Swinton College in 1948 provided a new centre for Conservative education which, like its institutional predecessor, Ashridge, offered lecture courses, summer schools, and the *Swinton Journal* as forums for the discussion and dissemination of Conservative ideas.[39]

As had been the case in the inter-war years, the Conservatives' electoral ascendancy in the 1950s did not quieten the level of debate within the party, and indeed the Conservatives' unprecedented third general election victory in a row in 1959, achieved with an *increased* majority, saw if anything an increase in the range of policy controversy. The early 1960s, especially in the wake of the 1961 'pay pause', the Macmillan government's economic planning initiatives, and the application to join the EEC, saw a burgeoning of differences of opinion on the future of Conservative policy and Conservatism. These differences were, again as in previous eras, evident at all levels of the party. In 1961 Macmillan's Cabinet was divided on the question of economic strategy, and grassroots resentments were again manifest in poor Conservative by-election results and restiveness at party conferences. After the Conservative defeat at the general election of 1964, calls for the party to change its

---

[36] E. H. H. Green, 'The Conservative Party, the State and the Electorate, 1945–64', in M. Taylor and J. Lawrence (eds.), *Party, State and Society: Electoral Behaviour in Britain Since 1820* (Aldershot, 1996).

[37] See ibid., and also K. Jefferys, *Retreat From New Jerusalem: British Politics 1951–64* (1997), 131–75.

[38] See e.g. *The Future of the Welfare State* (1958), a collection of seven essays from the CPC National Summer School at Oxford, 1957.

[39] In its first year Swinton had 2,000 students attend the 42 courses which it held. See Hoffman, *Conservative Party in Opposition*, 118.

approach were perhaps expressed most fully in the speeches of Enoch Powell, but he was voicing rather than creating the call for change. Under the leadership of Edward Heath, CRD committees explored possible policy directions, such as denationalization, that had been regarded as outside the mainstream of Conservative thought in the 1950s, and, likewise, think tanks such as the Institute for Economic Affairs, which had also been very much on the fringes of Conservatism, found audiences amongst the party hierarchy and grass roots increasingly receptive to their ideas.[40] This helps to explain why the party responded in the way it did to (erroneous) reports that the Conservative Shadow Cabinet's Selsdon Park conference of early 1970 had embraced a new policy agenda. The discussions at Selsdon Park were in fact largely anodyne, but the foment of ideas within the party had, by 1970, created a climate of anticipation for many Conservatives, and the response of the press and more especially the Labour leadership to the Selsdon Conference confirmed the hopes of significant sections of the Conservative grass roots. Indeed, it was precisely the long-running nature of the debate within the party which renders the disputes over Thatcherism after 1975 explicable. Particular aspects of the form and content of the post-1975 controversies were novel, but many were long-established in the subculture of Conservative intra-party debate. More important, however, the notion that what was new in and after 1975 was the 'ideological' nature of Conservative politics loses all validity, not only because aspects of 'Thatcherism' had existed *avant la lettre*, but because the history of the Conservative party in the twentieth century is steeped in ideological dispute.

Ideology, as it is for all political parties, is central to the history of the Conservative party. It may be that the Conservatives produce fewer 'great texts' (although they produce and refer to more than is frequently assumed), but if one sets aside the formal, 'canonical' notion of the forms of expression of political thought and examines speeches, policy-making discussions, exchanges of views and opinions in correspondence, and the construction of and response to legislation, the Conservatives' engagement with ideas is clear, rich, varied, and extensive. Politics is about argument, and arguments are about ideas. Politicians acting within an elective system of government seek to persuade people to give them power, and to achieve this end will deploy those arguments they feel will be most effective in terms of persuading their audience. But this raises a number of important questions. First, why do politicians choose some arguments over others? Second, how do politicians define their audience and how does the audience define itself?

[40] Cockett, *Thinking*.

Third, what are the dynamics of the relationship between the selection of argument and the nature of the audience? Any attempt to answer these questions immediately brings out the centrality of ideas and ideological assumptions in the political process. When politicians select a particular argument or range of arguments they are necessarily making a judgement, holding a view, expressing an idea as to why the form and content of one argument will serve their purposes better than another. Their selection in turn depends upon their perception of what their audience will respond to best, and this implies that they have ideas about the nature of their audience. But although politicians must have ideas as to how best to appeal to or even construct their audience, the audience is not simply a passive receptor of ideas: an audience may be indifferent to or may even reject a political argument. Here it is crucial to recognize that at no point do politicians and their audiences exist and operate in a historical vacuum. One does not have to accept Gilbert and Sullivan's aphorism that every child is born a 'little Liberal' or a 'little Conservative' to acknowledge that in any historical period there are political traditions, political identities, and political allegiances of long standing. In short, there always exists a range of assumptions amongst politicians and their audiences alike as to what it means to be a member or supporter of a particular political party, and this places constraints upon the range of arguments a politician can deploy. To take a simple example, some Edwardian Conservatives could have argued that the best way to alleviate poverty and social distress was for the government to introduce a strongly progressive fiscal structure, and redistribute wealth to the poor in the form of social reforms. However, they could not have done this and claimed to be Conservative. Such an argument would have lacked any verisimilitude in terms of ideas as to what constituted a recognizably *Conservative* answer to the particular problem in question. However, such constraints are not completely rigid. Some arguments will in some circumstances be deemed unacceptable, but it is self-evidently the case that politicians in the same party can advance differing arguments and ideas as to what constitutes the best expression of their party's beliefs, values, and interests. The purpose of this book is to explore aspects of the ideas, values, arguments, and beliefs that have informed Conservative thought in the last century.

The structure of the book has been designed to reflect the varied nature of Conservative ideas. An essay rather than a monograph format has allowed me to take different points of entry into Conservative thought at different times. The aim has been to deploy a 'cross-sectional' or 'core-sampling' technique in which the essays cut into Conservative ideological debate at a number of key points in the party's history through the twentieth century.[41] The first essay examines the political economy of the Edwardian Conservative leader Arthur Balfour, and seeks to open up new vistas on the complexities and nuances of the tariff debate which dominated Conservative politics in the first decade of the century. The second essay explores the influence of English Idealist thought on Conservatism in the period *c.*1880–1914, and suggests that the ideas of T. H. Green and his fellow Oxford Idealists may have had as important a resonance for Conservatives as they did for Liberals. Furthermore, by examining the ideas of an effectively unknown thinker, Arthur Boutwood, alongside those of better-known Conservative thinkers, the second essay presents the first of the book's attempts to stress the importance of the 'middlebrow' in Conservative thought. The third essay discusses the ideas of the Conservative politician Arthur Steel-Maitland as they evolved from the time of his involvement in the pre-1914 tariff debate through his engagement with the 'new economics' of the inter-war years, and thereby outlines perhaps the fullest, earliest Conservative response to Keynes. The fourth essay looks at the 'low politics' of the Conservative decision to end the Coalition with the Lloyd George Liberals in 1922, and examines the part played by the Conservative's identity as the party of anti-Socialism in this decision. The fifth essay examines the genesis and development of Conservative book clubs in the late 1930s, and shows how these organizations were part of a Conservative attempt to counter what was seen as a Leftist dominance of the world of letters. The sixth essay charts the development of the political economy of Harold Macmillan from the 1920s to his retirement as Prime Minister in the autumn of 1963, and outlines the changing nature of his concept of a 'middle way' between Socialism and unfettered capitalism and the similarly changing response of the Conservative party to his ideas. The seventh essay offers a new interpretation of the resignation of the Conservative Treasury team in January 1958, and suggests that this episode cannot be seen as a 'rehearsal' for future debates between 'monetarists' and 'Keynesians' in the party. Rather, it suggests that the events of 1958 must be seen as part of a debate that had profound but much more nuanced implications for the future development of Conservativive political economy. The eighth essay explores the ideological origins of the Thatcherite revolution, and indicates that the ideas which came to dominance in the Conservative party after 1975 had been prevalent amongst the middle and lower ranks of the party since the end of the Second World War. The final

---

[41] The approach is similar to that suggested by Sir John Elliott in his inaugural lecture as Regius Professor at Oxford. See J. H. Elliott, *National and Comparative History: An Inaugural Lecture* (Oxford, 1991).

essay discusses Conservative ideas on the role of the State in relation to economic and social policy over the course of the twentieth century, and offers a new interpretation of the nature of the ideological differences within the party on this question. Each essay offers a different point of entry into the Conservative ideological core, but the samples retrieved, it is hoped, add up to more than just the sum of the parts.

CHAPTER I

'No Settled Convictions'? Arthur Balfour, Political Economy, and Tariff Reform: A Reconsideration

ARTHUR BALFOUR's political career is somewhat of a paradox. As Lord Salisbury's nephew he enjoyed an almost automatic entry into the higher echelons of the Conservative party, and he became his uncle's Parliamentary Private Secretary in 1878. But family advantages aside, the beginnings of his parliamentary career were somewhat hesitatant, and his intellectual bent and apparent insouciance earned him the sobriquet 'pretty fanny'. In the 1880s and 1890s, however, Balfour became an important political figure in his own right. As a member of the 'Fourth Party' he earned Conservative plaudits for harrying Gladstone, and in Salisbury's second and third administrations he proved a tough and innovative Irish Chief Secretary and an adroit Leader of the House of Commons. It was thus his proven ability as a parliamentarian and administrator, and not simply the fact that he was the Prime Minister's nephew, which made him Salisbury's obvious successor when the old Conservative leader retired in 1902. Balfour's period as Prime Minister was, in many respects, a success. He could lay claim to presiding over the establishment of Britain's first genuinely national education system with the Education Act of 1902, and an important reorientation of Britain's foreign policy through cementing the alliance with Japan and pursuing the 'Entente' with France. Likewise, the Irish Land Act of 1903, the process of army reform that was set in train after 1902, and the Unemployed Workmen's Act and Aliens Act of 1905 showed that his administration was by no means 'unconstructive'. But if a case can be made for the defence of his premiership, his reputation as a *party* leader is, it seems, beyond repair. In 1906 he led the Conservatives to one of their worst ever electoral defeats, and in the process achieved the dubious distinction of being the only Prime Minister this century to lose his own seat. In 1910 his party suffered a further two, albeit close, electoral defeats, and when he resigned the leadership in the autumn of 1911 his record was three contests and three losses—in electoral terms he has proved the most unsuccessful Conservative leader of the twentieth century.[1]

At the heart of his failure as a party leader was the question of tariff reform. Confronted after May 1903 with an issue that brought about the resignation of five members of his government in September of that year, caused severe disputes within his party over the next two years, and ongoing internal strife during the rest of his leadership, Balfour appeared to suffer from political paralysis. Rather than controlling events, Balfour seemed to be controlled by them. Buffeted on the one hand by Joseph Chamberlain's 'raging, tearing propaganda' for imperial preference and protection, and on the other by the Conservative free traders' equally forthright opposition to tariff reform, Balfour sought ineffectively to find a 'middle ground'.[2] Only after the 1906 electoral defeat, when Chamberlain's cohorts dominated the Conservative parliamentary party and the constituency organizations, did Balfour come down on the side of tariff reform. But in spite of his announcement to the National Union in 1907 that tariffs were 'the first constructive work' of the party, Balfour never persuaded his followers that he was committed to tariff reform. His 'equivocation' was confirmed in the eyes of tariff reformers in 1910 when, before the December general election of that year, he publicly offered to submit tariffs to a referendum if the Conservatives were elected, as long as Asquith promised to do the same for Irish Home Rule. For Balfour this was a tactical ploy to dilute objections to tariffs whilst highlighting the Liberals' stance on Ireland. For hard-line tariff campaigners, however, the 'referendum pledge' indicated Balfour's lack of belief in the popularity of tariff reform, and communicated this to the electorate. After December 1910 Balfour had no credibility as a 'true believer' in the tariff cause, and his seeming want of conviction led to persistent and ultimately quite savage personal criticism of his leadership, culminating in the 'BMG' (Balfour Must Go) campaign of the *National Review* in the summer and autumn of 1911. As a consequence Balfour did go, and his resignation of 8 November 1911 must be seen as the result of his inability to cope with the politics of tariff reform.

Balfour's reluctance to commit himself unequivocally to the 'full tariff programme' has been explained in political and biographical terms. For the first two and a half years of the tariff controversy emphasis has been placed on Balfour's overriding desire to preserve the unity of his party.[3]

---

[1] I do not include Austen Chamberlain here as he never led the party in an election.

[2] For Balfour's quest for a *via media* see A. M. Gollin, *Balfour's Burden* (1965) and D. Judd, *Balfour and the British Empire* (1968).

[3] See in particular Gollin, ibid. 81–95; Judd, *Balfour, passim*; J. L. Garvin and J. Amery, *The Life of Joseph Chamberlain*, 6 vols. (1932–69), v. 225–384; A. Sykes, *Tariff Reform in British Politics, 1903–1913* (Oxford, 1979), 70–114.

Balfour himself publicly acknowledged that this was a priority, stating in his own constituency of East Manchester in January 1904 that, 'in all this controversy I have had few interests nearer my heart than the interests of the unity of the great Unionist party'.[4] At the heart of Balfour's attempt to mediate on the tariff question was his concept of 'retaliation'—the idea that Britain should introduce duties on imported goods as a way of forcing protectionist nations to negotiate their tariffs downwards. For Balfour 'retaliation' was a notion which both Chamberlainites and free traders could agree upon: Chamberlainites because it meant an adjustment of Britain's free-trade stance, and free traders because it represented an attempt to bring about 'real' free trade. Unfortunately for Balfour this *via media* failed to reconcile the warring factions in his party. Chamberlain famously scorned the policy, declaring that, 'for retaliation I would never have taken off my coat',[5] whilst the party's committed free traders were equally clear that it represented too much of a concession to the tariff case. Lord Robert Cecil, one of the leading Conservative free traders, summed up the situation best when he recalled that the upshot of Balfour's stance was that 'sometimes both sides . . . claimed him as an adherent. At others both rejected him.'[6] Nor did Balfour's position enjoy popular success outside the party. In 1904 the Conservatives' chief organizer in the North-East told Lord Lonsdale that 'In the North, as far as I am able to judge . . . there is no use in . . . waiting at the halfway house of 'Retaliation' as amongst working men the issues are too complex for them to grasp . . . With them it is just one or the other, Protection or Free Trade.'[7] Likewise, whatever the conflicting interpretations of the 1906 election result in the Conservative ranks, there was unanimity that Balfour's stance had proved a platform failure. That Balfour lost his own seat in 1906 did not exactly build confidence in his formula, but both sides of the tariff divide felt that his policy had been generally unpopular. Lord Robert Cecil argued that 'the body of the electorate regard[ed] his attitude as either intentionally ambiguous or else motivated by a culpable levity',[8] whilst the committed tariff reformer, Lord Morpeth, declared that, 'Whether A[rthur] B[alfour] has learned that his late policy is futile . . . I imagine that it must be apparent that ambiguity is no good'.[9]

---

[4] Balfour at East Manchester, 11 Jan. 1904, reprinted in A. J. Balfour, *Fiscal Reform* (1906), 137.

[5] Quoted in P. Clarke, *A Question of Leadership* (1991), 77.

[6] Lord Cecil of Chelwood, *All the Way* (1949), 109.

[7] E. H. Currie to Londsale, 7 Jan. 1904, Joseph Chamberlain papers, Birmingham University Library, JC 19/7/15.

[8] Cecil of Chelwood, *All the Way*, 109.

[9] Morpeth to L. J. Maxse, 25 Jan. 1906, Maxse papers, West Sussex Record Office, 455 S 295.

Balfour's attempt to use retaliation to bridge the gulf between the Chamberlainite and free-trade sections of his party between 1903 and 1906 was understandable, if perhaps unrealistic. But his problems after 1906 are less readily explicable in these terms. After the general election the much-reduced Conservative parliamentary contingent was overwhelmingly in favour of the full tariff programme, and the party grass roots showed, if anything, an even greater commitment.[10] Furthermore, the fact that Chamberlain was forced to retire from active politics in July 1906, following his stroke, meant that Balfour could not be seen as kow-towing to a potential leadership rival by moving towards the tariff camp. That Balfour, in his 'Valentine' exchange of letters with Chamberlain in February 1906 and in his addresses to the NUCA of 1907 and 1908, publicly endorsed the full tariff programme seemed to indicate that he had accepted the tariff reformers' case, or at any rate acknowledged the strength of their position in the party. And yet he never seemed comfortable with this position, and he was unable to convince his erstwhile followers that his heart was in the tariff cause.

Balfour's personal traits were looked to by contemporaries to explain his position as a 'reluctant' tariff reformer. Writing soon after the 1906 defeat, Andrew Bonar Law argued that 'Balfour . . . does not understand the man in the street'.[11] A year later the outspoken tariff-reforming MP Rowland Hunt stated that Balfour was unable to bring himself down from 'the olympian heights of philosophy and golf',[12] and commit himself to to a popular campaign. For his pains Hunt had the Conservative Whip suspended, but he was expressing a generally held view that Balfour was only at home in the rarified atmosphere of Westminster, and uncomfortable with the exigencies of popular politics. That the rabid tariff-reforming editor of the *National Review*, Leo Maxse, declared that 'the democracy understands Mr. Balfour as little as he understands the democracy',[13] could, given its provenance, be seen as a typically gratuitous insult. But in 1911 Lord Selborne, Balfour's cousin by marriage and a member of the 'Hatfield' circle, complained to his wife that 'Arthur's ideas of leadership out of the House of Commons are as scanty as his power of leadership in the House is wonderful'.[14] In the light of his successes as Irish Secretary,

---

[10] For the strength of Conservative tariff reform sentiment after 1906 see E. H. H. Green, *The Crisis of Conservatism* (1995), 145–55. For a case-study of local Conservative attitudes see L. Witherell, 'Political Cannibalism Amongst Edwardian Conservatives', *TCBH* 8 (1997).

[11] Law to L. J. Maxse, 30 Jan. 1906, Maxse papers, 456 S 334.

[12] R. Hunt in Parliament, 18 Feb. 1907, *The Times*, 19 Feb. 1907.

[13] L. J. Maxse, 'Episodes of the Month', *National Review*, 382 (Oct. 1910), 13.

[14] Selborne to Lady Selborne, 27 Apr. 1911, Selborne papers, Bodleian Library, Oxford, MS Selborne 102, fos. 17–18.

Leader of the Commons, and in his career after 1911, it is difficult to see Balfour as congenitally indecisive, but in his dealings with the tariff-reform issue this was precisely how he appeared to friend and foe alike. It is also how he has appeared to historians of his leadership, with one of his biographers encapsulating the general verdict that tariff reform 'revealed Balfour's inability to mould, or even sense, national opinion and to function effectively as head of a popular government'.[15] Balfour's problem, it seems, was that he was an 'intellectual statesman',[16] and that the considered appraisal, lack of dogmatism, and appreciation of nuance that were his strengths as an administrator were his weaknesses as a popular politician. The author of *A Defence of Philosophic Doubt* may have brought a healthy scepticism to the task of governance, but for a party leader engaged in a passionate public debate, it proved impossible to live down the declaration that he had 'no settled convictions'[17] on the main issue at stake.

It is not the intention of this essay wholly to overturn existing historical explanations of Balfour's stance on tariff reform. Rather, it will seek to add a further dimension to the story by fusing Balfour's political and personal positions on the tariff question. To begin with, this requires a brief biographical reassessment. With regard to Balfour's apparent indifference to 'popular' politics, and his inadequacies in that sphere, certain qualifications need to be entered. Given his aristocratic, intellectual, and aesthetic background and demeanour, it may seem only natural that Balfour found popular politics vulgar. His famous claim that he never read the newspapers, the established medium through which late-Victorian and Edwardian politicians sought to gauge and influence public opinion, epitomizes his seeming disdain for demotic politics. However, even if one accepts that Balfour personally did not read the newspapers (which is unlikely), the fact is that he did not need to, for the simple reason that he had others read them and keep him abreast of their contents. His Parliamentary Secretary, J. S. Sandars, and his secretary, W. S. Short, were in part employed to keep their chief's finger on the pulse of public opinion, and he could always turn to his friend and golfing partner, E. B. Iwan-Muller, the editor of the *Daily Telegraph*, for further counsel. Balfour's studied pose of aloofness was precisely that, a *pose*. Certainly Balfour did not like popular politics, but then neither did his predecessor, and that did not prevent Lord Salisbury from recognizing the importance of the wider political audience. Equally, Balfour probably realized that he was not a natural practitioner of the demotic

---

[15] S. Zebel, *Balfour: A Political Biography* (Cambridge, 1973), 128.
[16] See R. Mackay, *International Statesman: A Life of A. J. Balfour* (Oxford, 1985).
[17] Balfour in Parliament, 10 June 1903, in Balfour, *Fiscal Reform*, 52.

arts, and thus *cultivated* a political persona that emphasized his areas of strength as a parliamentarian and administrator. In the still relatively new age of mass politics, when the 'demagogue' was regarded with suspicion, especially in Conservative circles, Balfour's hauteur had political as well as personal recommendations. His great misfortune was that his period as leader coincided with a time when the demotic arts took on an added political significance. It may well be that he proved unable to adjust his style, but this was as much due to his having learned his political trade in a different climate as to inbuilt personal failings.

Staying with the biographical theme, one also needs to delve more deeply into Balfour's 'scepticism', and his apparent inability to cast himself as a 'true believer' or, to use an expression from the 1980s, a 'conviction politician' on the issue of tariff reform. At first glance Balfour's claim to have 'no settled convictions' on tariff reform seems to fit well with his 'indifference' to popular politics. After all, if there was nothing worth crusading for what was the point of a popular crusade? But it should be remembered here that the author of *A Defence of Philosophic Doubt* was also the author of *The Foundations of Belief.* Balfour may have been a sceptic, but that did not preclude his holding beliefs: rather, he merely asserted that the grounds for any belief be thoroughly scrutinized and tested. That Balfour *did* hold strong political beliefs cannot be gainsaid. Defence of the Union with Ireland stands out as a particularly powerful theme in Balfour's career, and the security of private property and the maintenance of established institutions (Church, Crown, Empire, aristocracy) were also intrinsic to his *Weltanschauung*. In some respects this is not surprising—what was he doing in politics unless he felt that there were certain values and institutions worth furthering and/or defending? Indeed, Balfour's very scepticism could, if one accepts the notion of 'intellectual imperfection' as a central aspect of the creed, be regarded as an essential part of his adherence to Conservative ideology.[18] In the light of this assessment, this essay will introduce its central 'revisionist' point about Balfour's position on tariff reform, namely, that his difficulties stemmed not from his having 'no settled convictions', but from the fact that he had very firmly held views as to the optimum path for British tariff policy.

At the root of Balfour's position on tariff reform were his views about political economy. He had studied political economy at Cambridge under the tutelage of Henry Sidgwick, and never lost his interest in the subject. From the outset of his political career this interest was evident. He made his maiden speech in the Commons on the subject of Indian

---

[18] See A. Quinton, *The Politics of Imperfection* (1975), a discussion of intellectual imperfection as the lemma of Conservative thought.

currency, and in the 1880s and 1890s Balfour showed a pronounced sympathy for the bimetallic cause.[19] This could be attributed to the fact that he sat for a constituency in Lancashire, where bimetallism had a powerful appeal to the cotton industry,[20] but it is difficult to see local interests as more than a partial explanation for Balfour's involvement with the currency question. He was one of the most inquisitive members of the 1887–8 Royal Commission on Currency, and during Salisbury's third administration Conservative bimetallists looked to Balfour as the senior figure who would press their case in Cabinet. Balfour's interest in and support for bimetallism is significant for two reasons. First, here was an economic issue renowned for its abstruse, even arcane, arguments which Balfour mastered and pursued with intelligence, tenacity, and some relish. Second, prior to the tariff controversy bimetallism was the most important debate with implications for Britain's commitment to 'orthodox' liberal political economy. In 1898 Robert Chalmers, one of the Permanent Secretaries at the Treasury, told T. H. Farrer: 'The more I have to do with these heterodox people [bimetallists], the more I realise the unity of the principles which lead you to maintain the two things—free trade and sound currency. One is the obverse of the other, the reverse of the same coin.'[21] Although there was by no means a simple correlation between advocates of bimetallism and critics of free trade,[22] there was an implicit willingness on the part of currency 'heretics' to question received economic wisdom. Moreover, the 'producerist' outlook which drove the bimetallic campaign of the late nineteenth century was also very much part of the later tariff-reform campaign.[23] In this respect Balfour's support for bimetallism was indicative of his acceptance that all was not right with Britain's economy, especially the agricultural and manufacturing sectors, and showed his readiness to consider alternatives to prevailing policy orthodoxies.

The reasoning that allowed Balfour to countenance economic 'heresy' was made clear in his 'formal' writings on political economy. His first significant intervention in this field was published in the

[19] See B. E. C. Dugdale, *Arthur James Balfour*, 2 vols. (1939), i. 168–81. Balfour was one of the voices sympathetic to bimetallism on the Royal Commission on Currency in the late 1880s.

[20] For bimetallism's particular appeal to the cotton industry and Lancashire see E. H. H. Green, 'Rentiers versus Producers? The Political Economy of the Bimetallic Controversy, 1890–98', *EHR* 102 (1988).

[21] Chalmers to Farrer, 19 Nov. 1898, T. H. Farrer papers, London School of Economics Library, vol. 1, fo. 28.

[22] For a discussion of the relationship between bimetallism and tariff reform see Green, *Crisis*, ch. 1, and id., 'The Bimetallic Controversy: Empiricism Belimed or the Case for the Issues', *EHR* 104 (1990).

[23] For the bimetallists' 'producerism' see Green, 'Rentiers versus Proucers?', and for the similar outlook of the tariff campaign see id., *Crisis*, chs. 5–10.

National Review in 1885. In this essay Balfour noted that political economy, as a discipline, had lost much of its cachet over the previous
decade. This, he argued, was due to misguided efforts to establish the
notion of economic orthodoxy. The net result had been that political
economy 'cease[d] to be a living science, and petrifie[d] into an
unchanging creed'.[24] Balfour felt that political economy was a vital
science, in that 'the study of economic facts is a necessary preliminary
to any judicious treatment of some of the most important problems of
the day', but he was was also clear that it was necessary to limit the
claims of political economy qua science to be an absolute guide to
policy. Political economy, he contended, only dealt with one aspect of
life, the pursuit of wealth, whereas politicians had to consider society's
needs in the round. Hence any conclusions produced by political economy had to be 'subject to revision', and notions like free trade and laissez faire had to be seen as '*maxims*' not 'truths'.[25] This line of thinking
led Balfour to declare that 'there is no question concerning either the
method or the results of political economy which I for one am not
prepared to question'.[26]

After 1885 Balfour did not publish any formal thoughts on the
nature of political economy. His *Economic Notes on Insular Free Trade*
of 1903 did contain some important theoretical implications, which
will be touched upon later, but it was largely a 'tract for the times'. But
between 1907 and 1911 he worked on the manuscript of a projected
major treatise on political economy, and although it was never
published (and probably did not deserve to be), it contains some interesting insights into his thinking. In his manuscript Balfour argued that
the 'fundamental' problem was, 'we live in a changing world, and in a
world where economic changes are at least as striking as any other . . .
by what causes are economic changes affected? and can these causes,
or any of them, be reduced to law?' His answer was pessimistic: he
noted that

Merely to state them [the above questions] is to show how small a fraction of the
economic problem can ever come within the scope of economic theory, or for the
matter of that, of any theory. New methods of manufacturing material, new methods of transporting it, the exhaustion of old supplies, the discovery of new ones,
war, conquest, colonisation, the diffusion through Eastern nations of Western
knowledge, revolutions in taste, in science, in organisation—who shall deny that
these are among the great causes of economic change? who shall assert that they can
be reduced to law? Evidently the task is hopeless.

[24] A. J. Balfour, 'Politics and Political Economy', *National Review* (May 1885), repr. in id.,
Essays and Addresses (Edinburgh, 1893), 232.
[25] Ibid. 229, 233–4.   [26] Ibid. 238.

But Balfour felt that some had mistakenly sought to establish such laws. The culprits were the classical economists, and he declared that 'where I venture to think Classical Economics has been to blame . . . is in the arbitrary emphasis it places on certain causes of change, in its defective account of them, and in the one-sided theory of economic development which has been the inevitable result.'[27] Balfour underscored this argument by further arguing that

some economists have been haunted by the notion that the infinite variety of economic effect exhibited in different stages of culture, display the workings of a single set of eternal and unchanging principles, which it was their business to disengage from their temporary setting . . . For my own part . . . I doubt whether much is gained in any branch of sociology by searching after laws of universal validity. The field of economic theory, at least, is no regime of unalterable outline, retaining its identity through every stage of social development. It depends for its content upon such variable elements as custom, law, knowledge, social organisation; nay on human nature itself which . . . is not necessarily the same from generation to generation . . . Every phase of civilization requires its own political economy.[28]

Balfour's manuscript on political economy represented a deepening and strengthening of the views he had articulated in 1885, and as such it indicates the consistency of his outlook over time. The scepticism which informed his views was perhaps to be expected, but of even greater importance is the historical relativism of his approach, for this brought him very close to the historical school of British economists.

The historical school,[29] whose leading lights were William Cunningham, W. J. Ashley, H. S. Foxwell, L. L. Price, and W. A. S. Hewins, first came to prominence in Britain in the 1880s, and from that point on developed a sustained critique of Classical economics and what it saw as its vulgarized derivatives, Manchesterism and Socialism. The basic objections to the classical school were, first, the deductive method used by the classical economists which had led them to 'isolate certain motives and measure them, and formulate laws according to which these motives act'.[30] This, the historical economists argued, was a fallacious procedure, because 'no economic principles have this mathematical character of being true for all times and places alike . . . [but were] approximately true as statements of the facts of actual life under certain social conditions'.[31] The second, related, objection was to the classical

[27] A. J. Balfour, unpublished drafts of a manuscript on political economy, n.d. 1907–11?, Balfour papers, Add. MSS, 49948, fos. 106–7.

[28] Ibid., Add. MSS 49950, fos. 10–14.

[29] For full discussions of the historical school see G. M. Koot, *The English Historical Economists* (Cambridge, 1988); J. Burrow, S. Collini, and D. Winch, *That Noble Science of Politics* (Cambridge, 1985), ch. 7; and Green, *Crisis*, ch. 5.

[30] W. Cunningham, 'A Plea for Pure Theory', *Economic Review*, 2 (Jan. 1892), 34.

[31] Id., *Politics and Economics* (1885), 3.

economists' abstraction of economic phenomena from the surrounding context. This 'immense simplification' of 'isolating wealth as a subject for study' was regarded by the historical economists as in some respects a good thing, but only as long as it was 'not forgotten that it was a tool of convenience'.[32] Where the classical school was seen to have gone wrong was in thinking that the 'science of wealth' represented the be-all and end-all of political economy, and ignoring the wider social, cultural, and historical influences on economic development.

For the historical economists, the classical school's deductive, abstract reasoning had ensured that they had 'lost touch with the actual phenomena of the present day'.[33] This was seen to be most evident in the individualist assumptions underpinning classical economics. Looking at the late nineteenth- and early twentieth-century world, the historical economists saw trusts, trade unions, and empire states as the characteristic features of economic life. In short, they saw *collective* agencies as the key actors on the economic stage. More particularly, they saw nationalism exercising a pervasive influence on the economic policies of Britain's rivals. The resurgence of protectionism was regarded by the historical economists as evidence of the desire of Britain's competitors 'to organize [their] economic life . . . in independence of [their] neighbours',[34] and therefore a comprehensive rejection of the 'cosmopolitan' assumptions of classical economics, which saw 'the interests of particular individuals'[35] as the basis of economic action and nations as 'non-competing groups'.[36] Looking at Britain's response to this environment, however, the historical school saw economists and governments still wedded to individualistic shibboleths of laissez faire and free trade, based on notions of the comparative advantage of individual 'economic men' in an international division of labour. In terms of both theory and practice, classical economic orthodoxies were seen to be out of step with contemporary conditions.

The net result of Britain's misconceived and misaligned thinking and policies was, the historical economists contended, a deterioration in the nation's relative economic performance. In particular they drew attention to the problems faced by Britain's 'productive' sector, by which they meant agriculture and manufacturing.[37] Here free trade was seen to have allowed unrestricted import penetration to weaken Britain's farming and industrial interests. Equally damaging, foreign manufacturers,

[32] Id., 'The Progress of Economic Doctrine in England in the Eighteenth Century', *Economic Journal*, 1 (Mar. 1891), 73–94.
[33] Id., *Politics*, p. vii.   [34] Ibid. 87.
[35] Id., *The Wisdom of the Wise* (1904), 61.
[36] L. L. Price, 'Economic Theory and Fiscal Policy', *Economic Journal*, 14 (Sept. 1904), 379.
[37] W. Cunningham, *The Alternative to Socialism in England* (Cambridge, 1885), 1–2.

aided by the state assistance of tariffs, had formed themselves into capital-rich trusts and cartels which had enabled them to adopt trading practices, such as 'dumping', which were driving British producers from foreign, 'neutral', and even home markets.[38] At no point did the historical economists contend that Britain was becoming poorer in an absolute sense. But they did argue that the nation's wealth was becoming imbalanced through an increasing reliance upon service sector and investment income.[39] This, they felt, brought home in practical terms the distinction between individual and collective/national prosperity. The historical economists frowned upon investment income on the grounds that it produced fortunes in the City of London but created only 'values in exchange'[40] for the nation, and did not lead to the diffusion of economic activity and employment that attended upon production.[41] They prioritized *productive* wealth as the basis of a nation's economic prosperity vis-à-vis other nations in a competitive world. Just as wealth in itself was an inadequate subject of study, so wealth in itself was no measure of a nation's economic health—what mattered most was *how* that wealth was created and what contribution it made to national well-being.

In terms of policy this emphasis on the need to foster Britain's productive capacities led the historical economists in the late nineteenth century to support the bimetallic cause. The price fall of the late nineteenth century, which the historical economists attributed to the gold standard, was seen to have benefited banking and investment interests at the expense of producer profits. Likewise, the historical economists felt that free trade had boosted *international* commerce and provided increased service income for 'the City', but left Britain's *national* productive base vulnerable.[42] Both the gold standard and free trade were seen as having committed Britain to a 'cosmopolitan' political economy which was out of keeping with the prevailing climate of cut-throat national rivalries, of benefit only to the 'unproductive' rentier element in society, and damaging to the interests of employers and employees in the productive sectors. As an alternative the historical economists advocated a neo-mercantilist approach, which culminated in their support for the tariff campaign. Tariffs were to provide British producers with a defence against their competitors and, through imperial preference, establish a

---

[38] Price, 'Economic Theory', 384.

[39] See W. J. Ashley, *The Tariff Problem* (1903), 212–15; W. Cunningham, *The Case Against Free Trade* (1911), 37.

[40] W. J. Ashley, *The Economic Organization of England* (1914), 91.

[41] Green, *Crisis*, 169–71.

[42] For the historical economists' support for bimetallism and tariffs see Green, 'Rentiers', and id., *Crisis*, 41–6, 169–71, 176–83.

large, sheltered market which would enable them to expand their activities. Britain's productive forces were to be actively encouraged by abandoning an economic strategy which had left them exposed to the whims of a market that was biased against them.

A close examination of Arthur Balfour's position indicates that he not only shared the historical economists' relativism but also many of their broader assumptions. He viewed the separation of economic phenomena from their wider context as an 'artificial simplification',[43] agreed that 'the industry of the world is evidently a corporate process',[44] and accepted that 'the State is something more than the individuals composing it'.[45] Equally important, he shared many of the historical economists' ideas about the nature of economic organization and the practical effects of contemporary economic developments. Like the historical economists, Balfour had no truck with the Smithean idea that 'the merchant has no country'. In his *Economic Notes on Insular Free Trade* he remarked that nations 'have not felt themselves bound to consider arguments drawn from cosmopolitan economics', and argued that this indicated that they were 'both unable and unwilling to turn the natural resources of the world to the best economic account'.[46] Balfour thus rejected the notion that there was a functioning international division of labour, and accepted that national interests were the basis of economic policy-making in the modern world.

When he addressed more particular issues, Balfour was also close to the historical economists. For example, on the effects of falling prices he argued that 'the fall of prices acts differently on the different members of the [social] group . . . On whom will fall the loss? Evidently on contributors who cannot withdraw their contribution and not on those who can.'[47] Balfour underlined his position by noting that: 'A man who merely serves does nothing for production. A man who merely invests, i.e. buys someone else's shares or stocks, does nothing . . . for production . . . Money makes nothing: therefore saving money does not accumulate the means of making anything . . . From all this it follows that an investing nation does not thereby become a producing nation.'[48] This was in keeping with Balfour's and the historical economists' bimetallist thinking, and it shows that Balfour accepted the historical economists' distinction between productive and unproductive groups. Furthermore, in his *Economic Notes on Insular Free Trade* Balfour was

---

[43] Balfour, unpublished treatise, BP, Add. MSS 49945, fo. 185.
[44] Ibid., Add. MSS 49948, fo. 1.
[45] A. J. Balfour, *Economic Notes on Insular Free Trade* (1903), 5.
[46] Ibid.
[47] Ibid., Add. MSS, 49946, fo. 36.
[48] Ibid., fos 120–4.

clear that 'As regards the national income from foreign investments, it has to be observed that while it must always be better for the inhabitants of any country to own capital than not to own it, it is better that the capital they own should be earning a profit at home', and he concluded that capital export could represent a loss to domestic capital and labour.[49] Balfour thus took the view that domestic production was of greater value in a national economic context than service income.

With regard to free trade Balfour also adopted a historicist position. In April 1902 he declared that 'the doctrine of Free Trade is not a mere speculative hypothesis . . . it is not a metaphysical theory, and it is not even a theological dogma, but . . . a practical thing'.[50] The implication of this argument was that *circumstances* rather than principle determined the efficacy of free trade, which paralleled the historical economists' view that if a policy had worked in the past 'there must be a strong presumption that it would be unsuitable in the present condition of society'.[51] In virtually all of his early statements on the tariff question Balfour insisted that the debate was not a repeat of the controversies of the 1840s for the simple reason that circumstances were entirely different, and he demonstrated great impatience with those who spoke of 'heresy' or who 'find some formula in a book of authority, and throw it at their opponents' head'.[52] In his *Economic Notes* he explicitly referred back to the 1840s, and declared that Cobden and his supporters had 'failed to foresee that the world would reject free trade and . . . failed to take account of the commercial possibilities of the British Empire'.[53] His message was constant and consistent—time and circumstance had changed and policy-makers needed to take note of that rather than rely upon a-historical formulations.

If in general terms Balfour acknowledged that changed circumstances required a re-think of policy, it was also the case that he felt that some changes in economic conditions were of particular importance. The development of trusts and their trading practices was one which he singled out for attention. In June 1903 Balfour stressed 'the provision of adequate capital for carrying on great modern industries'[54] as a *sine qua non* in an industrial world dominated by large-scale corporations. Here again he was in step with the historical economists, who felt that 'capital has become the dominating influence on production'.[55] In Balfour's

49　Balfour, *Economic Notes*, 15.
50　Balfour in Parliament, 22 Apr. 1902, in id., *Fiscal Reform*, 11.
51　Cunningham, *Politics*, 16.
52　Balfour in Parliament, 28 May 1903, in id., *Fiscal Reform*, 30, 36.
53　Balfour, *Economic Notes*, 8.
54　Balfour at the Constitutional Club, 26 June 1903, in id., *Fiscal Reform*, 61.
55　Cunningham, *Free Trade Movement*, 126.

view, Britain's ability to attract the level of capital necessary for its industries had been 'imperilled by the fact that foreign nations, under their protective system, are able and willing to import into this country objects which are largely manufactured in this country at below cost price either in the country of origin or in the country of importation'.[56] The advantage that protection gave Britain's competitors was, according to Balfour, that it enabled them to 'run their works evenly [and] . . . design their works on the scale which shall serve the greatest economy of production'.[57] In short, tariffs gave foreign industrialists the economies of scale and home-market security that enabled them to pursue 'dumping' tactics abroad. Balfour's analysis and description of the causes and effects of dumping was rarely matched, either by the historical economists or indeed by committed tariff-reform propagandists, and they provide an interesting example of his acceptance of the reasoning which underpinned a central element of the case for tariffs.

Balfour's basic precepts of political economy, and his arguments about the nature of economic developments in the late nineteenth and early twentieth century, were very close to those propounded by the 'house intellectuals' of the tariff campaign. Moreover, there was very little in his analysis of what was wrong with the British economy that the most ardent tariff reformer would have found alien. This makes it difficult to see his position as anything but sympathetic to the tariff cause, and the question that emerges is why he did not translate this intellectual sympathy into a more clear-cut support for the Chamberlainite campaign.

This question becomes all the more puzzling if one examines Balfour's position in the prologue to, and initial phases of, the tariff campaign. In his speech to the House of Commons of April 1902 Balfour had signalled his view that free trade was not an immutable policy, and his behaviour during the rest of that year confirmed his position. Here it should be remembered that, before he left for South Africa in November 1902, Joseph Chamberlain had, to his satisfacton, secured majority Cabinet support for using the one-shilling duty on imported corn imposed in spring of that year for the purposes of imperial preference.[58] Had Balfour as Prime Minister and chairman of Cabinet not been in agreement, it is difficult to see how the issue could have reached such an advanced stage of Cabinet discussion. Likewise, it is difficult to understand why Chamberlain should have reacted so angrily when, on

---

[56] Balfour at the Constitutional Club, 26 June 1903, in id., *Fiscal Reform*, 61.
[57] Balfour, *Economic Notes*, 24–5.
[58] For the most detailed description of the Cabinet discussions see Garvin and Amery, *Chamberlain*, v. 109–61.

his return, he found that the Chancellor of the Exchequer, C. T. Ritchie, had effectively blackmailed the Cabinet into accepting the duty's repeal. Unless Chamberlain was engaged in an extraordinary act of self-delusion, there is no alternative but to accept that the Cabinet, with Balfour at its head, had indicated its acceptance of the principle of Chamberlain's argument in the autumn of 1902.

The discussions and machinations that followed on from the repeal of the corn duty in the early summer of 1903 appear to confirm that Balfour was closer to Chamberlain than to the free-trade element in the Cabinet. Following a key Cabinet discussion in early May, Balfour informed the King that he was due to meet a deputation objecting to the corn duty's repeal later that month, and that he would speak 'in such terms as would indicate the possibility of a revival of the tax, *if it were associated with some great change in our fiscal system*.'[59] Given that prime ministerial correspondence with the sovereign is normally anodyne, this was an important statement, for it implied that Balfour had not discarded the idea of either imperial preference or a more comprehensive alteration in Britains's free-trade stance. On 15 May Balfour met the deputation against repeal, and told them that he was not 'one of those who can flatter themselves that our existing fiscal system is necessarily permanent'. He added that he was not a protectionist and that any policy change would require the consent of 'the great body and mass of the people', but he very much left the door open for critics of free trade.[60] On the same day Chamberlain made his famous 'demand for an enquiry' in Birmingham—the speech that has gone down as the public starting-point of the tariff debate. That both Balfour and Chamberlain spoke on the same day on essentially the same subject was a coincidence, and it would be wrong to assume some sort of 'conspiracy' theory concerning either the content or reception of their respective statements. However, given that Balfour and Chamberlain *knew* that they were both due to speak, it stretches the bounds of credulity to think that they had not reached *some* form of agreement before announcing their respective positions.

That Balfour and Chamberlain *did* have an agreement seems eminently plausible. In his diary for 15 May 1903 Edward Hamilton of the Treasury noted that Balfour's speech 'hinted obscurely at possible changes ahead fiscally', that 'such changes . . . could not be made without the express concurrence of the people', and that 'this was presumably or intended to be *what he and Chamberlain have agreed upon*'.[61]

---

[59] Balfour to Edward VII, 12 May 1903, in Amery, *Joseph Chamberlain*, 82 (my emphasis).
[60] Balfour at Westminster Hall, 15 May 1903, in id., *Fiscal Reform*, 26–7.
[61] E. Hamilton, diary entry, 15 May 1903, Hamilton papers, British Library, Add. MSS, 48680 (my emphasis).

Likewise Balfour, in writing to the Duke of Devonshire in late August 1903, referred to the Cabinet meeting of early May and noted that 'Chamberlain, if you remember, took the occasion to observe that *he* proposed to say at Birmingham much the same as what *I* proposed to say to the deputation, *only in a less definite manner*'[62]—a description of the two speeches of 15 May that was entirely accurate. However, Balfour added that Chamberlain's comments in the House of Commons in late May, referring to the use of tariff revenues to fund social reform, was 'a direct violation of an arrangement with me',[63] a strange remark to make unless there had been some form of 'pact'.

Piecing together evidence from the documents and events of 1902–3, and assessing it in the light of both Balfour's personal disposition and his statements on political economy, an intriguingly plausible story emerges. On the one hand there is Chamberlain: a dynamic personality, well-versed in the arts of popular politics and committed to a radical restructuring of Britain's commercial policy. On the other there is Balfour: a cautious man who fought shy of 'demagogic' appeals but who was also deeply sceptical about Britain's unilateral free-trade stance. In many ways the political division of labour between the two was perfect. Both felt that the time had come for a change in British trade policy, and both accepted that popular support had to be gained if such a change were to be politically viable. Balfour was not in a position, nor was he able, to engage in a popular crusade to persuade the electorate, but Chamberlain had greater freedom and the requisite political talents to pursue such a course of action. With Balfour as chief, Chamberlain could provide the indians.

At first glance the idea of such a political partnership may seem unlikely, but it would explain a great deal. To begin with, it would explain Balfour's tetchy remarks about Chamberlain's 'violation of an arrangement', which would otherwise make little sense. It would also explain Balfour's seemingly duplicitous behaviour in the late summer and autumn of 1903 over the Cabinet resignations. Balfour's public position on the tariff question in late 1903 was the *Economic Notes on Insular Free Trade*, which foregrounded a 'retaliationist' argument. However, two of the free-trade ministers who resigned in September, Lord George Hamilton and C. T. Ritchie, cited Balfour's so-called 'Blue Paper' to the Cabinet of 13 August as a major cause of their disquiet. In this paper Balfour, according to Lord George Hamilton, not only advocated retaliatory tariffs but also accepted 'food taxes' as a basis for

---

[62] Balfour to Devonshire, 28 Aug. 1903, in Amery, *Joseph Chamberlain*, 82 (original emphasis).
[63] Ibid.

imperial preference.[64] This, along with the Prime Minister's action in concealing Chamberlain's resignation until he had received the resignation of the free-trade members of his Cabinet, was taken to indicate that Balfour was closer to Chamberlain than he had been willing to admit. Given that there was a great deal of bitterness surrounding the Cabinet resignations of September 1903, it could simply be that sour grapes were being pressed particularly hard. But the fact that Balfour replaced Ritchie at the Exchequer with Chamberlain's son, Austen, hardly indicated even-handedness. More important, Balfour's public statements on the tariff question in late 1903 and over the next year tended to confirm the free traders' concerns.

Balfour's public exchange of letters with Chamberlain on the latter's resignation was hardly reassuring to free-trade opinion, with the Prime Minister saying that 'the time has come when a change should be made in the fiscal canons by which we have bound ourselves in our commercial dealings with other governments'.[65] This message was to be a consistent theme of Balfour's utterances from the autumn of 1903 onwards. At the Sheffield meeting of the National Union in October, Balfour stressed that whilst the move towards free trade in 1846 had been 'necessary and appropriate to the times', it had to be acknowledged that 'those times are not our times'.[66] Balfour went on to point out that Cobden had made an important error. 'Few who have studied . . . [Cobden's] life and writings', Balfour argued, 'will pretend that the sentiment of nationality had any large place in his philosophy of politics.' This, he declared, was a particularly relevant oversight, insofar as 'the sentiment of nationality has received an accretion of strength of which no man then living [1846] could have dreamed; and that contemporaneously with this growing sentiment of nationality we have found protection in foreign countries'.[67] For Britain and the Colonies not to take cognizance of this nationalist trend was, in Balfour's view, to live in an ideal world fit only for 'dreamers'.[68] Having neatly summarized the basic historical case against free trade, Balfour went on to point out the more particular dangers inherent in the contemporary situation, stating that, 'in the alliance of tariffs and trusts there is a danger to the enterprise of this country which threatens not merely the capitalist . . . but . . . the artisan and labouring classes'.[69] In the light of these developments Balfour posed himself a question, asking ' "Do you desire to alter fundamentally the fiscal tradition which has prevailed during the last two generations?" ',

---

[64] For Hamilton's and Ritchie's position on the 'Blue Paper' see Gollin, *Balfour's Burden*, 97–8.

[65] Balfour to Chamberlain, 16 Sept. 1903, in Balfour, *Fiscal Reform*, 69.

[66] Balfour at Sheffield, 1 Oct. 1903, in ibid., 99.

[67] Ibid. 100.   [68] Ibid. 101.   [69] Ibid. 104.

to which he replied, ' "Yes, I do".'[70] Mindful of the issue that had brought about the resignation of his free-trade Ministers, and concerned about the electoral implications of the 'food tax' aspect of the argument for imperial preference, Balfour entered some important caveats in his Sheffield speech. Whilst accepting that the idea of closer economic relations with the Colonies was an essential part of the case for tariffs, he contended that it was not a practical proposal at that time because 'the country will not tolerate a tax on food'. For this reason he felt that tariff reform could not be 'tried in its integrity',[71] and emphasized that he proposed to amend Britain's free-trade stance only in order to deploy 'retaliatory' tariffs for the purposes of commercial negotiation.

Speaking at Manchester in January 1904, Balfour reiterated his view that times had changed since 1846 and that this demanded a rethinking of free trade. He also went out of his way to launch an attack on H. H. Asquith, who had pursued Chamberlain around the country in the autumn of 1903 in an attempt to repudiate the case for tariff reform. Balfour in turn repudiated Asquith's arguments. He denounced Asquith's optimistic description of Britain's economic situation under free trade, and described the Liberal spokesman as a pseudo-free trader, on the grounds that retaliatory tariffs were the only means in the current climate of bringing about 'real' free trade through negotiation.[72] With regard to imperial preference, Balfour described this as 'the greater half of fiscal reform' which was motivated by 'more unselfish and nobler instincts than mere negotiation about tariffs', but he also stressed the obstacles in its path.[73] At the same time he denounced the free-trade argument that imperial tariffs would lead to arguments with the Colonies and asked: 'did anybody ever put his ideal of domestic felicity in a perpetual judicial separation?'[74] Balfour was particularly keen in this speech to emphasize the need for Conservative party unity, but his argument in this context was an interesting one insofar as he stated that 'fiscal reform itself will suffer more than any other cause if undue impatience or any other motive . . . forces a change so great either upon the party or the country in a manner which threatens even for a moment that there shall be a reaction'.[75] The very next day he underlined this message, declaring that 'Conservatism ought not to resemble Radicalism', and whilst stating that the Conservatives were 'a party and a Goverment of fiscal reform', he urged a cautious approach.[76] Timing, as much as principle, was Balfour's concern.

---

[70] Ibid. 111.   [71] Ibid. 112.
[72] Balfour at Manchester 11 Jan. 1904, in ibid. 131.
[73] Ibid. 135–6.   [74] Ibid. 132.
[75] Ibid. 140.   [76] Balfour at Manchester, 12 Jan. 1904, in ibid. 143.

Through all of his major set-piece speeches on the tariff question in 1904 and 1905 Balfour sang from the same hymn sheet. He consistently stated that Britain had to revise its tariff policy in order to bring protectionist nations to the negotiating table, counteract the effects of 'dumping', and, if possible, bring about closer commercial links with the Colonies.[77] His main emphasis throughout was on the retaliatory aspect of tariff reform, with imperial preference in close, if always qualified, attendance. It is important to note, however, that Balfour also consistently and explicitly rejected protectionism, which he flatly described at Edinburgh as 'not the best policy'.[78]

Balfour's caution on the tariff question is most easily explained in terms of his desperate desire to ensure party unity, but there is an alternative explanation. His views on the general nature of political economy and his stance on tariff reform were remarkably consistent, and indicated that Balfour had clear and strong views on these subjects. To begin with he evidently had no faith in free trade as an established wisdom. For him there was simply no such thing. He accepted the historical economic viewpoint that economic policy had to be shaped to its particular social, cultural, and national context. By 1903 Balfour had come to to the view that 'old fashioned' free trade had had its day, and that a new commercial policy better fitted to the prevailing climate had to be designed. Thus, in July 1903 he was able to tell his cousin, Lord Hugh Cecil, that 'the serious mistake into which you have fallen is that of supposing that the Unionist Party were put into office for the purpose of preserving, in every particular, a version of Free Trade doctrine which . . . I at all events, have never accepted'.[79] In this respect he was completely in agreement with Joseph Chamberlain that free trade in its established form had to go. The question remained, however, as to what was to replace it, and it was on this question that Balfour and Chamberlain's 'partnership' unravelled. Balfour accepted Chamberlain's and the historical economists' critique of free trade and their analysis of the damage it had done to the British economy, but he did not endorse their neo-mercantilist remedy.

With regard to imperial preference Balfour was in principle supportive. Had he not been then, as noted above, it is unlikely that the Cabinet would have approved the principle of preference at the Cabinet of 2 November 1902. Like Chamberlain, Balfour was struck by the voluntary support the Colonies had given to Britain during the Boer War and

---

[77] See e.g. Balfour in Parliament, 9 Mar. 1904, 1 Aug. 1904, at Edinburgh, 3 Oct. 1904, at Manchester, 26 Jan. 1905, at Newcastle, 14 Nov. 1905, in ibid. 162–8, 189–90, 197–200, 215, 263.

[78] Balfour at Edinburgh, 3 Oct. 1904, ibid. 200.

[79] Balfour to H. Cecil, 16 July 1903, BP, BL Add. MSS, 49759.

also by the unilateral 'Colonial Offer' of trade reciprocity at the Colonial Conference of 1902,[80] and he clearly hoped to exploit this outburst of 'imperial spirit'. In his Birmingham speech of May 1903, Chamberlain told his audience that the Colonies' outlook gave them 'an opportunity' which they had to seize or perhaps lose for good.[81] In a memorandum to Cabinet only six weeks later Balfour issued a similar warning. He criticized any dogmatic rejection of preferential duties on the grounds that 'if a tax is otherwise sufficiently desirable, the mere fact that it carries with it some flavour of Protection is by no means a conclusive argument against it', and he told his colleagues that if they rejected Canada's offer then this would lead the Canadians 'to an ultimate fiscal alliance with the United States' and do untold harm to the Empire, a contingency he described as 'not only probable ... [but] almost inevitable'.[82] Balfour had told his own audience of 15 May that he saw economic ties, rather than constitutional and political bonds, as the best means of securing imperial unity, and stated that 'if it were possible I should look forward to such a consummation with unfeigned pleasure'.[83] For Balfour the key phrase was 'if it were possible', and in this context his particular concern was popular antagonism to 'food taxes'. In Parliament at the end of May Balfour had agreed that 'you will never have a tax on food ... accepted by the people of this country except as an integral part of a large policy on which their hearts are set'.[84] This, however, does not indicate that Balfour was *against* imperial preference. Rather it reinforces the argument, developed earlier in this essay, that he looked to Chamberlain's campaigning abilities to deliver 'the heart, and conscience and the intellect of the great body and mass of the people'.[85] All the indications are that Balfour thought that imperial preference was *right*, but that he felt an 'educative' campaign was necessary before the party could embrace it as official policy.

The problem that arose for Balfour was that, partly as a result of Chamberlain's personal disposition and partly as a result of the complex political economy of the tariff argument, the 'educative' campaign got out of hand. Once the lid had been taken off the tariff issue, Chamberlain found that balancing the various demands and interests affected by the campaign required additions to the initial 'big idea' of

---

[80] For Balfour's references to the Colonies see his speeches in Parliament, 28 May 1903, and at Sheffield, 1 Oct. 1903 in Balfour, *Fiscal Reform*, 31, 98. For Chamberlain's response to the war see Green, *Crisis*, 75–7.

[81] J. Chamberlain at Birmingham, 15 May 1903, in C. Boyd (ed.), *Speeches of the Right Honourable Joseph Chamberlain*, 2 vols. (1914), ii. 128.

[82] Balfour, Memorandum to the Cabinet, 1 Aug. 1903, PRO, CAB 37/73/149.

[83] Balfour at Westminster Hall, 15 May 1903, in id., *Fiscal Reform*, 28.

[84] Balfour in Parliament, 28 May 1903, in ibid. 35.

[85] Balfour at Westminster Hall, 15 May 1903, in ibid. 28.

preference. The question of whether social reforms were necessary to sweeten the 'food tax' pill for the working-class electorate; whether domestic producers would accept the export emphasis of the argument for preference; whether rural and urban interests in tariffs could be reconciled. All of these issues came out of the woodwork once the tariff issue had been raised,[86] and Chamberlain's impulsiveness, and the fact that at 67 he was 'an old man in a hurry', only added to the problems. The considered, constructive debate that Balfour desired was thus lost in the heated controversy that surrounded the issue. Balfour's almost angst-ridden pleas for 'moderate' debate that marked his statements in early 1904 may well have been motivated by concerns about his own party's unity, but they also expressed his frustration that the sane, disinterested reappraisal of Britain's commercial policy which he desired had become submerged in a sea of factional dispute.

What was particularly worrying for Balfour, and ultimately to be instrumental in his downfall, was Chamberlain's endorsement of protective tariffs for British industry and indeed agriculture in the autumn of 1903, and the prominence of these issues in the tariff campaign thereafter.[87] Politically Chamberlain had very little option, and personally very little inclination, to avoid these issues, but Balfour regarded them as unnecessary and unwanted distractions from what he saw as the core issues at stake. For Balfour imperial preference was a 'noble', 'unselfish', and eminently desirable goal, but protectionism, which raised the spectre of American-style interest politics, was fraught with 'squalid' possibilities, and in December 1904 Balfour complained that Chamberlain had, through protectionism, hitched 'all sorts of particular and selfish interests to his Imperial car'.[88] But this was not Balfour's only objection. As noted above, he saw protection as a *wrong* policy, for the very good reason that he was a *committed* retaliationist.

Balfour's adoption of retaliation had an obvious, and oft-referred-to, political *raison d'être*.[89] But to see it simply as a politically convenient 'half-way house' between the 'whole hog tariff reform' and 'free food' positions is a one-dimensional view. Balfour himself dismissed this description of retaliation and argued that it was a cogent policy in its own right.[90] Balfour's defence of *his* policy was understandable, for he had adhered to it for many years. In June 1880, in the context of Anglo-French trade relations, the young Balfour had argued that circumstances had changed since Cobden had negotiated his famous commercial pact

[86] See Green, *Crisis*, 184–93 for a discussion of this problem.
[87] For the prominence of these aspects of the tariff campaign see ibid. 211–15.
[88] Balfour to H. Cecil, 2 Dec. 1904, BP, BL Add. MSS, 49759, fos. 55–61.
[89] See above, pp. 19–22.
[90] Balfour at Edinburgh, 3 Oct. 1904, in id., *Fiscal Reform*, 197.

with Chevalier. It was not true, he declared, that foreign countries had moved towards free trade spontaneously in the past, but rather that they had done so in exchange for mutual tariff reductions. But in 1880 he saw Britain at a disadvantage in any negotiations because, having no tariffs of its own, it could only use 'threats instead of bribes'. A possible way out of this problem, he suggested, was for Britain to introduce retaliatory tariffs as a bargaining instrument, a suggestion he repeated a year later when Parliament debated the new Anglo-French commercial treaty.[91] Likewise, during the election campaign of 1892 he stated that: 'I am not a Fair Trader nor a Protectionist, but I am of the opinion that, if foreign nations deliberately attempt to screw up their duties against English manufactured goods, there will be occasions on which it would suit us to bring them to a better state of mind by, in our turn, placing duties upon their manufactures.'[92] These arguments from the 1880s and 1890s were precisely the ones Balfour used in the early years of the tariff campaign. In his speech of 15 May 1903 he stated that: 'New conditions have arisen since the old Free Trade policy was fought out; and I can imagine contingencies under which, not so much by way of protection as by way of retaliation, it might conceivably be necessary for this country to say that it will no longer remain a passive target for the assaults of other countries living under very different fiscal systems.'[93] Similarly, in his Sheffield declaration he was clear that he looked to tariffs to provide 'liberty to negotiate'.[94] Balfour took what was in many ways an 'international relations' view of the tariff question, arguing that 'international commerce is largely regulated by treaty, in which trade flows along channels engineered not by Nature but by diplomacy'.[95] For Balfour, very much his uncle's protégé, national diplomacy, rather than bellicose economic nationalism, was the way forward. This required that Britain had something to negotiate with and hence the necessity of retaliatory tariffs, but protectionism *tout court* was a complete anathema to this approach and had no place in Balfour's schema.

When, in August 1904, Balfour told the House of Commons 'I am a Free Trader',[96] there was in terms of his own definition of tariff political economy an internal logic to his position. He accepted that many self-professed free traders did not acknowledge him as an adherent of their creed, but this he attributed to his being a 'new fashioned free

---

91 Balfour in Parliament, 24 June 1880, 9 June 1881, in ibid. 1–2.
92 Balfour at Manchester, 2 July 1892, in ibid. 5.
93 Balfour at Westminster Hall, 15 May 1903, in ibid. 27.
94 Balfour at Sheffield, 1 Oct. 1903, in ibid. 111.
95 Ibid. 105.
96 Balfour in Parliament, 1 Aug. 1904, in ibid. 189.

trader'[97] rather than a devotee of the old school. In Balfour's view his 'free trade' critics, unlike him, had failed to adjust to the times and could not appreciate or understand his idea of *freer* trade. Balfour saw no problem in reconciling his pursuit of freer trade with his support for imperial preference. Apart from contending that imperial reciprocity would produce freer trade within the Empire as the Colonies lowered their tariffs, Balfour also argued that retaliation would inhibit other countries from inflicting tariff 'punishment' on the Colonies for their actions.[98] In Balfour's view a combination of retaliation and preference would act to weaken protectionist barriers all round. Unfortunately for Balfour, the subtlety of his position was lost on devout free traders, and also failed to please the more autarky-minded imperialist and protectionist sections in the tariff campaign. In this respect Lord Robert Cecil was right in arguing that, although Balfour wished to be 'all things to all men', he ended up by being not much to hardly anyone. Balfour's formula was a subtle and sophisticated contribution to the debate on Britain's commercial policy. It undoubtedly did represent a critique of crude free trade, but it also avoided the cruder aspects of the tariff campaign. The consequence of Balfour's subtlety, however, was that his arguments failed to garner *immediate* support, but a strong case can be made for seeing his retaliationist position as gathering strength over time. In the long run Britain's business community proved more receptive to Balfourian than Chamberlainite logic, and the creeping success of retaliationist sentiment was to be an important indicator of weakening business faith in free trade.[99] But time, although it was what he wanted, was precisely what Balfour did not have.

Balfour's unwillingness to embrace the 'full tariff programme', as developed by Chamberlain and his followers between 1903 and 1910, did not stem solely from his desire to preserve party unity, or from his intrinsic inability to commit himself to a cause. To see Balfour's actions solely in these terms is to do a disservice to his ideas and to the history of the tariff debate. Balfour was committed to a particular conception of tariff reform, and his real problem was that he was asked to commit himself to another conception which he did not believe was *right*. In 1903 he had hoped to bring about a change in public opinion on free trade which would open the door to retaliation, a 'rational' readjustment of Britain's trading relations, and, if possible, closer commercial ties with the Colonies. Instead, the tariff campaign developed into a

[97] Balfour at Edinburgh, 3 Oct. 1904, in ibid. 206.
[98] Balfour at Manchester, 26 Jan. 1905, in ibid. 215.
[99] See F. Trentmann, 'The Strange Death of Free Trade', in E. Biagini (ed.), *Citizenship and Community* (Cambridge, 1996).

semi-autarkic programme of preference and protection linked to further schemes of domestic reform. Balfour may have been at fault for not realizing that this would happen, but in this respect he was by no means alone among his contemporaries. The net result was that Balfour became the leader of a party that had embraced a conception of tariff reform that was unrecognizable as his own and which he did not believe in. It may be a general assumption that politicians are good at saying and doing what they do not really believe, but the field of history is littered with the political corpses of those who have tried and failed to achieve this feat—and Arthur Balfour's is one of them.

CHAPTER 2

English Idealism, Conservatism, and Collectivism, 1880–1914

IDEALISM HAS rightly come to occupy a central role in the historiography of British political thought in the late nineteenth and early twentieth centuries. This is by no means a new historiographical phenomenon. The resurgence of interest in the New Liberalism, which began in the early 1970s[1] and which continues to burgeon, drew attention to the philosophical underpinnings of the Liberal party's turn to Collectivist social and economic policy initiatives. These studies showed that Idealism, and in particular the writings and influence of T. H. Green on a generation of Liberal thinkers and politicians, played an important role in the reshaping of Liberalism.[2] However, they also showed that there was not a straightforward link between philosophic Idealism and Collectivist social and economic thought. Green himself could not be described as espousing a positive role for the State. Whilst he saw society as an organism that was more than the sum of its individual parts, and was thus at odds with Liberal Individualists such as Herbert Spencer, the emphasis he placed on the role of the individual will in the realization of the social good was at variance with Statist thought. Green's death in 1882 meant that his views on the extension of State action in the social and economic spheres in the late nineteenth and early twentieth centuries could only be imagined or extrapolated from his fragmentary references to legislation, and such a process could be but inconclusive. Many of Green's fellow Idealists, both contemporaries and 'disciples', did witness the introduction of Collectivist legislation, but their

---

[1] The publication of P. Clarke, *Lancashire and the New Liberalism* (Cambridge, 1971) was the first milestone. The subsequent literature is extensive, but see in particular P. Clarke, *Liberals and Social Democrats* (Cambridge, 1978); M. Freeden, *The New Liberalism* (Oxford, 1977); S. Collini, *Liberalism and Sociology* (Cambridge, 1979); J. Allett, *New Liberalism: The Political Economy of J. A. Hobson* (Toronto, 1981).

[2] See M. Richter, *The Politics of Conscience* (1964); R. Plant and A. Vincent, *Politics, Philosophy, and Citizenship* (Oxford, 1984); I. M. Greengarten, *Thomas Hill Green and the Development of Liberal-Democratic Thought* (Toronto, 1981); J. Morrow, 'Liberalism and British Idealist Political Philosophy: A Reassessment', *HOPT* 5 (1984), id., 'Ancestors, Legacies and Tradition: British Idealism', in the *History of Political Thought*, 6 (1985); S. Den Otter, *British Idealism and Social Explanation* (Oxford, 1997).

views on these developments did not indicate any consistent relationship between Idealist thought and Statist or anti-Statist ideas. F. H. Bradley, D. G. Ritchie, Bernard Bosanquet, and Henry Jones all had 'views' on State action, but their positions varied over time and in relation to the particular legislative framework being contemplated or enacted.[3] Likewise, the response of Liberal politicians and self-professedly 'Progressive, New Liberal' writers and thinkers to Idealism was by no means wholly positive, and was in some cases notably hostile.[4] Furthermore, there were strong intellectual influences apart from Idealism which were important to the development of the New Liberalism, especially evolutionary and biological paradigms.[5] The importance of Idealism in shaping the intellectual context and framework of New Liberal Collectivism is clear, but both English Idealist thought and its influence on Liberal ideas were highly nuanced.[6] Insofar as any general conclusions can be drawn about its role, Idealist thought can be viewed as a key element in the 'search for a social philosophy' by thinkers and politicians in Britain in the late nineteenth and early twentieth centuries.[7]

The investigations that have been made of the varied and complex nature of Idealist thought and its influence have greatly enriched the historical understanding of the patterns and themes of British political, economic, and social thought in the period 1880–1914. Yet, there is one gap in the historiography which this chapter will seek in part to fill, namely, the influence of Idealism on Conservative thought. The starting-point for this chapter's investigation is in the same place and with the same individual that many studies of the relationship between Idealism and the New Liberalism began, that is, in late nineteenth-century Oxford and with T. H. Green. Oxford, and in particular Balliol College, have loomed large in the historiography of the New Liberalism. Green as a Tutor at Balliol and Benjamin Jowett as Master of that College were the leading intellectual figures in Oxford in the last quarter of the nineteenth century, exercising an influence that went beyond the walls of

[3] S. Den Otter, *British Idealism*, passim.

[4] R. B. Haldane stands out as the Liberal Cabinet Minister who expressed most admiration for Idealist thought, whilst L. T. Hobhouse was the New Liberal thinker who was most hostile.

[5] See Freeden, *New Liberalism*, 76–116, and id., 'Biological and Evolutionary Roots in New Liberalism in England', *Political Theory*, 4 (1976).

[6] See Den Otter, *British Idealism*, 88–119, 149–204; id., ' "Thinking in Communities": Late Nineteenth-Century Liberals, Idealists and the Retrieval of Community', in E. H. H. Green (ed.), *An Age of Transition: British Politics, 1880–1914* (Edinburgh, 1997); and S. Collini, 'Hobhouse, Bosanquet and the State: Philosophical Idealism and Political Argument in Britain, 1880–1914', *P&P* 72 (1976).

[7] See Den Otter, *British Idealism*, passim, and J. Harris, 'Political Thought and the Welfare State, 1870–1940: An Intellectual Framework for British Social Policy', *P&P* 135 (1992).

their own institution and which lasted beyond their own lifetimes. Apart from the emphasis they placed on scholarly achievement, Green and Jowett also saw Oxford's, and especially Balliol's, task as being to encourage and assist the devlopment of a sense of social and civic responsibility amongst the student body. Here they were by no means alone or unassisted. Other scholars, notably F. H. Bradley, another Idealist philosopher at Merton College, and Arnold Toynbee, a historian at Balliol, espoused similar views, and a range of undergraduate discussion groups, societies, and political forums emerged which fostered a philosophy of social and civic engagement and action. The Economic Society, the Oxford Extension movement, and the creation of the Oxford East End mission centre of Toynbee Hall were the most obvious examples of the attempt to bring scholarly and civic activities together, and the philosophy of Green, Jowett, and Toynbee had particular resonance as Oxford, like other sectors of the British social, political, and intellectual elite, heard the 'bitter cry of outcast London' and sought to understand and address the problem of 'the condition of the people'. Many of those who were exposed either directly to, or to the legacy of, the influence of Green, Jowett, Toynbee, and other Oxford mentors emerged as prominent voices and actors in the New Liberalism and the early Socialist movement. H. H. Asquith, Herbert Samuel, L. T. Hobhouse, J. A. Hobson, Sidney Olivier, and Sidney Ball were all products of this milieu, and the intellectual environment of 'Oxford Collectivism' was clearly influential in shaping their political development.

However, the 'Oxford Collectivist' milieu did not only produce New Liberals and Socialists, for a number of prominent Conservative politicians and thinkers who were equally interested in Collectivist answers to social questions emerged from the same environment. Alfred Milner was an undergraduate at Balliol from 1873 to 1876, when Green and Jowett's influence was at its height, and although he identified himself as a Liberal in his youth he had become disillusioned with Liberalism by 1885, became a Liberal Unionist in 1886, and in the Edwardian period emerged as one of the most articulate and influential advocates of State intervention in social and economic matters on the Right.[8] Leopold Amery was a student at Balliol from 1892 to 1896 when Jowett was still Master,[9] and was elected a Fellow of All Souls in 1897. He was one of Milner's 'kindergarten' in South Africa at the turn of the century, and, having become a Conservative candidate and then MP in the Edwardian

---

[8] Green, *Crisis*, 242–63.
[9] See L. S. Amery, *My Political Life*, 3 vols. (1953–5), vol. 1, *England Before the Storm*, 44–67.

period, Amery, like his political mentor, emerged as a powerful advocate of tariffs and social reform.[10] J. W. Hills also studied at Jowett's Balliol from 1885 to 1889, and, having stood successfully as the independent, tariff-reform Conservative MP for Durham in 1906, became one of the leading Conservative supporters of State social reform, being a member of the National Anti-Sweating League, an architect of the Conservative 'Unauthorised Programme' of 1908, and a leading figure in the Unionist Social Reform Committee (USRC).[11] Finally, Arthur Steel-Maitland was at Balliol from 1895 to 1899, and was elected a Fellow of All Souls in 1900. He too was a keen student of economics and political philosophy, attending lectures on these subjects at the LSE from 1900 to 1902. Like Milner, Amery, and Hills he was a committed tariff reformer, but he also developed a particular interest in social policy and was responsible for the establishment of the USRC in 1911.[12]

Conservative thinkers as well as politicians also emerged from this intellectual context, most notably the historical economists W. A. S. Hewins, W. J. Ashley, William Cunningham, and L. L. Price. Hewins, Ashley, and Price, all undergraduates in Oxford in the early 1880s, were active members of the Oxford Economic Society, with Ashley remaining a corresponding member after he left to teach at the University of Toronto.[13] Hewins was, until the early 1890s, a lecturer at Toynbee Hall, and acted as the organizing secretary of the Oxford Extension Movement's Summer Meetings, which had been established as a working memorial to T. H. Green.[14] At this point Hewins was 'beyond all question a very good Radical',[15] and applied for a post in the Publishing Department of the National Liberal Federation, but he moved into the Conservative orbit at the time of the Boer War because of his increasing interest in and commitment to imperialism.[16] L. L. Price was, like Hewins, involved with the Extension Movement, and his involvement with the Royal Commission on Labour in the mid-1890s was a further reflection of his interest in and engagement with social questions. Unlike the others, William Cunningham studied at Cambridge and became a Fellow of Trinity College, but he described T. H. Green as 'the man whom I looked upon as my master in all that I care about philosophy',[17]

---

[10] Green, *Crisis*, 161–2.

[11] Ibid. 257–8, 287–8, and id., 'J. W. Hills', entry for the *New DNB* (forthcoming).

[12] See Ch. 3.

[13] See Oxford Economic Society, membership list and term card, Jan. 1889, Hewins papers 42/4.

[14] See S. Barnett to Hewins, 21 June 1889, ibid., 42/15 and ibid., file 43 *passim*.

[15] J. Slater to C. Stanhope, 17 Mar. 1891, ibid., 43/52.

[16] See W. A. S. Hewins, *The Apologia of an Imperialist*, 2 vols. (1929), i. 44–61.

[17] Undated remark by Cunningham, in A. Cunningham, *William Cunningham: Teacher and Priest* (1953), 50.

and he shared the Oxford historical economists' 'Greenian' devotion to the quest for a social philosophy.[18]

The goal of this chapter will be to outline the influence of Idealism on Conservatism in Britain. It will do this in several stages. First, it will examine the ideas of a rather obscure Conservative writer, Arthur Boutwood. Second, it will link Boutwood's ideas to the work of the English historical economists. Third, it will look at how these ideas worked within the context of Edwardian Conservative politics. In so doing it will open a window onto a hitherto unexplored aspect not only of Conservative thought, but also the legacy of T. H. Green, English Idealism, and late nineteenth-century Oxford Collectivism.

I

In the annals of British political thought Arthur Boutwood is hardly a name to conjure with.[19] Boutwood was born in London in 1864 and died sixty years later in Brighton. His formal education ended at the elementary stage, but he was evidently an autodidact of some energy— an honours graduate of the Home University series. He joined the Civil Service in 1879 and rose to the hardly dizzying heights of Second Division Clerk with the Charity Commission. However, he clearly aspired to 'higher things', both financial and intellectual. From the late 1890s until his death in 1924 Boutwood produced a steady stream of publications, desperately seeking to break out of what he regarded as a humdrum existence and establish a reputation, and a living, as a 'thinker' and man of letters. As most of his writings either directly addressed or touched on political issues, he was obliged, by Civil Service regulations, to use pseudonyms, his favourite *noms de plume* being Ignotus and, more commonly, Hakluyt Egerton. As we shall see, his work led to his enjoying a brief period of lionization just before the outbreak of the Great War, but he was soon forgotten by his erstwhile patrons. His correspondence both during and after the war often referred to this fleeting moment of celebrity, but generally in the context of what were, in effect, begging letters. Having enjoyed five rather than fifteen minutes of fame, Arthur Boutwood and his works returned to obscurity. So why resurrect him and his perhaps deservedly forgotten oeuvre? This chapter will not present him as an 'undiscovered genius' or make any great claims about the intrinsic significance of his work.

---

[18] Cunningham, *William Cunningham: Teacher and Priest, passim.*
[19] The only reference to Boutwood the author has found is in W. H. Greenleaf, *The British Political Tradition*, 3 vols. (1983), vol. 2, *The Ideological Heritage*, 233–4.

Rather, it will seek to use his writings, and two texts in particular—
Patriotism (1905) and *National Revival* (1914)—as a point of entry into
a broader contemporary debate on the nature of Conservatism.

In *Patriotism* Boutwood addressed at length his chief philosophical
interests, the nature of the individual and the nation, and the relationship between them. For Boutwood 'man' (and he always used the
masculine pronoun) was an 'ethical organism', by which he meant three
things. First, he used the term 'organism' because he preferred biological to 'mechanical' metaphors—an organism, Boutwood argued, had
'its own end' whereas a machine was simply a tool.[20] Second, he
contended that an organism was 'determined by its own nature to an
end appointed by that nature, and that end is the organism itself'.[21]
Third, man was 'ethical' because it was 'characteristic of human life that
it has ideals' which 'set forth not only what man *desires* to be but what
he *ought* to be'.[22] 'Man', Boutwood argued, was determined by the
thought of himself 'as better or more perfect . . . an ideal of self realization . . . in which the soul itself is conceived as better or more
complete'.[23] As a consequence Boutwood saw the essence of man as
'self-realization . . . [the] realization of the self by the self . . . a transition of the potential into the actual, whereby the potential becomes
real'.[24]

In the same vein, Boutwood also saw the nation as an 'ethical organism'. A nation, he argued, was, like an individual, 'an organism self-
determined to self-realization'. But here there was a problem. If a nation
was an 'ethical organism' it could, in his logic, have 'no end other than
itself', and yet he also contended that 'every individual constituent of
the nation is . . . self-determined . . . to the completeness of his own
individual nature and life, and his characteristic end'. How was the 'self-
realization' of the nation to be reconciled with the 'self-realization' of its
individual constituents?[25] The answer Boutwood provided was that the
self-realization of both the nation and its individual constituents were
indivisible.

The ideal of individual self-realization was, according to Boutwood,
the 'completeness of individual life'. However, this was, he argued, 'an
ideal that cannot be reached by any solitary endeavour . . . man can
grow into likeness to his ideal only in and through society—only in and
through sympathy and co-operation'.[26] The reason was that, although
every individual had 'capacity for thought, for feeling, for various forms
of practical activity', this capacity could be exercised 'only in so far as

---

[20] H. Egerton (A. Boutwood), *Patriotism* (1905), 27–8.
[21] Ibid. 30.   [22] Ibid. 33.   [23] Ibid. 40.
[24] Ibid. 31.   [25] Ibid. 42–3.   [26] Ibid.

we have opportunity, and our opportunities are determined by our environment, partly by our natural environment, but partly and chiefly by our social environment.'[27] Individuals were not born into a state of nature or into chaos, Boutwood pointed out, but came into the world as citizens of a nation, and the nation, 'a growth, a result of the associated and interacting lives of men', was the key force that shaped, liberated, or constrained an individual's capacity for self-realization.[28] But precisely because the nation was such a 'growth', it did not, indeed could not, exist separately from its constituent individuals, but rather lived 'only in them'.[29] Nation and individual were bound together in a symbiotic process of realization. The nation was the key environmental agent in terms of shaping opportunities for individual self-realization, but at the same time the nation could only realize its true nature, or come to self-realization as an 'ethical organism', through 'the self-realization of each of the individual constituents in it, in whom alone it has concrete reality'.[30]

This organic conception of the relationship between the nation and the individual led Boutwood to explore the concept of citizenship. As the nation was, in Boutwood's view, an 'ethical organism', it followed that 'citizenship—membership in the nation—has . . . an ethical vocation'. 'Citizenship', he declared,

is not merely a franchise for the protection or furtherance of purely private interests . . . A franchise, indeed, it is, but the freedom it brings is a freedom for service, and not simply for private gain. In other words, citizenship is a freedom for duty—for a duty which is never *merely* self-regarding, can only, very rarely, be *directly* self-regarding. For what is our duty? To become truly and completely men, to grow into the measure of the stature of the fulness of life.[31]

Citizenship thus meant 'not only membership in a political society' but 'unselfish devotion to the common good', in that civic life was 'a collective following of the moral ideal'.[32] This did not mean that individual citizens were *subordinate* to the nation or to the common good, for an individual could not, in Boutwood's logic, be subordinate to something that was self-willed as part of the project of self-realization. Indeed, Boutwood argued that true freedom could only come through co-operative acts that were born out of a recognition and realization of mutual needs and goals. This, for Boutwood, was the essence of the Christian ideal in which 'manhood grows into its own completeness in and through love'.[33] 'In this ideal', he argued, 'all other ideals of self-realization are unified and consummated', and hence 'the end to which man

---

[27] Egerton (Boutwood), *Patriotism*, 42–3.   [28] Ibid. 43–4   [29] Ibid. 46.
[30] Ibid. 50.   [31] Ibid. 5.   [32] Ibid. 54.
[33] Ibid. 37–8.

as an ethical organism' was 'characteristically determined' was the Christian ideal of finding self-fulfilment through service to and fellowship with one's neighbours.[34]

But if the individual citizen had a 'duty' to attempt self-realization, the nation had a reciprocal duty which individuals could regard as a right. Boutwood described this 'ethical end' of the nation as 'general helpfulness', or the right of individual citizens to 'find the nation's life always availingly helpful' to the task of self-realization.[35] 'A man', Boutwood argued, 'has a right to demand that the national life, and the institutions and usages of national life, shall be helpful to him, helpful in all ways that make for fulness of life and completeness of manhood.'[36] Furthermore, this right had to apply equally to all citizens. 'In a true community', Boutwood stated, 'there is no room for merely tributary classes.'[37] The nation's 'general helpfulness' had to be truly 'general', and any nation that had an 'inequality of recognised right . . . contain[ed] within itself forces that will one day destroy it or transform it'.[38] Boutwood's basic conception of relations between the individual and the nation was thus that 'the individual is bound to serve the nation . . . but the nation is equally bound to be serviceable to the individual, and if in any given case it be not effectually and equitably serviceable, it should be made so'.[39]

It is at this juncture in Boutwood's schema that the State came into play. The State was not, he emphasized, synonymous with the nation, it was only an 'aspect of the Nation',[40] for the State was a 'body politic' whilst the nation was an 'ethical organism'; the State was a tool, or a means to an end, whereas the nation was an end in itself. But although the State was not the same thing as the nation, its role, according to Boutwood, was to use its legislative powers for national ends. If the State machinery was 'subordinate to interests that are merely personal or dynastic', Boutwood argued, it belonged to 'that . . . order of history which we rightly call "unmoralized" '.[41] The State's powers had to be 'incorporated into the National Organism' and become 'subordinate to the ends for which that organism exists', for it was 'only as thus subordinate' that government had 'any ground in ethical light'.[42]

The State was to achieve its 'moral conception' by engaging in what Boutwood called 'national work', which he defined as 'work that sustains and fosters [the nation's] life, that builds up its people into serviceable manhood'.[43] This required the State to 'make effective' what

---

[34] Ibid. 39. [35] Ibid. 56–9. [36] Ibid. 60.
[37] Ibid. 58–9. [38] Ibid. [39] Ibid. 60.
[40] H. Egerton (A. Boutwood), *National Toryism* (privately published, 1911), 8.
[41] Ibid. [42] Ibid.
[43] Egerton (Boutwood), *Patriotism*, 81.

Boutwood termed an individual's 'right to opportunity', that is, the right to attempt self-realization. Boutwood contended that this gave the State 'a double function'. It had to 'protect established rights' to opportunity, and it had 'to give opportunity when opportunity is refused'. As a consequence, the State's exercise of power had to be 'always National, never partizan', for if it adopted policies which were 'merely and self-ishly sectional' it would have 'cease[d] to discharge its characteristic function, and thereby [lost] its . . . claim to general allegiance'.[44] To secure its claim to general allegiance the State had to ensure that it was effectively and equally 'serviceable' to all citizens as they strove to real-ize their full potential.

These basic precepts reveal the paradigms within which Boutwood was working. Boutwood was an Idealist, and more specifically, was part of the very particular strain of English Idealism that flourished in the late nineteenth and early twentieth centuries. The idea of human life as a constant process of transition from 'potential' to 'actual', and as a progress towards an eventual realization of an 'ideal', was clearly and confessedly derived from Hegel. Closer to home, Boutwood's emphasis on individual self-realization through a self-willed acceptance of the idea of a common good, and his desire to promote an active civic consciousness, were drawn explicitly from T. H. Green. Likewise, Boutwood's view of the State as fulfilling its own ethical essence by securing opportunities for the citizenry's self-realization was very 'Greenian'. That Boutwood presented his concept of individual and national self-realization as an expression of Christian values further confirms his position in the specific intellectual context of late nineteenth-century English Idealism, for, as Raymond Plant and Andrew Vincent have shown, a key characteristic of this body of thought was that it situated collective action, the common good and freedom, 'within a metaphysical theory which claimed to state, in a more rational form, the real essence of Christianity'.[45]

But what has this to do with Conservatism? For Boutwood Conservatism was the most promising political creed available in the early twentieth century. The Liberal party, he argued, was 'the inheritor of an obsolete tradition of thought'. Liberalism's maxims were, Boutwood stated, 'chraracteristically abstract', and in particular were based on an atomistic individualism. In Boutwood's schema Liberalism contained 'no creative potency', because it could not grasp concrete historical subjects.[46] By way of contrast, Conservatives sought to

---

[44] Egerton (Boutwood), *National Toryism*, 17.
[45] R. Plant and A. Vincent, *Philosophy, Politics and Citizenship* (Oxford 1985), 6.
[46] Egerton (Boutwood), *Patriotism*, 319–20.

'conserve' because they recognized 'the spiritual continuity of English life . . . and mistrust[ed] changes that . . . threaten[ed] destruction or loss'.[47] Conservatives, in other words, instinctively recognized the organic nature of the nation and appreciated that individuals could not be abstracted from their historical environment. According to Boutwood, this meant that Conservatism was inherently better suited to the task of shaping a polity and society which would facilitate individual and national self-realization.

However, the problem, as Boutwood saw it in 1905, was that Conservatism had lapsed into an intellectual torpor in which mere negation of precipitate change had become its only 'principle', and it did not possess a distinctive, constructive philosophy. In the circumstances of the early twentieth century, such a philosophy was, Boutwood contended, urgently required. 'At one time', he noted,

it might have been possible to think of the nation as a relatively permanent polity . . . But the day for this pre-Darwinian and pre-Hegelian Conservatism has completely passed . . . We have learned that a nation's life is essentially dynamic, and normally progressive—that all forms of social, political and industrial polity are creations of this dynamic and progressive life . . . [and] that the need for reform arises not from merely secondary accidents of history, but from inner spiritual necessities.[48]

Boutwood concluded that, unless it wished to be bypassed by the current of intellectual development, Conservatism had to become 'a doctrine and a policy not only of preservation, but of progress'.[49]

If in 1905 Boutwood felt that Conservatism needed to adjust its outlook, he had grown even more convinced by 1914. In *National Revival* he explicitly addressed the question: 'In the present crisis of English affairs, what should the Conservative party do?'[50] Boutwood felt that the 'crisis' was quite generalized, but in particular he had in mind the Constitutional Crisis of 1909–10 and the labour unrest of 1911–12. He saw these conflicts as a product of the fact that 'In every part of the country men—and women too—are discontented with the opportunities which the existing social order affords them'. It was, he claimed, 'an uprising of life', a demand for a 'larger existence'.[51] That this had occurred was, Boutwood declared, due to the way in which 'the lives emancipated by the political and social changes of the last century grew to maturity outside the established order', with the result that the lower and lower-middle classes had developed a 'separate political mind which has no conscious debt to the established order, and discerns in

---

[47] Ibid. 312.   [48] Ibid. 324–5.   [49] Ibid. 326.
[50] H. Egerton (A. Boutwood), *National Revival* (1914), p. xiii.
[51] Ibid. 1–2.

that order merely a selfish contradiction of its own self-assertive claims'.[52] This in turn had fed political antagonisms, as demonstrated by the conflicts over the People's Budget, the House of Lords, land reform, and industrial conditions, all of which were indicative of a growing threat to the fabric of Britain's existing social and political order.[53]

Insofar as the existing order had 'failed to assimilate (to incorporate into itself) the classes which had been emancipated by the social and political changes of the nineteenth century', and thereby failed to meet their (legitimate) demands for a 'larger life', then the established order had only itself to blame.[54] The existing polity had failed to fulfil its ethical end, and was thus rightly challenged by its own internal contradictions. However, Boutwood also felt that the form the challenge was taking was in itself seriously flawed. Writing in July 1912 to the Diehard Conservative peer Lord Willoughby de Broke, he criticized the stance that the Liberal government had taken on industrial unrest,. 'Mr. Asquith', he argued, 'appears to regard "the nation" as a *mere aggregate*. Consequently he does not attribute "national character" to a trade dispute.' This was deemed wholly wrong, for the nation was

a 'spiritual construct' which progressively realises an idea (and ideal) of unity . . . [and] consequently a trade dispute derives its character from the 'idea' which it involves. In nearly every case the idea involved in a trade dispute is some form of the idea of 'social justice'. Now the idea of 'social justice' is the political expression of the idea (and ideal) of the nation. Therefore every trade dispute which involves a form of the idea of social justice has, in virtue of that fact, a national character, even though . . . the numbers affected be small.[55]

The point Boutwood was seeking to establish was that both the industrial unrest, and the responses to it, were informed by narrow class or sectional, and therefore non-national, interests. He saw nothing wrong with expressions of class interest or even legislation for the benefit of a particular class. In *Patriotism* he had noted that,

'Class legislation' is, it is true, a name of evil repute, not however, because it is purely for class benefit, but because it is thought, and sometimes with reason, to be only or disproportionately for class benefit.[56] [And he had added that:] In so far as a given act of 'class legislation' increases the patriotic helpfulness of the class it benefits, that particular legislation is so far justified. There is no harm in class legislation, but, on the contrary, much good if it widen or improve the national seviceableness of the benefited class.[57]

---

[52] Egerton (Boutwood), *National Revival*, 7.   [53] Ibid. 8.   [54] Ibid. 8–10.
[55] Boutwood to Willoughby de Broke, 5 July 1912, Boutwood papers, Corpus Christi College Library, Cambridge, Boutwood Letter Book, 1905–24.
[56] Egerton (Boutwood), *Patriotism*, 232.   [57] Ibid.

To Boutwood, legislation for a class *in itself* was quite acceptable, but legislation to benefit a class *for itself* was unjustified. Applying this principle to the political context of the late nineteenth and early twentieth centuries, he agreed that the British State and its legislative acts had been biased towards the interests of a privileged few, and that those privileges were no longer exercised in the national interest.[58] However, he also contended that the demands and actions of Socialists and the 'socialistic' Liberal government were simply seeking to replace one set of class interests with another, with the consequence that Britain was on the verge of 'a social war'.[59]

Boutwood's remedy for this crisis was what he called 'National Revival', and hence the appearance of the eponymous text. What Boutwood meant by this was 'a reawakening of the sense of social solidarity, a reassertion and reconstruction of national unity'.[60] This meant producing structures that gave proper expression to lower-class aspirations, a task Boutwood described as 'social reconstruction and moral reintegration', with the ultimate aim being to 'reconstruct the spiritual fabric of the nation's life upon a broader foundation and a larger, more generous plan' and thereby 'lift "labour" out of a mere class consciousness into the broader thoughts and loftier hopes of a life genuinely national'.[61]

National reconstruction and reintegration was, Boutwood argued, the primary task of the Conservative party, and it should be noted at this point that the original drafts of *National Revival* were entitled 'Notes Preliminary to a Revival of Conservatism'.[62] Unlike Liberalism and Socialism, with their respective emphases on individuals and classes, Conservatism was based on national, historical premises which recognized the organic nature of society. Conservatism, because of its 'attachment to certain relatively permanent elements in the existing order' had 'an inclination to make the new organically continuous with the old'.[63] But to achieve this Conservatives first had to recognize that 'our earliest work must be wrought in ourselves. We must clear our vision and enlarge our sympathies.' Conservatives, Boutwood argued, had to look 'beneath the extravagances of the moment' and 'discern the deep human needs which these crudely and aberrantly express', and then show the lower classes that they were capable of providing 'a better satisfaction than the tarnished triumphs of a class war'.[64]

[58] Ibid. 227–30.
[59] H. Egerton (A. Boutwood), 'The Budget—Conflict in England', draft MS of an article in the Boutwood papers, Box 3.
[60] Egerton (Boutwood), *National Revival*, 16.   [61] Ibid. 18.
[62] The drafts are dated Sept. 1913, Boutwood papers, Box 3.
[63] *National Revival*, 86–7.   [64] Ibid. 36–7.

'Constructive Toryism' was the term Boutwood used to describe his path to 'national revival', by which he meant a social reforming policy that showed that Conservatism had 'its own distinctive way of dealing with social problems'.[65] This entailed using the State to 'help those who cannot help themselves'. 'The helpless', Boutwood argued, 'have a right to be helped. Their need is their right. That right is not merely a moral or religious right—it is a civic right, a right which pertains to them in virtue of their citizenship, or (more accurately) in virtue of their membership in the nation.'[66] This did not mean, however, that the State was to become a source of universal bounty. Boutwood's stated aim was to find a middle ground between 'the Manchester School's discredited creed' and 'those who, Fabian wise or avowedly, desire the State to become a general providence and the one economic agent'.[67] In his schema the State was not to provide opportunity, but to give all citizens the right to opportunity, and make it an 'effective right' by removing the 'obstructiveness and hindrances created by the inequitable development of society'.[68] There are echoes here of Bernard Bosanquet's well-known remark about 'the hindrance of hindrances', but Boutwood's unequivocal criticisms of 'the superficial doctrines of . . . liberal political economy' clearly envisaged a more active State than Bosanquet.[69] One indication of the practical implications of Boutwood's thought was his support for tariff reform, expressed in the context of a discussion of the 'right to work'. He argued that

The alleged 'right to work', although extravagant, undoubtedly expresses a real right, but that real right does not require us to think that the State should provide work. If it be true that Tariff Reform would expand our industries, and thus increase the demand for labour, Tariff Reform would be—within the range of its efficacy— a complete discharge of the duty of the State towards those who are employable but not employed.[70]

However, although he mentioned a need for 'industrial reform' and supported old-age pensions, Boutwood remained vague as to the details of a 'Constructive Tory' programme, preferring to concentrate on broad statements of principle.

It would be easy to dismiss Boutwood as a crank. In every period it is possible to find eccentric thinkers who have, to their own satisfaction,

---

[65] *National Revival*, 38, 81–83.   [66] Ibid. 113.
[67] H. Egerton (A. Boutwood), 'Social Reform', draft article dated 26 Sept. 1913, Boutwood papers, Box 3, later published in *The British Review* (Nov. 1913).
[68] Egerton (Boutwood), *National Revival*, 90–2.
[69] Bosanquet was, of course, closely associated with the Charity Organization Society. For the COS position see C. L. Mowat, *The Charity Organization Society* (1961), *passim*, and A. MacBriar, *An Edwardian Mixed Doubles* (Oxford, 1987), 54–85.
[70] Egerton (Boutwood), *National Revival*, 91.

discovered the lodestone of politics and who present their ideas as the answer to either a party's or the nation's prayers, or, as in Boutwood's case, both. Boutwood appears eminently qualified for this role. His works were eclectic, opaque, and on occasion self-contradictory, perhaps as a result of their being composed during his lunch-breaks and on the train between Marylebone and Prince's Risborough. Nevertheless he clearly took himself seriously and hoped, even expected, that his contemporaries would do likewise. But did they, and should we? The answer to the first part of this question is yes, for a number of Conservative politicians gave his work some quite serious attention.

In late September 1911 Lord Willoughby de Broke, having come into possession of an unpublished essay by Boutwood, wrote to compare notes with him on the subject of 'Conservative principles'.[71] As a result of this correspondence Boutwood was invited to present a paper to a small gathering of Conservative peers and MPs, including Lord Selborne, Lord Hugh Cecil, W. A. S. Hewins, William Ormsby-Gore, the Duke of Northumberland, and Willoughby de Broke himself, all of whom were members of the Conservative Diehard movement. This paper was then privately published, with a foreword by Lord Selborne, as *National Toryism*. Over the next three years Boutwood continued to correspond with various Conservative grandees, in particular Selborne, Willoughby de Broke, and Lord Halifax, and in 1913 he presented another paper, 'Some Preliminary Notes on a Revival of Conservatism', to a Conservative country house party.[72] This too was published, as *National Revival*, with Willoughby de Broke providing a eulogistic foreword.

There is little evidence that Boutwood's writings had any direct impact on Conservative politics, although Willoughby de Broke's forays into political journalism between 1911 and 1913 do seem to bear the imprint of Boutwood's influence. But this is beside the point. What matters is that Boutwood's message clearly had a resonance for at least some Conservatives. His argument that 'the one thing the country is really earnest about is social reform, and on our side we have not a single constructive idea', whereas Lloyd George had convinced the people that 'he has genuine sympathy with them and an honest purpose to ameliorate their condition',[73] chimed in with a general Conservative

---

[71] See Boutwood to Willoughby de Broke, 29 Sept. 1911, Boutwood papers, Letter Book, 1900–24. The essay in question was entitled 'A New Statement of Political Conceptions'. Willoughby de Broke himself published an essay on Conservative principles the following month: see Willoughby de Broke, 'The Tory Tradition', *National Review*, 344 (Oct. 1911).

[72] For a discussion of this episode see Boutwood to Willoughby de Broke, 10 Sept. 1915, Boutwood papers, Letter Book, 1900–24.

[73] Boutwood to Lord Halifax, 15 Feb. 1912, Boutwood papers, Letter Book, 1900–24.

concern that the Liberals and their 'Socialist' allies held all the electoral trumps.[74] Likewise, Boutwood was by no means alone in calling for a bold rethink and restatement of Conservative principles. Fears provoked by the 'People's Budget', the Conservative electoral defeats of 1910, and the Parliament Bill controversy of 1911, saw the emergence of numerous groups within the Conservative party, all of which sought in some way to provide Conservatism with a fresh sense of direction,[75] and particularly prominent in this context were the Diehards,[76] who appear to have been the chief admirers of Boutwood's work. One cannot understand the brief lionization Boutwood enjoyed without reference to the pervasive sense of crisis in Conservative politics in the years immediately prior to the Great War. In difficult circumstances, Boutwood was thought by some Conservatives to be addressing the right issues in a helpful fashion.

II

That Arthur Boutwood's work attracted the attention of even a section of the Conservative party is in itself of interest. What makes it worth more than a footnote is that his political concerns, and the philosophical currents that informed them, were part of a broader intellectual dynamic in late nineteenth- and early twentieth-century Conservatism. Nowhere is this more evident than in the writings and activities of the English historical economists, a group who emerged as the 'house intellectuals' of the Edwardian Conservative party. The historical economists' critique of liberal economics, and their involvement with Conservative politics, are subjects I have dealt with in detail elsewhere.[77] This chapter will, therefore, present only an outline of the main features of their work. The lemma of their intellectual project— what made them historical economists—was their insistence that 'no economic principles have [the] mathematical character of being true for all times and places alike . . . they . . . become approximately true as statements of the facts of actual life under certain social conditions',[78] or, as W. J. Ashley put it, 'economic conclusions are relative to given

---

74 For a full discussion of this concern see Green, *Crisis*, 145–56.

75 Ibid. 267–306.

76 For the Diehards see ibid. 271–4 and also G. D. Phillips, *The Diehards* (Cambridge, Mass., 1979).

77 See Green, *Crisis*, 159–83. Their affinities with Balfour's economic thinking are discussed in Ch. 1, above.

78 W. Cunningham, *Politics and Economics* (1885), 3.

conditions'.[79] This historical relativism led the historical economists to restrict the realm of economic 'science', but to expand the scope of economic study, for they rejected the idea that economic phenomena could be abstracted from their broader context.[80] This in turn meant that the historical economists dismissed the idea of 'economic man', the rational individual associated with classical liberal economics, as a pure abstraction and a wholly inappropriate subject of study. Their contention was that 'real' historical phenomena were the only basis of a meaningful economic analysis.[81] Furthermore, looking around the world they found no perfectly competing, rational individuals, but saw collective groups, trade unions, trusts, cartels, and, above all, nation states as the main features of the age.[82]

If the historical economists were critical of the liberal model's general inability to appreciate the importance of collective entities, they were particularly concerned with the liberal view of nations as 'non-competing groups'.[83] This 'cosmopolitan' outlook was regarded as a logical necessity for an individualistic economic science which saw 'all as contributing to and drawing from the common stock of the world as a whole'.[84] But, the historical economists contended, the real world simply was not like this. Indeed, their view was that, in terms of both theory and practice, it was the case that 'with the rise of nationalities in modern times the nation has come to be a convenient unit, both for political and economic purposes'.[85] They argued that individuals were not engaged in 'atomistic' competition, because all individuals were members of a given polity and only had concrete existence as economic actors through membership of their particular polity.[86] Furthermore, the historical economists' analysis of trends in world politics in the late nineteenth and early twentieth centuries indicated to them that national rivalry rather than intra- or trans-national competition was the chief characteristic of the period.[87] As a consequence, they concluded that

---

[79] W. J. Ashley, 'On the Study of Economic History', repr. in N. B. Harte (ed.), *The Study of Economic History* (1971), 4.

[80] See e.g. W. Cunningham, 'The Relativity of Economic Doctrine', *EJ* 2 (1891), 1–16.

[81] For a full statement of this position see W. Cunningham, *Political Economy and Practical Life* (1893).

[82] See e.g. H. S. Foxwell, 'The Growth of Monopoly and its Bearing on the Functions of the State', 1888, repr. in id., *Papers on Current Finance* (1919), 262–80; W. Cunningham, *The Wisdom of the Wise*, 19–20; L. L. Price, 'Economic Theory and Fiscal Policy', *EJ* 14 (1904), 372–87; W. J. Ashley, *The Economic Organization of England* (1914).

[83] Price, 'Economic Theory', 379.

[84] W. Cunningham, *Christianity and Socialism* (1909), 9.

[85] Ibid.

[86] See id., *Politics and Economics*, 14–15.

[87] See id., *The Rise and Decline of the Free Trade Movement* (1904); L. L. Price, 'Free Trade and Protection', *EJ* 12 (1902), 305–19; W. J. Ashley, *The Tariff Problem* (1903).

if we are to have a body of doctrine which lays down maxims in regard to the pursuit of wealth, this body of doctrine can only be a political economy, not a Cosmopolitan Economic Science; for it must devote its attention to the particular needs and ambitions of a particular polity, and can only indicate the means to procure wealth-as-conceived and wealth-as-desired by that nation, not wealth in general.[88]

Thus, the historical economists were also national economists, and indeed derived their 'nationalist' outlook from their historicism.

This mixture of historical and national economic thought led the historical economists to denounce what they saw as the central policy maxims of liberal economics, namely free trade and laissez faire. The historical economists contended that the basic assumption underpinning free trade was—and here they were fond of quoting Adam Smith—that 'the merchant has no country'. Indeed, William Cunningham found it ironic that, 'though Smith entitled his book *The Wealth of Nations*, he was chiefly concerned in discussing the wealth of the separate citizens . . . the thought of the nation as a unit and of the gradual development of its resources was left somewhat in the background'.[89] Free trade was seen as economic individualism in the sphere of international economic relations, with the interests of a nation being regarded as a simple aggregate of the interests of its individually competing citizens. Hence W. J. Ashley described the repeal of the Corn Laws in 1846 as 'the culmination in England of a current of public opinion of far wider range than fiscal policy. It was the most signal triumph of the movement towards political and industrial individualism; towards the removal of restraint, Atomism or Cosmopolitanism.'[90]

In the mid-nineteenth century free trade had been a success, largely, the historical economists argued, because Britain had appeared to establish a position whereby it could 'dump English manufactures on every other part of the globe for all time'.[91] As a result, it had seemed to be 'perfectly clear that so far as England was concerned there was a complete harmony between the cosmopolitan ideal and the national interest'.[92] But according to the historical economists it was *circumstance*, and not the *principles* of free trade, which had brought about this situation, and in the late nineteenth and early twentieth centuries circumstances had changed. The free-trade ideal of an international division of labour based on comparative advantages enjoyed by individual producers had been rejected by the rise of economic nationalism,

[88] Cunningham, *Politics and Economics*, 14.
[89] Id., *Free Trade Movement*, 11.
[90] Ashley, *Tariff Problem*, 1.
[91] Cunningham, *Free Trade Movement*, 44.
[92] Ibid. 90.

protectionism, and 'the desire of most nations to organize the[ir] economic life . . . in independence of [their] neighbours'.[93] What is more, the historical economists felt that this development had not only robbed Britain of its trading ascendancy, but was also threatening to undermine Britain's productive base. The problem, as they saw it, was Britain's unilateral retention of free-trade, cosmopolitan, individualistic policies in a protectionist, nationalist, and increasingly corporate world. Britain's farming and industrial sectors were, the historical economists argued, being systematically destroyed by large-scale foreign enterprises whose governments gave them every assistance, whilst Britain continued to adhere to free trade.

The historical economists were equally clear that laissez faire in domestic policy was wrong in theory and dangerous in practice. The basis of their position here was that, contrary to the assumptions of both classical liberal and 'Manchester' economics, there was no conflict between State intervention and individual interests. 'The State', wrote Cunningham, 'is the embodiment of what is common to the different persons in the nation, it expresses the spirit which each shares . . . we cannot represent the State as antagonistic to the individual citizens. The State is concerned with the general interest—with what is common to all.'[94] In short, the historical economists posited an organic conception of the relationship between the State and the individual, and saw individuals' interests as indivisible from those of the State in which they lived. The critical point in the historical economists' schema was, however, that the common interest was not an aggregate of individual interests. Writing in 1893, Cunningham noted that:

in the eager competition of individuals with one another, public objects of general good and for the common advantage, may be overlooked. It is necessary that they should be consciously and deliberately taken in hand by public authority; and there must be some interference with private interests, favourable to some and unfavourable to others . . . [for] in so far as the national resources and the aggregate of individual wealth are distinct, it is desirable that the public authority should occasionally interfere.[95]

Such conflict only arose, he argued, because as individuals 'men give attention to the accumulations of the past and the activities of the present; this standpoint does not lead them directly to examine the possibilities of the future',[96] and as a result it was possible that future prosperity could be sacrificed by individuals whose desire for immediate gain led them to overlook society's and hence their own long-term

---

[93] Ibid. 87.   [94] Id., *Politics and Economics*, 135.
[95] Id., *Practical Life*, 28.   [96] Ibid. 24.

interests.[97] Cunningham illustrated this by the example of a factory-owner who overworked his employees. In the short term the owner would make additional profits, but at the expense of the health and well-being of his work-force who, when they retired prematurely or became infirm, would become a burden to their families and the community, including the factory-owner. In such a situation, or in any similar circumstances, there was, Cunningham argued, 'a strong case for enforcing a restriction'.[98] He agreed that there could be 'objection taken to class legislation on the grounds that laws should be passed in the interest of the whole, and not with regard to particular or private interest', but at the same time he and his fellow historical economists also felt that it was damaging to the interests of the community or nation as a whole to allow a class of its citizenry to suffer.[99] On ethical and economic grounds the preservation of national wealth necessitated the preservation of 'all physical objects which may be used for sustaining and prolonging national life',[100] and 'the weakness of laissez faire economics' was that they failed to appreciate the organic relationship between individual and common interests and thus did not 'formulate any national end as distinct from the interests of particular individuals'.[101]

On philosophical grounds the historical economists rejected liberal economic theory for misunderstanding the relationship between the State, society, and the individual. However, they also argued that unless the practice of liberal economics was abandoned then the British economy, and indeed British society, would collapse. It was at this juncture that their critique of laissez faire dovetailed with their attack on free trade, as they explained the causes and consequences of Britain's social problems in the late nineteenth and early twentieth centuries. Pointing to unemployment, widespread poverty, hunger, and poor health and housing, the historical economists placed the blame squarely on liberal economics. To begin with, the failure to defend the competitive position of British industry and agriculture through tariffs was presented as the root cause of many problems, but at the same time laissez-faire domestic policies were blamed for the failure to address the 'symptoms' of social distress. The need for action on both fronts was deemed a matter of urgency, not only because of the scale of the problems, but also because the deterioration of Britain's economic and social situation had created a climate in which 'an increasing number of persons are inclined to try a desperate remedy and look to some form of Socialism as offering a

---

[97] For a further statement of this argument see Price, 'Economic Theory', 379.
[98] Cunningham, *Politics and Economics*, 144–5.   [99] Ibid. 98–9.
[100] Ibid. 117.   [101] Cunningham, *Wisdom*, 61.

means of relief'.[102] The reason for the appeal of Socialism was, according to Cunningham, straightforward, in that 'the attraction of Socialism lies not in the reasoning which supports it, but in the hope it holds out ... with a strong sense of the grinding poverty and degradation in which millions of their fellow men are sunk, the generous spirits of our day can hardly fail to be eager to give every human being the opportunity of developing the best that is in him'.[103] The historical economists contended that, for a variety of reasons, Socialism would only exacerbate the problems it set out to solve,[104] but that, they pointed out, did not weaken the appeal of the Socialist call for great social justice: to point out errors in the Socialist 'solution' did not overcome the uncomfortable fact that there was much truth in Socialist descriptions of widespread social distress. As a consequence, H. S. Foxwell expressed the general view of the historical economists when he argued that: 'The State may become social reformer without becoming Socialist, but if the State does not become social reformer it will inevitably become Socialist.'[105]

The State intervention the historical economists put forward as the means of overcoming Britain's social and economic difficulties addressed what they saw as the external and internal failings of liberal economics. The historical economists' critique of free trade led them to advocate neo-mercantilist tariff policies as a way of reinforcing Britain's industrial and agricultural base. Tariffs were on the historical economists' agenda even before Joseph Chamberlain launched the tariff-reform campaign in the summer of 1903,[106] but once the tariff campaign proper got under way they devoted themselves to the cause. For example, W. A. S. Hewins became Chamberlain's chief economic adviser, was appointed secretary of the Tariff Commission, and became a Conservative MP. Likewise, Ashley, Professor of Commerce at the educational showpiece of Chamberlain's 'Duchy', Birmingham University, was a prominent tariff campaigner. His book *The Tariff Problem* was described by Chamberlain himself as 'the best manual we have',[107] and his advice on economic questions was sought by many prominent Conservatives, in particular by Andrew Bonar Law. Cunningham and L. L. Price were not as directly involved in tariff politics, but they both produced a steady stream of pro-tariff publications

---

[102] Id., *The Alternative to Socialism in England* (Cambridge 1885), 1–2.
[103] Ibid. 11.   [104] See Green, *Crisis*, 159–83.
[105] Foxwell, 'Growth of Monopoly', 277.
[106] See e.g. Price, 'Free Trade and Protection', which was published in Sept. 1902.
[107] J. Chamberlain to W. J. Ashley, 26 Apr. 1904, Joseph Chamberlain papers, Birmingham University Library, JC 19/7/2.

and were chairmen of, respectively, the Cambridge and Oxford University Tariff Reform Associations.[108]

The historical economists' support for tariff reform was a product of their belief that the State should regulate trade, and direct the nation's international economic relations, for the sake of the national economy considered as an integral unit. But it was not only in the sphere of international trade that they defined a positive role for the State. In the 1880s and 1890s Cunningham expressed sympathy with Charles Booth's schemes for old-age pensions, and advocated stronger rights for trade unions as a means of creating a more secure labour market,[109] and in the same vein Price was a powerful advocate of industrial arbitration schemes and wages boards.[110] However, it was in the Edwardian period that the historical economists became most closely associated with social-reform debates. Ashley argued from the outset of the tariff campaign that it was both logical and politically essential for the Conservatives to link fiscal reform to social reform, and he lost no opportunity to press his case at the highest level.[111] On this issue he was strongly supported by Hewins, and both of them became key policy advisers to the Unionist Social Reform Committee, a group set up in 1911 by the Conservative party Chairman, Arthur Steel-Maitland, to devise a programme of Conservative social reforms. By 1914 this Committee had proposed an extension of old-age pension rights, argued for minimum wages in certain trades, sponsored several schemes for working-class housing, and was close to presenting a blueprint for a national health service.[112] At various levels, the historical economsts were deeply involved with the Conservative party's attempt to formulate a response to the problems of a mature economy and offer a constructive, Collectivist alternative to the 'socialistic' challenge of the New Liberalism.

But what were the origins of the historical economists' ideas? Part of the answer to this question lies across the North Sea, in Germany. The importance of German economic thought to the English historical economists is almost impossible to overestimate. Wilhelm Roscher, Friedrich List, Adolf Wagner, and Gustav Schmoller were all major influences,

---

[108] H. S. Foxwell was the only leading historical economist not to involve himself in the tariff campaign. For a full discussion of the historical economists' contribution see Green, *Crisis*, 159–83.

[109] Cunningham, *Practical Life*, 17 and id., *Politics and Economics*, 88–9.

[110] Price, 'Industrial Reform', *passim*.

[111] See e.g. Ashley to Law, 19 Jan. 1906, Bonar Law papers, House of Lords Record Office, 21/1.

[112] For the development of Conservative social policy in the Edwardian period see Green, *Crisis*, 242–66. For the USRC's activities see ibid., ch. 11 and also J. Ridley, 'The Unionist Social Reform Committee, 1911–14: Wets Before the Deluge', *HJ* 30 (1987).

with List being decribed by Ashley as 'the only writer to be placed for his influence on the world by the side of Adam Smith'.[113] Ashley and Cunningham both spent periods in the early part of their academic careers at German universities (Göttingen and Tübingen respectively), and these visits, according to their biographers, were of great significance in shaping their maturing thought.[114] Hewins also had many close contacts with the German academic world, and his first major essay on Britain's trade position was published in Schmoller's *Jahrbuch* in 1899. Equally important, the English historical economists admired what they saw as the practical results of German national economics. The Bismarckian social reforms of the late 1880s were held up as evidence of the way the German State had taken steps to ensure the well-being of all of its citizens and thereby diluted the appeal of Socialism. But what was regarded as more significant than any individual measure of reform was the fact that German theorists and policy-makers had recognized the broader implications of taking such action, in that they had acknowledged

that a concession on this point [social reform] ought to involve a readjustment of the whole mental attitude . . . [and that] If in this field the State has a positive part to play then no longer could it be maintained that the 'natural' economic forces always worked out to the best result; that society cannot be safely trusted to the individual pursuit of self-interest; that the State had no right to 'interfere'.[115]

What the historical economists felt had been acknowledged in Germany was that 'individual competition is only a beneficient force when the conditions under which it acts are carefully regulated'.[116] Furthermore, it was not only in the domestic sphere that the Germans had learned this lesson. The German tariff regime, and the assistance it had given to the development of cartels, was taken as evidence of the broader benefits of neo-mercantilism for the German national economy. The use of tariffs to protect domestic producers and encourage large-scale enterprise was seen to reflect the way in which State intervention had been applied to all aspects of German social and economic life, with the aim being to regulate and organize economic activity for the benefit of the German nation conceived as an organic entity.

Given that the roots of German neo-mercantilism lay in Hegelian Idealism, it is difficult to disentangle the English historical economists from the Idealist nexus discussed at the beginning of this chapter. Most

---

[113] W. J. Ashley, 'Political Economy', 263.
[114] See A. Cunningham, *William Cunningham: Teacher and Priest* (1953), 12–16; A. Ashley, *William James Ashley: A Life* (1925), 25–40.
[115] Ashley, 'Political Economy', 262.
[116] Cunningham, *Free Trade Movement*, 150.

of the historical economists received their intellectual training in Oxford at the time when the influence of Idealist thought was at its strongest. The historical economists, often through further study in Germany itself or simply through reading German economic works, drew themselves still closer to a world of ideas steeped in Idealism. That the historical economists travelled in a very different direction from Progressive thinkers after having imbibed the Idealist brew may have indicated that, unlike their Liberal contemporaries, they shared the German head for spirits, but whatever the differences that developed, it is clear that the Conservative historical economists drew much of the inspiration for their Collectivist predispositions from fundamentally the same source as many Progressives.

III

That Conservative and Progressive Collectivism emerged from a common intellectual context is confirmed by further evidence of close correlation and contact between the schools of thought. For example, in 1894 Benjamin Kidd was transformed from an obscure, lower-grade civil servant into an intellectual celebrity through the publication of his book *Social Evolution*. Its theme, which Kidd was to reiterate to the point of tedium in later publications, was that man 'grows more and more social',[117] and that contemporary developments were witnessing the inexorable substitution of collective for individual action. Kidd criticized economists and social scientists for having been predisposed in the past to an Individualist approach to the study of social phenomena,[118] but he added that 'one of the most remarkable signs of the time in England has been the gradually spreading revolt against many of the conclusions of the school of political economy represented by Adam Smith, Ricardo and Mill'.[119]

Soon after the publication of *Social Evolution* Kidd received an invitation from Ramsay MacDonald to join the Rainbow Circle. The purpose of this group, MacDonald informed Kidd, was to discuss '1. The political, economic and ethical shortcomings of Philosophic Radicalism and the Manchester school; 2. the growth from these schools of the new-radical and Collectivist movements in politics and economics; and the ethical, political and economic principles which are to guide us in further social progress'.[120] Kidd refused the invitation,

---

[117] B. Kidd, *Social Evolution* (1894), 18.   [104] See Green, *Crisis*, 159–83.
[119] Ibid.
[120] J. R. MacDonald to Kidd, 9. Aug. 1894, Kidd papers, Cambridge University Library, Add. MSS, 8069.

and as a result has missed out on the historical attention which has been devoted to the Rainbow Circle.[121] However, the fact that he refused a part in the development of the New Liberal/Progressive modification of 'Manchesterism' and classical liberal thought should not be allowed to disguise his continued interest in overturning the Individualist assumptions of the Manchester and classical liberal schools. Kidd continued to develop his critique of Individualism throughout his career as a writer and publicist, and in his 1908 Herbert Spencer Lecture at Oxford, which he entitled 'Individualism and After', he took as his main theme that 'Individualism has no final meaning in itself . . . its real significance lies in the fact that it is the doctrine of a transition period preliminary to and preparatory to a more important stage'.[122] What is equally interesting in the context of this essay is that in March 1904 Kidd was invited by a rising young Conservative journalist and politician, Leo Amery, to join another discussion group, 'a small League that is being formed of people who are keen on the purely Imperial and constructive side of the Chamberlain movement'.[123] On this occasion the invitation was accepted, and Kidd became an active member of the Compatriots Club, an association which, from 1904 to 1914, functioned as a Conservative 'think-tank', with a membership made up of prominent Conservative politicians, writers, and intellectuals, including Cunningham, Hewins, Ashley, Price, Lord Milner, Leo Amery, J. W. Hills, and Arthur Steel-Maitland.[124] In spite of the political differences that separated the Compatriots and the Rainbow Circle, there was one important similarity in their attitudes and outlook which explains why Kidd should have received invitations to join both. When, in 1905, some *Compatriots' Club Lectures* were published, L. L. Price noted in his review of the collection that 'the creed which they advance is consistent and is also comprehensive. It embraces not merely fiscal but other matters . . . In their opposition to laissez faire . . . the contributors to this volume are fully agreed, and their abandonment of this principle is certainly consistent.'[125] The theme which linked Kidd, the Rainbow Circle, and the Compatriots was a shared hostility to laissez faire and Individualism, and an affinity for Collectivist thought and action.

The Compatriots' Club, as is evident from Amery's invitation to Kidd, was formed in the wake of Joseph Chamberlain's inauguration of the tariff campaign, but it would be a mistake to see its emergence as purely a result of Chamberlain's actions, for if one examines the earlier

---

[121] See Clarke, *Liberals*, 56–61; M. Freeden (ed.), *Minutes of the Rainbow Circle* (1988).
[122] B. Kidd, *Individualism and After* (1908), 13.
[123] L. S. Amery to Kidd, 4 Mar. 1904, Kidd papers, Add. MSS, 8069.
[124] For a list of the Compatriots' Club membership see Green, *Crisis*, 339–40.
[125] Review of *Compatriots' Club Lectures*, EcR, xv, 1905, 362–7.

careers of some of the most active Compatriots it becomes clear that they had held views critical of liberal 'orthodoxy' before Chamberlain officially launched his attack on free trade. The prime movers in bringing the Compatriots together were Leo Amery, Alfred Milner, J. L. Garvin, and Halford Mackinder, all of whom had previously been members of the Coefficients' Club, the cross-party society founded by Sidney and Beatrice Webb in 1902 specifically to discuss Collectivist ideas in an atmosphere of mutual hostility to Individualist politics and economics.[126] In fact there was a marked affinity between Fabians and Conservative Collectivists at this juncture, brought about in large part by a mutual interest in imperialism.

In 1900 L. T. Hobhouse described the Boer War as 'the test issue of this generation', in that attitudes towards it marked who was and who was not a 'genuine Progressive'. In 1904 Hobhouse expanded on this theme by denouncing those who held that 'a positive theory of the State in domestic affairs [should be] matched by a positive theory of Empire'.[127] He had two targets here. On the one hand he was attacking Joseph Chamberlain's efforts to link imperialism with social reform in the context of the tariff campaign, but he was also taking a side-swipe at the Fabians. The fact that he, and indeed other New Liberal writers, bracketed the Conservatives' 'constructive imperialism' with Fabianism is quite understandable. The Fabian hierarchy had lent support to the Boer War, and in 1903 Sidney Webb remarked of the tariff campaign that 'Chamberlain has hit on the fundamentally right idea'.[128] The Coefficients seemed merely to institutionalize an intellectual affinity.

To understand how Fabian Socialism and the 'constructive imperialism' of the Conservative Collectivists came to be regarded as related, it is essential to grasp that their area of agreement was a shared negative. Both Fabians and constructive imperialists looked to demolish 'Manchesterism', and thus they attacked all of its works, which meant laissez-faire 'administrative nihilism' at home, and Little Englandism abroad. The basis for the Fabian-constructive imperialist rapprochement, so marked between 1900 and 1904, was that both were, as Sidney Webb put it, 'in sympathy with . . . making the Empire the "unit of consideration" rather than the forty millions of this island',[129] and that both saw this as contributing to the destruction of mid-Victorian liberal individualism.

---

[126] For the Coefficients see G. R. Searle, *The Quest For National Efficiency* (Oxford, 1971), although an amusing fictional account of the club's activities can be found in H. G. Wells, *The New Machiavelli* (1911), in which the Coefficients appear as the 'Pentagram Circle'.

[127] L. T. Hobhouse, *Democracy and Reaction* (1904; Brighton 1974 edn.), 12.

[128] S. Webb to E. R. Pease, 30 May 1903, in N. Mackenzie (ed.), *The Letters of Sidney and Beatrice Webb*, 3 vols. (Cambridge, 1976), ii. 184.

[129] B. Webb to B. Russell, n.d. (May?) 1903, in Mackenzie (ed.), *Letters*, ii. 185.

What differentiated the Fabians from the Conservative constructive imperialists was that the former were not imperial enthusiasts. Like Hobhouse, the Fabians saw imperialism as a 'test issue', except that for them it revealed who was a closet Cobdenite, and helped to break up Individualism on a front on which they were not themselves fully engaged. For the Conservative constructive imperialists, however, Empire was an ideal which had 'all the depth and comprehensiveness of a religious faith'.[130] Indeed, at one meeting of the Coefficients one of the constructive imperialist members stated that he 'no more asked himself why he became an Imperialist than he asked himself why he fell in love'.[131] This stemmed from their view that Britain needed to organize the Empire to ensure that it could survive in an era of Empire states. For constructive imperialists like Kidd, the historical economists, the Compatriots, and Arthur Boutwood, the Empire did not really exist, insofar as it had not realized its potential. In some respects they agreed with J. R. Seeley's remark that Britain had conquered and peopled half the world in a fit of absence of mind, for they felt that although territories had been acquired, no attempt had been made to create a proper imperial structure. Britain's Empire was, according to Arthur Boutwood, the product of the British people's enterprise and industry and not an 'official' creation, because on imperial matters 'official activity . . . lags . . . far behind the non-official industry of . . . [the] people'.[132] That a popular imperial consciousness existed throughout the Empire was conclusively demonstrated to Boutwood and other constructive imperialists by the Boer War, when imperial enthusiasm in Britain had been matched by the voluntary support offered by the Colonies.[133] The task of constructive imperialism was thus to bring 'official' policy into line with this burgeoning imperial consciousness, and construct a genuine Empire State. Hence, Alfred Milner argued that imperialism was no longer about painting the map red, and that 'the age of expansion' was over and 'the age of organization' had begun.[134] This 'organization' was to be achieved by the construction of formal imperial political and economic ties, the first of which was to be the system

---

[130] A. Milner 'Introduction' to id. *The Nation and the Empire* (1913), p. xxxii.

[131] Coefficients' Club, Minutes of a discussion on the question 'For What Ends is a British Empire Desirable?', 15 June 1903, at 'The Ship', Whitehall, W. A. S. Hewins papers, Sheffield University Library, 17/1.

[132] Egerton (Boutwood), *Patriotism*, 64–6.

[133] Ibid. 66. Contemporary analysis of the 'Khaki' election of Sept. 1900, ranging from Chamberlain and Lord Salisbury to J. A. Hobson, emphasized the role of jingoistic popular imperialism in securing the Conservative victory. For 'constructive imperialist' comments about the 'imperial patriotism' of the Colonies see e.g. Chamberlain to Lord Beauchamp, 5 Mar. 1900, in J. L. Garvin and J. Amery, *The Life of Joseph Chamberlain*, 6 vols. (1934–68), iii. 629 and L. J. Maxse, 'Episodes of the Month', *National Review*, 177 (Mar. 1906), 8.

[134] Milner at Liverpool, 7 June 1910, in id., *Nation and the Empire*, 466.

of imperial tariff preferences advocated by Joseph Chamberlain. By such means the resources of the Empire, both human and material, were to be rationally organized, and the potential of the Empire fully realized — sentiment and interest were to be united.

By emphasizing and realizing the ideal of Empire a number of things were to be achieved. On the basis of the evidence of the period after 1870, constructive imperialists argued that 'the tendency everywhere in the world is towards organization',[135] and that 'the days are for great empires and not for little states'.[136] As a consequence they contended that 'the United Kingdom *alone* will be hard put to retain its place amongst the foremost nations of the world'.[137] This in turn led constructive imperialists to argue that imperialism and social reform were 'inseparable ideals, absolutely interdependent and complementary'.[138] In their view a failure to organize the Empire meant that Britain would become a 'fifth rate nation' without the wealth, markets, and materials to provide either military or economic and social security for its home population. Hence, the constructive imperialist journal *The Outlook* declared that 'no policy of social reform which leaves out of view the British Empire can be in the truest sense constructive',[139] and the social reforms of the 1906–14 Liberal governments were denounced not for being too Collectivist but for failing to use the powers of the State to organize imperial as well as domestic resources.[140]

The core of the constructive imperialist case was that whilst 'the maintenance of the Empire must depend to an overwhelming degree upon the power and the wealth of the island', it was also the case that 'the power and wealth of the island must depend . . . upon the maintenance of the Empire'.[141] This mutual dependence of Britain and the Empire led Arthur Steel-Maitland to declare that although constructive ideas ought to be 'Nationalistic', it was vital to recognize that 'Nation here = British Empire'.[142] This did not mean that either the Colonies or Britain were to surrender their sense of nationhood; rather, it implied that they should recognize that their independent existence was inextricably linked to

---

[135] B. Kidd, 'Colonial Preference and Free Trade', 2nd article, sect. i, of a printed MS in the Kidd papers, CU, Add. MSS, 8069.

[136] J. Chamberlain at Birmingham, 16 May 1902, quoted in Garvin and Amery, *Chamberlain*, iv. 17.

[137] Milner at Bath, 30 Apr. 1909, in id., *Nation and the Empire*, 376 (my emphasis).

[138] Milner at Manchester, 14 Dec. 1906, in ibid., 139.

[139] *The Outlook*, 9 Nov. 1907.

[140] For a full discussion of this critique see Green, *Crisis*, 194–206, 242–66.

[141] J. L. Garvin, 'The Principles of Constructive Economics as Applied to the Maintenance of the Empire', in *Compatriots' Club Lectures*, 44.

[142] A. Steel-Maitland, 'The Economics of Modern Industry and Imperialism', an outline for a 'standard economic work', enclosed with Steel-Maitland to Milner, 12 June 1908, Milner papers, Bodleian Library, Oxford, Ms Milner Dep. 34, fos. 179–97.

their membership of the imperium. Hence, when Leo Amery asked in 1910 'What do we mean when we speak of Imperial unity?', he answered by saying 'we mean that all its [the Empire's] members should remain citizens of a single world State with a duty and a loyalty to that State, none the less real and intense because of the coexistence with it of a duty and loyalty towards the particular nation or community within the Empire to which they belong'.[143] The constructive imperialists' conception of the relationship between Britain and the Colonies was thus strikingly similar to their description of relations between the State and the individual. Just as the rights and interests of individual citizens within each nation were realized through membership of the particular State to which they owed allegiance, so too both Britain and the Colonies could and would only realize their true potential as nations within the Empire. In turn this implied, not a contradiction, but rather a necessary and positive correlation between being a British or Colonial citizen and being a citizen of the Empire.

IV

Britain in the late nineteenth and early twentieth centuries was, as Jose Harris has remarked, 'perhaps the most urbanized, industrialized, and class-stratified society in the world', and was, moreover, a society that 'was only just in the process of opening itself up to popular democracy, and where the structure of the constitution appeared to indicate that popular control of the franchise would lead inevitably to some degree of popular control of the State'.[144] Against this backdrop all political groups in Britain were seeking to comprehend Britain's changing position in the world, cope with the problems emerging in Britain's maturing economy, and control the social and political transformations that were taking place. The Conservatives were no less involved with this 'search for a social philosophy' than any other party or organization. Indeed, for them the search was arguably more urgent than for anyone else. It was, after all, the Conservative party who were losing elections in the early twentieth century, and it was the values and interests most cherished by Conservatives—Britain's imperial supremacy, property rights, the House of Lords, and the Union with Ireland—that seemed to be most threatened by social, political, and economic change.

---

[143] L. S. Amery, 'Imperial Unity', a speech to the Chatham Club, 15 July 1910, in id., *Union and Strength* (1912), 2.
[144] J. Harris, 'Political Thought', 139.

It was this sense of a 'Crisis of Conservatism' that provided the impetus for the development of Conservative Collectivism. The fundamental aim of Conservative Collectivist thought, as developed by Arthur Boutwood, the historical economists, the Compatriots' Club, and the Unionist Social Reform Committee, was to provide the basis for a socially and politically integrative strategy that could overcome tensions and divisions within Britain and the Empire and thereby present a unified face to a hostile world. This was to be achieved by fostering the organic unity of the nation, which in turn required acknowledging that the nation was such an organic entity. It was here that a positive role for the State was essential, in that the State was to ensure that no particular section of society was to be systematically undervalued or over-privileged. In practical terms this meant two things: first, social reform in the domestic sphere to alleviate the privations of the poorer classes, but carried through without recourse to class-divisive rhetoric or actions; second, reordering imperial relations to create a more equal partnership within the Empire, thereby making the Empire a more effective and efficient unit. In short, a fusion of imperialism and social reform was the characteristic feature of Conservative Collectivism.

As was the case with the New Liberalism and British Socialism, Conservative Collectivist thought was quite eclectic, with biological, evolutionary, and geopolitical theories all contributing. At the same time, however, it would be a mistake to underestimate the input of English Idealism into Conservative thought in this period. Idealism, as many historians of the time have pointed out, was a very flexible philosophy which could be and was taken in a number of different directions, and Jose Harris has rightly pointed out that Idealism 'generated a vocabulary of social reform that transcended political parties'.[145] Its role in generating such a vocabulary for Conservatives has, however, been somewhat overlooked. Nevertheless, Idealism, in the hands of Arthur Boutwood and the historical economists, generated an idea of the nation that provided an ethical underpinning for a highly developed pattern of Conservative Collectivist thought—the idea of a nation, and indeed an Empire, in a process of becoming more powerful and therefore more supportive of its citizenry. In his Rectorial Address to Glasgow University in 1904, the Conservative Irish Secretary, George Wyndham, declared that 'the State must be large enough in contour to fire the imagination of all its citizens with faith in the future',[146] and in a period when 'a continuous trend towards complex political aggregation' was seemingly dominant he looked to 'the birth of an Organic

---

[145] Harris, 'Political Thought', 138.
[146] G. Wyndham, *The Development of the State* (1904), 11.

Empire State' as the key to Britain's imperial and domestic security.[147]
In fact, the title of Wyndham's address speaks volumes for the direction
Conservative political ideas were moving in at this point: it was called—
The Development of the State.

[147] Ibid. 32, 49.

CHAPTER 3

An Intellectual in Conservative Politics: The Case of Arthur Steel-Maitland

THE FIGURE of Arthur Steel-Maitland looms rather small in the twentieth-century Conservative pantheon. His political career began brightly. He was elected to Parliament in January 1910, and the following June he was appointed to the newly created position of Chairman of the Conservative party. In this post he had overall responsibility for the party's finances, was in charge of its organizational and electoral machinery, and had an important voice in policy discussions. Given this auspicious start, Steel-Maitland appeared set for a high-flying political career, but he seemed to stall soon after take-off. He was appointed to his first government post in Lloyd George's wartime coalition, but did not advance past junior ministerial level either during or immediately after the war, and he resigned from the post-war coalition government in 1919. After five years on the backbenches he was appointed to Cabinet as Minister of Labour by Stanley Baldwin in 1924, but only after the post had been offered to and turned down by Sir Robert Horne. In 1929 Steel-Maitland lost his seat at the general election, and although he quickly returned to Parliament he was not offered a post in the Conservative-dominated National Government formed in 1931. Steel-Maitland was thus once again consigned to the backbenches, where he remained until he died, 'a disappointed man',[1] in 1935.

This essay does not seek to explain in detail the reasons for the 'failure' of Steel-Maitland's career.[2] Rather, it will explore his political and economic ideas as they evolved from the Edwardian period until his death—focusing in particular on his ideas on tariff reform, social reform, industrial relations, 'the Slump' and mass unemployment. Steel-Maitland was self-consciously an intellectual in politics. From 1895 to 1899 he attended Balliol College, Oxford, where he enjoyed an

---

[1] Obituary of Steel-Maitland, *Sunday Dispatch*, 31 Mar. 1935.
[2] These are discussed in the author's entry on Steel-Maitland in the *New DNB* (Oxford, forthcoming).

outstanding undergraduate career. He gained two First Class degrees, in Classics and in Law, and in 1899 was the University's Eldon Law Scholar.[3] In 1900 he was elected a Fellow of All Souls. On leaving Oxford in 1900 he went to London to read for the Bar, but gave up the pursuit of a legal career and spent much of his time in London attending lectures on philosophy and economics at the then newly founded LSE.[4] Having married a wealthy heiress Steel-Maitland had no need to obtain well-paid employment, and from 1902 to November 1905 he acted as unpaid secretary to two Conservative Chancellors of the Exchequer, C. T. Ritchie and Austen Chamberlain, in which position he was able to observe economic debates at the highest levels of government.[5] Steel-Maitland stood, unsuccessfully, as a Conservative candidate at the general election of 1906, but in the four years between this reversal and his election in January 1910 his interest and expertise in economic and social questions broadened and deepened. In 1906 he was appointed a Special Commissioner to the Royal Commission on the Poor Laws, carrying out an investigation (with Rose Squire) of 'the relation of industrial and sanitary conditions to pauperism'[6] which apppeared as a separate appendix of the Commission's Final Report. He also undertook an independent study, with Norman Chamberlain, of the 'boy labour' problem. In 1908 he produced the draft outline for a book (which he did not write) on 'The Economics of Modern Industry and Imperialism',[7] and in the same year contributed an essay on 'Labour' to the *The New Order*, a collection of Conservative essays edited by Lord Malmesbury.[8]

That Steel-Maitland published in *The New Order* indicated that he was a member of the extreme tariff-reform group the Confederacy, for the book was a Confederate project. His involvement with this project and with the Confederacy more generally reflected the importance he attached to ideas in politics. It is well known that the main aim of the

---

[3] His reputation as a 'Renaissance Man' was also enhanced by the fact that he gained a rowing blue.

[4] Steel-Maitland's lecture notebooks for this period are preserved in his papers at the National Archives of Scotland, GD 193/50/2.

[5] Treasury papers covering a number of issues, most notably the tariff question, are also to be found in Steel-Maitland's papers. See esp. SMP, GD 193/88/1/147.

[6] See the official letter of invitation appointment from Lord George Hamilton to Steel-Maitland, 7 July 1906, SMP, GD 193/131/231. Steel-Maitland himself had defined the remit more broadly when he wrote to Canon Barnett a month earlier, stating that he was to look at dangerous, insanitary, underpaid, and overworked trades and their connection to pauperism, 26 June 1906, ibid., GD 193/131/167.

[7] Steel-Maitland, 'The Economics of Modern Industry and Imperialism', n.d. (1908), Milner papers, Bodleian Library, Oxford, MS Milner Dep. 34, fos. 183–97.

[8] A. Steel-Maitland, 'Labour', in Lord Malmesbury (ed.), *The New Order* (1908).

Confederacy was to purge the Conservative party of free-traders,[9] but their engagement in publishing indicates a less familiar Confederate goal, namely, their wish to establish the dominance of their ideas as well as their personnel.[10] This was why Steel-Maitland in particular was asked to contribute an essay to *The New Order*. He was informed by Thomas Comyn-Platt, one of the chief organizers of the Confederacy, that 'the greater brains of the Confederates are contemplating a book which will contain 12 essays on the most important political questions of the day ... [and] there is a general opinion that your assistance is essential'.[11] Steel-Maitland's brains and ideas were as much in demand as his organizational skills within the Confederacy as that body sought to reshape the ideological make-up of the Conservative party. This blending of intellectual and institutional change was a characteristic feature of Steel-Maitland's political activities in the Edwardian period, and was further demonstrated by his active membership of the Compatriots' Club. The Compatriots was the leading unofficial Conservative think-tank of the Edwardian period, and it organized lectures and seminars on economics, imperial matters, social questions, and other issues for the Club's membership of prominent Conservative politicians, journalists, and intellectuals.[12] It was ostensibly a purely 'intellectual' body, but after 1906 it became active in electoral work, establishing a subcommittee, of which Steel-Maitland was a member,[13] to offer the Club's help to 'to Parliamentary candidates *of sound views* at Bye-elections'[14] — in effect, seeking the same ends as the Confederacy but using different, and more subtle, means.

Steel-Maitland's involvement with the Compatriots reflected his desire to inject serious intellectual engagement into Conservative policy, and in particular to galvanize in-depth discussion of imperial, economic, and social issues within the party. In October 1910, having been an MP for only nine months, Steel-Maitland sought to set up a Committee of Conservative social reformers.[15] The December 1910 general election

---

[9] See A. Sykes, 'The Confederacy and the Purge of the Unionist Free Traders, 1906–10', *HJ* 18 (1975), and Larry L. Witherell, *Rebel on the Right: Henry Page Croft and the Crisis of British Conservatism, 1903–14* (1997), *passim*.

[10] Indeed, it was *because* certain members of party personnel held the wrong ideas that they were targeted for purging. For a fuller discussion of the relationship between ideas and internal party faction fighting see Green, *Crisis* (1995), *passim*.

[11] T. Comyn-Platt to Steel-Maitland, n.d. (1907 ?), SMP, GD 193/135/51.

[12] For the Compatriots see Green, *Crisis*, 160–1, 339–40. Apart from the one published volume of *Compatriots' Club Lectures* (1905, repr. 1998), surviving material relating to the Compatriots is scarce, and almost all the archival fragments are to be found in Steel-Maitland's papers. See esp. SMP, GD 193/130/56, 78, 347.

[13] G. C. Tryon to Steel-Maitland, 31 Mar. 1906, SMP, GD 193/130/347.

[14] Circular Letter to Compatriots' Members, n.d. (July ? 1906), SMP, GD 193/130/78.

[15] S. Rosenbaum to Steel-Maitland, 23 Oct. 1910, SMP, GD 193/149/4/28.

intervened, but in February 1911 the Unionist Social Reform Committee (USRC) held its first meeting.[16] Steel-Maitland's activities on this front remained very much to the fore after he became party Chairman. In September 1911 he wrote to Lord Milner,[17] inviting him to attend 'a little séance' which he and Leo Amery were organizing at All Souls,[18] 'in order to get a dozen Unionist members of Parliament to discuss some of the real social questions of the minute'.[19] This was the first of a number of such 'séances' which Steel-Maitland organized in the last years before the Great War; more important, he remained very much the driving force behind the USRC, which under his aegis had become an official party think-tank of Conservative politicians and intellectuals dedicated to formulating Conservative social policy.[20] But even with the USRC up and running as part of the Conservative apparatus, Steel-Maitland continued to organize weekend 'lecture courses' on social issues[21] to provide added stimulus and input for the USRC.

War and government interrupted Steel-Maitland's 'intellectual' activities, but certainly did not end them. He remained a Fellow of All Souls, and in 1916 became Chairman of the Governors of the LSE and was to play an active role in that position until his death, enjoying a productive relationship with the Director appointed in 1919, William Beveridge. After the war Steel-Maitland produced a number of publications presenting his ideas. He edited a short study of Marx's political and economic ideas in 1920,[22] published a collection of his articles written for the *Observer* as *The Trade Crisis and the Way Out* in 1931, and wrote a study of the early years of Roosevelt's New Deal, *The New America*, in 1934. This may not represent a vast formal oeuvre, but Steel-Maitland's activities and correspondence over the years reveal a politician with a profound interest in economic and social questions. Trade and tariffs, especially in the imperial context, were major, recurrent themes of his political life, but social investigation and social policy were equally prominent—as Minister of Labour he even disguised himself as a 'down and out' to visit Labour Registries and study 'dole queues'. The need for industrial reorganization and a new footing for

---

[16] Minutes of USRC Meeting, 28 Feb. 1911, SMP, GD 193/108/1/359.

[17] Steel-Maitland had acted as secretary to Milner during his tour of Canada in 1908, and the two had become and remained close friends, sharing an intellectual as well as personal affinity.

[18] As well as having been one of Milner's 'kindergarten' in South Africa, Amery was another leading Compatriot, and a Fellow of All Souls.

[19] Steel-Maitland to Milner, 29 Sept. 1911, SMP, GD 193/154/4/21.

[20] For the activities of the Unionist Social Reform Committee see J. Ridley, 'The Unionist Social Reform Committee, 1911–14: Wets Before the Deluge', *HJ* 30 (1987).

[21] See M. Woods to Steel-Maitland, 25 Oct. 1911, SMP, GD 193/155/4/5–6.

[22] *Foreword to the Socialists' Bible: Karl Marx's Theory Discussed* (1920).

industrial relations were leitmotifs of his discussion of both industrial disputes and the problem of unemployment. He also showed a keen interest in new departures in economic thought, and was the first leading Conservative to engage with the ideas of John Maynard Keynes. Steel-Maitland took ideas seriously, and his own ideas deserve equally serious consideration.

Economics was, from the outset of his involvement in politics, Steel-Maitland's main area of interest and expertise. This interest was in part a reflection of his intellectual curiosity, but it also had a broader purpose. In his *Foreword to the Socialists' Bible* of 1920 Steel-Maitland stated that, as 'quacks and frauds' were wont to exploit people's ignorance of economics, a good knowledge of the subject was politically essential, and he certainly made strenuous efforts to follow his own advice. In 1901–2 he attended lectures on economics at the LSE by the historical economist W. A. S. Hewins, the School's first Director, who, like Steel-Maitland, was to become a leading figure in the tariff-reform campaign and a Conservative MP.[23] Hewins's ideas were to exercise a strong and enduring influence over Steel-Maitland,[24] but although Hewins may have been the first prominent economist to excite Steel-Maitland's interest he was by no means the last. Over the next thirty years Steel-Maitland read widely in the field and consistently sought expert economic opinion and advice. His 1908 draft outline for his proposed 'standard economic work' indicated a familiarity with the German historical/national economists List, Wagner, Schmoller, Miquel, and Fuchs, and the American institutionalists Patten, Jenks, and Seligman.[25] Given that Steel-Maitland was clear that the 'point of view' of his study would be 'Nationalistic', the prominence he accorded the German historical/national school in his outline was logical. It was also a further reflection of his close intellectual affinity with Hewins, who was an admirer of the German school and had clearly transmitted this enthusiasm in his lectures at the LSE.[26] In 1910 Steel-Maitland was elected a member of the Political Economy Club at Oxford, read his first

[23] See SMP, GD 193/50/2 for his copious notes on Hewins' lectures. In 1911 he told one correspondent that the two years he spent at 'the school of economics . . . [were] of quite unusual worth', Steel-Maitland to L. Sutherland, 20 Oct. 1911, SMP, GD 193/155/2/27.

[24] For their influence see below, pp. 81–3.

[25] Steel-Maitland, 'The Economics of Modern Industry and Imperialism'.

[26] For the broad influence of the German historical/national economists on Hewins and the other British historical economists see Green, *Crisis*, 159–83, and G. M. Koot, *The English Historical Economists, 1870–1926* (Cambridge, 1987). See also Steel-Maitland's notes on Hewins's lectures, 5 Nov. 1901, 16 Dec. 1901, 13 Jan. 1902, GD 193/50/2 fos. 5–72. Steel-Maitland's comment in 'Economics of Modern Industry' that 'abstract economic statements' required 'limits to be imposed and changes made when applied to practical problems' was a commonplace of the historical economists' critique of classical liberal economics. See Green, *Crisis*, 159–83.

paper to the club that summer, and debated the merits of its argument in a correspondence with Charles Booth.[27] He continued with his economic 'studies' after he was elected to Parliament. In 1911, for example, he asked George Paish if he could recommend a lecturer to help him gain 'some practical insight into methods of finance and business in the City', and enquired as to whether H. S. Foxwell was, as he had heard, the best person.[28] Paish confirmed that Foxwell was indeed excellent, but also suggested, with pleasing irony for Steel-Maitland's future career, that if Foxwell was unavailable then he should talk to a young economist of whom he had heard good reports—J. M. Keynes.[29] The following year Steel-Maitland was again looking for economic experts to advise and sit upon the newly formed Unionist Social Reform Committee, and Hewins was brought on board, along with another noted historical economist and tariff expert W. J. Ashley. On labour questions William Beveridge was an important source for Steel-Maitland's writing and speeches on labour exchanges and national insurance before 1914, and, when Minister of Labour, he drew directly upon Beveridge's advice on the operation of unemployment insurance and on industrial relations. Steel-Maitland and Beveridge, in spite of their political differences, shared some perspectives,[30] and had a relationship based on mutual intellectual respect—as was made clear in Beveridge's obituary of Steel-Maitland, which warmly praised his contribution to social and industrial policy.[31] When it came to the central economic problem of the inter-war years, persistent large-scale unemployment, Steel-Maitland again demonstrated a readiness not only to canvass expert opinion but also to engage in high-level debate himself. His own writings and speeches indicate a familiarity with the work of Keynes, Ralph Hawtrey,[32] and Sir Henry Strakosch,[33] and his correspondence in 1929–30 in particular contains lengthy and detailed discussions of the economic causes and possible cures for unemployment with,

---

[27] Steel-Maitland to C. Booth, 27 July 1910, SMP, GD 193/148/2/27.

[28] Steel-Maitland to G. Paish, 5 Jan. 1911, SMP, GD 193/151/5/80–1x. Foxwell was another historical economist, who, although a Fellow of St John's College, Cambridge, was Professor of Political Economy at UCL and also lectured at the LSE.

[29] G. Paish to Steel-Maitland, 18 Jan. 1911, SMP, GD 193/151/5/82x.

[30] Beveridge was one of the members of the 1925–6 Royal Commission on the Coal Industry (the Samuel Commission), and both he and Steel-Maitland disliked the coal-owners and coal-miners in equal measure.

[31] Sir William Beveridge, 'Sir Arthur Steel-Maitland', *Listener*, 10 Apr. 1935.

[32] Hawtrey was, of course, the Treasury's main, indeed only, economist and Steel-Maitland would have come across his ideas in a governmental context, but he had also clearly read some of Hawtrey's works. See A. Steel-Maitland, *The Trade Crisis and the Way Out* (1931), 30–1.

[33] A banker, currency expert, and a member of the Financial Committee of the League of Nations.

amongst others, E. R. Peacock,[34] Hubert Henderson, and Montagu Norman. This prolonged and intense discussion of and reflection upon the unemployment question appeared to give Steel-Maitland a deep respect for the 'new economics' and an equally deep sense of frustration with the political obstacles to policy innovation. This highlights a crucial point about Steel-Maitland's *political* economy, which he summed up very well in Parliament in November 1934.[35] He argued that developments in the statistical and theoretical sophistication of economics had both transformed the subject and opened up new possibilities in the realm of policy: 'We have had', he said, 'brilliant economists doing brilliant work—Mr. Keynes and others', but the crucial step remaining was to find a policy strategy that would make the best use of that work.[36] Steel-Maitland was clearly profoundly interested in economics qua science, but he saw it as a discipline that provided tools and techniques for achieving what one saw as socially and politically desirable ends. The questions this essay will examine now, therefore, are how Steel-Maitland defined what was socially and politically desirable over the course of his career, and how these imperatives both informed and were informed by his economic ideas.

The first major issue that Steel-Maitland became involved with, and which in varying degrees was to remain an integral part of his political career until his death, was tariff reform. When he was attending the LSE, Steel-Maitland noted at one of Hewins's lectures that 'in the course of the next few years Free Trade policy will be a burning question',[37] which was a reasonably accurate prediction. Steel-Maitland was from the outset a committed supporter of the tariff cause. Indeed, he was in many respects a tariff reformer *avant la lettre*. In 1902, as noted above, he had taken up the position of unpaid private secretary to the Chancellor of the Exchequer, C. T. Ritchie, and in that post could not but have been aware of the internal Cabinet wranglings over whether to use the 1 shilling per quarter registration duty on imported corn imposed by Ritchie's predecessor as a vehicle for imperial preference. Whether or not Steel-Maitland knew the details of the argument, he certainly knew which side he supported. When Ritchie repealed the duty in the 1903 Budget Steel-Maitland resigned his position.[38] Six years

---

[34] A Director of Barings and a member of the Court of the Bank of England. He was also Steel-Maitland's friend and golf partner.

[35] He died on 30 Mar. 1935.

[36] Steel-Maitland in Parliament, 26 Nov. 1934, *Parliamentary Debates* (henceforth 'PD'), 295, c. 618.

[37] 'Notebooks on Economic Theory', n.d. (Nov. 1901?), SMP, GD 193/50/2.

[38] He took up the position again when Austen Chamberlain became Chancellor following Ritchie's resignation in the autumn.

later he had occasion to discuss this action, and noted with pride that: 'As a Tariff Reformer I left Mr. Ritchie when he took off the corn duty', and that 'mine was the first formal resignation on account of the tariff reform policy'.[39]

Steel-Maitland himself outlined one of the principal reasons for his commitment to tariff reform shortly before his death, when he declared 'I am an Imperialist and always have been'.[40] For Steel-Maitland, as for most tariff reformers, the cause of imperial unity, which lay at the heart of Joseph Chamberlain's argument for imperial preference, was just that—a *cause*.[41] In the wake of the Boer War, and with concern growing that Britain was not coping with the challenge of rival imperial, military, and economic powers, the Empire offered both a poweful symbol of Britain's greatness and a potential means of sustaining it. Tariff-reformers saw the ideal of Empire as something worth fighting for, and Steel-Maitland was no exception. What was exceptional about Steel-Maitland's devotion to the cause of Empire was the breadth of his argument for imperial tariffs and the scope of the connections he established between imperial and domestic economic policy. Steel-Maitland produced his fullest statement of imperialist economics in his outline book-proposal, 'The Economics of Modern Industry and Imperialism'. Here he argued that the 'Underlying Principles' of his outlook were, first, 'Nationalistic', and second, that the 'Economic object' was 'to increase aggregate strength in comparison with other countries combined with maximum production per head'.[42] Steel-Maitland's economic nationalism in part rested on the premiss that it was a world trend demonstrated by the revival of protectionism. Economic nationalism, he argued, showed the error of 'the basis of free trade theory', which was 'maximum production independent . . . of political boundaries'. Britain had become isolated in a sea of protectionism and 'Free Trade theory [had] become for [the] United Kingdom a Free Import theory'.[43] Tariffs were thus crucial to getting the British economy back in step with the trend of world economic developments. Imperial preference was to

[39] Steel-Maitland to Sir Charles Follett, 11 Nov. 1909, SMP, GD 193/144/100. Follett had been at the Inland Revenue at the time and had met Steel-Maitland. Typically Steel-Maitland was writing to him to gather expert advice on the effect which rejecting the 'People's Budget' would have on customs revenue.

[40] Steel-Maitland in Parliament, 14 Feb. 1935, *PD* 297, c. 2196.

[41] The best-known illustration of this is Leo Amery's description of how, on the morning after Joseph Chamberlain had opened the tariff campaign with his speech at Birmingham, Leopold Maxse had 'waltzed me round the room as he poured forth a paean of jubilation at the thought that, at last, there was a cause to work for in politics'. L. S. Amery, *My Political Life*, 3 vols. (1953–5), vol. 1, *England Before the Storm, 1896–1914*, 238.

[42] Steel-Maitland, 'Modern Industry and Imperialism'.

[43] Ibid.

boost exports by providing British industry with privileged access to Colonial markets, and protective tariffs were to stem the flood of 'free imports' that was robbing British industry and agriculture of their home market.

At first glance Steel-Maitland might seem to have been espousing straightforward neo-mercantilist economics, but to describe his ideas in such terms would be simplistic—his neo-mercantilism was by no means straightforward. When he described his economics as 'Nationalistic' he added the significant rider that 'Nation here = British Empire', in that he 'regard[ed] gain or loss to [the] Empire as a whole' as the true measure of 'national' prosperity. For Steel-Maitland the vital things were to examine 'How far [the] British Empire [was] at present an organism from [a] Nationalistic point of view (a) politically (b) economically', and to grasp the 'Need for promoting organic connection' within the Empire.[44] Steel-Maitland felt that the Empire did not have, either politically or economically, the appearance of a fully functioning organism, noting that the Colonies had no voice in the governance of the Empire and that commercial relations between Britain and the Colonies were undeveloped. This situation, he argued, had to be rectified in order both to counter 'tendencies to disintegration' and to construct 'a federal organism of developed parts'.[45] Here Steel-Maitland was articulating concerns and positions that were commonly held by 'constructive imperialists'.[46] The fear of imperial 'disintegration' was much discussed in imperialist circles in the Edwardian period. A particular worry was the rise of nationalism in the self-governing Colonies. That the Colonies had developed their own industries and tariff regimes was seen as in many respects a natural and welcome development, insofar as it was a reflection of the general growth of nationalism in the world and a product of the Colonies' increasing 'maturity'. However, it was also seen by many imperialists in Britain as a potential threat, in that if Colonial nationalism became too strong it could become a 'centrifugal force' which could cause the disintegration of the Empire into separate nation states. Closer political and economic ties within the Empire were the means of forestalling this, but the challenge was to construct ties that would bind the Empire and at the same time allow the Colonies scope to achieve economic maturity and develop their own identities. Hence

---

44 Steel-Maitland, 'Modern Industry and Imperialism'.

45 Ibid.

46 For 'constructive imperialism' see Green, *Crisis*, 59–77, 176–83, 194–206; P. Cain, 'The Economic Philosophy of Constructive Imperialism', in C. Navari (ed.), *British Politics and the Spirit of the Age* (Keele, 1995); and E. H. H. Green, 'The Political Economy of Empire, 1880–1914', in A. Porter (ed.), *The Oxford History of the British Empire*, vol. 3, *The Nineteenth Century* (Oxford, 1999).

imperial *preference* and not Empire free trade was at the heart of the tariff-reform movement's imperial economic policy. Empire free trade threatened the Colonies' 'infant industries' with a flood of cheap British imports, whereas preference offered British producers better treatment than foreigners but still allowed the Colonies 'developmental' tariff protection. In this way imperial and national goals could be harmonized.

The quest to achieve a balance between the 'national' and the 'imperial' carried some important implications for the broad political economy of Empire. Writing to Arthur Balfour in February 1907, W. A. S. Hewins argued that it was necessary to break away from the old mercantitilist conception of Empire. 'The Colonies', he wrote, 'had a definite place in this [mercantilist] system. But it was a subordinate place, both economically and politically . . . they were to supply . . . raw materials . . . which we could not produce and take in our manufactures.'[47] The problem with this crude mercantilist notion of imperial relations was that it could only fail to allow for Colonial development and was thus incapable of comprehending the issues confronting the British Empire in the early twentieth century. In October 1903 Joseph Chamberlain himself pointed out that the self-governing Colonies were 'all protective countries' because they were not content 'to be what the Americans call a "one horse country" ',[48] or, in other words, that they had rejected a division of labour based on themselves as producers of primary goods and consumers of British manufactures. In order to take proper account of this it was necessary to construct a new conception of Empire which recast the relationship between Britain and the Colonies. Joseph Chamberlain again stated the position very eloquently, when he argued that 'the British Empire is not an Empire in the sense in which that term has been applied before. The British Colonies are no longer Colonies in the sense in which that term was originally applied to them . . . We are sister States in which the mother country, by virtue of her age, by virtue of all that has been done in the past, may claim to be first, but only first among equals.'[49] What was being constructed here was a notion of imperial *partnership* which in economic terms would be based, almost literally, on a sense of common wealth and in political terms a sense of a common loyalty between the member States of the Empire. The essential aim, in the words of one of Steel-Maitland's

[47] W. A. S. Hewins to A. J. Balfour, 18 Feb. 1907, Balfour papers, Add. MSS, 49779, fos. 61–70.

[48] J. Chamberlain at Glasgow, 6 Oct. 1903, in C. Boyd (ed), *Speeches of the Right Honourable Joseph Chamberlain*, 2 vols.. (1914), ii. 159.

[49] L. S. Amery, 'Imperial Unity', a speech to the Chatham Club, 15 July 1910, in id., *Union and Strength* (1912), 2.

fellow Compatriots, Leo Amery,[50] was 'that all its [the Empire's] members should remain citizens of a single world State with a duty and a loyalty towards that State none the less real and intense because of the coexistence with it of a duty and a loyalty towards the particular nation or community within the Empire to which they belong'. This approach, in the words of another Compatriot, J. L. Garvin, would ensure that 'the physiological system of the Empire . . . [was] considered as a whole',[51] with the result that all of its parts would grow and benefit equally from membership of the Empire. In this way constructing an imperial organism of *developed* parts, as envisaged by Steel-Maitland, would avoid the errors of crude mercantilism and thereby promote the integrative rather than disintegrative potential of Colonial national aspiration.

For a constructive imperialist like Steel-Maitland the imperial aspect of tariff reform was central, but it was not the only element of the tariff programme that he deemed important. Tariffs to protect British industry and agriculture were also integral parts of his economic programme, and indeed the importance Steel-Maitland attached to industrial tariffs grew over time. 'Tariff Reform Means Work for All' was one of the most often-used slogans of the tariff campaign—the underlying argument being that tariffs would provide security of employment for workers in protected industries and, by allowing such industries to prosper and grow, expand the realm of employment opportunity. At the same time industrial tariffs were seen as essential to allow British industries to develop the kind of large-scale organizational structure characteristic of German and US industry, and thereby to enable them to realize economies of scale and continuous running of plant. That the first part of the title of Steel-Maitland's proposed book was 'The Economics of *Modern* Industry', was significant, for Steel-Maitland was certainly aware of the evolution of large-scale corporations abroad and felt that British industry under free trade was languishing. From Hewins's lectures at the LSE he had learned that 'National welfare depends . . . on (a) amount of industry per head (b) productiveness of that industry',[52] and tariffs were to ensure that all were at maximum level by allowing British industry to function on a level economic playing-field. Steel-Maitland had no time for the argument that free trade necessarily produced optimum economic results from a national point of view. A

[50] Amery (along with Milner and Halford Mackinder) was one of the people to whom Steel-Maitland sent his book proposal for comment/discussion. See Steel-Maitland to Milner, 12 June 1908, Milner papers, MS Milner dep. 34, fo. 179.

[51] J. L. Garvin, 'The Principles of Constructive Economics as Applied to the Maintenance of the Empire', *Compatriots Club Lectures* (1905), 45.

[52] 'Notebooks on Economic Theory', 5 Nov. 1901, SMP, GD 193/50/2, fo. 5. For the similarity with Steel-Maitland's own position see above, n. 41.

Treasury Memorandum of August 1903 criticized the argument that Britain would suffer if foreign industrial trusts drove British firms out of their home markets. US trusts, the Memorandum argued, would still have to compete with, say, German trusts for the British market, and this would result in cheapness for British consumers of items from this trade. Here Steel-Maitland noted in the margin, 'is it economically profitable in the end to allow such a thing to happen to secure temporary cheapness in one branch of trade?'[53] Clearly Steel-Maitland thought not, for he regarded *production* and productive employment as the essence of national economic well-being, not being able to buy in the cheapest market. Hence, he could argue that 'the duty on manufactured goods is still the sheet anchor' of Conservative policy even at a time when the party was back-tracking on the proposals for tariffs on imported foodstuffs that were necessary for imperial preference.[54] Protection without preference was not Steel-Maitland's ideal, but at least it offered a first step.

Steel-Maitland saw direct social benefit accruing from tariffs in the shape of higher and more secure levels of employment. In this respect he regarded tariffs as the coping-stone of an active social policy in that, like many Edwardian social investigators, he regarded unemployment and lack of regular employment as major causes of poverty. By reducing employment problems tariffs would, therefore, reduce the scale of social problems. But Steel-Maitland saw other potential benefits in tariffs, insofar as they could help boost revenue to pay for social reform. Here, once again, Steel-Maitland's argument provided a subtle twist to the case for tariff reform. The idea that tariffs could provide a fresh source of revenue to fund social reform was one which had been in circulation since at least the 1890s, and Joseph Chamberlain had, albeit briefly, raised the possibility in the early stages of the tariff campaign. There was, however, a seeming internal contradiction in this argument. If tariffs were to protect British industry and jobs then imports had to be shut out, but if they were to raise revenue then imports had to enter the country in order to pay duty. Steel-Maitland solved this problem by arguing that the revenue potential of tariffs was indirect rather than direct. Writing to Charles Booth in 1910, he contended that

The national revenue (and indeed local rates) is really contributed by men who earn their livelihood and their means to pay taxes by industry, either themselves producing articles, or helping in their distribution. Roughly speaking, therefore, for every shilling's work of production in England, rather more than 2d is contributed in rates

---

[53] Treasury Memorandum, 'The Fiscal Problem' 25 Aug. 1903, SMP, GD 193/88/1/147.
[54] Steel-Maitland, 'Suggested Policy', n.d. (Dec. 1912?), Jan. 1913 (?), SMP, GD 193/80/5/43–9.

and taxes. If therefore under a tariff we no longer buy a German article for 11d, but we buy instead a British article for 1/- we are really the gainers, because through that shilling the revenue is really twopence the richer.

This allowed Steel-Maitland not only to deny any contradiction between the protective and revenue aspects of tariffs, but to claim that the two functions were mutually supportive. Tariffs would secure the productive base, increase production, profits, and employment, and thereby increase the nation's taxable capacity and the flow of revenue to the Exchequer through existing taxes.[55] The scale of the social problems the government had to deal with would thus be reduced, and more revenue would be available to spend on those that remained.[56]

That greater revenue would be needed to fund social reform was generally acknowledged across the political spectrum in Edwardian Britain. Steel-Maitland would have been more aware of this than most, partly because of the time he had spent working with the Treasury and also because of his commitment to a wide range of social policy initiatives. Social reform was one of Steel-Maitland's main interests throughout his career, and this interest was particularly pronounced in the decade before the Great War, when political debate on the nature and scope of social policy reached a previously unknown intensity. Steel-Maitland's main aim was quite simple, namely, to construct a distinctive Conservative approach to and programme of social reform. He saw this as necessarily related to tariff reform, not only in terms of the revenue aspect noted above but also in broader social and political terms. In his 1908 book outline Steel-Maitland had a section dealing with social reform, which he deemed one of the 'Cognate Questions' of the economics of imperialism. This confirmed a remark he had made to Lord Milner in October 1907 when, having invited Milner to speak at Rugby,[57] he pointed out that 'we [the local Conservatives] have consistently placed imperialism and an advanced social policy in the fore-front—*as obverse and reverse of the same coin*'.[58] Milner had no difficulty falling in with the local party line, for his speech at Rugby in November expressed exactly this argument.[59] But then, only eleven

---

[55] For another statement of this argument see Leo Amery's letter to *The Times* as 'Tariff Reformer', 28 Mar. 1908.

[56] Steel-Maitland, and others who presented this argument on the revenue impact of tariffs, were in many respects advancing a primitive version of what came to be known as the multiplier, which has some interesting implications in terms of Steel-Maitland's later interest in Keynes's economic ideas.

[57] Steel-Maitland had stood for Rugby at the 1906 general election, and at the time he wrote to Milner was still the prospective Conservative candidate for the seat.

[58] Steel-Maitland to Milner, n.d. (Oct. 1907), SMP, GD 193/135/187 (my emphasis).

[59] Milner at Rugby, 19 Nov. 1907, in A. Milner, *The Nation and the Empire* (1913), 243–53.

months earlier, Milner had argued at Manchester that imperialism and social reform were 'inseparable ideals, absolutely interdependent and complementary'.[60] The point that Steel-Maitland, Milner,[61] and others in the constructive imperialist camp[62] were seeking to establish was that, just as the Empire had to be viewed in a 'holistic' way which recognized that 'the principle which lies at the root of . . . [the] Imperial aspect, is the national principle',[63] so the relationship between imperial and domestic policy had to be viewed in the same way. Imperial policy had its social side, for example, the employment that could be created by imperial preference, and, likewise, social policy had its imperial side, for example, nurturing the health and 'fitness' of the population in order that they could be more effective workers, servicemen, parents, and citizens: the 'condition of the people' and the 'condition of the Empire' were as one.

In terms of specific policies, the range of Steel-Maitland's interests and activities was very wide. His first publication was his essay on 'Labour' in *The New Order*, which addressed problems in the British labour market. The first things he singled out were casual labour and the related issue of seasonal unemployment. These, he argued, could be assuaged by the introduction of labour registries to 'regularise' employment in areas and trades where casual and seasonal labour were rife. Not only would this improve the lot of those who worked in these sectors of the labour market, but the higher numbers of people in regular employment would also increase the overall level of earnings of the poorer classes and increase their demand for other goods.[64] He also called for the establishment of wages boards to regulate pay in the so-called sweated trades and for the regulation of home work.[65] These proposals drew on his investigations with Rose Squire for the Poor Law Commission, but it was clearly his work with Norman Chamberlain on 'boy labour' which led him to argue for more rigorous apprenticeship schemes. Poor apprenticeships, Steel-Maitland contended, led to a lack of skills and increased the probability of casualization in later life, thereby exacerbating the general scale of labour-market problems.[66]

---

[60] Milner at Manchester, 14 Dec. 1906, in ibid. 139.

[61] The particularly close relationship between Steel-Maitland's and Milner's ideas was undoubtedly strengthened when Steel-Maitland acted as Milner's private secretary when on the latter's speaking tour of Canada in the winter of 1908–9. Milner's speeches on that tour dealt with the themes outlined here, and it seems implausible that they did not in part reflect discussions between the two men. For Milner's speeches on Canada see ibid. 302–64.

[62] Other exponents of this argument included, for example, F. E. Smith, Leo Amery, J. W. Hills, E. A. Goulding, W. A. S. Hewins, and W. J. Ashley.

[63] Milner at Edinburgh, 15 Nov. 1907, in ibid. 240.

[64] Steel-Maitland, 'Labour', in Malmesbury (ed.), *New Order*, 351–8.

[65] Ibid. 367–73.   [66] Ibid. 260–3.

Steel-Maitland recognized that all of these proposals would have administrative costs and would also raise the costs of production in some trades, but both of these problems were to be solved by tariffs, which would produce more revenue and provide protection against foreign producers with lower costs.[67]

Steel-Maitland's interest in labour questions was not, however, confined to his activities as a social investigator and to his publications. He was one of a number of Conservatives who played an active part in the National Anti-Sweating League (NASL), a group set up in 1906 to campaign for government regulation of conditions and wages in trades such as clothing, furniture, and nail- and chain-making. Although he did not enter Parliament until 1910, he was evidently involved in the work that went into a Private Member's Bill presented, with cross-party support,[68] by the Compatriot Conservative MP, J. W. Hills, in February 1909.[69] Although this Bill was not passed, the Liberal government did introduce and pass the NASL-backed Trade Boards Act in March 1909, which provided a regulatory framework that was almost identical to Hills's measure and which Steel-Maitland could only have approved. He was also, as one would expect, supportive of the introduction of Labour Registries, which were established in 1908. Although they were brought into being by a Liberal government, Steel-Maitland enthusiastically endorsed them. Writing to a Birmingham Poor Law official in September 1910, he stated

I am exceedingly glad that you think the Labour Registries are likely to have some good effect. It has been the fashion for people in politics on my side to decry them because they owe their existence to the present Government. As a matter of fact, however, the credit belongs to no political party, but really to one man, Mr. Beveridge. For myself, I believe in them, and in fact advocated them in my Poor Law Report.[70]

Nor were Labour Registries and the Trade Boards Act the only Liberal legislation that Steel-Maitland supported. He was also broadly in favour of the National Insurance scheme that was established in 1911. However, his support for this measure, like that of the Conservative party in general, was not unqualified. Before the National Insurance legislation was introduced, and during its progress through the Commons, Steel-Maitland canvassed opinion from a range of business contacts and interests, from the friendly societies, and from within the USRC, and the messages he received shaped his somewhat equivocal

---

[67] Steel-Maitland, 'Labour', in Malmesbury (ed.), *New Order*, 376.
[68] The Bill also carried the names of Sir Charles Dilke and Arthur Henderson.
[69] A copy of the Bill can be found in Steel-Maitland's papers, SMP, GD 193/352/7.
[70] Steel-Maitland to C. Fletcher, 29 Sept. 1910, SMP, GD 193/108/1/177.

view of the legislation. Three things in particular stood out in this extensive correspondence. First, there was concern in the industrial assurance business, and amongst the friendly societies, about the process of gaining 'approved status' and being brought under the umbrella of the State-sponsored system.[71] Second, some employer groups who had supported the principle of National Insurance 'for years' were concerned about not being given a voice in the control of the proposed unemployment insurance funds.[72] Third, there was anxiety lest the employer contribution to the National Insurance fund would be a disincentive for employers to take on workers, and whether this would be the case only for small businesses and 'pass unnoticed' in larger firms.[73] These concerns help to explain why Steel-Maitland upheld the principle of State insurance as embodied in the Liberal legislation whilst criticizing detailed aspects of its operation. It is interesting in this context that Steel-Maitland's research, and popular response, indicated that the National Insurance Act aroused significant opposition, and yet he still looked to 'make the best of the Act' and did not advocate either repeal or wholesale criticism.

While Steel-Maitland was fully engaged with National Insurance he received a letter from the Unionist Social Insurance Committee which gave notice of another social issue bubbling under the surface of British politics. The Committee pointed out that their work had been devoted to the immediate legislative question and had therefore focused on *urban* analysis, but they noted that 'there is also a rural problem more or less parallel'.[74] The 'rural problem' blew up in October 1913 when Lloyd George opened the 'Land Campaign', but the fuse had been smouldering for many years, and the Conservatives themselves had quickened the pace of their own rural policy deliberations through 1912 and 1913.[75] Steel-Maitland himself played a leading part in this intra-party debate on an issue which had personal as well as political importance for him—he was, after all, a major landowner as well as party

[71] See e.g. J. Durant to Steel-Maitland, 19–25 May 1911, SMP, GD 193/151/1/36.

[72] Birmingham Chamber of Commerce to Steel-Maitland, 16 Nov. 1911, SMP, GD 193/153/2/143. It was this, as much as anything else, which had prompted the Birmingham Chamber to propose dropping unemployment insurance from the legislation and referring it to a Royal Commission. See Birmingham Chamber of Commerce to Steel-Maitland, 26 Aug. 1911, SMP, GD 193/155/5/67.

[73] J. M. Mckillop to Steel-Maitland, 26 Apr. 1911, and forwarded by Steel-Maitland to Sir Thomas Wrightson, W. Paxman, Mumford and Co., Dudley Docker, and V. Nicholson—all prominent Conservative businessmen. SMP, GD 193/152/3/28. Mckillop was Secretary of the Unionist Social Insurance Committee.

[74] Letter/Memorandum from the Unionist Social Insurance Committee, 15 Nov. 1911, enclosed in Steel-Maitland to Milner, 29 Sept. 1911, SMP, GD 193/119/5/34–46.

[75] See Green, *Crisis*, 280–4, 289–94, and M. Fforde, *Conservatism and Collectivism, 1886–1914* (Edinburgh, 1990), 126–31, 156–8.

Chairman and chief doyen of the USRC. It was Steel-Maitland who persuaded the party leadership to commission Lord Milner to undertake a comprehensive survey of land policy, which was completed by early 1913 and which provided material for much subsequent discussion and policy-making.[76] Likewise, Steel-Maitland was, of course, the prime mover in prompting the USRC to produce its land proposals in September 1913.[77] Yet, in spite of this, Steel-Maitland was complaining in November 1913 that 'Our Party is drifting into a very serious situation as regards the land controversy', and expressed concern that farming opinion was no longer solidly Conservative, and that the question of agricultural labourers' wages was a 'sleeping dog [that] will not lie'. The wages question in particular troubled Steel-Maitland. 'It is', he argued, 'not a case where we can . . . forbear to raise the question. It is raised for us . . . [and] Our own men are already going in all directions like foxes in a cornfield.'[78] This was an accurate description of the problems the Conservative party faced on the 'Land Question'. There was indeed considerable disillusion with the Conservatives amongst farmers, which had been growing over time but had become especially pronounced following the decision by Andrew Bonar Law, the recently elected Conservative leader, to shelve proposals for tariffs on corn in January 1913.[79] However, it was the issue of wages that caused most difficulties. The Liberal Land Campaign promised the introduction of a minimum wage for agricultural labourers, an initiative widely regarded as a major vote-winner. The Conservatives were deeply divided as to how to respond. There was a general consensus that *something* had to be offered to the labourers, given that they were the largest element of the rural electorate, but exactly what was highly contentious.

The USRC was clear that the Conservatives could only counter the Liberals' appeal by embracing the minimum wage themselves. In September 1913 the USRC had sought to pre-empt Lloyd George, whose intentions on the wages front were well known before the official opening of the Land Campaign, by publishing proposals calling for the establishment of rural wages boards. These were to be appointed by County Councils, and were to indicate and if necessary enforce a minimum wage. This proposal ran into strong opposition, both from those

---

[76] See 'Lord Milner's Agricultural Memorandum', Milner papers, MS Milner Dep. 159, and for discussions of its ideas see MS Milner Dep. 38, 40. For Steel-Maitland's role in the genesis of this see Steel-Maitland to A. C. Glazebrook. 26 Aug. 1913, SMP, GD 193/159/6/15–18x.

[77] For these proposals see below.

[78] Steel-Maitland, Memorandum on the Land Question, n.d. Nov. ? 1913), SMP, GD 193/119/5/139–43.

[79] See Green, *Crisis*, 280–3 and id., 'No Longer the Farmer's Friend: The Conservative Party and Agricultural Protection, 1880–1914', in J. R. Wordie (ed.), *Agriculture and Politics in England, 1830–1914* (Basingstoke, 2000).

who opposed the minimum wage in principle, and from those who felt that a minimum wage was acceptable but that it ought to be voluntary. Faced with such diverse views, and fearing an intra-party feud, Bonar Law sought to postpone any decision on the issue by telling the party conference in November 1913 that the issue demanded a full inquiry. But peace did not break out, and over the following months the internal party debate grew quite acrimonious. In late January 1914 there seemed to be some room for agreement, when Lord Salisbury, one of the strongest opponents of the regulation of rural wages, accepted in a lengthy memorandum on the question that 'It is very difficult to resist the demand for some sort of State interference with the rate of agricultural wages'. However, Salisbury was clear that any regulation of wages should be locally and not centrally organized, was prepared only to accept a voluntary minimum wage, and argued that even then there was a danger that it would cause unemployment by pricing labour out of the reach of impecunious farmers. Moreover, Salisbury followed up his memorandum with a letter to Steel-Maitland which was strongly critical of a USRC-endorsed book on rural issues. At this juncture Steel-Maitland made his position very clear, for he produced a comprehensive critique of Salisbury's memorandum. He dismissed the idea that a minimum wage would cause unemployment, arguing that the demand for agricultural labour exceeded supply, and he was equally hostile to the idea of a voluntary minimum wage on the grounds that it would not provide a means for bringing underpaying farmers into line.[80] Steel-Maitland aligned himself with his 'protégés' at the USRC, and endorsed their minimum wage proposals of September 1913.

Steel-Maitland's stance on agricultural wages was consistent with his general aims and approach with regard to social policy. To begin with there was a clear electoral rationale to Steel-Maitland's interest in social reform. Writing in December 1913, he stated that:

We cannot outbid the Liberals or the Socialists, but we ought to realise that the bulk of the population are alive to their own interests, and have an exaggerated belief that these can be bettered by legislation to an extent that no-one could have dreamed of fifteen years ago. Even if we cannot outbid, we ought to show them that we sympathise, and are sincere in a desire to act along social lines.[81]

In Steel-Maitland's view a positive policy of social reform was, in an age of mass politics, an electoral necessity. This was a view shared by British politicians of all parties in the late nineteenth and early twentieth centuries. But if the popularity of social reform was generally accepted,

[80] Steel-Maitland, Notes on Lord Salisbury's Memorandum, 17 Feb. 1914, SMP, GD 193/119/5/15.
[81] Steel-Maitland to A. C. Glazebrook, 24 Dec. 1913, SMP, GD 193/159/6/9.

important questions still had to be addressed—namely, how exactly were social reforms to be constructed and upon what principles were they to be based. Some of the main tasks Steel-Maitland set himself in his early years in politics were to persuade his party of the electoral importance of social reform, and to provide an intellectual and institutional framework for the development of a Conservative social programme. He was by no means alone in the Edwardian Conservative party in seeing social reform as a *sine qua non* of electoral success, but he still found it quite hard going to persuade his party to accept the arguments for social reform. Only a few months after his election to Parliament, Steel-Maitland told one of his friends that he found politics, especially social reform politics, 'a little disheartening sometimes', because it was difficult to chart a course 'between the stupid reactionaries on our own side and the flabby sentimentalists on the other', and three years later he was still complaining about 'the old buffoons' in the Conservative party who were obstructing progress on rural policy. The creation of the USRC and Steel-Maitland's frequent use of extra-parliamentary experts bore testimony to his desire to ensure not only that policy was well thought out but also that his internal party opponents could be overwhelmed by intellectual weight of argument. In this way obstacles to the party adopting an electorally vital policy could be overcome.

Sheer force of persuasion was one strategy; the use of examples of successful social policy was another. As the Conservatives were not in government, central legislative action was obviously not possible, but Steel-Maitland canvassed support for local initiatives to bring about improvements in social and industrial conditions. He supported attempts by the Birmingham industrial magnate Dudley Docker to foster a sense of corporate partnership between employers and employees, which were essentially extensions of the employment practices pioneered by Joseph Chamberlain.[82] Mention of Chamberlain in this context is of particular relevance. In February 1910 Steel-Maitland told Milner that the reason he had become MP for a Birmingham constituency was because 'The town is potentially capable of corporate effort more than any other town in the country'.[83] Clearly he felt that the legacy of Joseph Chamberlain's mayoralty and the improvements it had brought were still part of Birmingham's civic culture. This was vital, because local schemes of social reform were a route to educating opinion on social issues.[84] In September 1910 he told one correspondent,

---

[82] R. Davenport-Hines, *Dudley Docker: The Life and Times of a Trade Warrior* (Cambridge, 1984), 73–4.
[83] Steel-Maitland to Milner, 19 Feb. 1910, SMP, GD 193/147/1/11.   [84] Ibid.

'we may be able to do something in Birmingham on lines that even Chatham would have approved of', in that all classes could be brought to co-operate in and benefit from industrial and civic harmony,[85] and two months later he suggested to the secretary of the Birmingham Imperial Tariff Committee that 'a housing and town planning policy should be made part of the Unionist platform in Birmingham'.[86] For Steel-Maitland municipal action provided one way of demonstrating to both sceptics in his own party and to the public generally that social reform *worked*.

Steel-Maitland saw the practice of social reform as crucial, but he was equally interested in the principles. Here his ideas and activities in the realm of social and economic policy are of particular interest, for both before and after the Great War he was effectively engaged in an attempt to structure a Conservative position on the role of the State. He succinctly outlined his basic view of the principle of State intervention when, in April 1911, he spoke in a Commons debate on the Labour MP Will Crooks's motion for the introduction of an industrial minimum wage. Steel-Maitland offered Crooks support for the principle of mini-mum-wage legislation, and declared 'We . . . have given up the old theory that the State should no longer interfere with industry at all. That has been relegated to the rubbish basket.'[87] At first glance this was an unequivocally Collectivist statement, and, insofar as it did reflect Steel-Maitland's belief in a positive role for the State, it was. However, there are, as Steel-Maitland himself was keen to point out, degrees of Collectivism, and he consistently set limits to State action. How he defined those limits was implicit in the policies he supported. The most straightforward limit was that State action should not be class-discrim-inatory in terms of its fiscal and economic effects. Social reforms were obviously to be of most direct benefit to the poorer classes, but this was not class discrimination because society as a whole would benefit from the general improvement of the condition of the people. The kind of class discrimination to be avoided was that exemplified in the 'People's Budget' of 1909, which imposed 'punitive' taxation on wealth (espe-cially landed wealth) to fund social reforms. In contrast, tariffs, which were paid either by all classes, or by foreign importers, or which increased the flow of existing taxes, were a non-discriminatory source of revenue. With regard to other possibly discriminatory economic effects, such as the increased costs that farmers might face under a mini-mum wage, or that employers would incur through National Insurance

---

[85] Steel-Maitland to W. L. Grant, 3 Sept. 1910, SMP, GD 193/148/7/25.
[86] Steel-Maitland to W. Jenkins, 19 Dec. 1910, SMP, GD 193/148/9/18.
[87] Steel-Maitland in Parliament, 26 Apr. 1911, *PD* 24, c.1896.

contributions, there were to be compensatory benefits in the shape of reduced local taxation on agricultural land and tariff protection against foreign manufactures. In this way the State could balance the effects of its action to secure maximum social benefit and minimal social disruption.

The idea that State intervention should have a socially balanced impact was one of Steel-Maitland's primary concerns. But if one considers, for example, his support for tariffs, the 1909 Trade Boards Act, National Insurance, and an agricultural minimum wage, another important aspect of his thought begins to emerge. With regard to tariffs, which contemporaries placed in the context of State intervention, the essential point was to provide British industry in particular with a level playing-field on which to compete. With many foreign markets closed by tariffs, imperial preference was to provide a fair opportunity for exporters. At the same time protective tariffs were to provide a shield against 'unfair' competition, such as 'dumped' foreign imports, and to enable British firms to develop economies of scale and to enjoy continuous running of plant. In this respect tariffs were to be an *enabling* device of which industries and firms could only take full advantage if they were well organized and efficient. Tariffs, as noted above, were also to have a beneficial social effect in terms of protecting and extending employment, but this in turn assumed that workers would be willing to take advantage of the opportunities for employment that would become available. That foreign 'sweated goods' were a particular target for tariff prohibition[88] provided a link with Steel-Maitland's stance on the regulation of sweated trades. A key point about workers in the sweated trades was that they were unorganized—the nature of their work militated against the formation of trade unions. Given that the workers could not bring about improvements in pay and conditions by their own actions, and given that their notoriously exploitative employers were unlikely to raise wages or cut hours voluntarily, State regulation was the only feasible route to improvement. Having achieved this improvement by regulation of sweating in Britain, tariffs against foreign sweated goods were deemed essential to protect workers from unregulated foreign competition.[89] On the question of insurance there were, before the introduction of the State scheme, private and voluntary health and unemployment insurance schemes available from industrial assurance companies, friendly societies, trade unions, and some employers.

[88] See Steel-Maitland, 'Economics of Modern Industry' for his emphasis on this point. It was also a point generally made by Conservatives.

[89] See the speeches made by Conservative spokesmen in the Commons' debates on the passage of the Trade Boards Act.

However, the adequacy of private and voluntary schemes had been called into question by the first decade of the twentieth century, largely because the scale and scope of the problems of a mature industrial economy were beyond their administrative and financial capabilities. State action was thus a means of addressing problems with which existing structures could not cope if left to themselves. There was a similar rationale to Steel-Maitland's support for an agricultural minimum wage. His great opponent on this issue, Lord Salisbury, noted that agricultural labourers' trade unions had proved difficult to organize and maintain, and that the labourers could not press their own case for higher wages effectively. But whereas Salisbury looked to voluntary action by farmers to solve the problem, Steel-Maitland thought that the farmers had failed in their way just as the labourers had failed in theirs, and could not be relied upon. Hence, once again, State intervention was necessary to rectify the systemic failings of a particular set of social actors.

The implications of Steel-Maitland's stance on State intervention in terms of the nature of Conservative thought on the subject will be examined in detail later in this book.[90] This chapter will concentrate on its implications for his own intellectual formation. The roots of his ideas on social reform are quite difficult to establish. The influences must largely be inferred. The economists who exercised the strongest sway over Steel-Maitland shared a common intellectual heritage in the shape of German Idealist philosophy. Hewins and the American institutionalists drew their inspiration from the German historical/national school, who were very much part of that heritage.[91] There is no evidence that Steel-Maitland ever read Hegel, though there are detailed lecture notebooks on Kant from his time at the LSE.[92] However, it is tempting here to point to the years he spent at Balliol, when the legacy and legend of T. H. Green was still strong, and it is also difficult to ignore Steel-Maitland's close personal and intellectual links with Alfred Milner, who had attended Balliol when Green and Benjamin Jowett were at the peak of their powers and who was also strongly influenced by German philosophy. The case for seeing Idealism as an influence on Steel-Maitland's stance on social questions is by no means watertight, but it becomes stronger if one takes into account his knowledge of and interest in Platonic thought, which he had studied as an undergraduate and at the LSE. A blend of Idealism and Platonism was, in varying degrees,

[90] See Ch. 10.

[91] For the links, both intellectual and personal, between the German and English historical schools and the American institutionalists see E. H. H. Green, 'Conservative Progressives or Progressive Conservatives? A Comparative Study of the Political Economy of the English Historical School and the American Institutionalists, 1880–1920' (forthcoming).

[92] SMP, GD 193/52/2.

an important aspect of late-Victorian and Edwardian social thought.[93] Steel-Maitland thus fits into the pattern of politicians and intellectuals in the late nineteenth and early twentieth centuries who were 'in search of a social philosophy', and his holistic approach to social and economic questions, his sense of personal civic and social duty, and his belief in an active role for the State at both central and local level are indicative of a social philosophy that carried Idealist inflections.[94] The question to which this chapter will now turn is how Steel-Maitland's search for a social philosophy developed in the very different historical context of the inter-war years.

Three main issues were the focus of Steel-Maitland's inter-war activites—tariffs, industrial relations, and above all unemployment. Except perhaps during the general election campaign of 1923, the debate over tariffs was never as intense after the Great War as it had been before, but it still excited passions, including Steel-Maitland's. One aspect of Steel-Maitland's involvement with inter-war tariff debates was somewhat surprising: he did not place anything like the same emphasis on the imperial dimension as he had before 1914. At the NUCA Conference in Birmingham in 1920 he urged the assembly to 'adhere to their old policy',[95] but the domestic, imperial, and international economic context had changed and the old 'full tariff' programme had less resonance than in the pre-war period. Steel-Maitland remained a devotee of the cause of Empire, but he stressed that imperial trade alone could not solve Britain's economic difficulties.[96] His emphasis was on the protective side of tariffs, and their use as a means of promoting industrial reorganization. He supported the Safeguarding tariff legislation of 1921 and was likewise supportive of Baldwin's tariff campaign in 1923. The November 1923 election saw Steel-Maitland reactivate a political career that had been largely dormant for four years;[97] the reactivation was completed when the Conservatives returned to power in November 1924 and he was appointed Minister of Labour. Steel-Maitland's first major speech in office was in a debate on a Labour

[93] See SMP, GD 193/52/4 for Steel-Maitland's lecture notes on Greek philosophy and Plato in particular. For the importance of the blend of Idealist and Platonic ideas in late 19th- and early 20th-century social philosophy see J. Harris, 'Political Thought and the Welfare State, 1870–1940: An Intellectual Framework for British Social Policy', *P& P* 135 (1992).

[94] See Harris, ibid., and S. Den Otter, *British Idealism* (Oxford, 1997).

[95] Steel-Maitland at NUCA Conference, Birmingham, 10 June 1920, NUCA Conference Minutes, Microfil Card 95.

[96] See in particular Steel-Maitland in Parliament, 14 Feb. 1935, *PD* 296, c. 2196.

[97] Steel-Maitland was a backbencher from 1919 to 1924. He had resigned his junior position in the post-war Coalition in 1919 and had become a strong critic of the government. From late 1922 to late 1923 he suffered a bout of ill-health, and was rendered *hors de combat* politically.

censure motion on unemployment, in which he presented a critique of the case for public works,[98] and defended the government against charges of inactivity. The centrepiece of this defence was tariffs. Turning the tables on Labour, he criticized their decision to repeal the 1915 'Mckenna duties' and indicated that the Conservatives would reintroduce them—which they did in 1925. Steel-Maitland's case for tariffs was essentially the same one he and many others had deployed before 1914—that tariffs would protect employment by protecting the source of employment. He did, however, add a twist to the argument which had rarely been made explicit in the pre-war debate. 'A believer in Free Trade', he contended, 'may think that a person who under a Free Trade system is thrown out of work in one industry will be absorbed in another; but the essence of that doctrine is that this can only happen in a time of brisk trade.'[99] In 1930 the same argument was to emanate from a very different source. In giving his 'private evidence' to the Macmillan Committee, J. M. Keynes pointed out that 'Free Trade . . . assumes that if you threw men out of work in one direction you re-employ them in another. As soon as that link is broken, the whole Free Trade argument breaks down.'[100] In the wake of the 1921 economic downturn British governments were confronted with previously unknown levels of unemployment, and as they sought to get to grips with this problem most previously established economic nostrums were re-evaluated. Steel-Maitland's recasting of the unemployment case against free trade and for tariffs was a contribution to this process of re-evaluation, and he was to make several more, of quite far-reaching significance.

Staying with tariffs, Steel-Maitland was a strong supporter of the renewal of the Safeguarding duties in 1925 and of their extension in 1926. Following the Crash of 1929 and the ensuing Slump, Steel-Maitland's support for tariffs grew still stronger, and in 1930 he was closely connected with the League of Industry (LI) and the National Council of Industry and Commerce (NCIC), two groups made up of prominent industrialists who campaigned for the introduction of a more comprehensive tariff regime.[101] But although both LI and NCIC publications held out promises that would have been familiar to a pre-1914 audience—work for all, imperial unity, secure home markets, and so on—it would be a mistake to see the tariff argument of 1929–32 as a

[98] Steel-Maitland's thoughts on public works will be discussed below.

[99] Steel-Maitland in Parliament, 26 Nov. 1924, *PD* 188, c. 1702.

[100] J. M. Keynes, 'Private Evidence to the Macmillan Committee', 28 Feb. 1930, *The Collected Writings of John Maynard Keynes*, 30 vols. (1973–82), xx. 117.

[101] Comprehensive documentation of Steel-Maitland's involvement with the groups can be found in SMP, GD 193/617–26, *passim*.

rehash of old ideas. This was certainly not the case with Steel-Maitland. In his book *The Trade Crisis and the Way Out* he made a strong case for tariffs, but did not present them as in themselves an economic *deus ex machina*. In particular, he linked tariffs with a discussion of industrial efficiency. Steel-Maitland started from the premiss that the 'widespread belief that the whole of our present trade depression is due to world causes ... is wrong and demonstrably so'.[102] Pointing to Britain's reliance on exports, he felt that the fact that the *value* of exports was significantly higher than in 1913 but that the *volume* of exports was not indicated that British industry was uncompetitive, and could not generate a great enough volume of production to sustain employment levels.[103] Here Steel-Maitland downplayed the significance of the return to the gold standard, arguing that the advantages enjoyed by other countries stemmed not from their having depreciated currencies. He agreed that the return to gold 'added to our difficulties', but insisted that this was 'only because of the rigidity of our economic system', and he concluded that 'Our loss of trade and decline in prosperity is due solely to our own shortcomings'.[104] To rectify these shortcomings British industry needed to rationalize its structures, and it was here that tariffs came in. Tariffs were to provide a shield behind which industries could shelter, free from disruptive competition, while they implemented organizational changes. At the same time, they were also to provide a shield for the labour market, and allow time for any labour displaced by rationalizations to be reabsorbed.[105] Steel-Maitland saw other potential benefits from tariffs,[106] but he was also clear that there were risks and that tariffs were not the sole answer to Britain's economic difficulties. He warned that steps had to be taken to ensure that tariffs did not bring about any increased costs of production, and he was also concerned that tariffs might postpone rather than facilitate rationalization.[107] Industrial *efficiency* was the end Steel-Maitland sought, rationalization was the most important means of achieving that end, and tariffs were potentially one of the best ways of assisting rationalization.

The language of industrial rationalization was very much an economic *lingua franca* of the late 1920s, in much the same way as 'planning' was to be in the 1930s.[108] Steel-Maitland was aware of this,

---

[102] Steel-Maitland, *Trade Crisis*, 10.
[103] A point reminiscent of his argument in 'Economics of Modern Industry' that volume of production per head of population was the truest measure of a nation's wealth.
[104] Steel-Maitland, *Trade Crisis*, 16.   [105] Ibid. 32.
[106] Here he did recycle one of his pre-1914 arguments on the indirect benefit to the Exchequer of increased production and business activity, ibid. 33.
[107] Ibid. 34.
[108] On the language of planning see D. Ritschel, *The Politics of Planning* (Oxford, 1997).

and noted that rationalization was 'often too glibly used'. It was not, he pointed out, a synonym for 'amalgamation', for the good reason that it was possible to have inefficient amalgamations. In Steel-Maitland's view the hallmarks of effective rationalization were the achievement of organizational structures that enabled firms and industries to realize economies of scale.[109] Here he felt the State could assist industries to reorganize and re-equip, as it had done in Belgium and France,[110] but his preference was for the State to play an arm's-length, facilitating role, and for financial institutions to take the lead in co-ordinating industrial reorganization. However, he was not convinced that this would happen in Britain. Thus, in mid-December 1930 Steel-Maitland proposed that the government should raise a large, low-interest loan to fund a major programme of rationalization under the management of a committee of businessmen. This scheme drew a lukewarm response. Edward Peacock told Steel-Maitland that both he and Montagu Norman were of the view that 'the Government should be kept out of intervention in the financing of industry', and that his scheme would be acceptable only as an alternative to schemes which threatened greater intervention.[111] Steel-Maitland's response, in two letters on Boxing Day 1930, was to seek to persuade Peacock, a member of the Court of the Bank of England, that the Bank should be more active on the industrial front. Earlier that year the Governor of the Bank, Montagu Norman, had set up the Bankers Industrial Development Corporation (BIDCo), which was designed to direct more investment capital to industry and to promote rationalization schemes, and by the end of the year the BIDCo was already heavily involved with the iron and steel and cotton industries.[112] Steel-Maitland told Peacock that he had 'great admiration for the Governor, both for his judgement and his courage in breaking through tradition, by taking a lead in industry', but he felt that Norman was still somewhat tentative in pursuing this new strategy and that there was a sense of too little, too late. He recalled that:

In 1918 before he [Norman] was Governor and I was at the Board of Trade, he came . . . to dine with me and two or three of my head officials, so that we might question him. I asked him then whether it would not be possible for the Banks to do with Industry just what he is doing now. I was not talking wildly or without thought. He was amused, quizzical, determindly negative; said that British banks weren't built that way. (It was the bankers, not the banks, who were not adaptable.)

---

[109] Steel-Maitland, *Trade Crisis*, 37. [110] Ibid. 23.
[111] E. R. Peacock to Steel-Maitland, 18 Dec. 1930, SMP, GD 193/119/1/8.
[112] For the role of BIDCo, and especially its involvement with iron and steel and cotton see S. Tolliday, *Business, Banking and Politics* (Cambridge, Mass., 1986), and J. H. Bamberg, 'The Government, the Banks, and the Lancashire Cotton Industry', unpublished Cambridge University Ph.D thesis (1984).

Now he is sharing the lead in doing it. Had the Banks taken the business in hand earlier, the cotton industry would not be in such a mess to-day; nor some of the other industries.[113]

Steel-Maitland's concern, even scepticism, about Norman's commitment to industrial reorganization was, in effect, what had prompted him to advocate his own scheme. In the second of his Boxing Day letters to Peacock, Steel-Maitland noted that: 'If the Bank with the BIDCo could multiply itself tenfold and deal with other industries as it is doing with cotton . . . [my] proposal would not be needed', but he added that it was clear the Bank could not do this, that 'others won't', and that a government-sponsored programme was necessary.[114]

Steel-Maitland was convinced that 'other industries need remodelling as well as iron and steel and cotton', and that this need was all the more urgent because there was 'every indication that the international competition we shall have to face will be increasingly keen'. Moreover, reorganizing industries to achieve more efficiency was, he argued, essential because it was obvious that 'protective duties of some sort are pretty certain [and] The organisation under . . . [my] proposal, well started, will . . . prevent any wrong advantage being taken of the duties'.[115] Steel-Maitland's proposal was wholly consistent with his perception of the shortcomings of British industry and the potential risks of tariffs unaccompanied by rationalization, but the economic rationale of his scheme carried a clear political rationale as well. One of Steel-Maitland's main aims was to keep the State as far away from the control and management of industry as possible. This was an aim shared by his party. For a minority of Conservatives, any State intervention in the economy was Socialism, but even those who were not pure anti-Statists viewed the idea of State control or management of business as distinctly Socialistic. Steel-Maitland, however, denied that his scheme carried any such danger. He told Edward Peacock, 'I should hate the Government to interfere in the management of industry as much as you or the Governor or anyone. A Government's sphere is to lay down general regulation, but not to manage', and claimed that his proposals would ensure that 'we can get the remodelling done now without the Government retaining any permanent control'.[116] Indeed, he argued that far from being 'Socialist', his proposal was a way of thwarting Socialism, and he suggested that had such a scheme been in operation 'Possibly the recent Coal Act would not have been passed'.[117] But in spite of his efforts to assuage concern over the implications of his

---

[113] Steel-Maitland to E. R. Peacock, 26 Dec. 1930, SMP, GD 193/119/1/5.
[114] Ibid., SMP, GD 193/119/1/6.   [115] Ibid.
[116] Ibid., SMP, GD 193/119/1/5.   [117] Ibid.

proposal, Steel-Maitland was unable to persuade any of his many corre-
spondents of its merits. Indeed, the general response was in accord with
Montagu Norman's view that it was 'really a means of reaching purga-
tory instead of hell'.[118]

Tariffs and industrial restructuring were subjects Steel-Maitland was
able to devote time and thought to after 1929. As Minister of Labour
between 1924 and 1929 he had, perforce, to focus on matters central to
his own departmental brief, namely, industrial relations and unemployment. With regard to industrial relations he was in office during a
period of intense conflict, with the coal dispute of 1925–6 and the
General Strike of 1926 marking the peak of the troubles. The details of
the coal dispute and the General Strike are well known, and will not be
explored here. This chapter will focus on the general aspects of Steel-
Maitland's position, and the light this sheds on his broader political
economy. Unlike many of his Cabinet colleagues, and certainly unlike
his party's backbenchers, Steel-Maitland was not a 'hawk' on the industrial relations front. During the coal dispute he was firm, insofar as he
did not wish the miners to achieve their aims through either the threat
of or actual strike action, but he was also keen to find a path to a concil-
iatory settlement. The Royal Commission on the Mines, chaired by
Herbert Samuel, was Steel-Maitland's main hope in this last respect, but
its Report failed to satisfy either side of the dispute, and Steel-Maitland
himself expressed reservations about some of its conclusions.[119]

Steel-Maitland was critical of both the miners and mine-owners, feeling that neither side showed an adequate understanding of their industry's situation. He felt that the miners were *more* to blame than the
owners, but at one point he described a meeting with the owners as
'lamentable'.[120] At first glance it may seem that Steel-Maitland was
sitting on the fence and saying 'a plague on both your houses', but his
position was more complex. This was clear when he wrote to the
Conservative party Chairman, J. C. C. Davidson, to discuss the ongoing
dispute in September 1926. Steel-Maitland suggested that Winston
Churchill's behaviour during negotiations then current had been
counter-productive, and that he had 'put all their [miners and mine-
owners] backs up' with his impulsive and combative behaviour. More
important, Steel-Maitland stated that, 'What has also put all their backs
up is that they think W. C. is activated by political and not industrial
reasons and of course that is true. He thinks out industrial policy in
terms of making a political speech.' He went on to argue that three

---

[118] M. Norman to Steel-Maitland, 18 Dec. 1930, SMP, GD 193/119/1/23.
[119] Steel-Maitland, Memorandum, 'Course of Action in the Coal Dispute', n.d. (May 1926), SMP, GD 193/109/5/69.
[120] Steel-Maitland to J. C. C. Davidson, 8 Sept. 1926, SMP, GD193/94/2/103–8x.

things were needed. The first was to consider 'what is best for the indus-try & industry generally; to judge by undustrial not political considera-tions predominantly'. The second was 'to get peace on conditions that should make it lasting'. The third was for the government to act as an honest broker between the two sides.[121] Here Steel-Maitland's views were close to those expressed in a letter that had been forwarded to him in June 1926 by Sir Harry Brittain, which stated that 'the crisis in the coal industry is not really a problem of labour . . . but a problem of Britain's reluctance to organize and re-adjust to meet the demands of a new age . . . the economic urge of a new industrial era the world over makes the reorganisation of the coal industry as inevitable as fate. Why not reorganize now and win peace and prosperity for the whole nation.' The author of the letter concluded by saying 'I may be out of chime with the Government's inner views [but] (not so far out of line with Sir Arthur's, I fancy)'.[122] Brittain's correspondent was right. Steel-Maitland did think that industrial reorganization was essential to better industrial relations in mining and other industries. His reasoning was straightfor-ward. Industrial reorganization was necessary in order to modernize British industry and improve its efficiency. This would lead to greater profitability and prosperity, which would reduce pressure on employers to seek cost-reductions in the shape of lower wages or longer hours for their workers, and this in turn would reduce the likelihood of industrial conflict.

But although Steel-Maitland saw industrial reorganization as crucial, this did not mean that he felt the structure of industrial relations could be left unchanged; far from it. For Steel-Maitland, better industrial rela-tions were a necessary complement to industrial reorganization—they were two sides of the same coin. Hence, in October 1926, while the coal dispute was still ongoing, he outlined plans to bring about harmony between employers and employees.[123] This was to be achieved by bring-ing both sides of industry together and promoting the idea of a part-nership of capital and labour. To achieve this end Steel-Maitland sought in the first place to persuade Stanley Baldwin not to pursue the Trade Disputes Bill, the measure then being drawn up to discipline the trade-union movement.[124] In this way a climate of reconciliation rather than recrimination was to be created. In addition, Steel-Maitland sought to bring the leaders of the employers and the trade unions together, with Lord Weir of the Confederation of Employers Organisations and Ernest

[121] Steel-Maitland to J. C. C. Davidson, 8 Sept. 1926, SMP, GD193/94/2/103–8x.
[122] S. Walton to Sir H. Brittain, 17 June 1926, SMP, GD193/109/5/331–3x.
[123] See Steel-Maitland, 'Memorandum on the Industrial Situation and its Bearing on Trade Union Legislation', 11 Oct. 1926, Baldwin papers, Trinity College, Cambridge, vol. 11.
[124] Ibid.

Bevin of the Transport Workers being the principal figures whose co-operation he sought. Steel-Maitland's initiative seemed, at first, to meet with some success, with Weir and Bevin making plans in February 1927 for a series of meetings. But, as Steel-Maitland had feared, the publication of the Trade Disputes Bill in March antagonized the trade unions and led Bevin to suspend his dialogue with Weir. Nevertheless, Steel-Maitland's efforts were not wholly wasted, for he had set in train the process that led to the Mond–Turner talks of 1928, which in turn led to further, sporadic discussions between the employers' organizations and the TUC over the next five years.[125] Steel-Maitland was, in this respect, one of the earliest advocates of restructuring employer–trade union relations along lines which would emphasize their joint, corporate interest in the efficiency of their industry.

Moving industrial relations away from conflict and towards concordat was eminently desirable on political grounds. Industrial peace, especially in the wake of the General Strike, was widely regarded as necessary for political and social stability. But industrial peace was inextricably linked in Steel-Maitland's mind with industrial efficiency. That Steel-Maitland, like many of his contemporaries, was an admirer of the US economy was in this context significant. The ability of US industry to match efficiency with high wages and industrial peace was something Steel-Maitland wished British industry to emulate, and in the summer of 1926 he sent an official mission to the USA to study industrial conditions and industrial relations there. When he visited the USA himself in 1933 Steel-Maitland was to express particular admiration of the 'business unions' that were a feature of US industry,[126] and in some ways they did offer a broad model of the kind of industrial relations structure he desired in Britain. Steel-Maitland viewed co-operative relations between employers and trade unions as the basis for higher productivity in industry, and argued that the resulting higher output per worker would enable employers to pay higher wages but at the same time enjoy lower unit costs.[127] He regarded trade-union resistance to new technical processes, and their restrictive practices, as significant obstacles to higher productivity, but these he felt could be overcome by the restructuring of industrial relations on co-operative lines. Trade unions were to be persuaded to lower their resistance to new techniques, and to relax their over-rigid rules of working, by being drawn into consultation and collaboration with employers. This required greater flexibility on the

---

[125] G. W. McDonald and H. F. Gospel, 'The Mond–Turner Talks, 1927–33: A Study in Industrial Co-operation', *HJ* 16 (1973).
[126] A. Steel-Maitland, *The New America* (1934), 73.
[127] Id., 'Memorandum on the Industrial Situation'.

part of employers too. Trade unions had to be convinced that concordat was in their interest.

Steel-Maitland also felt that government had a constructive role to play, as was made clear by his response to the 1924 Washington Hours Convention. This Convention proposed an international agreement on limiting working hours—the idea being that this socially ameliorative step had to be taken collectively or industry in non-adherent nations would gain a competitive advantage. The Labour government did not ratify the Convention's proposals, and the Conservative party, in office after November 1924, was largely indifferent or hostile. Steel-Maitland, however, was in favour of ratifying the Convention. On four occasions between 1925 and 1929 he presented memoranda to Cabinet advocating this course of action,[128] and when challenged in the Commons about his views in 1929, he stated, 'I have always been, and am now, a supporter of the principle of the Washington Convention'.[129] The reasons for his stance were twofold. First, a reduction of hours was something that had great appeal to the British workforce, and would serve to reduce industrial militancy. Second, bringing all countries into line on hours would reduce foreign competition for the basic industries. In short, it was a measure that would benefit both employees and employers, and would serve to demonstrate that their interests were best served by improving conditions in industry as a whole. He argued that some flexibility on the hours question was necessary, on the basis that different industries had different patterns of work, and he insisted that Britain could not act unilaterally.[130] On the hours question, as with providing a framework for bringing employers and trade unions together, the government could facilitate the process of industrial collaboration.

But if the hours that people worked were an important preoccupation for Steel-Maitland in his time as Minister of Labour, the problem that dominated his period in office was, as he stated in February 1929, 'the question of our unemployment, the causes of it, the character of it, and the lines on which alone treatment can proceed'.[131] With regard to the causes of unemployment, Steel-Maitland saw the decline in the volume of Britain's export trade as a major factor, accounting in his view for perhaps 800,000 of the then total of 1.2 million unemployed. However, as noted above, he felt the loss of trade was due to structural weaknesses

---

[128] See id., Memorandum on 'International Regulation of Hours of Work', 20 Apr. 1926, PRO, CAB 24/179; id., Memorandum on 'Washington Hours Convention', 18 July 1927, PRO, CAB 24/188; id., Memorandum on 'Washington Hours Convention', 28 Jan. 1929, PRO, CAB 24/201.

[129] Steel-Maitland in Parliament, 27 Feb. 1929, *PD* 225, c. 2076.

[130] Id., 1 May 1925, *PD* 183, cc. 527–35.

[131] Id., 27 Feb. 1929, *PD* 225, c. 2077.

in British industry which had rendered it uncompetitive. This explains why he saw industrial reorganization as the key long-term solution to unemployment, and also why he stressed that tariffs would only help if they were accompanied by rationalization. To a certain extent Steel-Maitland felt the unemployment problem had to be disaggregated, on the grounds that 'to get at the true character of unemployment we must not regard it as a whole . . . [but] take all the different parts'.[132] Each depressed industry had different needs, and rationalization schemes had to be tailored to suit those needs. This emphasis on the structural aspect of the problem underpinned the main legislative legacy of Steel-Maitland's time at the Ministry of Labour, the Industrial Transference scheme, introduced in 1928. The aim of this scheme was to facilitate the movement of unemployed workers from depressed areas and industries into areas of new industrial growth or, failing that, to the Colonies. The basic assumption here was that the depressed industries were unlikely to return to their previous manning levels, and indeed that the rationalization necessary to render them competitive might cause further redundancies. The unemployed had, therefore, to be transferred from structurally weak to structurally sound industries. Steel-Maitland argued that this was particularly true of the coal industry, in which, he declared, 'there is no conceivable way of solving the problem . . . except by the policy of transfer'.[133] The structural weaknesses of the mining sector were, he argued, beyond the scope of any reorganization to deal with. Hence, although Steel-Maitland thought that the best cure for unemployment was, if possible, to get people back to work in their own trades, in the coal industry this was simply not possible.

The emphasis which Steel-Maitland placed on the structural causes of unemployment might seem to indicate that the focus of his interest in the problem was essentially microeconomic, with greatest weight being attached to the supply side. This would, however, be a partial and misleading description of his position. The best indication of the complexity of Steel-Maitland's position on unemployment is the evolution of his ideas on the issue of public works. The idea that government could implement programmes of works to provide employment at times of economic recession was not a product of the inter-war years. The 'Chamberlain Circular' of 1885, the 1905 Unemployed Workmen Act, and Lloyd George's forestry and road schmes of 1909–11 had all, to varying degrees, presented public works as a means of reducing unemployment.[134] What was new in the inter-war years was the scale of the

[132] Ibid., c. 2081.   [133] Ibid.
[134] For the early discussions of public works and unemployment see J. Harris, *Unemployment and Politics* (Oxford, 1972), 75–7, 222–5, 334–46.

programmes advocated, the constancy of advocacy, and the emergence of radical economic theory to underpin the case for counter-cyclical action; all of which was a reflection of the unprecedented scale and duration of the problem, and the apparent inability of established economic wisdom either to comprehend or grapple with it. In particular, the argument for public works came to be associated with the work of J. M. Keynes, and Steel-Maitland's ideas on the issue of public works mark him out as the first leading Conservative figure to engage seriously with Keynesian economics.

Steel-Maitland first fully addressed the idea of public works when he responded to a motion of censure on the newly elected Conservative government's unemployment policy, moved by the Labour party, in a Commons' debate of November 1924. Dealing with the Labour party's call for 'relief works', Steel-Maitland argued:

I make a quite distinct difference between schemes which are merely for relief and schemes that a Government can put in hand, and which have a practical and economic value, which, as I always say, are few in number . . . Early in the year I said I thought that at best they were only palliatives and might, by the burdens they cast on rates and taxes, create greater troubles than they could cure. They are a transference of employment, and not an ultimate addition to employment. That transference may be well worth while in acute crises, or it may be right in the case of areas which are very hardly hit, but if a depression of trade is universal that is how you get the springs of vitality and resilience sapped. At times it may be right to undertake some work as a relief scheme . . . even if the price has got to be paid by the rest of the country . . . [but] we should not draw off from the normal channels of trade large sums for extemporized measures which can only be palliatives.[135]

His fatalistic conclusion was, 'I do not believe any Government can cure unemployment . . . directly by their own schemes'.[136] Steel-Maitland was by no means alone in the inter-war period in expressing such scepticism about public works. Indeed, the grounds for his objections will be very familiar to scholars of inter-war economic policy debate. The demand that works should show an economc return; the question of their cost and fiscal implications; the notion that they would only transfer labour from the private to the public sector rather than create new employment; and the concern that public 'artificial' investment would 'crowd out' private 'natural' investment: all of these were arguments commonly used against the case for public works Most famously, they were all central to the 'Treasury view' which was deployed as a critique of Keynes's position in particular.[137] That Steel-Maitland produced such

---

[135] Steel-Maitland in Parliament, 26 Nov. 1924, *PD* 188, c. 1699.
[136] Ibid. cc. 1699–1700.
[137] The literature on this topic is extensive, but see in particular P. Clarke, *The Keynesian Revolution in the Making, 1924–1936* (Oxford, 1988), 47–69.

an eloquent rehearsal of these arguments in 1924 would perhaps tend to indicate that he was an adherent of 'orthodox' economics. But a more careful scrutiny of his position reveals that his views changed over time. For example, in 1927 he reiterated the argument that public works would divert credit from its proper channels, stating that: 'There is, I will not say a fixed quantum of credit in this country, but there is credit which if it is used to-day for relief works, which are not the best economic kind of work for any set of men, will not be available to be spent in the expansion of industry which is of a more useful kind.'[138] Yet less than two years later he was telling one correspondent that 'the extreme view that £1000 raised in loans means £1000 denied to business' was 'absurd', and had no more validity than the extreme view in favour of public works.[139]

The increasing level of unemployment in the late 1920s, and the development of suggestions for a new approach to the problem emanating from Lloyd George and Keynes, were the catalysts for Steel-Maitland to subject 'orthodox' economics to considerable critical scrutiny. His concerns were, once again, an admixture of the political and the economic. With unemployment rising, and the Liberal party in particular promising dramatic action, there was much Conservative concern that the party's electoral prospects were weakening. The question was whether the government could take any steps to alleviate unemployment and cut the ground from under Lloyd George. In a memorandum to Cabinet in January 1929 Steel-Maitland proposed an £8 million road-building scheme, which was aimed at stealing some of Lloyd George's thunder.[140] Such a scheme fitted with his earlier views of the need for public works to be of practical and economic value, but the following month he broadened the scope of his argument. In another Cabinet memorandum, which endorsed proposals by William Joynson-Hicks, the Home Secretary, for a public-works programme, Steel-Maitland questioned the 'orthodox' case against such schemes—the case he had himself stated so well in November 1924. In particular, he demanded to know

Is it or is it not true that if capital be directed to such schemes it will not be forthcoming in the same abundance for more natural and more fruitful ordinary business? This question concerns a cardinal principle of finance and financial policy, on which, of course, my Department offers no opinion . . . [but] after 8 years of financial orthodoxy and 8 years of unabating unemployment, ought we not to ask for a reasoned proof, for some foundations of belief that the financial policy by which we guide our steps is right?

[138] Steel-Maitland in Parliament, 27 July 1927, *PD* ccix, c. 1372.
[139] Steel-Maitland to E. R. Peacock, 22 Mar. 1929, SMP, GD193/500/10–16.
[140] Steel-Maitland, Memorandum to Cabinet, 23 Jan. 1929, PRO, CAB 23/60.

He continued by asking whether expansive government action might not 'give a fillip to public confidence', and queried whether those who had so strongly advocated the return to the gold standard had foreseen the deflationary consequences it had brought about. Although he did not suggest abandoning the gold standard or risking inflation, Steel-Maitland thought it necessary to ask whether 'the settled financial policy of the country . . . [had] dominated our actions unduly and prevented us from adopting ameliorative measures which would have reduced the numbers unemployed, and, if so, is it expedient to continue to acquiesce in that domination?' And he concluded that 'we should have a full case stated, subjected to criticism and substantiated, for the financial policy we are asked to continue'.[141] The upshot of Steel-Maitland's request for a thorough scrutiny and statement of the basis for 'orthodox' policy was a Treasury paper to the Cabinet at the end of February 1929. This laid the foundations for the Treasury's contribution to the Government White Paper on employment policy in May, in which the 'Treasury View' of the case against extensive public works was most fully stated. The demands made by Steel-Maitland's memorandum were crucial to clarifying the economic doctrines at issue in the debate over public works.

In the early summer of 1929 Steel-Maitland seemed to have accepted that an effective case for orthodoxy had been made. In the Commons in late April he attacked Lloyd George's proposals for public works, which had been fully outlined in March in the pamphlet *We Can Conquer Unemployment*. He declared that he had taken 'expert advice' on Lloyd George's schemes and, after receiving it, was wholly against them. The proposals in *We Can Conquer Unemployment* were, he claimed, impractical, with one major problem being that, as 23.7 per cent of the unemployed were aged over 50, they were unsuitable for the heavy labour, such as road-building, which Lloyd George had placed at the heart of his programme. Moreover, he argued that those who could do the work envisaged would only obtain temporary work, and that what was needed was for them to find work in their own trades. Safeguarding tariffs, retraining, transference, and industrial de-rating were, Steel-Maitland declared, the only practical remedies for unemployment, and they were already part of government policy. He ended by asserting that unemployment would be brought down 'under a Conservative Government and by Conservative policy, and that it can only be made worse by any rash specific such as that of the Right Honourable

---

[141] Steel-Maitland, Memorandum to Cabinet, 'Unemployment', 16 Feb. 1929, PRO, CAB 24/201.

Gentleman the Member for Carnarvon Boroughs'.[142] An important point about this critique was that it concentrated on *practical* rather than theoretical objections. This may have been due to his being forced to focus on these issues by the constraints of inter-departmental protocol, but it perhaps also showed that it was the full range of the government's objections to public works, and not simply the Treasury's, that had persuaded Steel-Maitland to toe the 'orthodox' line. Steel-Maitland undoubtedly remained sceptical about the economic value of 'relief works', and the White Paper's emphasis on *practicality* was in accord with his long-established views. However, this did not mean that he accepted the Treasury's macroeconomic case against Keynes. He had told Edward Peacock in March 1929 that:

prima facie Keynes seems right in saying that you don't get an exact balance at any particular moment between saving and investment, and that in a time like the present, as in 1894, the home demand for money for business does not seem likely to absorb the maximum of credit available. In other words, provided that the object was suitable (a quite different point) credit could be made available, either from savings not utilized or by diversion from use abroad . . . As to the other question . . . it seems to me that this is all important. Loans to reorganise the iron and steel trade or the cotton trade would be the best use of all. A certain amount of road building etc would be justified, just as railways were a hundred years ago, because of extra facilities to trade. On the other hand, to swamp out tens of millions of money on roads could bring no immediate return in facilitating productive industry.[143]

In effect, Steel-Maitland was arguing for the use of the new, macro-economic case for government loan expenditure to address the micro-economic problem of industrial structure—precisely the scheme he was to present to a chorus of orthodox disapproval in the winter of 1930–1. In this way government action would help bring about Steel-Maitland's oft-stated goal of returning workers to their own trades, with infra-structural 'relief works' being used as a supplement.

But even Steel-Maitland's reluctance to embrace public works weakened after the Crash of 1929 and the ensuing Slump. In *The Trade Crisis and the Way Out*, written in November and December 1930, Steel-Maitland discussed public works at some length. He felt that practical problems were still an important objection, but he expressed interest in Ralph Hawtrey's argument that public works could stimulate demand for goods and credit and help revive trade. He stressed that, to achieve this, public works would have to be 'fully economic', and restated the need for caution.[144] However, he added an important rider, which was

---

[142] Steel-Maitland in Parliament, 24 Apr. 1929, *PD* 227, cc. 958–65.
[143] Steel-Maitland to E. R. Peacock, 22 Mar. 1929, SMP, GD 193/500/10–16.
[144] Steel-Maitland, *Trade Crisis*, 29–31.

that the psychological impact of public works could provide the impetus for economic recovery, but to achieve this impact they had to be large-scale. This was an argument he was to repeat with even greater emphasis in his study of the New Deal. Praising the work of Roosevelt's National Recovery Administration (NRA), including the works projects carried out under its aegis, Steel-Maitland wrote that 'the "Blue Eagle" [the symbol of NRA projects] screamed so loud that it woke everybody up'.[145] Because NRA works projects had strict codes to ensure their economic value, they provided genuine and useful employment and at the same time galvanized other sectors of the economy. This he deemed of particular importance, for increased confidence and spending provided a boost to the circulation of money, which then became a virtuous circle.[146] Steel-Maitland's sympathetic response to Roosevelt's New Deal was extended to take in the British version outlined by Lloyd George at the beginning of 1935. *The Times* report of a speech by Steel-Maitland in Warwickshire in January noted that

he said that he would like to congratulate Mr Lloyd George on the vigour of his speeches. There was a great deal in the 'New Deal' which was not new. He admitted this and called some of it a platitude. But often the greater the platitude the greater the truth, and with part of what Mr. Lloyd George had said he (Sir Arthur Steel-Maitland) was in hearty agreement.[147]

He confirmed these sentiments in Parliament the following month. Although he attacked the Labour party for seeking 'to have workmen set to work upon the roads' rather than in their own trades, he spoke in favour of Lloyd George's schemes for public works and stated that 'any Government ought to do its best to carry them out'.[148] Evidently the ideas of 'the Member for Caernarvon Boroughs' had improved since 1929. Not all of Steel-Maitland's reservations about public works had gone, but they had been considerably softened.

On hearing of Steel-Maitland's death, Leo Amery, an old ally from the days of the tariff campaign, noted in his diary: 'I do not think he would have achieved much more in life.'[149] In political terms he was right, for Steel-Maitland's career had effectively ended with his exclusion from the National Government in 1931. But although his career never fulfilled its early promise, Steel-Maitland's ideas are of great intrinsic interest, and open a window on to important aspects of

[145] A. Steel-Maitland, *The New America* (1934), 89–90.
[146] Ibid. 194–5.
[147] Steel-Maitland at Knowle Unionist Association, 22 Jan. 1935, *The Times*, 24 Jan. 1935.
[148] Steel-Maitland in Parliament, 14 Feb. 1935, *PD* 297, c. 2194.
[149] L. S. Amery, diary entry, 31 Mar. 1935, in J. Barnes and D. Nicholson (eds.), *The Empire at Bay: The Leo Amery Diaries, 1929–45* (1983), 393.

Conservatism and especially Conservative political economy in the early twentieth century. In his 1908 book outline Steel-Maitland described the scheme of imperial organization he was seeking to construct as 'opposed to (1) Laissez faire (2) Socialism'. Speaking in Parliament in July 1927 he reiterated this position, stating that 'The principles of Conservatism are these: we differ from the old Liberalism in that we do not allow things simply to take their own course, and we differ from modern Socialism in that we do not want the State to undertake managerial functions'.[150] The basic formula of these two statements is identical, but the ways in which Steel-Maitland sought to chart his path between laissez faire and Socialism shifted markedly over the years from the Edwardian period until his death.

Tariffs, the issue which dominated the initial phases of Steel-Maitland's career, provide a helpful route into the changes his ideas underwent. In the Edwardian era Empire was at the heart of the tariff campaign and Steel-Maitland's own devotion to the cause. But by the 1930s the imperial aspect of the tariff argument was no longer central. Steel-Maitland's main emphasis in inter-war tariff debates was on safe-guarding—protectionism rather than imperial preference. Following the Crash, imperial trade appeared as one route out of the worst of the Slump, but Steel-Maitland attached equal weight to the idea of negotiating multilateral tariff reductions to bring about a revival of trade with other markets. In 1930 he declared that, although he would like to see Empire Free Trade, which in itself marked a major shift from his Edwardian stance, or free trade with as many Colonies as possible,[151] he was never associated with Beaverbrook's Empire Free Trade campaign. He welcomed the Ottawa agreements of 1932, but did not, like some veterans of the pre-1914 tariff campaign, greet this as the belated triumph of the Chamberlainite ideal. Like the majority of the Conservative party, Steel-Maitland was still avowedly imperialist, but what that meant had shifted as the relationship between Britain and the Colonies had shifted.

The substance of Steel-Maitland's argument for protective tariffs also underwent important changes, and gained new features. During the Edwardian tariff campaign he had argued that protection would prevent 'unfair competition' and help British industry to match the organizational structure of the large-scale industries of its main competitors, and that these in turn would secure 'work for all'. In the 1920s he was still of the view that tariffs would assist in the achievement of these goals, but had come to the conclusion that they were not enough in themselves.

---

[150] Steel-Maitland in Parliament, 27 July 1927, *PD* 260, c. 1371.
[151] Steel-Maitland at Birmingham, 10 May 1930, *The Times*, 12 May 1930.

The reorganization of British industry required a micro-economic strategy that would see the government help recast the relationship between the financial and industrial sectors, and thereby assist the progress of industrial rationalization. Only if this was done, and industrial rationalization successfully carried out, would tariffs help the employment position, which, in Steel-Maitland's view, was dependent on the efficiency and competitiveness of Britain's industries. Steel-Maitland was consistent over time in arguing that volume of production per head of population was the best measure of national economic well-being—such was his stance in his 1908 outline book, and in his description of the US New Deal.[152] What changed over time was his view of how this measure of well-being could be maximized. The problems of British industry in the inter-war period, and the emergence of mass unemployment, led Steel-Maitland to scrutinize the institutional structures of British industry in particular and the British economy in general, and he found them wanting. Here he was by no means alone, but his advocacy of the need for a goverent-sponsored programme of industrial rationalization was both early and uncommon in Conservative circles.

Steel-Maitland's engagement with the 'new' economics of the interwar period was, for a Conservative, also uncommonly full. It would be simplistic to describe him as 'Keynesian' in a straightforward sense, although perhaps one of the most interesting aspects of the development of his ideas is that it raises the question of whether there was such a thing as a straightforward Keynesian. Steel-Maitland's insistence on 'sound finance' and 'sound money' revealed a tendency to caution which was certainly not Keynes's predisposition. Yet on some other points, such as the potential helpfulness of what Steel-Maitland called 'a Great Assize of the nation'[153] and Keynes called a 'national treaty' to secure a national agreement to reduce wages, the two men were in complete agreement. Similarly, by 1930 they were close on tariffs. On the issue that has, perhaps somewhat misleadingly, dominated much of the historiography of Keynes's ideas, public works, Steel-Maitland's cautious stance placed some distance between them. But even so there were overlaps between Keynes's and Steel-Maitland's views on unemployment and public works. It was because of pressure from Steel-Maitland on these questions that the Treasury was forced to define precisely what its 'view' was, and this was crucial in terms of providing Keynes with a clear target for his evolving critique of economic orthodoxy. Moreover, Steel-Maitland's own stated opposition to *We Can*

---

[152] Steel-Maitland, *New America*, 179.
[153] Steel-Maitland, *Trade Crisis*, 40.

Conquer Unemployment was based more on what has been termed the 'Whitehall view' than on the 'Treasury view', in that it stressed practical and administrative problems rather than theoretical objections.[154] Certainly Steel-Maitland's engagement with the principles of Keynes's ideas in 1929 indicated that he found them very persuasive. One thing which may seem to separate him from Keynes is his emphasis on industrial reorganization, in that this was a 'supply-side' emphasis whereas Keynes has been seen as a 'demand-side' thinker. But this oversimplifies the positions of both men. Keynes was fully aware of the structural weaknesses of British industry, and rationalization was one of the seven possible solutions for unemployment he outlined to the Macmillan Committee.[155] Equally, Steel-Maitland was clear that buoyant demand for goods was essential to sustain high levels of economic activity and employment. It would be reductionist to conflate Steel-Maitland's and Keynes's ideas, and this essay does not seek to do this. Rather, it seeks to point out that in the flux of inter-war economic debate the exchange, overlap, and imbrication of ideas was often as marked as tension and conflict between them, and that the picture was complicated still further by the fluid political context. What emerges from Steel-Maitland's engagement with Keynes's arguments is a Conservative intellectual who saw a potential for deploying aspects of Keynes's ostensibly radical economics for Conservative ends.

The central problem that Steel-Maitland sought to address in both the Edwardian and inter-war periods was how to rectify systemic social and economic problems in such a way as to ensure social and political stability. This he saw as a prime responsibility of government, and he had no hesitation in constructing a positive role for the State. But he set limits to the sphere of State action. His idea of the optimum State structure became increasingly clear over time, and reached full maturity in his inter-war stance on industrial reorganization and industrial relations. In both these spheres, which he saw as interdependent, Steel-Maitland defined the State's role as enabling rather than controlling. Rationalization was to be facilitated by government assistance in the shape of loan finance, tariffs, and information, but the actual process itself was to be in the hands of industry's own collective agency. The State would have an 'arm's-length' role in which it helped to shape strategy but had no part in the day-to-day management of affairs. This was

---

[154] For the 'Whitehall view' see in particular G. C. Peden, 'The "Treasury View" on Public Works and Employment in the Interwar Period', *EcHR* 37 (1984); id., 'Sir Richard Hopkins and the "Keynesian Revolution" in Employment Policy, 1929–45', *EcHR* 36 (1983); R. Middleton, 'The Treasury in the 1930s: Political and Administrative Constraints to Acceptance of the "New" Economics', *Oxford Economic Papers*, 34 (1982).

[155] J. M. Keynes, *Collected Writings*, xx. 109–13.

also the pattern Steel-Maitland envisaged for the structure of industrial relations. As with the genesis of the Mond–Turner talks, the government's role was to facilitate dialogue between employer and labour organizations, and to act as an 'honest broker' in discussions with the two groups. In this way the interests of industry and the nation as a whole, rather than those of particular, sectional interests, were to be the focus. Such a concordat would ensure that working practices would be geared to maximum productivity, which would allow maximum rewards to employers in terms of profit and utilization of plant, and maximum rewards for labour in terms of wages and security of employment. The nation as a whole would benefit from the gain in economic strength, lowering of social deprivation and lessening of social strife. Once again the State would be at arm's length, insofar as it would set a basic framework of industrial law, conditions of work, and assistance for both ongoing and transitional social ills, but would otherwise rely on the economic system's own devices. The political, economic, and social structure that Steel-Maitland envisaged was corporatist, in that it was based on the premiss of an essentially tripartite relationship between the State, trade unions, and employers, and saw collaboration between the three as the key to prosperity and social peace. Steel-Maitland was by no means alone in inter-war Britain in advocating this corporatist type of structure,[156] but few matched the scope of his argument.

As a Conservative politician and thinker Steel-Maitland's interests were uncommonly wide-ranging and innovative. But there was an underlying consistency of purpose in his arguments over time. In the Edwardian period he embraced tariffs and an ambitious programme of social reform on the grounds that the alternative would be the triumph of radical or Socialist ideas. An imperial-national economy was to provide security of employment and broader social securities under a tariff system that ensured maximum levels of production per capita and a non-class-discriminatory fiscal structure. This was to be the antidote to the 'Socialistic' programme of the New Liberalism. In the inter-war years a combination of government-sponsored industrial reorganization, tariffs, and any necessary relief works was to ensure social and industrial peace by facilitating harmonious industrial relations and alleviating the scourge of unemployment. Britain in the 1930s, according to Steel-Maitland, had to learn from Roosevelt's America, and grasp that abandoning the idea that the trade cycle would cure itself did not mean abandoning the entire economic system. 'If . . .', he argued,

---

[156] Another good example of early Conservative corporatist thought is W. Elliot, *Toryism and the Twentieth* Century (1927).

Great trade depressions can be prevented and capitalism pruned of its excesses, stability in industry may be combined with freedom of individual enterprise . . . capitalism is indeed on trial. So, too, is the freedom of individual initiative. If this is destroyed the chief responsibility for its destruction will lie with those who professed to believe in it, but were too remiss to try and remedy the admitted short-comings of the existing economic system.[157]

Steel-Maitland summed up the underlying rationale of his political economy in a speech shortly before he died, when he argued that the existing economic system could 'provide a cure for poverty in the midst of plenty',[158] and by so doing avoid the perils of political extremes. His search for a 'middle way' was to end soon after, but it was continued by a member of his Parliamentary audience.

[157] Steel-Maitland, *New America*, 208.
[158] Steel-Maitland in Parliament, 26 Nov. 1934, *PD* 295, c. 616.

CHAPTER 4

Conservatism, Anti-Socialism, and the End of the Lloyd George Coalition

THE YEAR 1922 witnessed one of the most dramatic episodes in modern Conservative party history. At a specially convened party meeting at the Carlton Club on 19 October Conservative MPs voted to bring an end to the Coalition government of Conservatives and Lloyd George's Liberals. It was not only the Coalition that was brought to an end in 1922. The careers of its leading figures and adherents were effectively broken. Lloyd George was the most obvious victim of the Carlton Club 'revolt'. In 1918 Andrew Bonar Law had stated that 'Lloyd George can be Prime Minister for life if he wants', but in 1922 Law himself was instrumental in ending Lloyd George's career at the highest levels of politics. A similar fate befell the political careers of the leading Conservative Coalitionists. The most notable casualty was the Conservative leader, Austen Chamberlain, who resigned his office. From 1924 to 1929 he was to be a successful Foreign Secretary, but his fall from the leadership cemented his reputation as the man who 'always plays the game and never wins it',[1] and gave him the unenviable record of being the only Conservative leader of the twentieth century never to have become Prime Minister.[2] Other Conservatives whose reputations and careers never fully recovered included the Earl Birkenhead, Sir Robert Horne, and the Earl Crawford and Balcarres.[3] In contrast, the careers of leading anti-Coalitionists were resurrected or made: Law came out of retirement to be Prime Minister, and Stanley Baldwin emerged from relative obscurity to establish his credentials as a future Conservative leader. The Conservative party as a whole also benefited; at the general election that followed the dissolution of the Coalition the

---

[1] W. S. Churchill to C. Churchill, 26 Dec. 1935, in D. Dutton, *Austen Chamberlain: Gentleman in Politics* (Bolton, 1985), 317.

[2] William Hague will join Chamberlain if the Conservative party loses the first election of the 21st century.

[3] Birkenhead's drink problem would have brought his career, as well as his life, to a premature end.

Conservatives won their first election as an independent force since 1900. The events and developments of 1922 have received a great deal of historical attention. Much of that attention has been focused, understandably, on the sphere of 'high politics'.[4] This essay will, however, concentrate on the 'low politics' of 1922, and in particular on how the events at the Carlton Club were part of a Conservative debate over how best to construct the party as an anti-Socialist bulwark.

The reasons Conservatives turned against the Coalition with the Lloyd George Liberals were legion, but three in particular stand out. The first was the Coalition's Irish policy, where the Anglo-Irish Treaty of 1921 was regarded by many Conservatives as a surrender to IRA terrorism, a betrayal of the Union, and of the Southern Irish Unionists in particular, and, even if the South was irredeemably lost, weak in terms of the guarantees it offered to Ulster. Within the Parliamentary party the Diehard contingent engaged in almost constant criticism of the government's Irish policy,[5] and the NUCA Conference of November 1921 witnessed significant rumblings of disquiet about Ireland amongst grass-roots Conservatives.[6] Both the Diehards and grass roots had quietened by the end of 1921, but this had taken no little effort by the party leadership. Significantly with regard to future developments, Law, who had resigned the Conservative leadership on grounds of ill-health in March 1921, chose in mid-December to signal his return to active politics by making his first major speech in Parliament since the spring on the question of the Irish Treaty. Although he spoke in support of the Treaty, and thereby helped quieten discontent in the Conservative middle and lower ranks, his stance was one of watchful rather than enthusiastic assent to the government's policies. In the summer of 1922 Law and dissenting Conservative opinion were brought together again in the wake of the assassination of Sir Henry Wilson by Irish Republicans,[7] an event which was seen to underline both the physical and political danger of attempting to achieve peace at any price in Ireland.

Ireland was in many respects Britain's closest and longest-running imperial problem, but it was by no means the only one. The governance

---

[4] M. Cowling, *The Impact of Labour* (Cambridge, 1971); M. Kinnear, *The Fall of Lloyd George: The Political Crisis of 1922* (1973); K. O. Morgan, *Consensus and Disunity: The Lloyd George Coalition Government, 1918–1922* (Oxford, 1978); Dutton, *Chamberlain*, 185–98; R. J. Q. Adams, *Bonar Law* (1999), 302–21.

[5] Morgan, *Consensus*, 246–8.

[6] See in particular the speeches by M. Archer-Shee, H. Gretton, and R. Sanders at the NUCA Conference, Liverpool, 17 Nov. 1921, NUCA Conference Minutes, Microfilm Card 97, and also L. S. Amery, diary entry, 31 Mar. 1922, 10 May 1922, 31 May 1922, in J. Barnes and D. Nicholson (eds.), *The Leo Amery Diaries, vol. 1, 1896–1914* (1980), 284–6.

[7] See Amery, diary entry, 23 June 1922, ibid. 287.

of the Empire posed new, complex problems after the Great War. For the Conservative party, which had been the self-professed guardian of Britain's imperial interests since the mid-1880s, these problems had a particular resonance. The growing 'maturity' and independence of the old, self-governing colonies was viewed as inevitable and even desirable. However, the development of Indian nationalist aspirations was another matter, and, as the Dyer case illustrated, Diehard Conservatives regarded any hint of concessions to Indian sensitivities as unacceptable.[8] In many respects the Irish question and the broad issue of imperial governance were seen, as they had been in the late nineteenth century, as two sides of the same coin, and the Coalition, like Gladstone's second administration, was regarded as too Liberal, in every sense of the word, to provide firm imperial government. For many Conservatives this lack of firmness, or at any rate *focused* firmness, was a particularly important failing in the post-1918 period. Britain had emerged from the Great War with an expanded Empire, but if in 1900 Britain had been a 'weary titan' struggling under the weight of its overseas commitments, this was still more the case after the war. The evident problem of 'over-stretch' meant that Britain had to adopt a less assertive global stance; it had to be very selective as to when and where it was assertive. Here, once again, Law was in tune with the concerns of the Conservative grass roots. He wrote in early October 1922, in relation to the 'Chanak Crisis', that Britain's interests in the Near East were involved and had to be defended, but that Britain, because of its 'financial and social condition' could not 'alone act as the policeman of the world', and that other powers had to bear their share of the burden of maintaining the integrity of the peace settlements of 1919. As had been the case with the Irish question, Law was ostensibly supportive of the government, but his suggestion that British policy should 'restrict . . . attention to the safeguarding of the more immediate interests of the Empire' implied that the Coalition, and in particular the Prime Minister, were being overly ambitious.[9]

By 1922 the Coalition had gravely offended the Unionist and imperialist sensibilities of many Conservatives. Nor did this by any means exhaust the list of Conservative complaints. The overwhelmingly Conservative farming community had been hit by the worldwide fall in agricultural prices, and felt let down, even betrayed, by the government's repeal in July 1921 of Part I of the wartime Agricultural Acts which had guaranteed the price of wheat and oats. Although the

---

[8] Morgan, *Consensus*, 238–42.
[9] Law to *The Times*, 6 Oct. 1922, in R. Blake, *The Unknown Prime Minister* (1955), 447–8.

Conservative party was no longer, and had not been for some time, simply the 'farmer's friend', the land was still an important part of the party's ethos and identity, and the Coalition was deemed guilty of failing to provide adequate support for rural interests. What added insult to injury was that Lloyd George himself was seen to have looked after his own interests and those of his 'cronies' without hesitation or shame. The 'Coalition stain' of 'corruption', associated with Lloyd George's sale of honours to his political benefactors, offended Conservative opinion at all levels of the party. Details of the scale of Lloyd George's activities in this sphere were available only to those with a full working knowledge of the honours system, but rumours abounded and were widely and not unreasonably believed in the lower echelons of the party.[10] Here, some of the resentment amongst the Conservative hierarchy may well have stemmed from the fact that Lloyd George was getting money which they could have expected to receive had they had control of the levers of patronage, but there is no doubt that Lloyd George's 'corruption' did offend the sense of political propriety of the Conservative grass roots.

For many Conservatives Lloyd George's behaviour as Prime Minister simply confirmed views they had held since the Marconi scandal of 1912–13, namely, that he used and abused high office for his own personal gain. However, it was not simply the connection between Lloyd George's pre- and post-war 'corruption' that led Conservatives to rebel against the Coalition. The domestic policies of the post-war Coalition also seemed far too redolent of Lloyd George's pre-war radicalism. Before the Great War Lloyd George was the figure Conservatives most loved to hate, his only rival being Winston Churchill. This loathing was a blend of the personal and political. The fiscal strategy of the New Liberalism, as embodied in Lloyd George's 'People's Budget' of 1909, was deemed by Conservatives to be at best 'Socialistic' and at worst simply Socialist. In the wake of Asquith's budget of 1908 the Conservative journal *The Outlook* had declared that 'all indications . . . point to a vast development of direct taxation . . . Our moribund fiscal system seems likely to expire in the arms of Mr. Philip Snowden'.[11] In 1909 it was thought that this was precisely what had happened, and in the January 1910 general election campaign one-third of Conservative candidates explicitly referred to Lloyd George's budget as 'Socialist'.[12] The People's Budget fulfilled the criteria for a Socialist measure laid

[10] G. R. Searle, *Corruption in British Politics, 1895–1930* (Oxford, 1987), 328–411.

[11] 'The Coming Fiscal Reform', *The Outlook* (6 June 1908), 782.

[12] N. Blewett, *The Peers, the Parties and the People: The General Elections of 1910* (1972), 323.

down by contemporary Conservative opinion. It was designed to fund State intervention for the benefit of the poorer classes through explicitly class-differentiated, 'confiscatory' taxation.[13] In the circumstances it was not surprising that many Conservatives accused Lloyd George of having 'gone over bag and baggage to Socialism'.[14] Lloyd George's radical pre-war actions and rhetoric left a legacy of bitterness that was difficult, if not impossible, to erase. As a result of this legacy Lloyd George himself and the wartime and post-war Coalition governments he headed were *never* popular with the middling and lower ranks of the Conservative party, and in particular with the grass roots.[15] Only eight months after Lloyd George's wartime Coalition had been formed, Arthur Steel-Maitland, who had then only recently given up the Chairmanship of the Conservative party, informed Austen Chamberlain that the constituency parties had a very low opinion of the Coalition and that 'the organisation outside is even more angry—and less malleable—than the House'.[16] The formation of the National Party in 1917 was the most tangible expression of Conservative dissidence at both the political centre and periphery, but it was by no means the only one.[17] From the outset, the Conservative rank and file viewed the Coalition with suspicion or hostility. Many would have made a pact with the devil himself to win the war, and in allying themselves with Lloyd George they felt they had done precisely that.

The 1918 general election illustrated the problems that many Conservatives had with both the principles and practice of Coalition. The politics of wartime had allowed the Conservative party at Westminster to re-enter the corridors of power through the back door, but neither the parliamentary party nor the constituency rank and file felt secure about the party's electoral position, particularly as universal manhood suffrage had been introduced. In these circumstances it seemed practical and indeed unavoidable for the party to align itself with 'the man who won the war'. The 'coupon' for candidates who gained the endorsement of Lloyd George and Law, and who thereby bound themselves to support the Coalition, embodied the Conservatives' acknowledgement of the Coalition's apparent importance to their electoral fortunes. During the 1918 election campaign Leo Amery told his wife that Lloyd George's national standing was of great assistance to the Conservatives, in that it compensated for the lack of

[13] Green, *Crisis*, 122–56, 140–4.
[14] C. A. Gregg to A. Steel-Maitland, n.d. (Jan. 1910), SMP, GD 193/147/7/1.
[15] See Bates, 'Conservative Party', 15.
[16] Steel-Maitland to Chamberlain, 27 July 1917, in ibid.
[17] See W. D. Rubinstein, 'Henry Page Croft and the National Party', *JCH* (1975).
[18] L. S. Amery to Mrs Amery, 26 Nov. 1918, in Bates, 'Conservative Party', 14.

party workers and was crucial in combating Labour's appeal to the new mass vote.[18] But if in 1918 the Conservative party generally accepted that alliance with Lloyd George was 'indispensable', this did not mean either that they liked the alliance or that there was no active dissent. In many constituencies where a Coalition Liberal received a 'coupon' there was pronounced irritation amongst the local Conservative associations, and this resentment grew rather than faded.[19] Relations between local Coalition Liberals and Conservatives varied from region to region and within regions, but overall it is fair to describe them as an 'armed truce' rather than an alliance. Such institutional tensions within the Coalition were in many respects unavoidable. It was difficult for local Conservative associations to give up their *raison d'être*—attempting to secure the return of a Conservative MP to Parliament. At the 1921 Conservative Party Conference the Sheffield constituency representative declared that the frustration this caused had led to apathy, with the result that 'in a lot of constituencies, the association had been closed down and furniture sold because of the Coalition'. In his view this was 'nothing more than the assassination of the Conservative party'.[20] This echoed the sentiments of a Newport representative the previous year who had accused the party of 'erecting their own guillotine—committing party suicide'.[21] Nor was it only the rank and file who felt frustrated, for within the parliamentary party there was resentment amongst Conservatives who felt that, in spite of their party being overwhelmingly the largest element in the Coalition, they were under-represented in terms of Cabinet posts and junior ministerial office.[22] Such institutional tensions were largely unavoidable, but they were made much more difficult to manage by the growth of Conservative resentment over Coalition policy.

At the 1920 NUCA Conference H. S. Foster, a member of the National Union's Central Council, outlined what he saw as the Coalition's *raison d'être*—to provide the political structure 'which will most effectively defend all classes against the well-organised and growing efforts of the Socialist Party'.[23] Foster's argument was reiterated by all of the party hierarchy who addressed the Conference and the following party meeting,

[19] See ibid., 17–21, and also Ramsden, *Balfour*, 140–1.

[20] W. J. Woolacott to NUCA Conference, Liverpool, 17 Nov. 1921, NUCA Conference Minutes, Microfiche Card 97.

[21] Councillor Clissett to NUCA Conference, Birmingham, 10 June 1920, ibid., Card 95.

[22] Here it is significant that the first major outburst of high-level discontent was at a meeting between senior Conservative members of the Coalition Cabinet and junior ministers. See Earl Crawford and Balcarres, Diary, 28 July 1922, in J. Vincent (ed.), *The Crawford Papers* (Manchester, 1984), 428–9.

[23] H. S. Foster to NUCA Conference, Birmingham, 10 June 1920, NUCA Conference Minutes, Microfiche Card 95.

including Law, and it was also to be at the heart of Austen Chamberlain's defence of the Coalition throughout his period as leader and at the Carlton Club meeting which brought the Coalition and his leadership to an end.[24] A Conservative desire to build 'the case against Socialism' and thwart the 'menace of Socialism' was not new. The emergence of the Labour party, and the 'Socialistic' strategy of the New Liberalism, had generated much Conservative concern before 1914, but such concern reached new levels after 1918. The 1920 NUCA Conference saw calls from the floor for the establishment of constituency labour committees 'to combat the socialists and extremists in the ranks of organised labour', whilst others expressed anxiety that Labour's interest in socialization and nationalization would lead, as in the Soviet Union, to 'the nationalisation of women'.[25] Frequent references to the Soviet Union reflected the fact that developments abroad, and the Bolshevik revolution in particular, fuelled Conservative fear of the spread of Socialism and, again at the 1920 NUCA Conference, Leo Maxse's speech denouncing Lloyd George for having recently 'hobnobbed with Bolsheviks' in Downing Street was cheered by the assembly for one minute.[26] But if the spread of Socialism was seen as an international phenomenon, it was its domestic manifestation that caused most concern, and in this context an increasingly powerful body of Conservative opinion regarded the Coalition government as not only failing to thwart but as actively contributing to the rise of Socialism.

The Coalition's chief failures on the anti-Socialist front were deemed to lie in the spheres of public expenditure and fiscal policy, with its 'extravagance' and 'waste' in the former having led it to make excessive demands on the taxpayer in the latter. Many areas of government expenditure aroused resentment. Economic assistance to Germany caused particular ire, with the representative from Peckham pointing out at the 1920 NUCA Conference that the 1918 general election had witnessed promises to make Germany pay for the war, but that 'our pockets were being searched to provide the money'.[27] Likewise, the government's Irish policy was deemed to have resulted in the British taxpayer footing the bill for damage caused by others, with Leo Amery noting in March 1922 that the only certain thing about the Irish settlement was 'that the British taxpayer should contribute £500,000 to relief in Belfast'.[28] However, it was the Coalition's social policies which attracted most hostility, in no

[24] See Dutton, *Chamberlain*, 196.
[25] T. J. Whittaker, Mrs J. Heard to NUCA Conference, 10 June 1920, ibid.
[26] L. J. Maxse to NUCA Conference, 11 June 1920, ibid.
[27] C. Hughes at NUCA Conference, Birmingham, 10 June 1920, NUCA Conference Minutes, Microfilm Card 95.
[28] Amery, diary entry, 31 Mar. 1922, *Amery Diaries*, i. 284.

small part because they were chiefly the responsibility of ministers who were members of 'Lloyd George's Stage Army' of Coalition Liberals in the Cabinet.[29] The expansion of educational provision introduced under the Education Act designed and implemented by H. A. L. Fisher, and the housing programme inaugurated by Christopher Addison's Housing Act of 1919, were viewed with particular hostility. In the same vein, the extension of unemployment assistance, and especially the introduction of 'uncovenanted benefits' in 1921, were regarded as further examples of 'Socialistic' generosity at the expense of the taxpaying classes. It could not be gainsaid that government expenditure on education, housing, and welfare reached record levels under the Coalition. Nor could it be denied that levels of taxation were historically high. In 1909 the 'Socialist' People's Budget had raised the standard rate of income tax to 1s 2d in the pound, but during the war it had risen to 5s and in 1919 had risen to 6s and remained at that level in 1922. The 1919 budget, with Austen Chamberlain at the Exchequer, had seen the introduction of an Excess Profits Tax of 40 per cent on business, and in 1920 the budget had raised this to 60 per cent and had also introduced a Corporation Tax of 1s in the pound, along with higher duties on beer and spirits. That the Labour party welcomed the 1920 budget did not exactly reassure Conservative opinion. Furthermore, in 1920 a Royal Commission on Income Tax and a parliamentary Select Committee on Wartime Wealth had been sitting, which had raised the spectre of yet higher basic taxes and the still more daunting prospect of a possible Capital Levy on wartime profits.[30] To the post-war Conservative constituency, dislike of the existing burden of taxation and concern about its possible increase was in many respects understandable. For the 'hard-faced men who had done well out of the war', whom Stanley Baldwin saw ensconced on the Conservative back-benches, the threat of a Capital Levy on wartime profits was very real, insofar as the Labour party advocated such a measure and some Conservatives flirted with the idea as a 'one-off' alternative to other taxation. Leaving aside the 'special interests' of war profiteers and the broader business community opposed to the Excess Profits Tax, the fact was that the direct taxpaying population of Britain had increased enormously in the years after 1914, largely because the combination of

---

[29] The phrase is taken from K. O. Morgan, 'Lloyd George's Stage Army: The Coalition Liberals, 1918–22', in A. J. P. Taylor (ed.), *Lloyd George: Twelve Essays* (1971).

[30] For post-1918 taxation see M. E. Short, 'The Politics of Personal Taxation: Budget Making in Britain, 1917–31', unpublished Cambridge University Ph.D thesis (1984); R. Whiting, 'Taxation and the Working Class, 1915–22', *HJ* 33 (1990); and M. J. Daunton, 'How to Pay for the War: State, Society and Taxation in Britain, 1917–24', *EHR* 110 (1996).

[31] Daunton, 'How to Pay', 889–90. In 1914 only 6% of the adult population paid direct tax, but by 1920 this had risen to 38%.

wartime increases in salaries and wages and inflation had pushed a great number of people over the taxpaying earnings threshold.[31] The bulk of the new taxpayers were members of middle and lower-middle class, and were regarded by Conservatives as a 'natural' constituency for their party as long as their desire for protection from Socialism and increased taxation—which were almost synonymous terms—was met. The problem Conservative Coalitionists faced was convincing this constituency that their interests were best served either by the Coalition's policies or indeed by its very existence.

The 1920 NUCA Conference, as noted above, saw loud complaints about the burden of taxation, and denunciations of the 'ruinous and socialistic legislation since the armistice'.[32] The Conservative leadership sought to address these concerns. Austen Chamberlain stressed that the government recognized the need for vigilance on public expenditure, and although he accepted that the tax burden was high, he argued that it was unavoidable if national credit was to be fully restored.[33] In the same vein, Law engaged in a very lengthy discussion of the tax question. He too agreed that there was a need for public economy, but insisted that the existing level of taxation was necessary to ensure budgetary balance and credit stability and emphasized, in a clear reference to the Excess Profits Tax and Corporation Tax imposed by the 1920 budget, that the government could only raise the necessary revenue from industry and business and not from the professional classes.[34] But the Conservative rank and file and, more important still, Conservative voters and potential voters were evidently unconvinced by these arguments. As early as May 1919 the Middle Class Union (MCU) had been founded to express the grievances of the 'hapless middle class' who were being crushed by the related demands of State taxation and organized labour,[35] but by early 1921 the MCU was by no means the only organ-ized expression of middle-class, taxpayer, Conservative rank-and-file anger. In January 1921 the Conservatives lost a by-election at Dover to an independent candidate whose electoral message was a call for 'Ruthless Economy'.[36] Given that Dover had been, albeit under the pre-1918 franchise, one of the few Conservative seats to have been held against the great Liberal landslide of 1906, its loss had an important psychological impact. This was rein-

[32] E. W. Bather at NUCA Conference, Birmingham, 10 June 1920, NUCA Conference Minutes, Microfil Card 95.

[33] A. Chamberlain at NUCA Conference, Birmingham, 10 June 1920, ibid.

[34] A. B. Law at NUCA Conference, Birmingham, 11 June 1920, ibid.

[35] Sir H. Brittain, 'Middle Classes, Mobilise!', *Review of Reviews* (May 1919). Before 1914 Brittain, a Conservative MP, had been one of the leading figures of the Anti-Socialist Union (ASU). For the ASU see F. Coetzee, *For Party or Country* (Oxford, 1990), 124–32, 155–60.

[36] See Cowling, *Labour*, 56.

forced soon after when the Anti-Waste League (AWL) was founded, with support from Lord Rothermere and the *Daily Mail*, to campaign for reductions in government expenditure and taxation. Between January and September the AWL adopted candidates in twenty seats, winning two at Westminster St George's and Hertford.

In themselves organizations like the MCU and AWL did not pose a serious institutional threat to the Conservative party. Their importance lay with the fact that they were indicative of serious discontent with the Coalition amongst the Conservative grass roots. Some local parties expressed concern that the appearance of the MCU and AWL could help to explain a worrying decline in membership, perhaps not surprisingly in the case of Reading, where by 1921 the MCU had 1,154 members and the Conservative party 250.[37] In the West Midlands the level of discontent and leakage of support away from the Conservatives was very marked, and was reflected in the social and political actions of local party grandees as well as the rank and file. For example, in Shropshire Lords Hatherton and Forester, respectively, sold land and rented their country houses to meet their tax bills, and by 1921 Forester, who had been President of the Wrekin Conservative Association, had become chief organizer of the Shropshire AWL.[38] Similarly, in Worcester the local brewing magnate Lord Hindlip declined the offer of the Presidency of the Conservative Association in 1920, and declared: 'I cannot pretend to approve of the present wild extravagance of the Government, or of their reluctance to force economy on the various departments . . . bureaucracy, together with the penal taxation proposed by the Chancellor of the Exchequer [Chamberlain], is rapidly forming a stranglehold upon industry.'[39] For some Conservatives, like the pre-1914 Diehard peer Lord Forester, loathing of Lloyd George and all his works came easily, but general distrust and dislike of the Coalition was too general and too deep to be attributed to past grievances and personal antagonisms, and the issues of public economy and taxation underpinned much of the animus. As early as August 1919 the *Conservative Agents' Journal* had noted that: 'The mind of the people is setting steadily against lavish Government grants and interference, and it is probable that a sound financial policy and a strong lead against Socialism and Nationalisation may yet find favour within the country.'[40] This view only gained in strength over time, and at the Annual General Meeting of the Conservative Eastern Provincial Division in April 1922 a unanimous resolution was passed:

[37] J. W. B. Bates, 'Conservative Party', 24.
[38] Ibid. 21–2.
[39] Lord Hindlip in *Berrow's Worcester Journal* (5 June 1920), in ibid. 22.
[40] *Conservative Agents' Journal* (Aug. 1919), 32–3, in ibid. 23.

That the attention of the Government be drawn to the urgent need of effecting immediate reduction in the heavy burden of taxation in order to revive trade and promote employment [and that] In furtherance of this object the meeting . . . recommends as a first step that the existing taxes upon tea, beer, & income be substantially reduced.[41]

The emergence and activities of the MCU and AWL expressed widespread Conservative discontent with the Coalition's domestic policies. This was increasingly acknowledged by the Conservative hierarchy. The NUCA Central Council noted in its Report to the NUCA Conference in 1921 that one resolution passed *inter alia* at its meetings 'urg[ed] upon the Cabinet the increasing necessity for the strictest economy in public expenditure, both imperial and local'.[42] It further noted that: 'On the question of economy we do not believe that any definite end is obtained by denouncing Ministers as "squander maniacs" or by forming independent groups or parties whose sole cry is "anti waste". The Government has already reduced expenditure enormously.'[43] As is so often the case, attempts by a party hierarchy to deny the importance of fringe groups, mixed with an assertion that the aims of those groups were already being addressed, provided a most eloquent testimony to the significance of the MCU and in particular the AWL. Nor was this the only 'high political' admission of the 'low political' problem. It was largely as a consequence of anti-waste opinion that the Geddes Committee was appointed in the summer of 1922 with a brief to cut public expenditure, which it did by wielding its 'axe' to the military, health, housing, and education budgets.[44] Furthermore, the Geddes Committee's Reports were published in February 1922, after much pressure from the government Chief Whip, Sir Leslie Wilson, in an attempt to demonstrate to the anti-waste lobby that the government had acknowledged and acted upon its demands.[45] Other examples of anti-waste influence abounded through 1921–2. Shortly after the AWL had been established, another, parliamentary, group, the People's Union for Economy (PUE), had been set up. This organization was in effect a 'respectable' AWL,[46] with its leading figures being Lords Selborne, Robert Cecil, Cowdray, and Sir Arthur Steel-Maitland. Unlike the AWL, it did not enter candidates in by-elections, but acted as a parliamentary

[41] Conservative Eastern Provincial Division, Minutes of AGM, 24 Apr. 1922, CPA, ARE 7/1/6.

[42] NUCA Central Council Report, 17 Nov. 1921, NUCA Conference Minutes, Microfilm Card 97.

[43] Ibid.

[44] Morgan, *Consensus*, 245–6, 269–73, 288–94.

[45] See Minutes of Cabinet Meeting, 6 Feb. 1922, PRO CAB 23/29.

[46] This description is taken from Cowling, *Labour*, 73.

catspaw for the anti-waste movement. In the wake of the AWL by-election victory over the Conservatives at Westminster in June 1921, the PUE played an important part in co-ordinating the backbench Conservative disaffection that forced Addison, the AWL and MCU's 'squander-maniac' *bête noir*, to resign from the government.[47] In addition, the PUE was instrumental in organizing a written demand from 150 Conservative MPs calling for greater control of government expenditure.[48] If the Westminster by-election gave an impetus to anti-waste activity in parliament, the Conservatives' loss of the Hertford by-election to the AWL only nine days later further reinforced this trend. Lord Salisbury was particularly affected by this reversal, for the Hertford constituency was close to his country seat at Hatfield. As a consequence, Salisbury became convinced that the Coalition was no longer serving the Conservative cause and that taxpayer grievances had to be addressed. The conversion of an influential figure like Salisbury was an important individual indication of the growing strength of the dynamic between anti-waste ideas at the periphery and the centre of Conservative politics. This was made even more clear in early 1922, when two of the PUE's leaders, Lord Robert Cecil and Arthur Steel-Maitland, circulated a Memorandum to Conservative MPs that was highly critical of the government. This Memorandum argued that the Coalition had failed in every area of foreign and domestic policy, but many of the generally supportive responses they received expressed anti-waste sentiments. For example, Viscount Bledisloe told Cecil that: 'I am a stiff and heart-whole social reformer, but social reform is in many—in fact in most—spheres a luxury which we cannot now afford ... [and] yours and Arthur [S]teel-Maitland's letter seems to me to be the expression of sane Conservatism to which two-thirds of the honest Conservatives should give heart-whole adherence.'[49] In similar fashion, one of Steel-Maitland's businessman constituents complained that: 'The thing that is killing us at the present time is taxation; it is difficult, of course, to see how this can be reduced so long as the national expenditure goes on at the present rate, but what with the taxation and the almost entire absence of overseas trade, due to unfavourable exchanges, British industries are unquestionably fading away.'[50] This reference to fading industries indicates that the economic downturn of late 1921 had added to middle-class grievances and anxieties with regard to the economy in general and the burden of taxation in particular. By the spring of 1922

---

[47] Ibid. 74; Morgan, *Consensus*, 98–104.
[48] Cowling, *Labour*, 74.
[49] Bledisloe to Cecil, 2 Mar. 1922, SMP, GD193/276/64.
[50] A. McCormack to Steel-Maitland, 6 Feb. 1922, SMP, GD193/95/4/62.

the Coalition was faced with an ongoing leakage of Conservative confidence and support in the constituencies, and this in turn fed the anti-Coalition forces at Westminster.

At the heart of the differences between the critics and supporters of the Coalition was the question of whether the Conservative party and Conservatism were best served by staying in or leaving the Coalition. In this context the question of anti-Socialism was crucial. All Conservatives, arguably since 1906 and certainly since 1918, were agreed that Socialism was *the* enemy which had to be confronted and defeated. That Conservatives at all levels insisted that the Labour party be referred to and 'exposed' as Socialist (or even 'Bolshevist')[51] reflected this agreed identification of the political foe.[52] Indeed, the preference for labelling Labour as 'the Socialists' continued not only through the inter-war years but also in the period from 1945 to the 1990s. But agreeing who the enemy was and what to call them did not translate into agreement as to the best means of fighting them. For committed Coalitionist Conservatives, the Coalition itself was the best instrument of anti-Socialism. To a certain extent this reflected a perhaps understandable electoral caution. The Conservative party had not won a general election since 1900, and it was possible to argue that even then they had been beholden to Liberal Unionist support. Moreover, many Conservatives thought that the 1918 Representation of the People Act had enfranchised a mass of voters who were preternaturally inclined to vote Labour and support Socialism,[53] and that political and electoral allies were thus necessary to combat Labour's 'natural' advantage. This was where the Coalition came in. At the 1920 NUCA Conference H. S. Foster argued that there was a clear divide in British politics between those of *all* parties who defended the constitution and the Socialists who sought to subvert it, and he was supported by an alderman from Brighton who proposed a resolution 'calling for a combination of all parties to combat Socialism'.[54] Austen Chamberlain endorsed these sentiments, and went so far as to say that the Coalition was neither the old Conservative party nor the old Radicals, 'but a great middle body of opinion' which was needed to

---

[51] Although few went as far as the Conservative MP for Handsworth, Oliver Locker-Lampson, who drove around his constituency with an effigy labelled 'Bolshie' hanging from a gibbet.

[52] See e.g. J. Whittaker to NUCA Conference, Birmingham, 10 June 1920, NUCA Conference Minutes, Card 95. For a general examination of the importance of this labelling process see D. A. Jarvis, 'Stanley Baldwin and the Ideology of the Conservative Response to Socialism, 1918–31', unpublished Lancaster University Ph.D thesis (1991).

[53] See D. A. Jarvis, 'British Conservatism and Class Politics in the 1920s', *EHR* 110 (1996).

[54] H. S. Foster, D. Davis at NUCA Conference, Birmingham, 10 June 1920, NUCA Conference Minutes, Card 95.

deal with the new issues that had emerged since the war and to combat the threat of revolution.[55] In similar, but importantly not identical vein, both Lord Salisbury[56] and Law[57] stated that the Coalition was indeed crucial to the fight against Socialism, but they also argued that co-operation did not mean fusion, and were keen to stress that membership of the Coalition did not mean a betrayal of Conservative principles.

The language used by Salisbury and Law was designed to deal with the strong body of opinion hostile to the Coalition that had been voiced at the NUCA Conference. In response to Alderman Davis's motion for a combination against Socialism, Mr Collingwood Hughes from Peckham proposed an amendment which called for 'the formation of a Conservative Government which *alone* can apply the financial, economic and industrial principles necessary to stabilise the position of Great Britain'. He also stated that proposals to continue the Coalition would and should be viewed with 'utmost detestation and fear', and that Lloyd George in particular had to be 'turned out', as he was 'the man who was the greatest danger to the Conservative party.'[58] Hughes was supported by Councillor Clissett from Newport, who argued that working-class voters would support Labour if the Conservatives remained in the Coalition, and he urged the party to escape from the influence of the 'hypnotic little Welshman . . . [and] stand fast for the tenets of Conservatism'.[59] The outcome of the debate was intriguing, insofar as Alderman Davis's motion in favour of co-operation with other parties in the face of Socialism was carried, but only on the understanding 'that the organisation of the Unionist party in each constituency be kept in full efficiency'.[60] At the following year's NUCA Conference at Liverpool this debate continued. W. J. Woolacott from Sheffield proposed a motion that called for a strict enforcement of the National Union's constitutional rule that required local associations actively to pursue the Conservative cause. He suggested that associations in constituencies where Coalition Liberals sat had ceased to function, and that in other areas Coalitionism was fostering apathy. In these circumstances, Woolacott argued, Conservatives could not combat Socialism effectively because local parties were either not being allowed

[55] Chamberlain at NUCA Conference, Birmingham, 11 June 1920, ibid.

[56] Salisbury at NUCA Conference, Birmingham, 10 June 1920, ibid.

[57] Law at NUCA Conference, Birmingham, 11 June 1920, ibid., Card 96.

[58] C. Hughes at NUCA Conference, Birmingham, 10 June 1920, ibid., Card 95.

[59] J. Clissett to NUCA Conference, Birmingham, 10 June 1920, ibid. That Clissett was from Newport is of some interest, in that the by-election at Newport on the day before the Carlton Club meeting in October 1922 was to see a Conservative candidate, standing against the wishes of CCO, defeat the sitting Coalition Liberal MP.

[60] NUCA Conference, 10 June 1920, ibid.

or were too discouraged to fight.[61] The Conservative Chairman, George Younger, defended CCO against what was, in effect, a charge that it had stymied local party activity, but in spite of this the motion was carried.[62] Small wonder that Austen Chamberlain, who had become Conservative leader in March, stated in his speech to the Conference that 'it would be foolish to deny and futile to ignore the existence of great anxiety among the party today'. But although he acknowledged this 'unrest', he urged patience, and declared that if 'we of the present Coalition dissolve' it would mean 'breaking the forces of order'.[63]

The tensions apparent at the NUCA Conference of November 1921 continued into the New Year. Lloyd George's hint that there might be a dissolution and election necessarily raised the question of whether the Conservatives would fight independently or continue the Coalition. Chamberlain was livid, and complained to his sister that 'Lloyd George put the fat in the fire with his talk of dissolution'. The Prime Minister, he argued, risked

Upsetting and perhaps permanently ruining my effort to join all that is reasonably progressive in the Unionist Party with what is sound & not too tied up in old party shibboleths in the Liberal Party. Most unfortunately he was encouraged by the Lord Chancellor [F. E. Smith, Lord Birkenhead], & now . . . I do not know that the anger & excitement in the Unionist Party can be allayed. My letter bag is heavy with protests & threats never to stand again as Coalitionists.[64]

Chamberlain's heavy letter bag could only be cause for concern, given that a general election had to be held at some point before the end of 1923, and convincing the Conservative party of the need for continuing the Coalition seemed to be growing increasingly problematic as time went by. Chamberlain attributed this to the 'local Associations . . . [being] full of old pre-war Tories, who have learned nothing & forgotten nothing',[65] but whether or not it was due to the 'Bourbon' tendencies of local Conservatives, the fact that the Coalition was increasingly reviled by the party grass roots could not be denied. Moreover, as pressure from the constituencies grew, so restiveness in the upper echelons of the party increased. In response to their Memorandum criticizing the Coalition, circulated in early 1922, Steel-Maitland and Robert Cecil received only only five replies that were unequivocally supportive of the

---

[61] W. J. Woolacott at NUCA Conference, 17 Nov. 1921, NUCA Conference Minutes, Microfilm Card 97.

[62] Ibid.

[63] Chamberlain at NUCA Conference, Birmingham, 18 Nov. 1921, NUCA Conference Minutes, Microfilm Card 97.

[64] Chamberlain to I. Chamberlain, 7 Jan. 1922, in R. C. Self (ed.), *The Austen Chamberlain Diary Letters* (Cambridge, 1995), 178.

[65] Chamberlain to H. Chamberlain, 4 Mar. 1922, in ibid. 182.

government. Others were openly hostile: John Buchan declared, 'I want to get back to a real Tory party . . . without any suggestion of a working alliance with Independent Liberals',[66] and Viscount Bledisloe asked 'why modern day Conservatives must necessarily be either Diehards and follow Page Croft and co, or Coalitionists and follow George and "F. E."?'[67]

The desire amongst Conservatives to re-establish the independence of their party grew apace in the first half of 1922, and in July the Earl Crawford noted, after a meeting of the most senior, committed Coalitionists, that:

It appears that some of our Whips and under-secretaries are very apprehensive about the future. They dislike Coalition as such, their constituency associations are hostile to its continuance, and in some case, especially in the South of England, the Liberal Coalition candidate will be denied our support. In some cases too a Conservative candidate will be run against him.[68]

By September, evidence that local Conservative associations were increasingly willing to disregard the orders of CCO and run independent candidates was indeed widespread.[69] Sir Leslie Wilson told Chamberlain that 180 constituencies had decided to follow this course, and that, 'When a General Election comes you may find a majority of your followers not following but, under the influence of their Associations, finding themselves forced into a position which will leave you, as Leader of the Party, in a position in which none of your friends and none of your colleagues would wish or intend you to be'.[70] Chamberlain and his Coalitionist colleagues were thus wholly aware of the burgeoning antagonism towards the Coalition in the localities, but they were also clear that this movement of opinion was not only wrong but dangerously counter-productive. Writing to his old Liberal Unionist colleague Joseph Parker Smith shortly before the fateful Carlton Club meeting, Austen Chamberlain summed up his view of the underlying political and electoral situation, and declared that:

Those who think that the Conservative Party, standing as such and disavowing its Liberal allies, could return with a working majority are living in a fool's paradise. Confronted with such a danger [Socialism] I conceive that it is our business to rally all the conservative elements of the country, for we shall need all the strength that we can muster.[71]

---

[66] J. Buchan to Cecil, 1 Mar. 1922, SMP, GD 193/276/24.
[67] Bledisloe to Cecil, 2 Mar. 1922, SMP, GD 193/276/64.
[68] Crawford and Balcarres, diary entry, 26 July 1922, Vincent (ed.), *Crawford Papers*, 428.
[69] See Bates, 'Conservative Party', 24–43.
[70] Sir L. Wilson to Chamberlain, n.d. (Sept. 1922), A. Chamberlain papers (ACP), Birmingham University Library, AC 33/2/26.
[71] Chamberlain to J. Parker Smith, 11 Oct. 1922, ACP, 33/2/38.

The problem for Chamberlain, which was to become all too evident eight days later, was that the bulk of his party did not share this view.

The situation, as it unfolded at the Carlton Club, could be taken to indicate that there was a stark polarity of opinion in the Conservative ranks, namely, between those who saw the Coalition as essential to the political and electoral security of the Conservative party and Conservative values and those who saw it as unnecessary and indeed inimical to them. To a certain extent this was the case, for the victorious Carlton Club 'rebels' gave voice to a visceral grass-roots loathing of the Coalition: William Bridgeman noted in his diary that: 'One thing is certain about the crisis [which] is that it certainly was not the result of a Carlton Club plot, but came up from below with great force from the constituencies.'[72] Shortly before the Carlton Club meeting the news was announced that an independent, anti-Coalition Conservative had won the Newport by-election, which underscored the synergy of 'high' and 'low' anti-Coalition politics. But, although the idea of a simple, straight-forward dichotomy has obvious and plausible attractions, there are other dimensions and complexities which need to be added to the story.

For a number of commentators, both at the time and since, the break-up of the Coalition was not inevitable, and Chamberlain's 'mishandling' of the situation has been singled out as a contributory factor to the government's and his own downfall.[73] In this context Chamberlain's particular error was, it has been suggested, his excessive loyalty to Lloyd George. The logic of the argument here is that, if the key thing for Chamberlain was to continue the coalition of anti-Socialist forces, then he could have achieved this by sacrificing Lloyd George and recasting the Coalition leadership. This was not an implausible strategy. In March 1922 Steel-Maitland had felt obliged to explain to Chamberlain the reasons for his non-attendance at a party meeting in Birmingham, and had stated that 'I do not believe myself in the advantage of the continuance of the Coalition *under the present Prime Minister*'.[74] The clear implication of Steel-Maitland's statement was that his view of the Coalition might change if it was led by another Prime Minister. Similarly, Steel-Maitland was told in the spring, by Archibald Salvidge and Walter Elliot respectively, that Liberal assistance had been crucial in the fight against Socialism in Liverpool, and that any non-Socialist government had to be a coalition.[75] The Coalitionist Conservative argument that the

---

[72] W. C. Bridgeman to R. Bridgeman, 22 Oct. 1922, in id., diary entry, Oct. 1922. P. Williamson (ed.), *The Modernisation of Conservative Politics: The Diaries and Letters of William Bridgeman, 1904–1935* (1988), 162.

[73] See e.g. Kinnear, *Fall*, 56–8, 99, 110, 126–7; Dutton, *Chamberlain*, 195–8.

[74] Steel-Maitland to Chamberlain, 21 Mar. 1922, SMP, GD 193/95/4/41 (my emphasis).

[75] A. Salvidge to Steel-Maitland, 20 Mar. 1922, SMP, GD 193/120/3/385; W. Elliot to R. Cecil, 1 Mar. 1922, SMP, GD 193/276/26–7x.

Coalition was a means of cementing non- and anti-Socialist forces into a cohesive bloc was one to which many Conservatives were sympathetic, and had the Conservative Coalition leadership been willing to jettison Lloyd George much of the anti-Coalition bile in the middle and lower ranks of their party might have been purged.

In many respects what lay at the heart of the dispute between Coalitionist and anti-Coalitionist Conservatives was the role each ascribed to Liberals in the construction of an anti-Socialist bloc. That the Liberal party was in decline as a major political force had been evident since at least 1918, but the question remained as to what would happen to the decaying Liberal vote. In March 1922 Walter Elliot asked Steel-Maitland to give his 'attention to municipal politics generally, particularly in the North', where, he argued, there was a 'process . . . taking place of a two-party system—Socialists and non-Socialist—[which] will be reproduced in the Imperial Parliament much more rapidly than present leaders of opinion are willing to admit'.[76] In fact it was the emergence of precisely this bipolar political world which Austen Chamberlain and his fellow Coalitionists stressed as the *raison d'être* of the Coalition. Indeed, one major political reason why Chamberlain and his colleagues described the 'new' world of British politics in almost Manichean terms was to send a message to Liberals that there was no political space outside the Coalition for a non-Socialist. Where Chamberlain lost touch with the majority of his party was through his apparent willingness to make too many concessions to Liberal sensibilities and Liberal personalities, and thereby compromise the Conservative party and Conservatism. His reference at the 1921 NUCA Conference to the possible emergence of a new political party after the Coalition eventually dissolved[77] gave the impression that he was willing to embrace the possibility of fusion between the Conservatives and Coalition Liberals, whereas Law had publicly played down any such idea. That the 'Diehard' opponents of the Coalition appeared to become devout anti-Socialists only *after* the collapse of the Coalition was not because they had suddenly discovered the Socialist enemy, or needed to sublimate 'their crusading energies on Socialism'[78] once the Coalition 'enemy' had been slain, but rather because they felt that it was *only* after the Coalition had been removed that serious anti-Socialist work could begin. There are parallels here with the situation in the first half of the 1880s, when both Sir Stafford Northcote and Lord Salisbury had seen

---

[76] Ibid.
[77] Chamberlain at NUCA Conference, Liverpool, 18 Nov. 1921, NUCA Conference Minutes, Microfilm Card 97.
[78] Kinnear, *Fall*, 141.

the defection of the Whigs and moderate Liberals as the key to Conservative political success. However, Northcote was regarded as too ready to meet disillusioned Liberals on a middle ground, whereas Salisbury's position was deemed, rightly, to be simply to establish the Conservative position and wait for Liberal defectors to be driven over by their disgust with Gladstone and Radicalism. This 'no compromise' position was to underpin the Conservative appeal to Liberals after 1922, and was at the centre of Stanley Baldwin's self-conscious and successful construction of an anti-Socialist political and electoral coalition. The Conservative party was presented as the party of sound finance, low taxation, economic stability, Christian duty, and national unity. The Socialist Labour party was, in contrast, portrayed as an economically irresponsible tax-and-spend party, concerned only with the sectional interests of the trade unions, and also atheistic.[79] In this bipolar world, Conservatives argued, Liberals who were committed non-Socialists could only turn in one direction, towards the Conservative party. Ironically, Austen Chamberlain fell in with this strategy very easily. He told one correspondent in the spring of 1924: 'We shall have no small increase of strength from the Nonconformist traders, shopkeepers and the like who were the backbone of the old Liberal party.'[80] It was, of course, exactly this constituency that Chamberlain had sought to cement to the anti-Socialist cause through the Coalition, whereas his opponents on that issue had argued, rightly as it turned out, that a more effective route to this end was to establish the Conservative party in itself as the great anti-Socialist bulwark.

The events of 1922 were an important staging-post in the Conservative party's ongoing construction of its identity as the quintessential anti-Socialist force. This process had begun in the 1880s, when British Socialism first appeared as an important political force, and continued to be an integral part of the shaping and reshaping of Conservative ideas up to the close of the twentieth century. A closely related aspect of the Conservative party's identity was its development as the quintessential representative force of the middle class. Once again, the late nineteenth century had seen the first important stages in this process, in the shape of the Salisburyian party's acknowledgement

---

[79] For detailed discussions of the construction of the inter-war Conservatives' anti-Socialist strategy see R. McKibbin, 'Class and Conventional Wisdom', in id., *The Ideologies of Class* (Oxford, 1991); P. Williamson, *Stanley Baldwin* (Cambridge, 1999); D. A. Jarvis, 'The Shaping of the Conservative Electoral Hegemony, 1918–39', in J. Lawrence and M. Taylor, *Party, State and Society: Electoral Behaviour in Modern Britain Since 1820* (Aldershot, 1996); and id., 'Conservative Response to Socialism', *passim*.

[80] Chamberlain to Dr Garfield, 9 Apr. 1924, ACP, AC 35/4/17, in Jarvis, 'Conservative Response', 348.

of the centrality of suburban 'Villa Tories' as a key electoral constituency, the increasing prominence of businessmen and professionals in the parliamentary party, and the staffing of the party's organizational apparatus at the central and local level by members of the middle class.[81] Both during and after the Great War the importance of the middle classes to the party's electoral position and within the party increased still further,[82] as was in part reflected in the fact that all four of the inter-war party leaders were from urban, middle-class backgrounds. Yet, in spite of their centrality to the social make-up of the party and to the social geography of the Conservative vote, the middle classes were neither secure nor politically at ease in the immediate postwar period. In part, the causes of this unease were the economic difficulties and fears of the middle classes. Businessmen and employers may have 'done well out of the war', but this had been balanced by the growth of trade-union membership and a concomitant challenge to managerial authority at the workplace. Moreover, the end of the postwar boom and the onset of a severe recession in late 1921 saw business doing considerably less well than during the war. For the professional and salaried middle classes life was made more uncomfortable in two important ways. First, inflation had emerged as a significant problem after 1914,[83] and, unlike the trade unions, the middle classes did not have the organized power to protect their incomes. Inflation was also a source of grievance, insofar as the middle classes were the section of the community most likely to hold savings, with many having invested in war bonds in particular. Charles de Gaulle once referred to the French middle classes of the inter-war years as the 'generation of 3%', whose savings were particularly vulnerable to inflation. This would also have been a fair description of the British middle class, who tended, like their French counterparts, to favour the political economy of deflation. Second, the middle classes were the majority of the newly expanded taxpaying community, and felt that they were footing the bill for the expansion of government welfare expenditure on benefits for the non-taxpaying lower classes. As a consequence, the middle classes were, *in extremis*, supportive of the MCU and AWL, and opposed a Coalition government they deemed economically 'unsound'. If the Great War and

---

[81] For this development see J. Cornford, 'The Transformation of Conservatism in the Late Nineteenth Century', *Victorian Studies*, 7 (1963); F. Coetzee, 'Villa Toryism Reconsidered: Conservatism and Suburban Sensibilities in Late-Victorian Croydon', in E. H. H. Green (ed.), *An Age of Transition: British Politics, 1880–1914* (Edinburgh, 1997); R. Shannon, *The Age of Salisbury* (Harlow, 1996), 98–131, 314–43; Green, *Crisis*, 101–17.

[82] As a consequence of the redistribution of seats that accompanied the extension of the franchise in 1918 the number of predominantly middle-class seats rose to 200. See J. A. Ramsden, The Age of Balfour and Baldwin (1978), 119–25.

[83] From 1914 to 1921 prices rose by almost 130%.

the immediate post-war period saw a rise in 'class consciousness', this was as much a trend in middle-class social and political life as it was in the much more extensively studied world of working-class life, labour, and politics.[84] There are intriguing parallels here with the 'social politics' of the decade after the Second World War, when the questions of trade- union power and inflation saw a 'middle-class revolt', expressed in organizations like the British Housewives League, the People's League for the Defence of Freedom, and the Middle Class Alliance, against not only the Attlee government but Conservative governments that were deemed to be 'me-tooing' Socialist welfare policy and insufficiently responsive to middle-class concerns about public expenditure and its contribution to inflation.[85] The Conservatives' position as the 'party of the middle classes', like its position as the 'anti-Socialist party', was a problematic aspect of the party's twentieth-century identity, and the debate surrounding the end of the Coalition in 1922 was a crucial moment in an ongoing process of the negotiation and renegotiation of both of these aspects of its identity which was to continue in the decades thereafter.

[84] The literature here is extensive, but helpful summaries are B. Waites, *A Class Society at War* (Leamington Spa, 1987) and G. de Groot, *Blighty: British Society in the Era of the Great War* (Harlow, 1996), 290–333. For a similar discussion of middle-class political consciousness see Morgan, *Consensus*, 280–301.

[85] For the 1950s see E. H. H. Green, 'The Conservative Party, the State and the Electorate, 1945–64', in Taylor and Lawrence (eds.), *Party, State and Society*.

CHAPTER 5

The Battle of the Books: Book Clubs and Conservatism in the 1930s

THE CONSERVATIVE Party dominated British politics in the inter-war years, enjoying a political and electoral ascendancy that was in marked contrast to its pre-1914 experience. Yet, in spite of their success, the Conservatives remained strangely insecure; it was almost as if they felt they had stolen votes that really belonged to Labour, that this theft would be discovered, and that the electorate would be returned to its rightful owners.[1] This general sense of insecurity was, however, particularly pronounced in relation to the realm of political ideas, where Conservatives felt the Left enjoyed a clear ascendancy. At the NUCA Conference at Birmingham in June 1920 Alderman David Davis drew attention to the fact that the Labour party had established a college and thirty 'schools' for the purpose of instructing members, activists, and members of the public in Socialist ideas. In order to counter this Socialist propaganda effectively, Davis argued, the Conservatives needed to consider establishing similar institutions to spread their party's message.[2] In September 1923 the Sir Philip Stott College opened at Overstone in Northamptonshire, to act as a political education centre for Conservative speakers, candidates, and officials. The creation of this college had been announced the previous year, and by the spring of 1923 the Conservative Eastern Provincial Division had already decided to urge all local Associations in the Division to send representatives there 'for an instructional course in Anti-Socialist organisation'.[3] The Stott College functioned for five years, but in 1928 a new institution was founded, which came into being in 1930 as the Ashridge Bonar Law Memorial College at Berkhamsted. The new college, which came to be known simply as 'Ashridge', was funded from the will of Urban H. Broughton, and its purpose was defined as providing education in citizenship, 'with special reference to the development of the British constitution and growth and

---

[1] For discussion of the Conservatives' sense of insecurity see Jarvis, 'British Conservatism' and id., Conservative Electoral Hegemony'.

[2] D. Davis at NUCA Conference, Birmingham, 10 June 1920, NUCA Conference Minutes, Microfilm Card 95.

[3] Eastern Provisional Division, Minutes of AGM, 24 Mar. 1923, CPA, ARE 7/1/6.

expansion of the British Empire'.[4] Ashridge, because it was a trust foundation, was not owned or directly funded by the Conservative party, but its political role was clear. Urban Broughton, as CCO noted in 1954, had 'created the Trust because he was deeply concerned at the danger of what in those days was known as "Bolshevism" and he believed the best way to preserve liberty under a constitutional government was by educating the electorate in the responsibilities of citizenship'. Furthermore, Broughton had viewed the Conservative party as the best safeguard against 'Bolshevism', and the great repository of 'responsible citizenship', and hence only Conservatives had been asked to be governors of the college.[5] In the 1930s[6] Ashridge functioned as centre of Conservative political education, and certainly fulfilled its benefactor's wishes in that it provided a base for the discussion and dissemination of anti-Socialist ideas. Institutionally, the Conservatives appeared to have responded well to the demand from the constituencies for an educational forum that would match those enjoyed by the Left.

Ashridge provided an institutional structure where individuals could receive a training in Conservative principles, but this was regarded as only one aspect of the battle against Socialist ideas. Equally important concerns were the content and form of the intellectual training Conservatives received, and securing a wide audience for Conservative ideas. With regard to the first, Arthur Bryant, who was appointed as Secretary of the Education Department of Ashridge in the summer of 1928, outlined a curriculum of five essential subjects—Conservative principles, citizenship, economics, the historical development of modern industry and agriculture, and the British Empire.[7] In order to study these subjects students were to be provided with 'pioneer texts'. With regard to particular subjects, Bryant argued that the textbook on citizenship should outline the evolution of the rights and duties of the English citizen over time, with a particular stress on the role of ordinary people in local government and the principle of liberty under the law. He put foward J. H. Morgan, KC as a possible author. For economics he suggested that there was no better introduction to the subject than Fiennes and Pilkington's *Getting Our Living*, but noted that as it had been written for children it needed some amendment. On industry and agriculture, and on the Empire, Bryant did not recommend particular

[4] Summary of Reasons for the Ashridge (Bonar Law Memorial) Trust Bill, n.d. (1954), CPA, CCO 3/4/29.

[5] Ibid.

[6] After the war Ashridge experienced both financial and administrative problems, which led to the terms of the original trust being changed. For indications of these problems see Bryant to Lord Woolton, 27 May 1949, ABP, D12.

[7] Memorandum by A. Bryant, 13 June 1928, ibid., C13.

authors, but on Conservatism he suggested that 'I should be instructed to start writing it at once', and the result was his *The Spirit of Conservatism*, published in 1929. Whatever their individual merits, the purpose of these books was, in Bryant's view, that they would provide

a very simple historical and philosophical discussion of the great national problems to-day from the Conservative point of view. The books will avoid detail and try to attract the reader to a further study of the subject . . . Above all the purpose of the books would be to present Conservatism as an instructive philosophy of life. They would, in fact, aim at performing the same pioneer service for Conservative Education as that of the early Fabian publications for Socialism.

Those attending course at Ashridge were to be the primary audience for these 'pioneer texts', but other audiences were also envisaged, namely, 'Conservative students and members of existing study circles, week-end schools and correspondence courses. Students of Citizenship in Universities and schools . . . [and] the general reading public'.[8] In this way, like the Fabians, Ashridge would, through its courses and books, 'postulate, perorate and permeate' the Conservative and hopefully a wider public.

Reaching out to as wide an audience as possible was one of the main aims of Conservative propagandizing in the inter-war years. The Conservatives possessed a well-funded and innovative publicity machine, which produced a steady flow of printed matter in the shape of magazines, pamphlets, and posters, and a flood of material during general election campaigns. Often this material was at the cutting edge of contemporary political publicity in terms of the way it was produced, and, equally important, often targeted to resonate with particular audiences.[9] In addition, the Conservatives made early and adroit use of the new media of radio and film.[10] In this respect the Conservatives not only far outmatched the Left in terms of the quantity of publicity material they produced, but also in the quality and nature of the media they deployed.[11] Yet, in spite of the Conservatives' undoubted success as a 'propaganda machine', many Conservatives did not see their party dominating this field. Indeed, particularly in the realm of political literature, the Left was often described by Conservatives as enjoying almost complete ascendancy. Shortly after the publication of *The Spirit of*

---

[8] Ibid.

[9] D. A. Jarvis, 'Mrs. Maggs and Betty: The Conservative Appeal to Women Voters in the 1920s', *TCBH* 5 (1994).

[10] Baldwin's 'fireside chats' on the radio are a well-known example, but he was also at home with film: see J. Ramsden, 'Baldwin and Film', in N. Pronay and D. Spring (eds.), *Politics, Propaganda and Film, 1928–45* (Basingstoke, 1982).

[11] For a summary see R. Cockett, 'The Party, Publicity and the Media', in Seldon and Ball (eds.), *Conservative Century*.

Conservatism, Arthur Bryant was told by one correspondent that he had 'thoroughly appreciated and enjoyed it', particularly because 'for years . . . propaganda of the Tory outlook in a popular form was a national need' in order to counter 'the harm done by the Whig Radical monopoly of political thought and historical interpretation'.[12] This letter evidently expressed the views of someone who felt Toryism had been submerged under a flood of Leftist literature, and, even though it emanated from deepest Chelsea, it was by no means an isolated viewpoint.[13] In his autobiography, published in 1937, the Conservative writer Douglas Jerrold argued that nations were governed by words, and that in Britain a new aristocracy of the pen and the desk had replaced the landed classes as rulers of the country.[14] For Jerrold, however, the problem was that pens and desks were overwhelmingly used and occupied by writers of the Left, with the result that 'To go Right is to go wrong in journalism to-day',[15] and he himself attempted to break the Left's 'monopoly' by establishing the *English Review* as a journal of the Right in the late 1920s.[16] Jerrold's opinions and actions were mirrored by another Conservative writer, Francis Yeats-Brown, the author of *Lives of a Bengal Lancer*. In 1939 Yeats-Brown announced plans to publish his own magazine, on the grounds that there was 'not only an urgent need but a real public demand for an organ in which the fallacies of the Left can be exposed, and in which fair reviews of Right wing books can be read'. Yeats-Brown expressed particular concern about the way J. M. N. Jefferies's book on Palestine had been 'practically boycotted, because "Bloomsbury" doesn't want to hear the case for the Arabs', but he felt that 'the Right wing writer generally has very little chance of making himself heard'.[17]

The reference to Bloomsbury indicated a particular target of Conservative concern and enmity. As a political, intellectual, and cultural phenomenon, the 'Bloomsbury Group' embodied everything that Conservatives despised. Bloomsbury was 'highbrow' intellectual, iconoclastic of tradition, irreverent towards established historical institutions and figures, morally questionable, and, of course, strongly Left politically. If 'Bloomsbury' had just existed it would have been merely objectionable, but what made it a subject of intense Conservative loathing was its apparent success in extending its influence through the dissemination of its ideas. In this context an object of particular concern

[12] J. H. Blaksley to Bryant, 10 June 1929, ABP, C17.
[13] The author lived in Cheyne Court.
[14] D. Jerrold, *Georgian Adventure: The Autobiography of Douglas Jerrold* (1937; 1938 RBC edn.), 51.
[15] Ibid. 299.   [16] Ibid. 310.
[17] F. Yeats-Brown to Bryant, 26 May 1939, ABP, C39.

was the Left Book Club (LBC), which was seen as, in effect, the publishing arm of the Bloomsbury Group. In his 1938 publication *Ordeal in England*, Philip Gibbs, passing critical remarks on Harold Laski, noted that 'He [Laski] and [Victor] Gollancz run a Left Book Club, which has . . . been very successful. If it isn't one of the most subversive influences in this country I am very much mistaken.'[18] A year later another Conservative writer, Donald Cowie, clearly had the LBC in mind when he declared that, 'we have been treated in recent years to a flood of books on European affairs, mainly from a subversive viewpoint by intelligent but short-sighted publicists of the Left',[19] and he expressed the hope that there would come a time when 'we should no longer find our printing presses practically monopolised by the dangerous effusion of so-called intellectual idealists'.[20]

That 'Bloomsbury' and the LBC had established such a powerful position was, for many Conservatives, not only due simply to their 'cleverness', but also to the fact that Conservatives had let them go largely unchallenged. In Douglas Jerrold's view it had been the case in the nineteenth century that 'Toryism, as the creed of the governing classes had no intellectual aspirations'.[21] However, he also felt that little had changed in the twentieth century. The middle classes, rather than the old governing classes, were, he thought, the dominant force in society, but 'middle class culture', he declared, 'has never been an adventure of the mind or soul. It was, even at its best, a little asphyxiating.'[22] Jerrold felt that Conservative politics reflected this intellectual torpor. When he confessed that at Westminster school he had played soccer because it was a sport for which one could be awarded colours, he could not resist remarking that, 'when it came to games that earned no colours, there was as much interest as there is in the Conservative Central Office on questions of Conservative principles'.[23] As a consequence of this lack of interest, Conservatives had been unable to expose the fallacies of the Left, even to themselves, with the result that 'to suggest any opposition at all to Socialistic measures is . . . fatal at the Carlton Club'.[24] Jerrold himself, as noted above, had sought to launch his own publishing counter-attack on the Left, and in 1933 he tried to galvanize the Conservative party to greater anti-Socialist assertiveness through an internal party movement centred on Lord Lloyd.[25] At the same time Jerrold was also active as a lecturer at Ashridge, which he

---

[18] P. Gibbs, *Ordeal in England* (1938 RBC edn.), 222.
[19] D. Cowie, *An Empire Prepared* (1939 RBC edn.), 9.   [20] Ibid. 10.
[21] Jerrold, *Georgian Adventure*, 17.   [22] Ibid. 275–6.
[23] Ibid. 48.   [24] Ibid. 331.
[25] For this episode see J. Charmley, *Lord Lloyd and the Decline of the British Empire* (1987), 188–90; G. C. Webber, *The Ideology of the British Right, 1918–39* (1986), 42.

evidently regarded as one area of Conservative intellectual activity with the potential to offer real assistance in the struggle against the Left. Here he was not alone. Francis Yeats-Brown was also an Ashridge lecturer, as were the Conservative historians Charles Petrie, F. J. C. Hearnshaw, and Keith Feiling,[26] and other Conservative writers such as Sir Arnold Wilson and William Teeling. Their view of the purpose and potential of Ashridge was summed up by Teeling, who stated in 1938 that: 'If only the older Conservatives would take a little more interest and listen as seriously to the ideas of young people back from Ashridge, as they do to more out of date retired supporters with large cheque books there might be a more progressive activity in the Conservative party.'[27] The kind of ideas the 'young people' were bringing back from Ashridge were likewise summed up by Sir Arnold Wilson, whose lecture at Ashridge in October 1935 stressed that 'Toryism is not only a Party spirit but a way of life; not only a political attitude of mind but a regenerative social and moral force'.[28] But Toryism, Wilson argued, could only be such a force if it grappled with issues such as pensions, health, and welfare provision, which were 'examples, taken almost at random, of the sort of questions as to which the Tory Party should be thoroughly well informed'.[29] The Conservatives, he suggested, 'include in their ranks men and women of leisure, and a great number of educated persons . . . who could and should master the intricacies of these subjects and learn where the yoke galls and how the burden may be lightened'.[30] Equipped with such knowledge, Conservatives could confront 'forces now at work' which were, in Wilson's view, 'deeper and more powerful than those which caused the French and the Industrial Revolutions', of which Socialism was the most threatening.[31] Ashridge thus contributed to the fight against Socialism, in that it helped to provide Conservatives with the requisite knowledge for the struggle.

Ashridge was not regarded as enough in itself to counter the influence of Socialist ideas. For some Conservatives it was necessary for the Right to deploy the power of the written word as effectively as the Left had done. In particular, Conservatives looked to imitate, match, and perhaps surpass the success of Victor Gollancz's LBC. First into the 'battle of the books' in the Conservative cause was the Right Book Club (RBC), which was established in late 1936. The original idea for the RBC came

---

[26] For the anti-Socialist activities of Hearnshaw and Feiling see R. N. Soffer, 'The Long Nineteenth Century of Conservative Thought', in G. K. Behlmer and F. M. Leventhal (eds.), *Singular Continuities: Tradition, Nostalgia and Identity in Modern British Culture* (Stanford, 2000). For Petrie see below.

[27] W. Teeling, *Why Britain Prospers* (1938 RBC edn.), 113.

[28] Sir A. Wilson, *Thoughts and Talks* (1939 RBC edn.), 77.

[29] Ibid. 75.   [30] Ibid. 76.   [31] Ibid.

from Edgar Samuel, who worked for W. & G. Foyle, the booksellers of Charing Cross Road, and who was married to Winifred Foyle. He suggested to William Foyle, his father-in-law and senior partner in the company, that a book club of the Right was necessary to counter Gollancz's influence.[32] The RBC was established in early 1937, and its 'moving spirit',[33] until it ceased operations with the onset of the war, was Christina Foyle. Unlike its Left adversary, the RBC did not for the most part publish books specially written for it, but reprinted already-published works in RBC editions. A number of its authors, for example, Douglas Jerrold, Arnold Wilson, Philip Gibbs, Charles Petrie, William Teeling, and Francis Yeats-Brown, were Ashridge lecturers, and others, notably Cuthbert Alport and Reginald Northam, were to become figures of some importance in the post-war Conservative party. The RBC selection committee, which chose the books to be published, included two men, Anthony Ludovici and Derek Walker-Smith, who were prominent figures in Conservative 'fringe-group' activities in, respectively, the inter-war and post-war period,[34] and the RBC's patrons included thirty-three (mainly obscure)[35] Conservative MPs. In April 1937 the *Observer* announced that the RBC could claim 10,000 members, but its very appearance and the not-insignificant backing it received from within the Consevative fold, mark it out as an intriguing and often overlooked aspect of the late 1930s Conservative subculture.

Nor was the RBC the only Conservative combatant in the 'battle of the books', for 1937 saw the founding of the National Book Association (NBA). The moving spirit behind the NBA was Arthur Bryant, the head of the Education Department and leading member of the Central Council at Ashridge. According to Bryant, the idea of establishing a Conservative book club was raised by Stanley Baldwin at a meeting of the Governing Body of Ashridge in the summer of 1936, when the then Prime Minister had suggested that 'steps should be taken to get books written to counterbalance the propaganda of the Left'.[36] Later that summer Bryant laid the foundations of the NBA, by securing promises of backing from CCO and Ashridge and negotiating an agreement with

[32] W. R. Christopher Foyle to the author, 4 May 2000.
[33] Bryant to R. Northam, 3 Aug. 1938, ABP C46.
[34] Ludovici was the author of *A Defence of Conservatism: A Further Text-Book for Tories* (1927). Walker-Smith was to be a critic of Macmillan and a leading figure in the Anti-Common Market League in the early 1960s: see R. F. Dewey, 'British National Identity and the First Application to Europe', unpublished Oxford University D.Phil. thesis (2001).
[35] Leopold Amery, Lord Winterton, and Sir Henry Page-Croft were best-known at the time, but David Maxwell-Fyfe, Duncan Sandys, and Alan Lennox-Boyd would become prominent in the post-war period. The former MP Sir Harry Brittain provided a link with earlier anti-Socialist activities.
[36] Bryant to Baldwin, 5 May 1937, ABP, C49.

the publishers Hutchinsons. All of this preparation was done in secret, for Bryant believed that careful planning was essential if the Conservative effort was to match the LBC, given that Gollancz's organization had been in existence for ten years. However, Bryant's patient planning was thrown into disarray by the apperance of the RBC. He told Stanley Baldwin that:

Unfortunately the sensational success of Gollancz's Left Book Club caused other publishers to imagine that there would be money in a Right Book Club and to seek about for politicians in our own Party to support their attempts to form such clubs. Hackney and Gower at the C[entral] O[ffice] did their utmost to suppress these rash attempts—but we needed to move fast to stop being smothered by rivals. A few weeks later the ground was cut from under Hutchinsons' feet by Messrs. Foyle's announcement of a Right Book Club, backed not only by the names of several prominent Conservatives of the extreme Right, but also ... two Conservative Ministers, Lord Halifax and Sir Samuel Hoare, the Principal of Ashridge and the leading Conservative man of letters, Lord Tweedsmuir [John Buchan].[37]

Bryant was furious at the emergence of a rival 'voice of the Right'. He denounced 'fools on our side [who] made our path more difficult', and pointed out that the NBA's publishers, Hutchinsons, 'after months of preparation and expenditure . . . are being outbidden by rivals who are cutting the ground from under their feet by appealing for Conservative support under a parade of Conservative names'.[38] Bryant complained that the upshot of this was that 'Hutchinsons have been hopelessly paralysed in competition with a firm who without any policy that can further our cause (Foyle's are not to publish but merely to chose existing books . . .) and with a complete freedom from political responsibility, have divided our ranks and confused even our most loyal supporters'.[39]

Bryant had a number of reasons for writing to Baldwin. To begin with, they were friends as well as political allies. In addition, Baldwin, throughout his time as party leader, had displayed a clear sense of the importance of propaganda and, as noted above, had himself suggested the idea of a Conservative book club. Most important, however, Bryant was seeking to persuade Baldwin to act as Honorary President of the NBA. Bryant informed Sir Geoffrey Ellis, shortly before he wrote to Baldwin, that the Conservative leader was 'proposing to devote himself exclusively to political education after his retirement'. The NBA was, Bryant hoped, precisely the kind of project Baldwin would support, but he was concerned that rival projects, such as the RBC, might tempt Baldwin into lending his name to their activities, and hence the concern he expressed to Ellis that 'the NBA [is] struggling in the water and if we

[37] Bryant to Baldwin, 5 May 1937, ABP, C49.   [38] Ibid.   [39] Ibid.

do not get the word go from S. B. soon we may find ourselves beaten there too'.[40] Bryant thus began his letter to Baldwin with a plea, stated that 'Only you can help save the National Book Association', and, in effect, pressed the soon-to-retire Prime Minister to take up the club's Presidency.[41] Bryant's attack on the RBC, its supporters, and its lack of political purpose were in this respect part of his attempt to convince Baldwin that only the NBA possessed a clearly thought-out political strategy that was worthy of his endorsement. But although the strength and bitter tone of his criticisms may have been indicative of Bryant's personal irritation with the RBC, and of his desperation to gain Baldwin's public support, he also presented a closely reasoned case for the NBA's superior political utility. When the idea of a Conservative book club was first mooted in the summer of 1936, Sir Geoffrey Ellis had warned that it would have to be kept at arm's length from the party apparatus. He told Bryant:

From what I know of the C[entral] O[ffice] I have a certainty in my mind that they will produce just the potted 'one side of the question' which can be used as quick-firing fodder by the lazy minds of our political supporters. They and we appeal to two totally different types of mind . . . We are trying honestly to educate not only our own people (most of whom are so static and sub-consciously frightened that they will never vote anything but 'agin Socialism' but the large & indeterminate (& increasing) mass which honestly does demand reason (rather than dogmas) for how they are to order their lives & cast their votes.[42]

The 'we' Ellis referred to here was Ashridge, for both he and Bryant clearly viewed the college's educative role as being primarily but not wholly concerned with preaching to the converted. Likewise, they viewed the proper role of a Conservative book club as being to reach out beyond the party faithful. In May 1938 Bryant summed up the general philosophy. He declared that the purpose of the NBA and associated Ashridge publishing ventures 'was to combat the growing tendency in political, academic and educational literature to represent Left Wing propaganda as if it were an expression of middle opinion, and to ignore altogether facts and opinions that defend the traditionalist point of view'. He added that: 'Nothing that has happened in the last two years has diminished the necessity for the publication and circulation of popular political and educational books and current affairs. The Right Book Club, though it possesses a large circulation, has no effect whatever outside Conservative circles; its books are ipso facto labelled propaganda and Right.' Bryant felt that the LBC also faced this problem, insofar as it was self-evidently

[40] Bryant to Sir Geoffrey Ellis, 23 Apr. 1937, ibid., C44.
[41] Bryant to Baldwin 5 May 1937, ibid., C49.
[42] Sir G. Ellis to Bryant, 10 June 1936, ibid., C44.

associated with the Left, but that it had proved less of a difficulty for them in relation to the dissemination of Leftist opinion, because 'the printing presses of the country as a whole are turning out literature . . . [which is] overwhelmingly in favour of the Left'. This was true, he argued, even if the literature produced was not openly, or pretended not to be, Left-leaning, as was the case with Penguin and Pelican books.[43] In short, the secret for a Conservative book club, if it was to be a long-term political and publishing success, was for it to have a not-overtly Conservative identity. In October 1937 Bryant told Geoffrey Ellis that:

Ever since the Spring of 1936, in what to-day has become the National Book Association . . . we would greatly value all the co-operation and help we can receive from the Conservative Education Committee . . . But it must be frankly recognised that, both on account of Lord Baldwin's insistence on the widest possible appeal for our venture, and on the score that literature, unlike propaganda, cannot be rigidly partisan, that certain of our books will not be representative of the strictly party point of view.[44]

It was for precisely this reason that Bryant resisted suggestions from R. A. Butler that the Conservative Education Committee be merged with the Ashridge Fellowship. The whole point of the 'non-party' nature of the Fellowship, Bryant argued, was 'to draw into our net those whom the Party Organisation cannot send us'. The party, he pointed out, sent only one-third of the students that attended Ashridge, which indicated that the college attracted 'new apostles'.[45] If Ashridge was wholly identified with the party organization it would, Bryant suggested, be regarded simply as a propaganda machine and 'Nobody would come to . . . lectures except those who were already fully converted, and we should cease to make any appeal to the Centre which at present constitutes our main support and whose unconscious conversion by our educational methods is our main contribution to the Conservative cause'.[46] The political education role envisaged for the NBA was the same, namely, to provide literature which, through its balanced and *therefore* quietly Conservative nature would draw more 'unconscios converts' to Conservatism.

This desire on the part of Bryant and the NBA to pursue a political aim 'unpolitically' might seem strange, but it made perfect sense to them, and indeed fitted well with important aspects of the Conservative political culture of the inter-war years. The underlying reasoning was made clear by Bryant in the spring of 1937, when there was, briefly, talk

---

[43] Bryant, 'Notes on Mr. Graham's Confidential Memorandum of 20 May 1938', n.d. (May 1928), ibid., C49. (Graham was Secretary of the NBA.)
[44] Bryant to Ellis, 20 Oct. 1937, ibid., C44.   [45] Ibid.
[46] Ibid.

of the NBA merging with the RBC. Bryant thought a merger a good idea, provided it could be achieved 'on our own political terms'. It would, he argued, 'avoid wasteful competition, which we can ill afford in the face of a powerful enemy, strengthen our hands in dealing with any further attempts on the part of other groups to found political book clubs, and end a great deal of confusion among our own followers'.[47] But he had strong reservations. Bryant admitted that the RBC had, 'by vigorous propaganda … stolen a march on the National Book Association', and had a much larger membership.[48] But he felt that this was largely due to the fact that the RBC was 'unhampered either by the need of providing books or of studying political susceptibilities'.[49] These were, he suggested, helpful in terms of short-term commercial success, which suited the founders of the RBC, given that 'Mr. and Miss Foyle admitted … that they had founded the Right Book Club as a literary and bookselling venture rather than for any long term political and educational purpose'.[50] For the latter purpose, however, which the NBA wished to achieve, more consideration and, paradoxically, 'some proper political control'[51] was deemed essential. What Bryant meant by this was made clear in the principles he laid down to 'govern our terms for amalgamation'.[52]

To begin with, Bryant regarded it as essential to establish that

> our main business for the present is not so much to select books furthering political and educational aims as to get them written and published. Owing to the long predominance of the Left in the intellectual world, there are very few books of our kind being written: those that are mostly emanate from a small group of clever Catholic propagandists of the extreme Right, whose writings it would be almost impossible to popularise in a Protestant country.

He further insisted that the only way to run a book club effectively was along business lines in association with an established publisher, and that this meant cementing the agreement he had reached with Hutchinsons. He was also clear that any amalgamation should 'make it possible to obtain the general support of, and publish books by all (whether Right, Centre or Left) who are opposed to the principles of revolutionary dictatorship now being advocated so arrogantly by the Left Book Club [and] Retain the active backing of the Conservative Party Organization and the Ashridge Fellowship'. This, Bryant argued, required that 'Mr. Baldwin's name should be secured as President as

---

[47] Bryant, 'Memo: On Suggested Proposal for Amalgamation of the Right Book Club with the National Book Association, 29 Apr. 1937', ibid., C49.

[48] The RBC was reported as having 10,000 members while the NBA had 'no more than 2,000', ibid.

[49] Ibid.   [50] Ibid.   [51] Ibid.   [52] Ibid.

soon as possible with the support of one or two other non-party names of great standing such as that of G. M. Trevelyan'. It was, he felt, also necessary that 'The name of Right Book Club, which is likely to antagonise academic and university opinion, should be dropped or merged'. He suggested that it 'might be best to choose a name embodying the ideal of the defence of Freedom, which is likely to be the common ground on which all who dislike the propaganda of the Left Book Club will join hands'. Bryant concluded that,

Though it does not matter how diverse in opinion those whose names appear as members of its Council may be, the executive direction of the Association politically must remain as at present in the hands of those who have experience both of politics and political education and who are united as to what they wish to achieve . . . [and that] as the business of the Association is to get the right kind of books written and to give them a common purpose, it is vital that the publication should be supervised by a common Editor.[53]

Bryant's thoughts on a possible merger between the NBA and RBC provide valuable insights into his plan of campaign in the 'battle of the books'. He clearly had a strong personal investment in the subject, most notably when he suggested that one person who could be considered for the position of 'common Editor' of books to be produced by the merged clubs was himself.[54] But even such personal considerations were informed by a broader political agenda. Bryant viewed the RBC's list as too inchoate to provide readers with a clear political message, with such books as Clarence Street's *Union Now* serving only to sustain criticism of the Conservative government's foreign policy.[55] Closer editorial control was to ensure greater thematic unity and a clearer sense of political direction. But this political direction was to be made evident by the subject-matter of the books rather than by open political statements and allegiance. This was why Bryant wished to remove the 'Right' label from any merged organization, and for precisely the same reason he was keen that the NBA, when it experienced financial difficuilties in 1938, and requested financial assistance from Ashridge, should not change its name to the Ashridge Book Association because the College was too closely associated with the Conservative party.[56] Bryant's choice of the 'National' label for the NBA reflected a desire to present the club as an organization which could appeal to all groups and interests in the country, the underlying assumption being that Conservatism and the

---

[53] Bryant, 'Memo: On Suggested Proposal for Amalgamation of the Right Book Club with the National Book Association, 29 Apr. 1937', ibid., C49.
[54] Ibid.   [55] Ibid.
[56] Bryant, 'Notes on Mr. Graham's Confidential Memorandum of 20 May 1938', n.d. (May 1928), ibid., C49.

Conservative party were the best expression of national as opposed to sectional interests and values.[57] This was also the main reason why Baldwin was Bryant's choice for President of the NBA. An important part of Baldwin's political persona, as Bryant himself outlined in his own NBA book about the Conservative leader in 1937, was that he was somehow 'above politics' and had cross-party, cross-class, and cross-sectoral appeal. Neville Chamberlain told his sister that Baldwin 'holds the mugwumps and the clericals and the conscientious, earnest, theoretical liberals as no one else in any party can', and this was precisely the kind of appeal Bryant and his colleagues wished the NBA to have, that is, to all those, of Right, Centre, and Left, who opposed attempts to subvert the 'national' interest. As Bryant explained to the NBA's Secretary: 'Our work has to be of a very different kind from that of the other Book Clubs, for if we are to receive the support from the Centre and the Left centre which we can hope for, we must proceed very cautiously and refrain scrupulously both from propaganda and the showier kind of advertising.'[58] The chief concern here was not to alienate that 'middle opinion' which had grown exasperated by attempts of the LBC and other Left sympathizers to pass themselves off as representative of the middle ground.[59] Such middle opinion was not regarded by Bryant as Political, except insofar as it equated politics with extreme or over-strongly voiced opinions. Baldwin, with his deliberately consensual, moderate approach, embodied the kind of unpolitical politics which was thought to appeal to this particular middle opinion, and it was this appeal that Bryant wished the NBA to replicate. Having Baldwin as NBA President would, Bryant argued, 'Serve the double purpose of keeping the Conservative interest behind us and of realigning the intelligent centre and Liberal opinion we're out to capture. No other name could achieve this double role.'[60] Ironically, it was a clumsy attempt at political 'even-handedness' by the NBA that drove Baldwin to resign as its President in the spring of 1939. In February that year the NBA published as its book of the month an English translation of *Mein Kampf*. The choice of the book was 'the unanimous one of the NBA Committee', who chose it, according to Bryant, 'not because they agreed with it, but because it was a work which every political student would naturally want to read'.[61] Bryant justified the choice in his editorial note

---

[57] For this common inter-war Conservative assertion see McKibbin, 'Class and Conventional Wisdom'.
[58] Bryant, Memorandum to T. N. Graham, n.d. (Feb. 1938), ibid., C47.
[59] Bryant, 'Notes on Mr. Graham's Confidential Memorandum of 20 May 1938', n.d (May 1938), ibid., C49.
[60] Bryant to W. Hutchinson, 24 June 1937, ibid., C49.
[61] Bryant to G. Fry, 14 Feb. 1939, ibid., C62.

on the grounds that people should be given the same chance of reading Hitler as Rousseau and Marx, and also warned readers of the book's 'intolerable attack on Jewry'.[62] That the NBA had published the old Bolshevik Victor Serge's memoirs[63] and, in December 1938, a collection of Neville Chamberlain's speeches, *In Search of Peace*, appeared to lend some credibility to Bryant's claim that the club sought political 'balance'. However, it is also the case that the decision to publish *Mein Kampf* reflected Bryant's own strong pro-German, and indeed pro-Nazi, sympathies.[64] Bryant, like many on the Right, was a strong supporter of Appeasement, and NBA publications, such as his own *Humanity in Politics*, W. J. Blyton's *Arrows of Desire*, the collection of Chamberlain's speeches, and *Mein Kampf* itself were designed to support and proselytize the case for Anglo-German rapprochement. In this respect the NBA, and Bryant in particular, carried the case for Appeasement further and for longer than most, and Bryant himself visited Germany under the aegis of the Berlin-sponsored German–English Friendship Society as late as July 1939. The actions of Bryant and the NBA in 1938–9 were at best naive and at worst deeply suspect, a point which Bryant himself acknowledged thirty years later, when he wrote to the then Prime Minister's office expressing concern about the pending release of PRO documents dealing with his German visit, on the grounds that they might present his actions as foolish and unpatriotic.[65]

The NBA's publication of *Mein Kampf* has biographical significance in Bryant's case, but it also opens a window on a range of aspects and connections in the political subculture of the Conservative book clubs of the 1930s. The pro-Appeasement, pro-German, and pro-Nazi tenor of much of the NBA's activities had many overlaps with the position espoused by denizens of the RBC. For example, in his *Why Britain Prospers* William Teeling praised the labour camps he had seen on a visit to Nazi Germany, and noted that most of the inmates had 'gained in health'.[66] He also stated that the Nazis provided an excellent training in leadership, and noted: 'as against this, what are our Conservatives doing in this country to develop our political leaders of tomorrow?'[67] Teeling's view of German labour camps was shared by Philip Gibbs, who suggested in his *Ordeal in England* that the young men 'loafing'

---

[62] Bryant, MS of Editorial Note to *Mein Kampf*, n.d. (Jan.? 1939), ibid., C44.

[63] That Serge had been purged by Stalin somewhat complicated the political meaning here.

[64] See A. Roberts, 'Patriotism: The Last Refuge of Sir Arthur Bryant', in id., *Eminent Churchillians* (1994), esp. 295–307, and see below.

[65] Bryant to J. Hewitt, 28 Nov. 1968, ibid., H1. The papers were, probably as a consequence of Bryant's concern, reclassified, and were only released in 1989. For this reclassification see Roberts, 'Patriotism', 302.

[66] Teeling, *Prospers*, 57, 58–67.

[67] Ibid. 111.

outside labour exchanges in Britain 'should be rounded up, and put in labour camps, willy nilly, for at least a year's service instead of being allowed to drift into vice and demoralisation'.[68] The Nuremburg Rallies were also much admired by RBC authors, with Teeling and Sir Arnold Wilson seeing them as the embodiment of a nation reborn through strong leadership and patriotic fervour.[69] Wilson's *Thoughts and Talks*, which expressed admiration for Fascist Italy as well as Nazi Germany, was reviewed positively by Bryant, who saw Wilson as having rightly praised the dictators who had 'restored their native countries ... to some measure of order, common decency and self-respect', and having been wrongly criticized by 'petulant, shrill-voiced, mean-tempered men' who wished to sour relations with those countries.[70] This admiration for Hitler's Germany and Mussolini's Italy underpinned the commitment of both the NBA and the RBC to Appeasement. In a radio broadcast soon after the Munich Agreement, Neville Chamberlain declared that it was wrong for Britain to contemplate going to war 'because of a quarrel in a far-away country between people of whom we know nothing'. His sentiments were echoed, with an additional political edge, by Philip Gibbs, who asked: 'Are we to complete our ruin by bloody adventures on behalf of Russia or Czechs? The answer, I believe in the minds of the English people, outside the range of the Left Book Club, is very definitely: No!'[71] The British Left, Gibbs argued, were blinkered by their hatred of Nazism to the point where they were willing to risk war and jeopardize Britain's true interests, whereas the Chamberlain government's foreign policy was wholly in keeping with both the British tradition of moderation and tolerance in foreign affairs and immediate British interests.[72] William Teeling specified the rationale here when he argued that peace in Europe was the key to the protection of British interests, 'else we may lose what is far more valuable to us in the Far East',[73] while Francis Yeats-Brown provided further general support for Appeasement as the safest path in *The European Jungle*.[74] These were exactly the kind of arguments deployed by Bryant in a letter to Chamberlain in late September 1938, in which he expressed strong support for the Prime Minister's policy and dismissed any criticism as simply the product of 'organs of public opinion ... controlled by the publicists of the Left and the little noisy minority of the extreme Right'.[75]

[68] Gibbs, *Ordeal*, 417.   [69] Teeling, *Prospers*, 1–4; Wilson, *Thoughts*, 116.
[70] Bryant, review of Sir A. Wilson, *Thoughts and Talks*, *Ashridge Journal* (Mar. 1938), in Roberts, 'Patriotism', 297.   [71] Gibbs, *Ordeal*, 410.
[72] Ibid. 400–9.   [73] Teeling, *Prospers*, 208.
[74] F. Yeats-Brown, *The European Jungle* (1938 RBC edn.).
[75] Bryant to N. Chamberlain, 28 Sept. 1938, ABP, C11.

The close correlation between the views expressed by Bryant and RBC authors was in many respects hardly surprising. Teeling, Gibbs, Yeats-Brown, Wilson, and Charles Petrie, all of whom were strong supporters of Appeasement,[76] were, as noted above, lecturers at Ashridge, and Bryant was in fairly constant contact, and enjoyed cordial relations, with all of them. Nor was this the only connection between the RBC and NBA. Some RBC patrons, most notably Leo Amery, Yeats-Brown, and Lord Halifax, were also subscribers to the NBA, and two RBC authors, Cuthbert Alport and Reginald Northam, had offered their books to the NBA, and had been turned down and pointed towards the RBC by Bryant.[77] Although the NBA, and Bryant in particular, expressed considerable anger and frustration at the RBC's activities and even its very existence, the fact was that the two book clubs had important overlaps in terms of shared personnel. Furthermore, the political assumptions that underpinned both organizations were similar, and a number of common themes informed the outlook of the organizers of both clubs and the works they produced. Support for the Conservative-dominated National Government in general terms, and for its foreign policy in particular, were obvious correlations, but there were others. The idea of the Conservative party as the best expression of English national identity,[78] and the equation of that identity with the country-side and rural life, were marked features of both the NBA and RBC *Weltanschauungen*. In Bryant's *English Saga*, published in 1940, England's past was presented in terms of a pastoral idyll which, in the Middle Ages especially, had produced a social cohesion and social order based on a sense of community and reciprocal relations between the responsibilities and duties of the higher and lower orders.[79] For Bryant and other Conservative writers this idyll had been largely destroyed by nineteenth-century industrialization, urbanization, and the attendant philosophy of laissez-faire individualism. Reginald Northam felt that the manorial system had been replaced by a fractured urban life in which class divisions were a characteristic feature, with the result that 'the squire sleeps with his fathers'.[80] Sir Arnold Wilson also saw the freeborn Englishman as having been transformed into a 'city-bred

---

[76] For Petrie's position see his *The Chamberlain Tradition* (1938 RBC edn.), 268–70.

[77] Bryant to R. Northam, 11 Aug. 1938, ABP, C46. See also Bryant to H. Newts, 7 Sept. 1938, suggesting that he publish a book with the RBC, and L. Dickson to Bryant, 31 July 1938, requesting that the NBA, like the RBC, publish an edition of Petrie's *The Chamberlain Tradition*, ibid.

[78] The emphasis here was very much on *English* rather than British.

[79] Bryant, *English Saga* (1940), *passim*.

[80] R. Northam, *Conservatism: The Only Way* (1938 RBC edn.), 79–81, 77. Bryant had wished the NBA to publish Northam's book, but had been overruled by Hutchinsons after an adverse reader's report. See Bryant to Northam, 11 Aug. 1938, ABP, C46.

slave',[81] and Philip Gibbs demanded that England should not be judged 'by the monstrous ant-heap called London ... [but by] the English countryside where life goes on traditionally in old farmsteads and small villages'.[82] There were echoes in these hymns to England's rural past of the English Mistery, a Conservative fringe movement of the early 1930s which had advocated the restoration of the feudal system as a solution to Britain's social and political problems.[83] Moreover, Bryant himself organized numerous pageants under the aegis of Ashridge in order to present the spectacle of these past glories to the public. The rural past, 'Merrie England', and myths of a stable, hierarchical social order untroubled by class conflict were leitmotifs in the subculture of inter-war Conservatism, and the Conservative book clubs reflected this.[84]

One reason for the prevalence of these eulogies to, or perhaps elegies for, rural life and the rural past was that the essence of country life was deemed to be simpler, not only physically but also intellectually and morally. Intellectual simplicity, or at any rate the *appearance* of such simplicity, was greatly valued by many Conservatives and Conservative thinkers. Stanley Baldwin expressed this outlook very well when, in January 1938, he wrote to Arthur Bryant to thank him for sending a copy of his latest book. Baldwin told his friend that he had greatly enjoyed the book, and then added 'I never regarded you as an intellectual! When you have got over the shock you may realise that that is the very nicest thing I could say of you.'[85] Baldwin, of course, had deliberately cultivated the image of himself as a simple countryman during his time as leader of the Conservative party, and had famously stated in his speech 'On England' that, 'To me, England is the country, and the country is England', and had described the 'sounds of England' as 'the tinkle of the hammer on the anvil in the country smithy, the corncrake on a dewy morning, the sound of the scythe against the whetstone, and the sight of a plough team coming over the brow of a hill'.[86] In the same speech he had also noted that, although the English were 'less open to the intellectual sense than the Latin races', there was 'hardly any line in

---

[81] Wilson, *Thoughts*, 18.

[82] Gibbs, *Ordeal*, 421.

[83] For the English Mistery see Webber, *British Right*, 42, 61. Anthony Ludovici, a member of the Selection Committee of the RBC, was a leading figure in the English Mistery. Ludovici's book *A Defence of Conservatism* (1927) was a sustained plea for the restoration of aristocratic governance and 'the arrest of urbanisation, and the encouragement and development of agriculture', *passim*, and 227.

[84] This subculture is of course a particular aspect of the broader 'pastoral' theme discussed in M. Wiener, *English Culture and the Decline of the Industrial Spirit* (Cambridge, 1981). However, Wiener does not address the party-political aspects of the question.

[85] Baldwin to Bryant, 19 Jan. 1938, ABP, C62.

[86] Baldwin at the Hotel Cecil, London, 6 May 1924, in S. Baldwin, *On England and Other Addresses* (London 1926), 7.

which the nation has not produced geniuses'.[87] Baldwin saw the 'English genius' as being a talent for quiet, even serene, contemplation and wisdom which was no less profound than the more ostentatiously cerebral thought produced and valued by 'Latin' minds.[88] Bryant recognized and shared Baldwin's position, and in his NBA book on Baldwin described how the Conservative leader had triumphed over the 'clever men who sneered at him'.[89] Smart 'cleverness' of an openly Intellectual nature, as Iain Macleod and Enoch Powell were to discover, was not regarded as an advantage in Conservative circles, and it was precisely this kind of thought and this impression which both the NBA and the RBC sought to avoid. Here their position chimed, perhaps somewhat surprisingly, but nevertheless gratifyingly, with at least one noted Liberal thinker's concerns. Writing to Bryant in late 1938, Ernest Barker stated:

I am bothered to-day by the abstract intellectualism of them with whom I used to associate, and by the conventional lip service to phrases in my old party—the Liberal party. I admit more and more the practical wisdom of the good ordinary Englishmen, facing the facts and 'feeling' the right way through them—as a countryman feels his way through the countryside.[90]

The 'little intellectuals of the Left'[91] who produced books for the LBC epitomized everything that the organizers of the book clubs of the Right despised. Such intellectual thinkers and writers were the reason the Labour party and organized labour had fallen under the spell of Socialist *ideology*, whereas Conservatives possessed simple principles and a 'spirit'.[92] Books were crucial in helping to articulate and reinforce these principles and this spirit, but *bookishness* was another matter. Abstract ideas and logic were suspect because they were just that, and as such were removed from the British, and especially English, preference for inductive as opposed to deductive reasoning, or the wisdom of experience as opposed to mere reason.

This distrust of bookishness and 'high-falutin' intellect was an intrinsic part of the ethos of the Conservative book clubs. The organizers of the NBA and RBC, and most of the authors whose books they published, were 'thinkers', but, largely for reasons of political identity, they would not have described themselves as intellectuals. Equally

[87] S. Baldwin, *On England and Other Addresses* (London 1926), 2–3.

[88] For Baldwin's political ideas and values see P. Williamson, 'The Doctrinal Politics of Stanley Baldwin', in M. Bentley (ed.), *Public and Private Doctrine* (Cambridge, 1993), and id., *Stanley Baldwin* (Cambridge, 1999).

[89] Bryant, *Baldwin*, 88.

[90] E. Barker to Bryant, 7 Oct. 1938, ABP, E1.

[91] Gibbs, *Ordeal*, 230.

[92] See Bryant, *Spirit*, *passim*, and Northam, *Conservatism*, 39–40.

important, the audience they saw themselves as appealing to were thought to be the kind of people who were instinctively suspicious of intellectuals. The secretary of Hutchinsons, writing to Bryant in March 1938 to discuss advertising strategy, noted that advertisements in *The Times* had produced far fewer responses than those in the *Daily Telegraph*. The reason for this, he suggested, was that '*The Times* class of reader is not interested in book clubs. [But] The *Daily Telegraph* public is the lower middle class and slightly upwards, where it is obvious we shall find most of our supporters.'[93] As a consequence of their desire to play down their own status as 'men of ideas',[94] and the nature of the audience they sought to address, the NBA and RBC were self-consciously and unashamedly middlebrow. Highbrow was 'Bloomsbury', the literature and politics of the Left and the metropolitan cultural elite, as expressed in the novels of Virginia Woolf and the 'dreary high-brow articles' of the *Spectator* and *New Statesmen*.[95] Middlebrow was the novels of Hugh Walpole, James Hilton, John Buchan, and the like, which expressed the social and moral values of certitude and simplicity that embodied what came to be known as 'middle England'.[96] It was also the politics of Baldwin and Neville Chamberlain, with their moderate, practical, and steadfast resistance to the ideological advocates of change on the Left. The NBA and RBC provided, in subtly different but crucially similar ways, a corpus of literature which offered support for and affirmation of the Conservative cause.

Neither the NBA nor the RBC could lay claim to a mass membership. In May 1939 the NBA had 5,000 subscribers, which, in the view of their publishers, was cause for quiet celebration,[97] although this raising of glasses may have been due to the fact that in the previous year membership had been at 3,500 and subscription renewals had been dropping.[98] In April 1937 the *Observer* claimed that the RBC had a membership of 10,000, but Arthur Bryant felt that the true figure was closer to 5,000.[99] Bryant had his own reasons for playing down the number of RBC subscribers, and documentary evidence confirming either the *Observer*'s

---

[93] F. Heath to Bryant, 4 Mar. 1938, ABP, C47.

[94] An interesting aspect of the Conservative book clubs is that they were almost exclusively *men* of ideas: the NBA and RBC published very little work by women authors.

[95] F. Yeats-Brown to Bryant, 26 May 1939, ABP, C39.

[96] See R. M. Bracco, *Merchants of Hope: British Middlebrow Writers and the First World War, 1919–39* (Oxford, 1993), passim, and also A. Light, *Forever England: Femininity, Literature and Conservatism Between the Wars* (1991).

[97] W. Hutchinson to Sir G. Ellis, 15 May 1939, ABP, C44.

[98] T. N. Graham, 'Memo. On Present Position With Suggestions for Reconstruction', 20 May 1938, ibid., C47.

[99] Bryant, 'Memo: On Suggested Proposals', ibid., C49.

or Bryant's estimate does not appear to have survived. However, even if one simply accepts the *Observer*'s figure, that means that total NBA and RBC membership was only 15,000, whereas in 1936 the LBC had a membership of 50,000, and on this basis the Right lost the 1930s 'battle of the books'. That it comprehensively won the war for electoral supremacy was doubtless some compensation, but the fact that Conservatives spent such thought, time, effort, and money[100] on book clubs is an intriguing aspect of 1930s Conservative activity.

The Conservative party's engagement with the book club projects was clear, but was hardly straightforwardly enthusiastic. The NBA emerged out of the Conservatives' main political education forum, Ashridge, which consistently supported the NBA throughout its existence,[101] and five Conservative MPs were on the NBA Advisory Committee.[102] Members of the party hierarchy, most notably Baldwin and Chamberlain, gave it their support,[103] and some other leading Conservatives, such as Leo Amery, Oliver Lyttelton, and Ralph Assheton, were individual subscribers.[104] However, only five Conservative constituency associations are on a 1939 list of subscribers, and in May 1938 Bryant complained that 'we [the NBA] do not possess the wholehearted support of the Conservative Party organisation, and if we had it the National Book Association would be an assured success'.[105] In this context the NBA's 'unpolitical' strategy hampered its commercial prospects, in that full backing from both CCO and local Conservative associations would have given the NBA privileged access to a sizeable market of potential subscribers. But, whatever the reason, the NBA did not gain any substantial benefit from the Conservative party's mass membership. Rather, the benefits it gained were from the close relations its organizers enjoyed with the party hierarchy and the central Conservative political education machinery. Even in this context the NBA did not enjoy an entirely smooth ride. As noted above, the NBA's 'rival', the RBC, also attracted the support of some members of the party hierarchy, and, much to Bryant's annoyance, the Principal of Ashridge, General Hoskins, briefly served as a patron of the RBC.[106] Whilst the party hierarchy clearly agreed that a Conservative book club to counter the LBC was a good idea, and were predisposed to favour the

---

[100] In 1938 the NBA made a net loss of £4,360 8s. 4d. NBA Profit and Loss Account 1 Jan.–31 Dec. 1938, ibid., C51. Due to these losses the NBA sought support from Ashridge.
[101] Bryant, 'Notes on Mr. Graham's Confidential Memorandum, 20 May 1938', ibid., C49.
[102] Bryant to W. Hutchinson, 24 June 1937, ibid.
[103] Baldwin through acting as NBA President and Chamberlain through publishing his speeches with the NBA.
[104] See the list of NBA subscribers, n.d. (1939), ABP, C49.
[105] Bryant, 'Notes on Mr. Graham's Confidential Memorandum, 20 May 1938', ibid.
[106] See Bryant's reference to 'the General's unfortunate mistake', ibid.

NBA once it came into existence, there was evidently some confusion as to the best means of achieving the basic end. Nor was confusion confined to the party hierarchy. The NBA Secretary received a letter from one Scottish Conservative who stated that she was an RBC subscriber and had been using RBC books as a personal lending library for propaganda purposes in her constituency. She said that she had assumed the RBC was working with CCO, and had been surprised to discover the existence of the NBA and to find that its claims to 'official' status were much stronger, and still more surprised to find that amongst the founder members of the NBA were fourteen patrons of the RBC.[107] As Bryant had feared, the Scottish Tory member found the apparent duplication and division of effort as indicative of an 'utter lack of cohesion within the party'.[108] Conservatives saw the 'battle of the books' as an important, even essential, part of the struggle against Socialism, but it was one which generated tension and confusion within the Conservative ranks.

The outbreak of the Second World War saw both the NBA and RBC cease activity. In this respect the 'battle of the books' was a period-specific phenomenon, for, like the RBC and NBA, the LBC's existence also ended with the war. But some of the personnel involved in the Conservative campaign in the battle of the books, along with their concerns and ideas, continued to play a role in Conservative politics during and after the war. Bryant continued his connection with Ashridge until it was taken under CCO control in 1954, and he remained deeply involved in Conservative politics. In the early 1960s he played an important role as a propagandist for the campaign against British entry into the EEC,[109] and he retained close links with the Conservative hierarchy, especially Margaret Thatcher,[110] until his death. Two RBC authors, who also had close contact with the NBA, went on to play interesting roles in post-war Conservative politics. Reginald Northam, whom Bryant had advised to publish with the RBC, became the first principal of Swinton College, the successor institution to Ashridge as the centre for Conservative political education. Cuthbert 'Cub' Alport, one of a number of Ashridge lecturers who published with the RBC, is best remembered as a founding member of the One Nation group of Conservative MPs, which saw its key task as being to design a distinctive Conservative approach to social questions and counter the

---

[107] E. D. Coates to NBA, 30 Jan. 1939, ibid., C47.
[108] Ibid.
[109] For Bryant's role in the anti-EEC campaign see R. F. Dewey, 'British National Identity and the First Application to Europe', unpublished Oxford University D.Phil. thesis (2001).
[110] See Bryant's correspondence with Thatcher, ABP, E64.

notion of a Socialist monopoly on ideas of social reform.[111] But he was also the first Director of the Conservative Political Centre (CPC), which was set up in 1945, and which, in the words of R. A. Butler, was designed to be 'a kind of Conservative Fabian Society which would act as a mouthpiece for our best modern thought'.[112] If the CPC was to counter Socialism by learning from the Fabian model, so too the CPC bookshops established in 1946 were specifically designed, by Alport, to imitate the pre-war LBC's activities.[113] The battle of the books may have ended, but the war of ideas continued, and themes and strategies from pre-war engagements still had resonance as the post-war Conservative party sought to regroup.

[111] For One Nation see below, pp. 247–9. For Alport's role see M. Garnett, *Alport* (1999), 997–120.
[112] R. A. Butler, *The Art of the Possible* (1982), 136–7.
[113] Ibid. 74.

CHAPTER 6

Searching For the Middle Way: The Political Economy of Harold Macmillan

HAROLD MACMILLAN was the most self-consciously intellectual Conservative leader of the twentieth century. In spite of the fact that the Great War ended his undergraduate studies at Oxford, or perhaps because of this, Macmillan displayed a voracious scholarly appetite for books throughout his active political career. His diary for the period from the end of the Second World War to his resignation as Prime Minister in the autumn of 1963 shows he read an extraordinary range of literary, historical, and political works, and on this basis alone Macmillan has good claims to being the most 'bookish' Prime Minister since Gladstone. But Macmillan's intellectual activities were not confined to reading. Leaving aside the six volumes of memoirs he published in retirement, he wrote three books on economic questions, was joint author of three more, and made a major contribution to another in the inter-war years.[1] In the 1930s he enjoyed a fruitful exchange with John Maynard Keynes, and in the 1950s engaged, often to the irritation of Treasury officials, in an ongoing correspondence with Keynes's biographer, the Oxford economist Roy Harrod, on questions of economic theory and policy. His official correspondence as both a Minister and Prime Minister was characterized by often lengthy discussions of the underlying principles of policy, and, in the realm of economic policy, theoretical stones were rarely left unturned. Macmillan's approach to problems is encapsulated in an entry in his diary for March 1962—'Luncheon—Sir R. Harrod, Sir Donald Maclachlan, Professor Cairncross, Mr. Prior (Board of Trade) and Tim Bligh. A splendid argument.'[2] For Macmillan, engagement with ideas

---

[1] Macmillan's publications as sole author were *The Next Step* (1932), *Reconstruction* (1933), and *The Middle Way* (1938); as a joint author, *Industry and the State* (1927), *Planning for Employment* (1935), and *Economic Aspects of Defence* (1939). He was a major contributor to *The Next Five Years* (1935).

[2] H. Macmillan, Diary, 9 Mar. 1962, Macmillan papers (hereafter MP), Bodleian Library, Oxford, MS Macmillan Dep. d. 45,

and arguments was clearly a source of great enjoyment, but also an essential part of the policy-making process. The range of his intellectual engagement was wide and, necessarily, so too were his policy interests, but this essay will focus upon the realms of economic ideas and policy which were of particular interest and importance to Macmillan throughout his career.

Economic questions played a central role in the early stages of Macmillan's political career. At the 1923 general election he stood, unsuccessfully, for Stockton-on-Tees as a committed supporter of tariff protection, and, having been elected for the same seat in 1924, made his maiden speech in the House of Commons on the Budget of 1925. The following year, in the wake of the General Strike, he pressed for government reorganization of the coal industry, and argued for the introduction of statutory arbitration procedures to deal with industrial disputes.[3] Underpinning Macmillan's interest in the industrial situation was his concern over unemployment. As MP for Stockton, Macmillan was all too aware of how badly the North-East labour market had been affected by the difficulties faced by the mining, steel, and shipbuilding industries. But although his most immediate and pressing experience of the problem was at a local level, he saw unemployment as a national problem. With the onset of the Slump, unemployment reached unprecedented levels in the North-East and in the rest of Britain's industrial heartlands, and Macmillan's political activities and publications in the 1930s were focused on attempts to define and promote remedies for the depression and mass unemployment. Macmillan's commitment to solving 'this cruel problem of the depressed areas'[4] in the inter-war years was clear. So too was his commitment to preventing its recurrence after the Second World War, for he declared in 1958 that 'I am determined, as far as it lies within human power, never to allow this shadow to fall again upon our country'.[5] The depth of Macmillan's commitment can in part be explained in biographical terms,[6] but this essay will not pursue the question of his personal motivation. Rather, it will focus on the nature and rationale of the policy initiatives he advocated both before and after the war to solve and prevent the return of mass unemployment.

Industrial reorganization was the linchpin of Macmillan's inter-war economic strategy. In 1926 he argued that the government should step in to rationalize the coal industry, on the grounds that it had proved

---

[3] H. Macmillan to *The Times*, 10 Dec. 1926.
[4] Id. *Winds of Change, 1914–39* (1966), 304.
[5] Id. *The Middle Way: Twenty Years After* (1958), 13.
[6] Macmillan's experiences during the Great War appear to have been crucial in shaping his lifelong desire to ease living conditions for the British working class.

incapable of doing so on its own initiative. Macmillan felt that had the industry been reorganized along the lines advocated by the Samuel Commission, the miners' strike of 1925–6 and the General Strike could both have been avoided.[7] In the wake of the General Strike Macmillan, along with three other Conservative MPs, produced a study which argued that the structural problems of the coal industry were not an isolated example, but that organizational weakness was endemic in British industry.[8] To overcome these weaknesses, Macmillan and his co-authors called upon the State to act. State *ownership* of industry was not a favoured solution. Indeed, Macmillan and his colleagues were clear that, generally speaking, 'nationalisation as a substitute for private ownership must fail . . . [and that] except where competition and risk are absent, the results of nationalisation must be inferior to those of private enterprise'.[9] In their view the State's role was not to engage in direct intervention but to create a climate which would encourage industrial reorganization.[10] In particular, they wished the State to facilitate industrial amalgamation. Adjustments to the tax regime were one route to this, and government loans were another. However, the State had to exercise careful control over the destination of any credit made available, on the grounds that it had to be 'granted not for the purpose of adding a new competitor to an industry already sinking under the weight of competition, but for the purpose of assisting all the existing members of the industry to reorganise themselves upon modern and scientific lines'.[11] The models for 'modern' and 'scientific' industrial organization were Germany and the United States, where the economies of scale available to trusts and combinations had secured competitive efficiency.[12] If British industry could adopt similar organizational structures, then it would follow that both firms and their employees would be more secure.

Macmillan remained an advocate of industrial combination throughout the 1930s. In *Reconstruction* he argued that one of the benefits of the introduction of tariffs in 1932 was that they encouraged cartelization. Industries organized on a small-scale, competitive basis were, he suggested, incapable of preventing, and indeed encouraged, over-production, whereas large-scale, corporate structures could regulate the production, supply, and even marketing of goods.[13] Macmillan was keen to stress that tariffs alone could not solve industry's problems, but

[7] Macmillan, *Winds*, 216.
[8] R. Boothby, H. Macmillan, J. Loder, and O. Stanley, *Industry and the State* (1927), *passim*.
[9] Ibid. 133.   [10] Ibid. 35–41.   [11] Ibid. 52–3.
[12] Ibid. 43–6. The British chemical and tobacco industries were also seen as exemplars.
[13] Macmillan, *Reconstruction*, 5–9, 20–1, 73–9, 91–100.

they could assist the crucial process of reorganization. This could only be achieved by industry itself acknowledging the need for and benefits of such restucturing. In Macmillan's schema the role of the State was in many respects limited. He was clear that it was unwise and ultimately impossible for government to reorganize industry; it was 'a task which can only be performed by Industry itself'.[14] The State was to *enable* industry to reorganize, and its key function was to be the creation of a legislative and administrative structure that would allow industries to regulate and reorganize themselves. Each industry was to establish a National Industrial Council (NIC) which would draw up a reorganization plan for its sector and have the power to force firms to act in accordance with that plan. A central National Economic Council, made up of members drawn from each NIC, government representatives, and independent experts, was to provide an overview of the national situation and enable the NICs to co-ordinate their plans.[15] Such co-ordination was deemed essential on the grounds that the experience of the 1920s and the Depression had demonstrated that 'The economic policy of a nation cannot be made up of a conglomeration of policies pursued by separate units of industry commerce or finance operating in isolation from one another'.[16] This system was to bring British industry fully into line with the modern industrial world, in which the 'whole trend of development . . . [was] in the direction of greater integration, and the supercession of unrestrained competition by methods of co-operation'.[17] With older, small-scale 'forms of ownership, management and organisation . . . proved obsolete by the relentless movement of history',[18] British industry needed to adopt the large-scale structure of industrial enterprise pioneered by its main competitors. This would enable it to maximize efficiency and competitiveness, which in turn would ensure that displaced labour could be more rapidly reabsorbed.[19] For Macmillan, industrial reorganization and the efficiencies it would bring were prerequisites for solving the problem of mass unemployment.

In Macmillan's economic strategy the State was assigned an essentially supportive rather than a controlling, managerial role. Over-extending State intervention was, in his view, economically unnecessary, and politically dangerous insofar as it could curtail or restrict freedoms. In *Reconstruction* Macmillan stressed that an important political

---

[14] Macmillan, *Reconstruction*, 32.

[15] For this scheme see ibid., and the Self-Regulation of Industry Bill brought before Parliament in 1934. See also D. Ritschel, 'A Corporatist Economy in Britain? Capitalist Planning for Industrial Self-Government in the 1930s', *EHR* 56 (1991).

[16] Macmillan, *Middle Way*, 176.

[17] Ibid. 172.   [18] Ibid. 174.   [19] Ibid. 69.

consequence of industrial reorganization would be that, 'If . . . industry is so organized that it is capable of intelligent anticipation and response in the market conditions indicated by prices, then . . . bureaucratic methods of regulation will be unnecessary'.[20] Macmillan expressed some scepticism about the efficacy of the price mechanism,[21] but argued that the State should only intervene in areas where existing economic structures had 'failed'. In the industrial sphere direct State intervention was deemed necessary only in those sectors which had proved incapable of reorganizing themselves, such as the coal industry.[22] In *The Middle Way* Macmillan outlined his preference for limiting State action when he spoke of the danger of pressing intervention to combat poverty into other realms of economic activity, stating that, 'upon this argument . . . I wish to base a defence of private enterprise in the production and distribution of a wide range of goods lying outside the field of minimum human needs'.[23] The key phrase was 'minimum human needs', for it was here that Macmillan felt that existing market structures had clearly failed. Hence he declared:

I do not propose to employ this defence of private enterprise in the fields for which it is best suited in order to condone or excuse the poverty and insecurity in the basic necessities of life, which we have today as a legacy of unrestrained competition and uneconomic waste and redundancy. I shall advocate all the more passionately on grounds of morality, social responsibility, as well as economic wisdom a wide extension of social enterprise in the sphere of minimum human needs.

In the sphere of 'social enterprise', as in the industrial sphere, Macmillan advocated the adoption of 'the most economical methods of large-scale, co-operative enterprise', but also concluded that:

The volume of the supply of these necessities, the prices at which they are sold, and the power of the consumer to buy them should not be left to the determination of the push and pull of competitive effort. We have to evolve a new system by which the supply of those articles which we have classified as being of common need and more or less standardized in character, would be absorbed into an amplified conception of the social services.[24]

Such an 'amplified conception' was necessary because the 'satisfaction of those [minimum] needs . . . [was] a duty which society owes to its citizens', and the structures of private enterprise had proved themselves unable of carrying out that duty unaided.

---

[20] Boothby *et al.*, *Industry and the State*, 73.

[21] Macmillan, *Reconstruction*, 16–17.

[22] See id., *Middle Way*, 230, for a description of coal-mining as 'an industry that has long passed out of the phase in which social purposes can best be served by the private profit incentive'.

[23] Ibid. 94.   [24] Ibid. 102–3.

Macmillan felt that the State had a major role to play in the provision of social services, but this did not mean that he drew a hard-and-fast line between 'economic' and 'social' spheres. In his view the two were inextricably linked in terms of both principles and practice. 'Economic reconstruction', he argued in 1938, was 'the only possible or sound basis for social reform.'[25] The simple fact, according to Macmillan, was that 'we can only reduce our social burdens by making the economic system work in a much more efficient way'.[26] Industrial reorganization was thus socially essential in that it would serve to reduce unemployment and the ills attendant upon it. If private enterprise functioned at full efficiency the State could concentrate on social problems, such as ill-health and old age, that private enterprise was not best suited to dealing with. Private enterprise and social enterprise were in this respect complementary. For Macmillan the crucial things were, first, to acknowledge that 'When we look back at history we find that productivity has been increased and the standard of life raised by methods of co-operation, many of them directed by the State',[27] and, second, to draw 'a clear differentiation . . . between the proper sphere of State, social or co-operative activity, and the proper sphere to be deliberately reserved for private enterprise'.[28] The net result of this would be the creation of what Macmillan termed a 'mixed system',[29] in which the State and private enterprise worked alongside each other and the State would rectify the economic and social failures of private enterprise. Such a system was, he argued, already largely in place, inasmuch as examples such as the National Grid, the BBC, health insurance, reorganization of the mining industry, and a plethora of municipal enterprises indicated that the State could undertake certain actions and provide some goods and services where private enterprise had either failed to act or to meet demand.[30] This quasi-partnership between the State and private enterprise lay at the heart of Macmillan's 'middle way' between laissez faire and Socialism, with the State playing an enabling, supportive, and 'hands-off' role except where 'the failure of private enterprise to meet the new demands of a developing society makes it essential for public authorities to step in'.[31]

Industry was not the only sector of the British economy that Macmillan felt was 'failing'. In *Industry and the State* he and his co-authors expressed concern over the lack of co-operation between financial and industrial interests; this concern was shared by other Conservative advocates of industrial reorganization,[32] and lay at the

[25] Ibid. 36.
[28] Ibid. 95.
[31] Ibid. 127.

[26] Ibid. 114–15.
[29] Ibid. 186.

[27] Ibid. 94.
[30] Ibid. 129–57.
[32] See pp. 96–9.

heart of the investigations of the Committee on Finance and Industry chaired by Macmillan's namesake in 1929–30. In the 1930s his own interest in this problem developed considerably. In his 1932 pamphlet *The Next Step* he advocated the creation of an investment and development board made up of a membership drawn from government, industry, and the financial sector. This board was to 'direct investment into the correct channels as advocated by the Macmillan Committee's Report . . . [and] the Federation of British Industry', which meant directing 'new money into capital modernisation' and, if 'unfavourable market conditions discouraged borrowers', engaging in investment activity itself.[33] Keynes read this pamphlet, and told Macmillan that, although he liked it 'very much', he found its 'proposals for developing the investment functions of the State . . . not nearly bold enough'. In Keynes's view the main problem was 'the sort of middle position' Macmillan occupied, which meant that he overestimated the level of private investment that could be encouraged in a depression, and underestimated the extent of direct State investment necessary to reflate the economy and provide a stimulus for private investors.[34] Not for the first or last time, Keynes was sceptical that market actors could be moved without being pushed by both the pressure and example of State action. Macmillan accepted much of Keynes's criticism, and argued that political considerations had led him to moderate his position. 'I am still trying', he explained, 'the perhaps hopeless task of incluencing [*sic*] the Government . . . [and] I have to conceal a certain amount and to preserve certain political decencies!'[35]

Political caution may well have influenced Macmillan, for there were those in his party who viewed State action with suspicion.[36] But whether this explains his stance completely is open to question. That Keynes pointed to Macmillan's 'middle position' as a problem is important here, insofar as for Macmillan finding a 'middle way' was the whole point. Certainly his position changed little through the 1930s. He sat on the committee that drafted *The Next Five Years*, which was clear that 'the existing capital market in Great Britain leaves very much to be desired'.[37] *The Next Five Years* did not advocate State ownership and control of either the Bank of England or the joint-stock banks, but it did call for the creation of a National Investment Board (NIB) to regulate and encourage the capital market. Regulation was to include not only powers against fraud but also to discourage share issues 'of a kind

[33] Macmillan, *Next Step*, 31–2.
[34] J. M. Keynes to Macmillan, 6 June 1932, J. M. Keynes papers (hereafter 'JMKP'), Microfilm Reel 61.
[35] Macmillan to Keynes, 9 June 1932, ibid.
[36] See pp. 98–101, 242–5.   [37] *The Next Five Years*, 116.

which it considered to be already overdone' and to 'encourage issues in directions where further investment seemed to be desirable'.[38] In addition, the NIB was to monitor the volume of savings available for investment and to 'endeavour to see' that they were 'sensibly distributed'.[39] 'Encouragement' meant that the NIB had 'the duty of creating an active and adequate capital market and watching over its development'. This was to include the establishment of a 'domestic issuing house', which would perform the function for home investment that the merchant banks performed for overseas lending, and thereby rectify the institutional bias against domestic lending that characterized the existing British capital market.[40] However, much as it wished the new institution and existing banks and finance houses to invest in the reorganization of old and the creation of new enterprises, *The Next Five Years* also stressed that 'None of these functions can properly be performed by the State'.[41] The State was to act as a 'midwife' not a 'mother', on the assumption that having created the requisite institutional framework investors would want to lend and industrialists borrow. The State could rectify 'defects of the capital market' which had rendered it 'by far the weakest section of the nation's financial machinery',[42] but it was not to replace it.

Whether or not political niceties separated Macmillan from Keynes on the issue of direct State investment, they were certainly not divided when it came to criticism of the British capital market and the British banking system. In his *General Theory* Keynes famously looked forward to the 'euthanasia of the rentier',[43] on the grounds that investment was far too important an activity to be left in the hands of a casino-like financial market. Macmillan shared this disdain. In *The Middle Way* he pointedly remarked that 'Finance is a service. Its function is not, or ought not to be, to dictate or determine the condition under which industry and commerce have to be conducted.'[44] The State, Macmillan contended, needed to exercise a greater influence over the capital market, which was 'dominated by irrational and anti-social speculation in the fluctuating volume of securities'. Credit and investment, he argued, were needed by 'productive industry', but they tended to be used for the 'speculative purchase of existing securities', and, as a consequence, were 'performing no useful social function'.[45] Like Keynes, Macmillan thought that British financial institutions, and the City in particular, needed to change their outlook and their practices and that the State had an important role to play in helping to bring this about.

[38] *The Next Five Years*, 120.   [39] Ibid. 119–20.
[40] Ibid. 120–1.   [41] Ibid. 122.   [42] Ibid. 123.
[43] J. M. Keynes, *The General Theory of Employment, Interest and Money* (1936; 1973 edn.), 376.
[44] Macmillan, *Middle Way*, 194.   [45] Ibid., 257–8.

Criticism of the failings of the British capital market was not the only common ground shared by Macmillan and Keynes. They were also close on the question of government action to reflate the economy. Keynes's favoured solution to the problem of unemployment was large-scale public works, expenditure on which would, through the multiplier effect, trigger a virtuous circle of investment, production, consumption, saving, and reinvestment. Famously—infamously for some—Keynes argued that to achieve this it was necessary for the government to be willing to run a short-to-medium-term budget deficit.[46] Macmillan was sympathetic to this approach. In March 1933 he called for reduced taxation and a boost to government capital expenditure on public works, arguing that these actions would in turn boost business confidence and stimulate private investment. If this resulted in a budget deficit it was, he suggested, acceptable in what was a crisis situation.[47] Macmillan repeated these arguments the following year, and was one of very few Conservatives in the 1930s who was willing to accept deficit finance.[48] But his enthusiasm for budgetary unorthodoxy was by no means unreserved. In 1932 Keynes had chided him for 'paying far too much lip service to [fiscal] economy', and had urged him to embrace greater public expenditure on the grounds that the severity of the Slump demanded a stimulus to purchasing power that private investment was unwilling and unable to bring about.[49] Macmillan's parliamentary intervention the following year seemed to indicate that he had taken Keynes's message to heart, but it is noticeable that *The Middle Way* does not mention unbalanced budgets. Although he agreed that it could have an important reflationary effect, deficit finance was not central to his outlook.[50] Keynes and Macmillan were close insofar as they saw reflation as essential, and felt that the State had to be a key player in any reflationary strategy, but it would be wrong to exaggerate their affinity in the realm of fiscal policy.

[46] The literature on Keynes's response to the Slump is extensive, but see in particular Clarke, *Keynesian Revolution*; id., *The Keynesian Revolution and its Economic Consequence* (Cheltenham, 1998); A. Booth, *British Economic Policy 1931–49: A Keynesian Revolution?* (1989).

[47] Macmillan in Parliament, 22 Mar. 1933, in Macmillan, *Winds of Change*, 367–8.

[48] Another was Macmillan's collaborator on industrial arbiration from the mid-1920s, J. W. Hills. See J. W. Hills, *Managed Money* (1937), 115–17.

[49] Keynes to Macmillan 2 June 1932, JMKP, Microfilm Reel 61.

[50] Of course it was not *central* to Keynes either. *The General Theory* only refers to budget deficits twice, on 98 and 128–30, and the first reference is bound in with Keynes's light-hearted suggestion that the government bury money to stimulate employment digging it up. However, the *General Theory* was a work of *theory*, and in Keynes's works on *policy*, such as *The Means to Prosperity* (1934), deficit finance did play an important role. For a full discussion of the complexities of Keynes's thinking on this question see P. Clarke, 'Keynes, Buchanan and the Balanced Budget Doctrine', in id., *Economic Consequences*, esp. 199–205.

The area in which Macmillan and Keynes were perhaps closest was monetary policy, where both wished to break the 'deflationary mind set'[51] of economic orthodoxy. In *Industry and the State* Macmillan and his co-authors expressed agreement with the quantity theory,[52] but by the late 1930s Macmillan, under Keynes's influence,[53] had modified his position. In the section of *The Middle Way* that dealt with monetary policy, the importance of which Macmillan felt 'could hardly be exaggerated',[54] he argued that the rate of interest was the 'price' which equilibriated the desire to hold wealth in cash with the available quantity of cash, and that 'in given circumstances' the quantity of money *in conjunction with* liquidity preference could determine the rate of interest.[55] Macmillan, like Keynes, was an advocate of 'cheap money', seeing low rates of interest as an important stimulus to borrowing, investment, and consumption. However, he felt that the availability of money did not necessarily lead either to investment or consumption, and that the price level was not, therefore, determined simply by the supply of money. The key thing, in Macmillan's view, was the relationship between the speed and quantity of the production of goods and the expenditure of money upon their production and consumption. Money, he argued, was not necessarily invested or spent but could be saved in 'idle balances' in banks or other institutions. Savings and investment *could* balance, in which case the economy would be at a healthy equilibrium of production and prices, but if they did not then there would be deflation or inflation as either savings exceeded the supply of goods or as investment and consumption outran production. It was here that the institutional structure of the economy had a part to play, insofar as it was 'the function of the financial system to keep money circulating in the purchase of goods and services . . . [and] the function of industry to see that these goods and services are produced'.[56] The State could assist the smooth functioning of the system by fostering the reorganization of the industrial and financial sectors and, if necessary, providing the stimulus of its own investment and expenditure. For Macmillan, like Keynes, markets did not necessarily clear, and prices did not adjust simply in response to variations in the supply of money. Money could have 'real' effects, but these were dependent on other 'real' factors, especially the liquidity preferences and behaviour of individual and institutional holders of capital.

[51] Keynes to Macmillan, 2 June 1932, JMKP, Microfilm Reel 61.
[52] Boothby *et al.*, *Industry and the State*, 95.
[53] For an acknowledgement of his debt to Keynes see Macmillan, *Middle Way*, 247–8.
[54] Ibid. 249.
[55] Ibid. 248 (my emphasis).
[56] Ibid. 246.

The banking system had a particularly important role in Macmillan's analysis, in that it could offer business ventures long-term loans at low rates of interest or place cash in public hands by selling securities, in both cases releasing money which would otherwise have been kept in 'idle' blances or 'hoarded'. This action would stimulate business activity and 'recovery . . . would have been directly initiated as the result of an act of monetary policy'.[57] Once initiated, recovery would increase general business confidence and, as 'confidence begets confidence', a virtuous circle would have been set in motion. To achieve this goal meant, in Macmillan's view, charting a careful path through the 'maze of economic fact and psychological fantasy'.[58] A necessary first step here was the creation of 'a more rational financial mechanism'. Such a mechanism, he argued, required five main elements. First, the accumulation of idle balances was to be prevented. Second, the volume of credit and the quantity of money was to be regulated in accordance with the needs of production rather than being 'dominated by irrational and anti-social speculation in the fluctuating value of securities'. Third, the price of goods was to be determined by the cost of production rather than manipulation of the value of the medium of exchange. Fourth, money was to be a measure of value and medium of exchange and not a store of idle value. Finally, the central bank was to be made a public institution and be in a position to 'influence the *direction* of investment' as well as its volume.[59]

The points of intersection between Keynes and Macmillan on monetary questions were clear. Both were critical of the classical quantity theory of money, and viewed any veracity it held as contingent upon circumstance.[60] Although Macmillan did not enter into extensive theoretical discussion of the relation between savings and investment, and did not address the multiplier effect, his position represented an implicit acceptance of Keynes's arguments. Keynes himself saw Macmillan as a kindred spirit in the fight against 'reactionary forces' opposed to any break from orthodoxy,[61] whilst Macmillan felt Keynes provided the kind of 'expert and informed opinion' required in the Depression.[62] But it was more a general accord than the specifics of theory and policy that drew Macmillan and Keynes towards one another. To begin with they both saw deflation as the main enemy to overcome, and saw the government's predisposition to adopt a deflationary strategy as a political

---

[57] Ibid. 251–2.   [58] Ibid. 256.   [59] Ibid. 256–8.
[60] Neither would have had any difficulty accepting that the quantity theory was applicable in an economy *at full employment equilibrium*. See Macmillan's position in the late 1950s, discussed below and on pp 211–17.
[61] Keynes to Macmillan, 7 Sept. 1932, JMKP, Microfilm Reel 61.
[62] Macmillan to Keynes, 29 Aug. 1932, ibid.

rather than a technical choice. Late in life, Macmillan stated that Keynes had told him that 2.5 per cent inflation was the optimum price situation, which he accepted on the grounds that: 'If you had *deflation* of $2^{1}/_{2}$% a year, ultimately the claims of the creditors become too great (after all, the creditor doesn't create wealth—it's the entrepreneur). If you have permanent *inflation* that's too high, it's not fair to the savers, the creditor, who is normally in the saving classes . . . between $2^{1}/_{2}$ to 3%, then nobody would notice.'[63] Macmillan and Keynes shared a suspicion of, even contempt for, bankers and rentiers, and although they would not have gone so far as to describe inter-war deflationary policy as a 'bankers' ramp', they had no doubts over the financial sector's preferences or the power of their influence.

A related, general point of agreement between Keynes and Macmillan was the importance of 'psychology' in economics. The creation of a climate of confidence was central to their calls for reflationary action and policy. Public expressions of belief by influential economic actors that an economy was picking up, and actions by them commensurate with that belief, were essential to creating a positive interaction between the psychology and reality of recovery. Confidence bred confident actions and vice versa, whilst poor expectations produced poor results. *Expectation*, so prominent a feature of Keynes's work, was also built into Macmillan's argument. It was in many respects in this context that the policy and actions of the State were important, in that the level of government expenditure and influence made it the largest actor in the economy: if government spoke and above all acted in a confident manner this would encourage others to follow suit.

Keynes and Macmillan both saw positive action by the State as essential, with Keynes inveighing in a letter to Macmillan against the reactionaries who 'conscientiously disbelieve in the kind of schemes for planning etc which you and I favour'.[64] But it would be wrong to exaggerate the closeness of their positions on this point. 'Planning' was a lingua franca of the 1930s, but different individuals and groups spoke it with very different accents.[65] For Macmillan, planning involved State action, but his emphasis was upon business planning its own affairs, with the State very much in the background. For Keynes, however, the State had a central role. Moreover, there were differences between the two in terms of the focus of economic policy. In his memoirs, Macmillan noted that 'Keynes quite naturally put the greatest stress on reflation and monetary policy generally. I, for my part, and many agreed with me,

[63] Macmillan, taped interview with A. Horne, in A. Horne, *Macmillan*, 2 vols. (Basingstoke, 1989), ii, 70.
[64] Keynes to Macmillan, 7 Sept. 1932, JMKP, Microfilm Reel 61.
[65] See Ritschel, *Planning, passim*.

felt that this was only one part of the policy; that the efficient organisation of industry, and everything that was involved in the term 'rational-
isation', was just as vital.'[66] In short, Macmillan felt that Keynes's
emphasis was on macro-economics whereas his own was more microeconomic. He was indeed not alone in feeling that Keynes underplayed
the 'supply-side' aspect of the causes of and cures for the Depression,[67]
and this in itself reflected Macmillan's greater faith in and commitment
to encouraging industry and even finance to reorganize and rationalize
the British economy into recovery. Keynes was right when he noted in
1932 that Macmillan wished to 'minimise the part which the state must
play', and sought 'to get . . . results by a combination of private enterprise and subsidy'.[68] Keynes felt that this was unlikely to succeed, and
that only the State possessed the capacity to stimulate recovery.[69]
Macmillan's retrospective judgement was accurate, for although he and
Keynes were close, there were important differences between them.

Prior to the Second World War, Macmillan's economic ideas were
politically unacceptable to the Conservative party, and as a result his
political career was stymied: he had been in Parliament for fifteen years
by the outbreak of war, but had not held even junior ministerial office.
During and after the war, however, his career took off, culminating with
his accession to the Premiership in 1957. Macmillan himself argued that
his ideas did not change, but that the Conservative party was educated
into accepting them, in part by the war but largely by the experience of
electoral defeat in 1945. Broadly speaking, this is an accurate account
of the trajectory of Conservative economic ideas in the immediate post-
war period. The shock of defeat did prompt the Conservatives to
rethink their economic and social policies. Moreover, Macmillan played
a significant role in this process, and found the party unwontedly receptive to his ideas.

Writing in 1969, Macmillan summed up his attitude to the Attlee
government, noting 'I tried to criticise and even attack their policy without abandoning the progressive policies which I had preached in the
past'.[70] In many respects the situation was tailor-made for him.
Organizational defects and the legacy of the 'guilty men' of
Appeasement took some of the blame for the 1945 defeat, but the
prevailing Conservative wisdom was that the 'hungry thirties', the
memory of mass unemployment, and Labour's unequivocal endorsement of the Beveridge Report were chiefly responsible for the

[66] Macmillan, *Winds*, 363–4.
[67] See pp. 76–8 for Sir Arthur-Steel-Maitland's similar position.
[68] Keynes to Macmillan, 2 June 1932, JMKP, Microfilm Reel 61.
[69] Ibid.
[70] H. Macmillan, *Tides of Fortune* (1969), 70.

Conservative debacle. The Conservative quest after 1945, therefore, was to produce a policy stance which would enable them to criticize the Labour government, but at the same time allow Conservatives to differentiate themselves from their own pre-1945 antecedents. *The Industrial Charter* of 1947, which Macmillan helped draw up, was a textual embodiment of this quest. The *Charter* accepted the 1944 White Paper's central argument that 'the government must be responsible for a high and stable level of employment',[71] and stressed that workers should not only have jobs but should also enjoy more respect and status at the workplace in the shape of proper contracts of employment, consultation, and, if possible, co-partnership and profit-sharing schemes.[72] Employment and the need to 'humanise' the workplace had been important elements in *The Middle Way*, which helps to explain why the *Charter* was often referred to at the time as a 'second edition' of Macmillan's book. In his memoirs, Macmillan emphasized that the *Charter* had embraced his pre-war position, in that it accepted full employment and the mixed economy.[73] However, this was a misleading oversimplification of both the *Charter*'s and Macmillan's post-war position. To begin with there is the important fact that the *Charter*, echoing the 1944 White Paper, did not use the term 'full employment', but 'a high and stable level of employment'. The White Paper had been produced in part to 'scoop' Beveridge's book *Full Employment in a Free Society*,[74] and it had studiously avoided using the term 'full employment'.[75] The *Charter* adopted the Treasury's cautious vocabulary and, by implication, its hesitant, even equivocal, stance on employment levels. Macmillan himself had no hesitation in saying in June 1950 that a main duty of government in the economc sphere was 'to maintain "*full* employment" '.[76] He may have equated 'high and stable' with 'full' employment, and if so he was not the only person to do so, either at the time or subsequently, but the two were very different in terms of both their literal and historical meaning. Macmillan argued for, and was not afraid to use the term, 'full employment', but he may have flattered himself that his party accepted his position unequivocally, and was perhaps deceived by Britain's post-war employment record when he came to write his memoirs.

With regard to the mixed economy, Macmillan oversimplified both his party's and his own position in the immediate post-war years. Far from

[71] *The Industrial Charter* (1947), 36.
[72] Ibid. 32–4.
[73] Macmillan, *Tides*, 302–8.
[74] G. C. Peden, *The Treasury* (Oxford, 2000), 354–5.
[75] The White Paper only used the term *once*.
[76] H. Macmillan, 'Principles', 29 June 1950, CPA, CCO 20/1/3 (my emphasis).

'accepting' the mixed economy, *The Industrial Charter* stated in its 'Summary of Proposals', designed as a ready reference for party activists, that 'We are opposed to nationalisation in principle'.[77] In the main body of the text this position was qualified, and the *Charter* declared

We are opposed to nationalisation as a principle upon which all industries should be organised. If all industries were nationalised Britain would become a totalitarian country. If only a few industries are nationalised, they become islands of monopoly and privilege in a diminishing sea of free enterprise . . . Moreover, we consider that the bureaucratic method is highly inefficient when applied to business matters.[78]

Macmillan, who had spoken of his desire to see a 'mixed system' in *The Middle Way*, took an almost identical stance. He agreed with the nationalization of coal and the Bank of England, and saw rail, gas, water, and electricity as effectively in public ownership already, but he strongly opposed further direct State intervention in the economy. In 1946 he argued that the nationalization of 'selected and suitable undertakings' was acceptable, but expressed concern that the Attlee government's ongoing programme indicated 'the totalitarian tendencies of modern Socialism'.[79] In the run-up to the 1950 general election Macmillan stated that full employment and rising living standards were what most citizens wanted from the economy, but that 'these depend in the long run, not on restriction, but on abundance, and abundance comes from enterprise and is fed by freedom'.[80] This emphasis on removing restrictions and allowing 'freedom' was wholly in keeping with the burgeoning Conservative critique of the Labour government's economic controls, which were depicted as the cause of austerity and the growth of an impersonal, interfering bureaucracy. Macmillan's view of the mixed economy was one in which free enterprise and 'personal responsibility'[81] were the predominant features.

There are a number of ways in which Macmillan's position in the immediate post-war period could be explained. Political and electoral considerations were to the fore. He noted that internal party critics of the *Industrial Charter*, such as Sir Waldron Smithers and Sir Herbert Williams, attacked the *Charter* as 'not Tory policy' on the grounds that it was too Statist.[82] Such criticism, Macmillan felt, falsely equated Conservatism with the 'Manchester *laissez faire* school' and nineteenth-century Liberalism. This was in keeping with his long-standing hostility

---

[77] Ibid. 39.   [78] *Charter*, 24–5.

[79] Macmillan at Chatsworth, n.d. (July ? 1946), Macmillan in Parliament, 11. Nov. 1946, in *Tides*, 291, 81.

[80] Macmillan, 'Principles'.

[81] Macmillan, 'The New Crusade', n.d. (June? 1950), CPA CCO 20/1/3.

[82] Macmillan at Church House, Westminster, 14 June 1947, in *Tides*, 306.

to laissez faire, but his broader public attitude to Liberalism was notice-
ably accommodatory. In his memoirs, Macmillan stated that when he
spoke at Chatsworth in 1946 he was conscious of the alliance forged
between the Liberal Unionists and the Conservatives in 1886, and that
this provided a model for the Conservatives to build new alliances with
'those who rejected Socialism but wanted progress'.[83] Here he had the
Liberals in mind, and both his historical and immediate sense of possible links with the Liberals was strengthened when, at the invitation of
Charles Gladstone, he spoke at Hawarden in September 1947.[84]
Macmillan even toyed with the idea of making the Conservative party a
more congenial home for such new allies by changing its name to the
New Democratic party. This last idea was short lived and barely serious,
but it has significance insofar as it indicates that Macmillan saw the key,
common ground between Conservatives and Liberals as the defence of
individual liberties and economic freedom against the threat of Labour's
incipient Socialist 'totalitarianism'. There were faint echoes here of
Churchill's 'Gestapo' speech in the 1945 general election campaign, and
clear harmonies with the Conservative effort to build a 'United Front
Against Socialism' with the National Liberals most particularly and
Liberal opinion in general.[85] In this context it made sense for Macmillan
to play down the more Statist aspect of his middle way, and instead to
emphasize the question of whether 'the *free society* which Conservatives
and Liberals have built up over centuries . . . [is] to be sustained and
strengthened . . . [or] to pass quite rapidly into the full *Socialist State*?'[86]
At the same time, however, he reminded Liberals of their own interventionist past, when he noted that 'The "Welfare State" is the work of a
long line of Liberal and Conservative reformers'.[87] He thereby opened
a route to an argument that the Conservatives offered the best available
defence of economic freedom, whilst at the same time preserving the
positive freedoms first introduced by the social reforms of the New
Liberals.

   Macmillan himself presented his position as wholly consistent with
the one he had held in the inter-war years and expressed most fully in
The Middle Way. His argument was a straightforward version of the

[83] Ibid. 289. Macmillan's historical sense on this subject was in part a result of his own
extensive reading of political history, but was doubtless also informed by the fact that his wife
was the granddaughter of the Liberal Unionist leader and owner of Chatsworth, the 8th Duke
of Devonshire.
[84] Ibid. 308–9.
[85] See pp. 251–4, and for the Conservative appeal to the Liberals see Green, 'Conservative
Party, the State and the Electorate', in Lawrence and Taylor (eds.), *Party, State and Society*; J.
Ramsden, *The Age of Churchill and Eden* (Harlow, 1995).
[86] Macmillan, 'Principles'.
[87] Ibid.

familiar politician's story that his views had not changed, but that circumstances had. His claim was that in order to keep to the middle way one had to correct the over-steer to the Left caused by the Labour government's wrench on the wheel. Writing in 1950, Macmillan argued that in the nineteenth century laissez faire had 'inflated the rights of the individual to the point at which social responsibility for the welfare of all citizens threatened to be ignored'. In post-1945 Britain, he contended, 'The Socialists have inflated the rights of the State to a point at which they [have] threatened the rights of men', with the result that 'In reaction against one extreme, we are in danger of rushing, or of being rushed, towards the other'.[88] On this basis he could claim that he was, as he had been before the war, seeking to devise a 'compromise . . . between the extreme individualism of the early nineteenth century and the totalitarian tendencies of modern Socialism'.[89]

There were clear continuities between Macmillan's pre- and post-war ideas, but there were important differences as well. It would be all too easy to attribute these changes simply to the fact that he faced new circumstances and different political opponents. But the relationship between the new context and subtle shifts in Macmillan's ideas requires close appraisal. The most important change in Macmillan's outlook was a dilution of his views on the role of the State. He had not been a great proponent of State ownership, management, or control of industry, except in those cases where private enterprise had failed to take the necessary steps to organize itself efficiently. However, he had outlined an important role for the State in terms of using its power to construct an institutional environment conducive to enterprise, and to influence and even guide the structure of industry. In this respect the main emphasis of his arguments in the 1920s and 1930s had been on the microeconomic environment. Elements of this were still evident in his post-war ideas. The removal of restrictive practices, whether those of capital or labour, was one theme which recurred in his speeches and writings after 1945, but this in itself marked a shift: before the war he had been anxious to *encourage* cartelization, whereas post-war he sought to 'throw the searchlight of enquiry on all monopolies or restrictive practices . . . [to] encourage enterprise and efficiency'.[90] That problems of over-capacity had given way to shortages, and that restriction was no longer either necessary or in the public interest, was Macmillan's explanation of his position, but his adoption of a more unfettered language of free enterprise marked a change of emphasis. But the most important

88 Macmillan, 'New Crusade'.
89 Macmillan in Parliament, 20 Nov. 1946, in *Tides*, 81.
90 Macmillan, 'Principles'.

shift in his position concerned the general governance of the economy. He defined the main economic tasks of government as being to secure full employment and rising living standards, and he argued that 'The instruments for these tasks are the control of credit and currency, the supervision of the location of industry, taxation policy and the like. They cannot be secured by the direct intervention of the State in the ownership and management of industry and commerce.'[91] His desire to avoid State ownership, management, and control was consistent with his pre-war position, but his emphasis on monetary and fiscal controls marked a departure. Macmillan had altered the parameters of his economic policy strategy, with the macroeconomic variables being given greater weight than the micro. He had inverted his pre-war priorities and, in effect, moved towards an acceptance of what came to be known as Keynesian demand-management techniques. He was not alone in this. The Labour government, as it found microeconomic industrial planning difficult to implement, looked to the indirect controls offered by fiscal and monetary policy as an easier way of managing the economy.[92] At the same time, many Conservatives saw demand management as the means to achieve the politically crucial goals of high and stable employment and rising living standards whilst avoiding direct State intervention. Macmillan's position is thus best understood when placed within the context of the 'retreat to consensus' that characterized the direction of British economic policy debate in the last years of the Attlee government, with demand management emerging as the best available, or most politically acceptable, form of government action.[93]

Conservative governments of the 1950s adhered to the demand-management strategy for governing the economy, and sought, where they felt it was politically feasible, to withdraw the State from direct intervention in the economy. Rationing and controls were ended and removed, two industries were denationalized, and scope for the private sector was extended.[94] Macmillan, as housing minister from 1951 to 1954, was fully in accord with this strategy, and indeed played an important part in it. When he was offered the Housing Ministry Macmillan's response was, 'Oh dear, it is not my cup of tea',[95] but his success in fulfilling the Conservative promise to build 300,000 houses

[91] Macmillan, 'Principles'.

[92] J. Tomlinson, *Democratic Socialism and Economic Policy, 1945–51* (Cambridge, 1997).

[93] For the idea of a retreat to consensus see L. Minkin, 'Radicalism and Reconstruction: the British Experience', *Europa*, 5 (1982). See also Tomlinson, *Democratic Socialism*; P. Hall, *Governing the Economy* (Cambridge, 1986), 69–77; N. Rollings, 'Poor Mr. Butskell: A Short Life Wrecked by Schizophrenia', *TCBH* 4 (1994).

[94] See K. Jeffreys, *Retreat From New Jerusalem* (1997), 9–35.

[95] Macmillan Diary, 21 Oct. 1951, MP, MS Macmillan Dep. 9.

was his springboard to senior Cabinet office. His strategy for housing in many ways encapsulated the Conservatives' broad economic policy, insofar as, without by any means abandoning public housing, he sought to deregulate the housing market and encourage both private building and the private rental market.[96] But when Macmillan took the position of Chancellor in 1955, and then Prime Minister in 1957, and perforce focused his mind on economic policy in the round, he began to confront problems which led him to question the adequacy of demand management.

When he became Prime Minister in January 1957 Macmillan's chief concern was to end the Suez imbroglio and repair the damage it had done to Britain's international standing and to the Conservative party. However, by the end of the year his difficulties were chiefly economic. Above all, inflation emerged as a significant economic and political problem, generating a 'revolt' amongst the Conservatives' middle-class core constituency in particular.[97] Macmillan himself was more than aware of the economic aspects of the problem, for it was during his tenure of the Exchequer that the Treasury produced the 1956 White Paper *The Economic Implications of Full Employment*, which underlined inflation as the chief such implication. Moreover, he publicly signalled his awareness of the political implications of the problem in July 1957, when, speaking at Bedford, he stated that the 'constant concern today is—can prices be steadied while at the same time we maintain full employment in an expanding economy? Can we control inflation? This is the problem of our time.'[98] On the day he made this speech Macmillan recorded in his diary that the Cabinet meeting had been dominated by the question of inflation. He also noted that the newspapers were 'still running the "Rising Prices" and . . . demand . . . that the Prime Minister should act', but added with irritation, '*How* he is supposed to act, no one ventures to propose'.[99] For most of 1957 Macmillan supported the strategy for controlling inflation adopted by his Chancellor, Peter Thorneycroft, which was to deflate the economy by reducing public expenditure and investment. This was hardly surprising, in that, leaving aside his sense of political urgency, Macmillan had pursued this strategy himself when Chancellor.[100] In early September he

[96] For full details of Macmillan's housing policy during his time at the ministry and thereafter see P. Weiler, 'The Rise and Fall of the Conservatives' "Grand Design" for Housing, 1951–1964', *CBH* (2000).

[97] For the 'middle-class revolt' see Green, 'Conservative Party'; Jeffreys, *New Jerusalem*, 66–73, 166–74.

[98] Macmillan at Bedford, 20 July 1957, in id., *Riding the Storm, 1956–1959* (1971), 351.

[99] Macmillan Diary, 19 July 1957, MP, MS Macmillan Dep. d. 29.

[100] See pp. 200–10.

drew up a Memorandum on inflation which gave strong support to the Chancellor's deflationary policies.[101] Macmillan recorded in his diary that this Memorandum was written 'primarily for the Chancellor', but after he had completed it he noted that 'I may decide to circulate it to the whole Cabinet'.[102] He duly did so, indicating it seemed that Nos. 10 and 11 were wholly in accord. But, also in September, he was being warned by his economic guru, Roy Harrod, that Thorneycroft was creating the impression that the government adhered to a simple monetarist view of inflation. 'The idea', Harrod declared,

that you can reduce prices by limiting the quantity of money is pre-Keynesian. Keynes spent half his energy inveighing against precisely that idea. Hardly any economist under the age of 50 would subscribe to it. If it were supposed that the Conservatives were associated with such an idea, that might drive many middle of the road economists into the ranks of Labour . . . I do sincerely hope that no Govt. speaker will use words implying that the Govt. subscribes to such an antiquated doctrine.[103]

Harrod's criticisms were cleverly aimed, for he knew that Macmillan admired Keynes and that the last thing the Prime Minister wished to appear was 'antiquated'. Macmillan may have found Harrod's arguments persuasive, or he may have become concerned that Thorneycroft had indeed fallen under the influence of his monetarist-inclined Treasury ministers, Enoch Powell and Nigel Birch, and was pressing for too strong a deflation on the wrong policy lines. However, Macmillan did not support his Chancellor, either in the run-up to or at the crucial Cabinet meeting of 6 January 1958 which saw the resignation of the entire Treasury team. Macmillan's position, although he was not alone here, was that the 'swingeing cuts in . . . Welfare State expenditure' demanded by Thorneycroft were 'more, I fear, than is politically feasible'.[104] The fact is, however, that one of the reasons they were not politically feasible was because the Prime Minister, having stated in August that his Chancellor 'must be bold',[105] was unwilling to be bold himself. Harold Wilson famously remarked with regard to the Suez crisis that Macmillan was 'first in, first out', and perhaps the same thing was true of the 'inflation crisis'.

Although Macmillan's Treasury team went away, the problem of inflation did not. Soon after the Treasury team's resignation Macmillan left for a Commonwealth tour, and told journalists at the airport that he

---

    [101] See p. 195.
    [102] Macmillan Diary, 1 Sept. 1957, MP, MS Macmillan Dep. d. 29. For the contents of this Memorandum see p. 195.
    [103] R. Harrod to Macmillan 7 Sept. 1957, PRO, PREM 11/2973.
    [104] Macmillan Diary, 22 Dec. 1957, MP, MS Macmillan Dep. d. 30.
    [105] Macmillan Diary, 24 Aug. 1957, ibid.

had more important things to consider than 'little local difficulties'. Six weeks later, in a speech to mark the twentieth anniversary of the publication of *The Middle Way*, Macmillan admitted that he had been less sanguine. He noted that in 1938 unemployment had been the most pressing problem, whereas in 1958 reconciling full employment with stable prices was 'for us *the* problem',[106] and that the 'middle way' in 1958 was to be found between inflation and deflation. He confessed that, 'The day I left for my Commonwealth tour I had a feeling that the strict puritanical application of deflation was in danger of being developed into a sort of creed'.[107] However, he congratulated himself and his government upon having avoided extremes, and used a metaphor that for many commentators summed up the Conservatives' management of the economy in the 1950s, to wit, that just as 'both a brake and accelerator are essential to a motor car', so they were for an economy as well.[108] The 1958 Budget applied a touch on the brake in the form of a milder deflationary package than the one Thorneycroft had called for, and inflation fell accompanied by only a small rise in unemployment. The following spring the government pressed the accelerator with an expansionary, pre-election Budget, but in early 1960 Macmillan was being warned that the inflationary consequences of this action were already apparent, that the problem of reconciling full employment and stable prices was unresolved,[109] and that the political difficulties that had been extant in 1957–8 were being reawakened.[110] The latter-day 'middle way' was proving difficult to find.

The difficulty of balancing employment and prices, affluence and stability, raised doubts as to the adequacy of the instruments of economic control available to the government and the overall efficacy of demand management as a means of governing the economy. Demand management placed emphasis on government use of fiscal and monetary policy as the key instruments of policy. The fiscal levers appeared, in the shape of the Budget, to be completely in government hands, but control of spending by relatively autonomous local government authorities, and even that of central government departments, was not unproblematic, as was acknowledged by the appointment of the Plowden Committee in 1959 and subsequent creation of the Public Expenditure Survey Committee in 1961.[111] But, in the first instance, it was control of the

---

[106] Macmillan, *Twenty Years After*, 13.
[107] Ibid. 14.   [108] Ibid.
[109] 'Future Policy Study, 1960–1970', 24 Feb. 1960, PRO, CAB 134/3757.
[110] M. Fraser, CRD Memorandum to Macmillan on 'The Economic Outlook', 14 June 1960, PRO, PREM 11/3291.
[111] R. Lowe, 'The Core Executive, Modernization and the Creation of PESC, 1960–4', *Public Administration*, 75 (1997).

monetary levers that most exercised Macmillan. After the nationalization of the Bank of England in 1946, control over interest rates lay with
the Treasury, but there were no government controls over the banks and
financial system. On two occasions in the 1950s enquiries were made of
the Treasury Solicitor as to whether the government could issue directives to the banking system through the Bank of England, but on both
occasions the reply was in the negative.[112] This absence of government
control over the banking system, especially in relation to banking
advances and the availability of credit, was an issue that Macmillan had
raised as Chancellor, and, as will be shown in the following chapter, it
was a key aspect of the debate on monetary causes of inflation in
1957–8.[113] In early 1957, largely as a result of pressure from Macmillan
when he was at No. 11, the government established a committee—the
Radcliffe Committee—to inquire into the workings of the monetary
system and to investigate the possibility of strengthening governmental
powers. The Radcliffe Committee, which reported in 1959, recommended increasing the government's authority, and in particular advocated the introduction of a Bank of England Special Deposits scheme to
limit bank advances.[114] Its recommendations were implemented, but
concern, especially Macmillan's, was by no means fully assuaged.

In the inter-war years, as noted above, Macmillan had entertained a
profound suspicion of the banking sector, and his views did not change
dramatically after the war. In 1952, when Housing Minister, Macmillan
had felt that the encouragement of long-term investment held the key to
Britain's future prosperity, and that short-term balance-of-payments
problems should not dominate policy decisions. When Treasury officials
sought to counter his argument by 'appealing to the views of the City
and the Bank of England', Macmillan was 'tempted, perhaps improp-
erly, to make the disrespectful reply that while the authority of the City,
and particularly the Bank of England, must always be great, yet the
most tender critic of the financial policies proposed by successive
Governors could scarcely maintain that the Bank had always given wise
advice'.[115] Although in public hands, the post-war Bank of England still
tended, in Macmillan's view, to see itself as the voice of 'the City', and
he could not resist recording that even a Governor whom he admired,
Lord Cromer, was 'not a Baring for nothing' when it came to policy.[116]
As regards the clearing banks, Macmillan's views veered between irritation and contempt. During the 'inflation crisis' of 1957–8 he had been

[112] See E. H. H. Green, 'The Influence of the City Over British Economic Policy, 1880–1960',
in Y. Cassis (ed.), *Finance and Financiers in European History, 1880–1960* (Cambridge, 1992).
[113] See Ch. 7.   [114] See pp. 206–8.
[115] Macmillan, *Tides*, 387.
[116] Macmillan Diary, 20 June 1962, MP, MS Macmillan Dep. d. 46.

frustrated by their apparent unwillingness to curtail their advances. He had high hopes of the Radliffe Committee, and was greatly disappointed when it did not produce suggestions for more far-reaching government controls.[117] What irritated Macmillan most, however, was that the banks seemed willing to bypass the controls that had been introduced on the Radcliffe Committee's recommendation. In August 1960 Macmillan was furious when he learned that the Midland Bank, having been asked to make a Special Deposit, had proceeded to sell £15 million of Treasury Bills to replenish their liquidity. Writing to his newly appointed Chancellor, Selwyn Lloyd, the Prime Minister launched into what can only be desribed as a diatribe, arguing that:

The City, especially the Clearing Banks, seem to me to be out of touch with modern conditions. It is all very well for them to say it is their job to make money for their shareholders and that they won't co-operate with the Treasury on something which may cause them losses or may reduce their profits. If capitalist society as a whole were still to take that view we should be very near the crash ... If the Chancellor says he wants the base of credit restricted he ought to be able to have a meeting with them, tell them what he wants, and rely upon them to carry it out ... At present it is all kept as a sort of mystery, very much on an 'old boy' basis. This is all very well, but it needs some new look at it all.[118]

Given that this statement was made less than a year after the Radcliffe Comittee's report had supposedly provided such an in-depth 'new look', the Prime Minister's outburst was indicative of a deep-seated frustration.

For Macmillan, the point of 'the whole question of the Bank of England, the Clearing Banks and the Treasury' was 'to make a real partnership out of the three',[119] and to bring the financial sector into line with the government's overall economic strategy. With regard to monetary policy this meant greater control over the *quantity* of bank lending, but in broader terms the *quality* of lending, in terms of its purpose, was also crucial. In March 1959 the former Minister of Labour, Lord Monckton, wrote to Macmillan advocating an expansionary economic strategy, based on a 'considerable' increase in the supply of money and, if necessary, a budget deficit. He added, however, that 'the fillip to personal spending on "consumer durables" has probably exhausted itself ... [and that] what is needed now is to provide inducements to private capital expenditure'.[120] This message was underscored in the spring of 1960 by one of Macmillan's close allies in his earlier battles

---

[117] Macmillan to Harrod, 12 Nov. 1959, PRO, PREM 11/2973.
[118] Id. to Selwyn Lloyd, 1 Aug. 1960, PRO, PREM 11/3883.
[119] Id. to D. Eccles, 1 Aug. 1960, PRO, PREM 11/3756.
[120] Monckton to Macmillan, 16 Mar. 1959, PRO, PREM 11/2667.

with the banks, David Eccles, who argued that the City's penchant for overseas lending had to be curbed, and domestic investment increased, on the grounds that 'it is better to be a strong manufacturer and producer of food than to be a weak lender overseas'.[121] Selwyn Lloyd attempted to bring about this boost to domestic investment between 1960 and 1961. To begin with, he introduced generous investment allowances for business in his Budgets, but, approaching the problem from the other end, he noted in July 1961 that 'The banks have been asked that, when reviewing existing commitments or considering new lending, they should be particularly severe on proposals related to personal consumption, including finance for hire purchase, as well as finance for other speculative purposes, so that all possible room should be left for the finance vitally needed for exports and productive industry'.[122] Lloyd enjoyed only limited success, and in the spring of 1962 Eccles was again writing to Macmillan to stress that 'increases in purchasing power going to consumers' through simple reflation were not wanted, and that the economy needed 'a transfer of resources from consumption to various forms of investment'.[123] In 1963 Macmillan pressed his fourth and last Chancellor, Reginald Maudling, to shape his Budget for the 'encouragement of private investment', on the grounds that this was the soundest way to bring unemployment down before the impending election. But 'encouraging' investment did not necessarily ensure that banks would lend to industry or that industry would borrow. At the same time, Macmillan looked to the Budget to 'touch the accelerator' by giving a boost to consumer spending, but here too he confronted problems. In the late autumn of 1963 the clearing banks raised their overdraft interest rates, which prompted a 'furious' reaction from Macmillan who saw the banks undermining the government's expansionary policy.[124]

The ongoing technical and institutional difficulties presented by managing demand through fiscal and monetary policy had, by the early 1960s, raised important doubts about their adequacy as tools of economic governance. These doubts were only further strengthened by the problems which the British economy faced. Reconciling stable prices with full employment was the first problem to surface, but another problem emerged in the late 1950s and early 1960s which led Macmillan to call for a new approach to governing the economy—the problem of slow growth. The modern 'discovery' of British economic decline took place in the period from 1958 to 1960. The key to this

---

[121] D. Eccles to Macmillan, 22 Apr. 1960, PRO, PREM 11/3756.
[122] S. Lloyd, paper on the economic situation, n.d. (July 1961), PRP, PREM 11/3757.
[123] D. Eccles to Macmillan, 30 Apr. 1962, PRO, PREM 11/3765.
[124] This is discussed in a series of letters through Oct. and Nov. 1963, PRO, PREM 11/4199.

discovery was the burgeoning number of comparative, international economic surveys by both individuals and organizations, such as the OECD, which showed that Britain's rate of economic growth lagged well behind those of other industrialized nations. These surveys had a marked impact on and were internalized by both politicians and civil servants engaged in the 'official' discussion of Britain's economic situation,[125] but they also gained a wider audience. Britain's growth rate was the main topic of debate at the Federation of British Industry's [FBI] annual conference in 1960, and in early 1961 the runaway success of Michael Shanks's *The Stagnant Society*, in which slow growth was a central feature of Britain's economic stagnation,[126] was accompanied by widespread discussion of Britain's relative failure in the press. Small wonder that in July 1961 the Chancellor and his Treasury officials noted that, 'In the past year public interest in the rate of economic growth in this country has been intensified'.[127]

The problem was obvious, but for Macmillan, like Lenin, there remained the question of what is to be done? The Treasury Report of July 1961, cited above, was clear that 'Experience in the 1950s has shown conclusively that merely to increase demand in the short run in relation to the resources available does not increase national efficiency'. The Report went on to point out that when demand was 'managed' to reach a peak, imports flooded into the country, indicating that even at peak capacity British manufacturers were neither productive nor competitive enough. It suggested that, to overcome this problem, 'the modernisation of our market economy needs to be accelerated by a revolution of attitudes parallel to the revolutionary achievement of full employment and social services', and it further contended that, 'In this revolution the Government has a part to play by striving to remove obstacles to the effective operation of a market economy in the production of goods and service'. The Report ruled out extensions of public ownership, and was forthright in its view that 'The exploitation of the most rewarding investments by private industry is better secured through the operation of the market', on the grounds that the market was better than the government at 'picking winners'.[128] The policy implications of the Treasury's arguments were that arm's-length governance of the economy, through the use of fiscal and monetary levers to manage demand, had not brought the British economy to optimum

---

[125] See 'Future Policy Study, 1960–1970', for an emphasis on Britian's comparative weakness.
[126] M. Shanks, *The Stagnant Society* (Harmondsworth, 1961).
[127] 'Economic Growth and National Efficiency', Treasury Report circulated by S. Lloyd to Cabinet, 10 July 1961, PRO, CAB 129/105.
[128] Ibid.

levels of efficiency, and that a more active role for the State was required.

Since taking up the Chancellorship in July 1960, Selwyn Lloyd had been moving towards advocating a more 'hands on' role for the government in the economy, and had discussed the general direction of his ideas with Macmillan in early summer 1961. In May Macmillan told Lloyd, 'I like your idea of a little more planning in the economy',[129] and, shortly after Lloyd's July circular to the cabinet, he told his Chancellor:

I do not think we ought to be afraid of a switch over towards more direction. Our party has always consisted of a number holding the laissez faire tradition, but of an equal number in favour of some direction. So far as I am concerned I have no fear of it because these were the policies I recommended before the war. Therefore I shall be able to claim, like Disraeli, that I have educated my party.[130]

Educating the party and the country at large began in earnest in September 1961, when Lloyd, in consultation with the Cabinet, drew up a letter to employers' organizations and trade unions inviting them to join a new consultative body that was to become the National Economic Development Council (NEDC).[131] This body was to have a membership drawn from employers, trade unions, and government, and was to provide

a more effective machinery for the co-ordination of plans and forecasts for the main sectors of our economy . . . study centrally the plans and prospects of our main industries . . . correlate them with each other and with the Government's plans for the public sector, and to see how in aggregate they contribute to, and fit in with, the prospects for the economy as a whole.[132]

Macmillan threw his weight behind this proposal in a memorandum to Cabinet in mid-September, and also suggested that the NEDC be 'supported by the establishment of a high grade planning staff in an office, which, while it would be linked with and use the information of the Government machine, would have a considerable measure of independence and authority'.[133] This 'planning staff' came into being as the National Economic Development Office (NEDO), and began operating in adjunct to the NEDC from March 1962.

The new planning machinery did not enjoy an easy birth. The TUC

---

[129] Macmillan to Lloyd, 21 May 1961, PRO PREM 11/3883.
[130] Id. to Lloyd, 15 July 1961, PRO, PREM 11/3883.
[131] See 'Revised Draft of Letter from the Chancellor of the Exchequer to the Two Sides of Industry', Sept. 1961, CAB 129/106.
[132] Ibid.
[133] Macmillan, 'Economic Planning' Memorandum to Cabinet, 16 Sept. 1961, CAB 129/126.

was initially suspicious of and reluctant to co-operate with the NEDC, largely because it felt that the new organization would place the blame for Britain's slow growth on the 'wages problem', and would bring pressure to bear for the introduction of a restrictive incomes policy.[134] The employers' side was more positive: the President of the FBI agreed that something had to be done about low rates of growth, and stated that as 'all of us plan in our businesses' there was 'no reason why we should be afraid of the word'.[135] In Cabinet, Macmillan and Lloyd encountered 'a surprising degree of hostility' to aspects of the new planning strategy:[136] the President of the Board of Trade, Reginald Maudling, expressed scepticism as to whether an 'independent body' would carry weight with either trade unions or employers, and concluded that, 'in a free enterprise system there is no real room for central planning in the proper sense of the word'.[137] Macmillan, however, sought to assuage the concerns of his Cabinet colleagues about the NEDC's purpose, and argued that its object was 'not to dictate or enforce measures of economic planning, but to influence the attitudes and independent decisions of employers and unions'.[138]

When Macmillan was preparing to meet with his Cabinet on 21 September 1961, he asked his civil servants to add a paragraph to a memorandum he had written 'setting out the purpose of the new Council [NEDC] and *the middle way* which was possible and desirable between extreme laissez faireism and rigid planning'.[139] Macmillan, as his correspondence with Lloyd in the summer of 1961 had shown, consciously constructed the new departure as a renaissance of his pre-war principles.[140] It is easy to see why Macmillan made this connection. The role he envisaged for the NEDC was advisory rather than directive and controlling, which was very similar to the position he had envisaged for the NEC in *The Middle Way*. Likewise, the idea of the NEDO as a body of independent experts was akin to the body of 'informed opinion' working as an institute 'outside Party shackles' that he had suggested to Keynes in 1932.[141] The most important echo of *The Middle Way*,

[134] See S. Lloyd, minutes of a meeting with the TUC, 28 Nov. 1961, and also T. Caulcott to T. Bligh 24 Jan. 1962, PREM 11/4707.
[135] C. E. Harrison to Macmillan, 20 Sept. 1961, PRO, PREM 11/4207.
[136] Lloyd to Macmillan, 8 Sept. 1961, ibid.
[137] 'Economic Planning', Memorandum by the President of the Board of Trade, 20 Sept. 1961, PRO, CAB 129/106.
[138] Macmillan at a Cabinet meeting, 21 Sept. 1961, PRO, CAB 128/35.
[139] P. W., Record Note on Economic Planning, 19 Sept. 1961, PRO, PREM 11/4207 (my emphasis).
[140] Macmillan saw this very clearly himself, and was prompting his advisers and not, as some have suggested, being prompted by them: see A. Ringe (ed.), 'Witness Seminar: The National Economic Development Council, 1962–7', *CBH* 12 (1998), esp. remarks by Mcintosh.
[141] Macmillan to Keynes, 29 Aug. 1932, JMKP, Microfilm Reel 61.

however, was the emphasis on the NEDC's role as a forum which would bring together the most important actors in the national economy, in the public and private sectors, and enable them to co-ordinate their individual plans in terms of agreed national economic goals. This was to overcome the problem of economic interests acting in a disaggregated fashion with no national purpose—a problem which, as noted above, Macmillan had outlined as central in 1938.

The interdependence of all sectors of the national economy was built into the practical goals as well as the principles of the NEDC. By May 1962 the NEDC had announced that the target rate of growth for the economy was 4 per cent, which the FBI leadership thought was feasible if conditions allowed. One important condition was the position of trade unions on wages. The 'wages problem' had been ongoing since the mid-1950s, and in 1960–1 the government had implemented a 'pay pause' in the public sector and urged the private sector, without success, to follow suit. At a Cabinet meeting in January 1962 Macmillan stated that 'the main objective at this stage was to secure the co-operation of the TUC in long-term planning directed towards economic growth'.[142] The way to achieve this was, the Cabinet agreed, to convince the trade unions that growth rather than industrial action was the best route to higher wages. This was an argument Macmillan repeated in the autumn, when he told Oliver Poole: 'There is nothing that I can see inconsistent between an incomes policy and an expansionist policy. Indeed an expansionist policy must lead to trouble unless some reasonable incomes policy can go with it.'[143] But the question remained as to how to persuade the trade unions to agree to 'planned wages'. Alongside the NEDC the government established the National Incomes Commission (NIC) to monitor and advise on wage settlements, but it had no statutory powers and, like the NEDC, its tools were to be persuasion and influence. But persuading the TUC required that there be persuasive arguments and *actions*. In July 1961 Macmillan had suggested that increased welfare benefits and pensions could be a means to obtain union agreement to six-monthly assessments of the level of wage increase commensurate with the rate of growth.[144] In January 1962 the Cabinet felt that restrictions of prices and dividends could be a persuasive quid pro quo for trade union agreement to wage restraint.[145] However, the most important action that Macmillan set in train in the spring of 1962 was the abolition of Resale Price Maintenance (RPM).

---

[142] Macmillan in Cabinet, 8 Jan. 1962, PRO, CAB 128/35.
[143] Id. to Poole, 21 Oct. 1962, PRO, PREM 11/3765.
[144] Id. to Lloyd, 4 July 1961, PRO, PREM 11/3883.
[145] Minutes of Cabinet Meeting, 8 Jan. 1962, ibid.

The decision to abolish RPM appears at first glance somewhat paradoxical, insofar as it represented a withdrawal of State intervention at a time when Macmillan was arguing for a greater role for government in the economy. But the logic here was that if RPM went then high-street prices would fall, and with government having demonstrated a commitment to lowering the cost of living, trade unions could be persuaded to accept wage restraint.[146] The connections between growth, industrial relations, wages, and prices were all thrown into relief once the new search for 'the middle way' was begun in earnest.

But although Macmillan was keen to acknowledge the interdependence of all sectors and aspects of the economy, he wished to avoid the macroeconomic trap of the 1950s. By the winter of 1962 the NEDC, NEDO, and NIC had been established, but Macmillan was clear that only the first objective had been reached in the new era of planning. In a memorandum to Cabinet he stressed that 'We have now reached a stage in our post-war history where some more radical attack must be made upon weaknesses of our economy, both productive and structural'.[147] The removal of restrictive practices in order to boost industrial productivity was one of Macmillan's priorities, but he also argued that the imbalance in British society between the North and South had to be addressed, and stated that:

Our efforts in this have been mainly directed to influencing the economy as a whole; and whether we have been concerned to stimulate it or to restrain it, our methods and techniques have been largely indiscriminate. But this concept of influencing the economy as a single entity has led to a situation in which, in order to reduce unemployment to an acceptable level in some areas, we have to stimulate excessive employment in others. 2–3% overall OK, but 5% in some areas.[148]

The implication of this was clear. The microeconomic emphasis of Macmillan's inter-war political economy had resurfaced. Industrial growth, restructuring, and regeneration were once again the focus of his interest, with an emphasis on the need for a regional bias in order to 'rectify the imbalance between south and north—between the "rich" areas and the "poor" areas, the over-employed regions and the under-employed regions—and redress the grave social anomalies which are created by this'.[149] As in *The Middle Way*, economic efficiency was the basis for the amelioration of social ills: government influence over the location of industrial growth would ensure that prosperity was evenly

---

[146] See R. Findley, 'The Conservative Party and Defeat: The Significance of Resale Price Maintenance for the Election of 1964', *TCBH* (forthcoming).

[147] Macmillan, 'Modernization of Britain', Memorandum to Cabinet 30 Nov. 1962, circulated 3 Dec. 1962, PRO, CAB 129/111.

[148] Ibid.   [149] Ibid.

distributed, and the attendant buoyancy of government revenues would provide funds for social welfare without recourse to increased taxation.[150]

Harold Macmillan's political economy represented a lifelong quest for the middle way. The most obvious balance he sought to strike was between Socialist Statism and laissez-faire capitalism.[151] In 1994 one Thatcherite Conservative described *The Middle Way* as a work of 'nearly Bennite Socialism',[152] but it would be difficult to construct a more inaccurate description of Macmillan's view of the State either in 1938 or indeed at any stage in his career. Speaking at Cranbrook in November 1946, Macmillan outlined what in his view differentiated the Conservative from the Socialist position: 'We accept, and indeed demand, the broad strategic planning which, especially in a period of post-war reconstruction, is of vital necessity. We reject day to day and detailed interference with industry on a tactical level. Most of all we protest against the actual ownership and management of individual industries by the State.'[153] Macmillan's view of the role of the State, which shifted only within very narrow boundaries over the whole of his life and career, was that it should assist, enable, and advise free enterprise but should only play a direct role when all else, and in particular free enterprise itself, had failed. In his view the two things that were important about the State were that its duty was to the national interest rather than to any sectional interest, and that, as a consequence, only it possessed the information to see which economic developments would best serve the national interest. Given that particular economic interests in a nation were themselves part of the national economy, there was no intrinsic need for the State to own, control, or direct them. If the State provided information, co-ordination, and support, the interests of free enterprise and the national interest would for the most part naturally coalesce. It was for this reason that Macmillan advocated the self-regulation of industry in the 1930s, rejected day-to-day State interference in the immediate post-war years, and spoke of his dislike of detailed planning in 1961. At the same time, however, he had no time for laisssez faire, which, he felt, had produced the economic and social waste of the inter-war years.

Finding a balance between the State and free enterprise was one aspect of Macmillan's middle way, but a social balance between the

---

[150] Macmillan, 'Modernization of Britain'.

[151] This helps to explain why *The Middle Way* was republished in 1978, in that Macmillan was clearly concerned by the early signs of the liberal economic trend of Conservative thought under Thatcher's leadership.

[152] D. Willetts, *Civic Conservatism* (1994), 19.

[153] Macmillan at Cranbrook, 7 Nov 1946, copy in CPA, CRD 2/50/11.

classes was equally important to him. This was one reason why he rejected laissez faire, in that the abdication of social responsibility attendant upon this nineteenth-century Liberal philosophy had resulted in the social neglect of the working class and chronic social deprivation. Macmillan supported the introduction of the Welfare State, but above all he campaigned for and sought to maintain full employment as the best means of helping the working class to help themselves. That one consequence of full employment was a growth in the bargaining position of organized labour was undoubtedly a political and economic irritation for Macmillan, but for political and social reasons he proved willing to tolerate this. Politically, Macmillan felt that full or near-full employment was an electoral necessity, and that any government that allowed unemployment to rise would be punished by the electorate.[154] He was, in this respect, the first Prime Minister fully to adhere to and articulate what was to become a received wisdom, that the electoral fate of governments was determined by a few, key economic indicators. Trade-union militancy was 'tolerated' for a different, though related, reason, in that Macmillan resisted calls from the Conservative party rank and file for a reform of trade-union law on the grounds that it might alienate trade unionists who were, in Macmillan's eyes, unwontedly voting Conservative.[155] But in addition to reasons of *Realpolitik*, Macmillan had a predisposition to give the working class the benefit of the doubt, partly because he disliked the middle class. His well-known request to Michael Fraser at CRD to note down on a sheet of paper what the middle class wanted can be read as typical of Macmillan's *sang froid* in the face of the 'middle-class revolt'. But it was perhaps also indicative of the fact that middle-class wants were not worth more than a single piece of paper. In 1951 he described the *Economist*'s assaults on the Labour government as ' a mixture of fear and middle class jealousy towards the Conservatives',[156] and in 1962 he attributed poor by-election results to the revolt of the middle classes, 'who resent the vastly improved condition of the working classes, and are envious of their apparent prosperity & the luxury of the rich'.[157] For Macmillan, the most active, if largely unseen, proponents of class envy were the middle classes, and as a consequence he held a low opinion of them.

But Macmillan's dislike of the middle classes was as nothing compared to his dislike of the financial community. In *Reconstruction*,

[154] See, e.g. his instruction to Reginald Maudling in January 1963 to use the Budget to 'get the unemployment figures down in time before the election'. Macmillan to Maudling, 28 Jan. 1963, PRO, PREM 11/4202.
[155] See Green, 'Conservative Party'.
[156] Macmillan Diary, 30 Aug. 1951, MP, MS Macmillan Dep. d. 9.
[157] Ibid., 24 Mar. 1962, MP, MS Macmillan Dep. d. 45.

his call for a more rational financial system in Britain implied that
bankers were irrational, but when in *The Middle Way* he stated that
their speculative activities performed no useful social function, he was,
in effect, implying that they were parasites. In 1961, when involved in
discussions with the International Monetary Fund, Macmillan noted
that they would call for reductions in government expenditure before
allowing Britain to draw money, and also remarked that, 'if the package
[of reductions] is not good enough the international usurers—bankers—
will turn us down'.[158] Although the particular 'international usurers' in
this case were the IMF, this comment summed up Macmillan's general
criticism of bankers and financiers, which was that they were interested
only in their own sphere of economic activity and had no sense of social
or national responsibility. The IMF's 'usurious' behaviour came less
than a year after the Midland Bank's 'anti-social' behaviour had
provoked his diatribe against the City, and only served to confirm
Macmillan's prejudices. That the banking community had no part in
Macmillan's plan for the 'Modernization of Britain' in the early 1960s,
and the Bank of England actively discouraged banks from participating
in the NEDC, both reflected and confirmed Macmillan's view that the
financial sector could not and would not tread the middle way.

Harold Macmillan was referred to, in the title of one biography, as
The Last Edwardian at No. 10,[159] not simply because he had grown to
adulthood in the Edwardian period, but because of his dress, public
manner, and patrician lifestyle. But his political economy also had
distinct inflections of Edwardian Conservatism. The fact that when he
first stood for Parliament it was as a tariff reformer should not be *over*-
estimated: rather, the broad sweep of Macmillan's ideas on economic
policy as they evolved over the course of his career prompts the comparison. His dislike of the financial sector was very reminiscent of that
voiced by Edwardian Conservatives. Where he referred to bankers as
'international usurers', they had denounced them as 'cosmopolitan
finance',[160] but the underlying objections were the same, namely, that
financial interests were too international and, therefore, not concerned
with the economic health of Britain's domestic, productive economy. In
this respect Macmillan adhered to and developed aspects of the *nationalist* political economy that had underpinned the Edwardian tariff
campaign.[161] His advocacy of tariffs, both for protection and imperial
preference, in the 1920s and 1930s is one obvious echo, but the overall
rationale of his economic strategy in the inter-war years indicates a

---

[158] Ibid., 23 July 1961, MP, MS Macmillan Dep. d. 42.
[159] G. Hutchison, *The Last Edwardian at No. 10* (1980).
[160] See Green, *Crisis*, 235–40.
[161] Ibid., *passim*.

broader resonance. In *Industry and the State*, Macmillan and his co-authors were clear that inductive rather than deductive reasoning was the best way of approaching questions of economic policy, and in *The Middle Way* he stressed that history and economics had to be taken together as the essential guides in such matters,[162] positions which were entirely in keeping with the historical economic philosophy that had informed the tariff campaign.[163] Moreover, as had been the case with the late-Victorian and Edwardian historical economists, Macmillan saw the historical evolution of monopoly capitalism as evidence of the redundancy of laissez-faire, Liberal economics, with its emphasis on individualist, small-scale production.[164] The essential logic and shape of Macmillan's economic ideas was very similar to that of the Edwardian tariff reformers.

The trajectory of Macmillan's ideas after the Second World War reflected the way in which Britain's retreat from Empire and its decline in world economic status brought about an intriguing shift in the nature of his national economics. The basic aim of securing the economic strength of the nation remained a given, but the post-war liberal world trading order structured by the United States placed constraints on the room for economic manoeuvre. In late 1957 Macmillan launched what he saw as his big theme in terms of defining Britain's role as it lost its Empire, which was the concept of 'interdependence'.[165] In specific, diplomatic terms this meant cementing Britain's alliances with the United States and within NATO, but in more general terms it meant acknowledging that Britain, without its Empire, could not stand either militarily or economically *contra mundi*. This in turn meant that it was in Britain's national interest to build and participate in partnerships with other nations, which was, in this respect, the 'nationalist' logic behind Macmillan's 'grand design' for British entry into the European Economic Community. Unlike 'isolationists', such as Lord Beaverbrook, Viscount Hinchingbrooke, and other opponents of the idea of interedependence in general and the EEC in particular,[166] Macmillan, and some other inheritors of the national-imperial mantle,[167] sought to 'turn their

[162] Boothby *et al.*, *Industry and the State*, 11; Macmillan, *Middle Way*, 94, 105.

[163] Green, *Crisis*, 159–83.

[164] For a statement of the historical economists' position on this point see H. S. Foxwell, *Papers on Current Finance* (1919), 262–77. See also Green, *Crisis*, 163–5. For Macmillan's full discussion of the evolution of large-scale enterprise see *Middle Way*, 163–74.

[165] See Macmillan Diary, 5, 9 Nov. 1957, MP, MS Macmillan Dep. d. 30; ide., *Riding the Storm, 1956–9* (1971), 358–9.

[166] The use of the term 'isolationist' in this context is Macmillan's own. See Macmillan Diary, 5, 10 Nov. 1957, 5 Aug. 1961, MP, MS Macmillan Dep. d. 30, d. 43.

[167] A good example is Julian Amery, who was the son of one of Joseph Chamberlain's young lieutenants, Leo Amery. See Amery, *Chamberlain*, vi. 1050–4 for a discussion of the relationship between Chamberlain's tariff campaign and entry into the EEC.

minds from the old Imperialism . . . to a new concept of Britain's ability to influence the world'.[168] For Macmillan, Britain's ability to influence the world was and always had been dependent on its possession of economic strength, and in a post-imperial era that national economic strength would come from an acknowledgement of the need for economic partnership with other nations striving for similar goals in an interdependent world.

The failure of Macmillan's 'grand design' to gain entry to the EEC did not bring an end to his attempt to 'modernize' the British economy. Quite the reverse. In December 1962, when he circulated his memorandum on the 'Modernization of Britain' to the Cabinet, he already knew that de Gaulle was likely to veto Britain's entry. Membership of the EEC was certainly an important element in his design to bring about the political and economic modernization of Britain,[169] but the domestic economic aspects were just as important, and became even more so when the assistance of EEC membership was denied. Hence, on the day before the formal announcement of the EEC's rejection of Britain's application, Macmillan wrote to his Chancellor of the Exchequer to advise him that: 'In view of the probable break down at Brussels I feel that the Budget ought to be concentrated on help to industry, especially exporting industry as well as to the encouragement of private investment . . . [and that] lower rates of income tax and other such reliefs [are of] less importance than our industrial and commercial interests.'[170] In the wake of the European disappointment, the role of the NEDC, the NIC, and assaults on restrictive practices such as RPM took on, if anything, an increased significance for Macmillan as he pressed on with his quest to modernize the British economy.[171] This was confirmed by a meeting at Chequers in April 1963, at which members of Cabinet and Conservative party research officers discussed the whole range of the modernization strategy. The meeting concluded that problems of slow growth, lack of investment in British industry, and the inadequacy of industrial research and development required the State to 'take a more active role', not in terms of ownership but in terms of 'conscious Government support' to show the country that, 'while we were giving people every chance to take advantage of their opportunities, the

---

[168] Macmillan to the Queen, 7 Oct. 1962, in Horne, *Macmillan*, ii. 358.

[169] That the Cabinet decision to apply for membership was taken on 22 July 1961, at the same time that the new economic planning initiatives were being formulated, was no coincidence.

[170] Macmillan to Maudling, 28 Jan. 1963, PRO, PREM 11/4202.

[171] See J. Tomlinson, 'Conservative Modernisation, 1960–64: Too Little, Too Late?', *CBH* 11 (1997).

Government was taking a hand in shaping the economy'.[172] In the autumn of 1963 ill-health forced Macmillan to abandon this quest in person, and he was concerned that his party might do so as well. In July 1961 he had, as noted above, expressed the hope that he had 'educated his party' to accept the notion of a 'middle way', but as the contest to succeed him as leader and Prime Minister took shape he evidently had doubts about this. He recorded in his diary that a ' "draft" Home' movement was underway, and that Quentin Hogg, the contender whom Macmillan himself had initially favoured, 'had almost thrown it away'. But he also stressed that, 'What worries me in all this is the underlying struggle. It is really the old one. I find Hogg . . . represents what Stanley, & John Loder, & Boothby, & Noel Skelton & I had tried to represent from 1924 onwards',[173] with the implication being that the other contenders, including Home, did not. Realizing that Home's emergence as leader was least likely to result in a party split, Macmillan accepted that he was the most acceptable candidate in the immediate circumstances. But having attempted throughout his career to steer Conservative political economy along the middle way, Macmillan retired unsure of whether his party would continue on the course he had set.

[172] Minutes of a meeting at Chequers, 28 Apr. 1963, CPA, Steering Committee Minutes and Papers, 1963–4.
[173] Macmillan Diary, 14 Oct. 1963, MP, MS Macmillan Dep. d. 51.

CHAPTER 7

The Treasury Resignations of 1958:
A Reconsideration

ON 6 JANUARY 1958 the Chancellor of the Exchequer, Peter Thorneycroft, the Economic Secretary to the Treasury, Nigel Birch, and the Financial Secretary, Enoch Powell, resigned from Harold Macmillan's Conservative administration. This was a serious blow to the Prime Minister and the government: to lose one Treasury minister could be deemed unfortunate, to lose two looked like carelessness, but to lose three was unprecedented. Only in September 1903 had more ministers left a government simultaneously, and then at least the Prime Minister had engineered their departure. That Macmillan successfully limited the political impact of the resignations was an impressive achievement, but this should not detract from the historical significance of the event. Moreover, the Treasury team's actions have gained rather than lost importance over time. The cause of their departure was that Thorneycroft and his juniors, seeking to combat inflationary pressures, had demanded a £153 million reduction in estimated government expenditure for 1958–9 in order to deflate the economy, but had only achieved agreement for cuts of £105 million. At the time Macmillan described the £48 million difference as a trifling sum, and had it not been for later developments the events of January 1958 might well have come to seem much ado about very little. However, because they failed to convince the Cabinet of the need for public-expenditure reductions to counter inflation, even if it meant a higher level of unemployment, the Treasury team's action has been seen as an anticipation of developments in the 1970s and 1980s—a prefiguring of the debates between 'Keynesians' and 'Monetarists' that were to characterize the last two years of Edward Heath's leadership of the Conservative party and dominate the Thatcher era.[1] That Enoch Powell emerged in the 1960s as one of the earliest advocates of 'monetarism', and appeared to have an

---

[1] Thus, for example, Martin Pugh has described the 1958 resignations as 'the first shots in the battle for monetarist policy in the Conservative party', M. Pugh, *State and Society* (1994), p. 248, whilst Richard Lamb has seen the resignees position as 'Thatcherism and Friedmanism with a vengeance', R. Lamb, *The Macmillan Years: The Emerging Truth* (1995), 48.

important influence on Thatcherite political economy, has only served to reinforce this view,[2] as has the fact that Margaret Thatcher brought Thorneycroft out of political retirement to be her first party Chairman. This essay seeks to explore both the short- and long-term historical significance of the 1958 resignations at the Treasury, and attempts to clarify whether or not the episode was 'a little local difficulty' or had implications which went beyond the immediate circumstances of the late 1950s.

I

The resignation of the Chancellor of the Exchequer and his Treasury colleagues was a novel political development, but the issue that was at the root of their resignation—inflation—had become very familiar over the previous two years. When, in late January 1958, Thorneycroft sought to explain the reasons for his resignation, he stated that 'he alone in the Cabinet stood against inflation'.[3] Macmillan's subsequent reputation as a dyed-in-the-wool 'expansionist' has lent retrospective plausibility to Thorneycroft's claim, and has assisted his canonization as an early monetarist martyr.[4] However, the fact is that the whole Conservative Cabinet, including the Prime Minister, were aware of and concerned about the economic, political, and electoral impact of inflation throughout the whole of 1957. Indeed, it would have been difficult for them not to be. The Conservative party conference of October 1955 had seen grumblings of discontent about rising prices and in particular their effect upon the middle classes. The representative from Peckham, for example, put in a 'plea for the so-called middle classes', who, he said, were 'rapidly arriving at the position where some of them can hardly afford even a theatre ticket'.[5] A year later conference speakers were more blunt. The inflationary trend was denounced as 'legalised robbery', and there were calls for 'drastic measures' to defend the 'harassed middle class' from the scourge of rising prices.[6] The

---

[2] Powell himself described the 1958 resignations in these terms. See J. E. Powell, 'The Conservative Party', in A. Seldon and D. Kavanagh (eds.), *The Thatcher Effect* (Oxford, 1989), 81. Powell's latest biographers have advanced similar claims. See R. Shepherd, *Enoch Powell* (1996), 163–4 and S. Heffer, *Like the Roman: the Life of Enoch Powell* (1998), 217–38.

[3] Thorneycroft in Parliament, 23 Jan. 1958, *PD*, 5th series, vol. 580, c. *Conservative Century*, 1295.

[4] A. Seldon, 'Conservative Century' in Seldon and Ball (eds.), 49.

[5] D. Smith to NUCA Conference, Bournemouth, Oct. 1955, Conservative Party Archvive (CPA), Microfilm Cards 12–13.

[6] See R. Winston Jones (Bradford South), Councillor E. Hartt (Farnham) and others to NUCA Conference, Llandudno, Oct. 1956, CPA, Microfilm Cards 14–15.

Conservative leadership were not surprised that the Llandudno conference was an uncomfortable experience. Earlier in 1956 the founding of the Middle Class Alliance (MCA), which placed the problem of inflation at the heart of its agenda, had given institutional expression to middle-class grievances. Chaired by the Conservative MP for Lewisham, H. A. Price, the MCA attracted an investigation by Conservative Central Office (CCO), which concluded that although the new organization was not a major threat to the Conservative party, it was indicative of genuine dissatisfaction within a social grouping that was normally regarded as a core element of the Conservative constituency. From mid-1956 on messages from area officers and local party officials to CCO continually warned of the problem of middle-class anger, and the poor Conservative showing at by-elections that year, even in places like Tunbridge Wells, Hereford, and Torquay, indicated that a number of issues, but in particular inflation, were alienating some of the Conservative government's supposedly strongest supporters.[7] The early months of 1957 saw no respite for the Conservatives. By-elections, including the loss of Lewisham-North (which bordered on H. A. Price's seat), continued to show a decline in Conservative support, and the 'middle-class revolt' gathered pace through the rest of the 1957. By the end of the year both Oliver Poole and Lord Hailsham, the party's Chairman and Vice-Chairman, were moved to speak of a 'Poujadist' tendency in middle England that was threatening the Conservative heartlands.[8]

This party-political concern provided the context and impetus for Thorneycroft's 'obsession' with inflation. In early September the Chancellor launched his autumn Cabinet campaign for vigorous action by telling his colleagues that:

It is perfectly true that many people feel that they are doing well out of the inflation, but there is no evidence that we [the Conservative party] are picking up many recruits from the prosperous majority. What is certain is that a great many of those who are suffering from inflation are just the people who form the hard core of the Tory party—the men and women who do the hard slogging in the constituencies.[9]

Thorneycroft added that the Conservatives might lose the next election anyway, and that if this was to be the case then it was better they went down having demonstrated that they had done their utmost to

[7] For CCO's view of the MCA, the warnings of the local parties, and the Conservative reaction to by-election trends see Green, 'Conservative Party', in Taylor and Lawrence (eds.), *Party, State and Society*.

[8] For Poole's remarks see J. Ramsden, *Winds of Change: The Age of Macmillan and Heath* (1996), 29. For Hailsham's identical fears see Hailsham to Macmillan, 25 Oct. 1957, PREM 11/2248.

[9] Thorneycroft, Memorandum to the Cabinet, 'The Economic Situation', 7 Sept. 1957, CAB 129/88, C (57) 195.

overcome Britain's economic difficulties. This, he contended, was the course of action most likely to ensure a rapid return to office in the event of defeat.[10] Thorneycroft's blending of the need to reassure the party's core constituency with a desire to 'do the right thing' might, in terms of historical reputations at least, seem to distinguish his outlook from that of his Prime Minister, given that Macmillan has 'enjoyed' the label of 'opportunist'.[11] But Macmillan's position was very similar. Writing to Thorneycroft shortly before the Chancellor addressed the Cabinet, Macmillan noted that

the £ is weak . . . costs are rising all the time, and there is a sense of frustration, amounting almost to despair, among certain classes of the community, who do not believe that the Government have either the knowledge or the courage to handle the problem, and while the great mass of the people have never 'had it so good' there is a growing feeling that if the situation is allowed to drift too far, it may end in disaster. It therefore becomes not an economic but a political decision as to what we are to do.

Looking at the political situation, Macmillan went on to argue that '[t]he Conservative Party cannot approach the next election with any confidence'. In part he thought history was against the government, in that no party had won three elections in a row since 1832, but his main concern was that, 'while the great mass of the working population and the majority of the entrepeneur class have gained from the inflation, those who have been injured by it are disproportionately represented in the Party organisation in the constituencies'. The easy way out, Macmillan contended, would be to have a 'row' with the trade unions over wages, but this, he argued, would be to treat the symptoms and not the causes of the inflationary problem. What was needed, the Prime Minister stated, was a reduction in demand. If this meant 2–3 per cent unemployment then the government should face that problem, on the grounds that 'we shall lose no votes and injure nobody' as this would only prevent a hoarding of labour and reduce overmanning.[12] Just like his Chancellor, Macmillan blended his economic analysis with the underlying political/electoral imperative of quelling the 'middle-class revolt' through a bold stance against inflation.

The debate within the Conservative party at large, and within Macmillan's Cabinet, indicates that the Treasury ministers' stand against inflation in the autumn of 1957 enjoyed broad support. Against this backdrop Macmillan's view that the £48 million difference between Thorneycroft and his juniors and the rest of the Cabinet was 'trifling',

---

[10] Ibid.
[11] See J. Boyd-Carpenter, *Way of Life* (1980), 137.
[12] Macmillan to Thorneycroft, 1 Sept. 1957, T233/1369.

and by implication not worth their resignations, has a great deal more intrinsic plausibility than the ex-Chancellor's assertion that he (and Powell and Birch) were 'standing alone'. There was, to use a somewhat historically dangerous phrase, a consensus in the Conservative Cabinet that inflation *was* a vital issue and that deflation was necessary. That Thorneycroft, Birch, and Powell were not able to achieve the full measure of reductions they demanded had less to do with any disagreement over basic policy than with the (common) desire of 'spending ministers' to defend their departmental budgets, and indeed for ministers generally to resist Treasury encroachment on their 'patches'. Thorneycroft's demands, for example, implied that public-sector wages be either frozen or at any rate that increases be severely curtailed. This was queried in Cabinet by both the Minister of Labour and the Minister of Health, who both had their own departmental interests to consider.[13] Likewise, the fact that Thorneycroft wished to reduce family allowances was seen to contradict the government's electoral pledges, and was not smiled upon by the Pensions Minister, John Boyd-Carpenter.[14] The Cabinet's disagreement with the Treasury team was, therefore, not over the importance of inflation or even spending reductions per se, but over questions of degree and timing. That the government had already undertaken a major review of Social Services expenditure, with a view to finding economies,[15] and that the Conservatives were to set up their own Policy Committee on the Future of the Social Services (PCFSS) in 1959, at the same time as the Plowden Committee was engaged in the exercise that led to the establishment of the Public Expenditure Survey,[16] are all indicative of the fact that the 1958 resignations cannot be seen as an isolated event. Rather, they have to be seen as part of a broader, ongoing debate within the Conservative party[17] over how to reconcile the desires of their own core support with what were felt to be wider political,

[13] See I. Macleod (Minister of Labour), Memorandum to Cabinet, 'Wages: Collective Bargaining and Arbitration', 11 Nov. 1957, in which he insisted that 'we must try to make it clear . . . that we have not got a national wages policy', CAB 129/90 C (57) 264, and also H. Watkinson (Minister of Transport), Memorandum to Cabinet , 'Wages: NHS', 21 Nov. 1957, which stated that the Chancellor's desire to fund wage increases out of retrenchment or increased charges was not 'practical politics', CAB 129/90, C (57) 280.

[14] For a critical appraisal of Macmillan see P. Clarke, *A Question of Leadership* (1991), 211–34.

[15] See R. Lowe, 'Resignation at the Treasury: The Social Services Committee and the Failure to Reform the Welfare State', *Journal of Social Policy*, 18 (1989).

[16] On the PCFSS see R. Lowe, 'The Replanning of the Welfare State', in M. Francis and I. Zweiniger-Bargielowska (eds.), *The Conservatives and British Society* (Cardiff, 1996), and on the Plowden Commitee see id., 'The Plowden Committee: Milestone or Millstone?', *HJ* (1997).

[17] As Lowe has pointed out, there was a parallel debate taking place within the Treasury over how to achieve *its* traditional goal of a tighter grip on public expenditure. One intriguing issue which this essay has not the space to deal with is the dynamics of the relationship between the Conservatives' and Treasury's aims.

social, and electoral considerations. Lord Hailsham has suggested that Thorneycroft effectively abandoned the pragmatic politics that was required and allowed himself to be swayed by the more dogmatic Powell and Birch,[18] and hence took what was indeed a trifling sum to be a matter of *principle*. This is difficult to demonstrate conclusively, but what is clear is that Thorneycroft, Powell, and Birch were not fighting a lone battle, but simply insisted on fighting it at *their* pace, and this was what left them isolated in January 1958.

II

In terms of placing the 1958 Treasury resignations in a long-term perspective, the questions of the prioritization of inflation over unemployment and whether 1958 saw a dress-rehearsal for the debates of the 1970s and 1980s are crucial issues. That inflationary pressure might attend a fully employed economy had, by the late 1950s, long been recognized as a problem. John Maynard Keynes had indicated that this could be a difficulty as early as 1943,[19] and through the 1950s, especially after 1955, there was increasing concern in the Treasury, and in the Conservative party, that inflation was indeed a serious question. After 1945 Treasury officials, like their inter-war predecessors, had continued to see control of inflation as one of their primary goals, albeit one to be achieved by using a new set of policy implements.[20] This concern had grown rather than lessened over time, and in the spring of 1955 the Treasury Committee that produced the 1956 White Paper, *The Economic Implications of Full Employment*, had mooted the idea of producing a 'popular' version entitled 'Must Full Employment Mean Ever Increasing Prices?', in order to bring the problem home to the public.[21] That the Conservative Research Department (CRD) had an input into the discussions that led up to the 1956 White Paper[22] reflected the party hierarchy's desire to stem concern amongst the Conservative rank and file about prices, and in early 1957 Harold Macmillan's statement at Bedford that the reconciliation of full employment with stable

[18] Lord Hailsham, *A Sparrow's Flight* (1990), 317. See also the discussion in Horne, *Macmillan* ii. 75–8, which also stresses the role of Birch and Powell.

[19] For a summary of Keynes's views on inflation under full employment see R. Middleton, 'Keynes's Legacy for Post-War Economic Management', in A. Gorst *et al.* (eds.), *Post-War Britain, 1945–64* (1989), 28.

[20] See G. C. Peden, 'Old Dogs and New Tricks', in B. Supple and M. Furner (eds.), *The State and Economic Knowledge* (Cambridge, 1992); J. Tomlinson, *Employment Policy: The Crucial Years* (Oxford, 1988), 111–13, 168–71.

[21] See T 234/94 for this discussion. For more of the Treasury's concerns see T 234/91.

[22] See M. Fraser (CRD) to E. Boyle, 13 Jan. 1956, T 234/94.

prices was the great issue of the day confirmed the importance of inflation in Conservative thinking.[23] The summer of 1957 saw the government set up the Council of Prices, Productivity, and Income (the 'three
wise men') to monitor and advise on inflationary pressures, thereby
institutionalizing official concerns,[24] whilst the Conservatives' Policy
Study Group (PSG) discussed inflation in depth.[25] Thus, Thorneycroft's
series of memoranda to the Cabinet in the late summer and autumn of
1957, which highlighted the dangers of inflation,[26] were hardly surprising documents given the tenor of both Civil Service and Conservative
party discussions during the preceding twelve to eighteen months. In
official as well as Conservative circles there was general agreement that
inflation was, 'in both technical and human terms . . . the most difficult
issue which this country has to face'.[27] The question was how to deal
with it.[28]

The abandonment of direct controls over the economy, which had
proceeded apace since the Conservatives' return to office in 1951, had
left the government increasingly dependent upon fiscal and monetary
levers to manage the economy. 'Demand management', as it came to be
known, was based on the premiss that if government relaxed credit
facilities, via a lowering of short-term interest rates and/or an easing of
hire-purchase conditions, and/or reduced taxation and/or increased
government expenditure, then economic activity would increase, and
vice versa. These were, to use the vernacular of the time, 'the touch on
the accelator or the brake' which constituted economic 'fine tuning',
and which A. W. Phillips, in his eponymous 'curve', indicated would
lead to higher levels of employment and inflation or vice versa depending on whether the accelerator or brake was pressed.[29] During his brief
period as Chancellor of the Exchequer between 1956 and 1957 Harold
Macmillan, still living with the consequences of R. A. Butler's 'give-
away' pre-election Budget of spring 1955, had sought to curb public
expenditure in order to 'touch the brake'. In February 1956 he had even
threatened to resign if his colleagues did not agree to a reduction in food

[23] Macmillan at Bedford, 20 July 1957, *The Times*, 21 July 1957.

[24] That in its first report in 1958 COPPI argued that curbing inflation required control of
the money supply and a rise in unemployment serves to confirm that these ideas were in
general circulation.

[25] See 9th Meeting of the PSG, 15 July 1957, CPA, CRD 2/53/28.

[26] See the Chancellor of the Exchequer, 'Inflation', 17 July 1957, 'The Economic Situation',
1 Sept. 1957, and 'The Economic Situation', 7 Sept. 1957, CAB 129/88, C (57) 168, 195, 209.

[27] P. Thorneycroft in Parliament (Budget Speech), 9 April 1957, *PD*, 5th series, 568, c. 968.

[28] For a complementary analysis of contemporary views of the inflation problem, with a
different set of emphases, see A. Booth, 'Inflation, Expectations, and the Political Economy of
Conservative Britain, 1951–64', *HJ* 43 (2000).

[29] A. W. Phillips, 'The Relation Between Unemployment and the Rate of Change of Money
Wage Rates in the United Kingdom, 1861–1957', *Economica* 25 (1958).

subsidies,[30] and the day before he left the Exchequer in January 1957 he requested a £200 million reduction in defence expenditure and an £80–100 million cut in social-service spending. His successor, Thorneycroft, was persuaded of the need to continue dampening economic activity. His first Budget speech of April 1957 endorsed the 'disinflationary' strategy deployed by his predecessor, and he stressed the need for 'the maintenance of a satisfactory budget balance' to ensure that the economy did not overheat.[31] In the late summer of 1957 Thorneycroft felt that inflationary pressures and, partly as a consequence, the position of sterling were cause for deeper anxiety. He thus asked Macmillan to issue a directive to ministers to limit expenditure in 1958–9 to 1957–8 levels, and hoped to maintain this restraint into 1959–60. The 'September Measures' of 1957—particularly the raising of Bank Rate to 7 per cent, the highest rate since 1921—were in keeping with this strategy, as was Thorneycroft's ultimately unsuccessful demand that the 'spending ministries' find economies of £153 million in their 1958–9 estimates in order to hold the line on public expenditure. The question that emerges at this juncture is whether in late 1957 Thorneycroft took the approach to 'disinflation' to a new level, and whether his underlying reasoning and methods were fundamentally at odds with 1950s economic management.

When he first expressed his anxieties on the topic of inflation to the Cabinet in July 1957, Thorneycroft argued that 'we should lose no opportunity of making it clear in public that the source of our inflationary disease is wages increasing out of all proportion to increases in production'. He thus advocated restraint on the part of the chairmen of nationalized industries in settling wage claims, stated that the government should strictly control Civil Service pay-rises, and argued with regard to the private sector that 'arbitrators [should show] . . . more awareness of the needs of the community than is likely to be observed in bilateral agreements between employers and workers'.[32] Here Thorneycroft's emphasis was very much on a 'wage-push' notion of inflationary pressures, which was in keeping with much 'popular' and academic discussion of the problem.[33] By the end of the month, however, Thorneycroft was indicating an alternative line of thinking, telling Macmillan that if inflation was to be addressed properly, 'the

---

[30] R. Hall, diary entry 20 Feb. 1956, in A. Cairncross (ed.), *The Robert Hall Diaries*, 2 vols. (1991), ii. 62.

[31] Thorneycroft in Parliament (Budget Speech), 9 Apr. 1957.

[32] Chancellor of the Exchequer, 'Inflation', 17 July 1957, CAB 129/88, C (57) 168.

[33] For Conservative rank-and-file complaints about 'wage push'—the most vocal protests— see Green, 'Conservative Party'. For academic economic opinion see T. W. Hutchison, *Economics and Economic Policy in Britain, 1946–66* (1968), 131–59.

only resolute action which is really within the power of the Government would be to restrict the supply of money to the point where cost and price increases were checked by severe unemployment. It sounds simple . . . but it would involve cuts in public investment . . . and checking private investment by a savage credit squeeze'. He further argued that 'the present high level of Government expenditure . . . provides a level of demand which is in itself a potent cause of wage increases'.[34] In early August, in a memorandum to his Treasury staff, Thorneycroft again stressed the need for control of the money supply as a means of enabling the economy to 'inflate at a pace somewhat slower than our competitors',[35] and although he emphasized that he was 'not urging a full-blooded deflation on the lines of 1930', he stated that 3 per cent unemployment was a fair target for providing the 'lee-way' in the economy which he felt was necessary.[36] These arguments indicated a shift in emphasis in Thorneycroft's position which was underlined by his memorandum to the Cabinet of early September, where he argued that 'the continual increase in wages and prices *rests in the last resort on the belief that the Government will always make enough money available* to support full and indeed over-full employment'.[37] Thorneycroft had moved the agenda from the 'real' economy to the 'money' economy, and foregrounded the role of government expenditure rather than the behaviour of employers and employees as a determinant of inflation. This shift in the Chancellor's outlook was perhaps reinforced by the influence of his Economic and Financial Secretaries, who, the government's Chief Economic Adviser noted, had been expressing such 'mad' opinions for some time.[38] Equally, Lionel Robbins, who Thorneycroft had summoned back from holiday in late August to advise him on the 'crisis',[39] was also keen to establish monetary matters as 'the cause of all the trouble', and exercised some sway over the Chancellor's thinking.[40] The evidence seems to suggest that Thorneycroft was moving in a monetarist direction in the summer and autumn of 1957.

But to see the differences between Thorneycroft and his Cabinet colleagues as a dispute between 'monetarist' anti-inflationists and 'Keynesian' supporters of full employment would be simplistic. In his memorandum to the Cabinet of early September Thorneycroft noted

[34] Thorneycroft to Macmillan, 30 July 1957, T233/1369.
[35] Thorneycroft, 'Inflation', 7 Aug. 1957, ibid.
[36] Ibid.
[37] The Chancellor of the Exchequer, 'The Economic Situation', 7 Sept. 1957, CAB 129/88, C (57) 194 (my emphasis).
[38] Hall, diary entry, 8 Jan. 1958, in Cairncross (ed.), *Hall Diaries*, ii. 143.
[39] For Robbins's influence see A. Cairncross and N. Watts, *The Economic Section, 1939–61* (1989), 229.
[40] Hall, diary entry, 29 Oct. 1958, in Cairncross (ed.), *Hall Diaries*, ii. 126.

that his thoughts had 'been moving very much in the same direction as the Prime Minister's',[41] and Macmillan, as demonstrated by his own actions at the Exchequer, by his Bedford speech, by his comments to the PSG,[42] and by his acceding to Thorneycroft's request for a directive to the spending ministries in August 1957, had demonstrated sympathy and support for his Chancellor's desire to take a tough line on inflation and the apparent contribution of government expenditure to the problem.[43] Indeed, on 1 September 1957 Macmillan wrote to Thorneycroft from Balmoral outlining his views on the economic situation, and, having acknowledged the centrality of the inflationary problem, had indicated his willingness to accept an unemployment level of 3 per cent, and stated that the necessary reduction in demand required 'reducing the total volume of money'.[44] Small wonder that the Chancellor felt able to tell Macmillan that he felt 'greatly strengthened by your support'.[45] In terms of 'practical politics', the electoral damage being done by inflation, particularly in relation to the Conservative government's core, middle-class constituency, was generally acknowledged by the Prime Minister and the Cabinet.[46] The differences between Thorneycroft and his colleagues were, in the most basic of terms, not that great. That the Cabinet came close to meeting Thorneycroft's target of reduced expenditure levels for the 1958–9 fiscal year is itself testimony to this. There was general agreement in the Conservative hierarchy that the economy needed a 'touch on the brake' for both economic and political reasons. Thorneycroft and his Treasury colleagues felt, however, that the shortfall represented a 'matter of principle',[47] and resigned. But was it a matter of *economic* principle?

With regard to the issue of full employment, Thorneycroft had stated in his 1957 Budget speech that: 'To slash production, to drive down investment, to push up unemployment to a level at which, despite high world demand, we have manufactured our own depression is, to say the least of it, a high price to pay for price stability.'[48] Three months later he evidently felt that the situation had worsened, and argued in Cabinet that it was necessary to let unemployment rise in order to achieve the

[41] Thorneycroft, Memorandum to the Cabinet, 'The Economic Situation', 7 Sept. 1957, CAB 129/88, C (57), 195.

[42] See Macmillan to the meeting of the Policy Study Group, 19 July 1957, CPA, CRD 2/53/28.

[43] For the similarities between Macmillan's and Thorneycroft's positions see Macmillan, Memorandum to Cabinet on the Economic Situation, 1 Sept. 1957, CAB 129/88, C (57) 194.

[44] Macmillan to Thorneycroft, 1 Sept. 1957, T233/1369.

[45] Thorneycroft to Macmillan, 3 Sept. 1957, ibid. Macmillan's support for Thorneycroft is also stressed in M. Jarvis, 'The 1958 Treasury Dispute', *CBH* 12 (1998).

[46] See above, pp. 193–5.

[47] See Cairncross and Watts, *Economic Section*, 230.

[48] Thorneycroft in Parliament (Budget Speech), 9 Apr. 1957, *PD*, c. 970.

requisite 'disinflationary' effect, but he still insisted that 'I have never held the view that massive, large-scale unemployment was a solution to our problems'.[49] The seeming inconsistencies in Thorneycroft's position can in part be explained by the fact that he did not see the 'full employment versus inflation' issue as the *only* factor in his calculations. In his Budget speech earlier in the year he had begun by noting the special difficulties the British economy faced as a consequence of 'our function as banker for a large part of the world',[50] and, following the devaluation of the French franc in August 1957, pressures on sterling and the exchange rate were as important as inflation per se in shaping the Chancellor's thinking in the autumn. In his October memorandum to the Cabinet Thorneycroft stressed not the *domestic* situation but the fact that Britain had lost £185 million from its gold and dollar reserves in the previous two months, and that those reserves stood at only two-thirds of their 1954 level in spite of drawing £200 million from the International Monetary Fund.[51] In this important respect Thorneycroft did not look at all unique. He was simply another post-war British Chancellor trying, like his predecessors and many of his successors, to balance internal pressures with sterling's role as an international reserve currency. His willingness to tolerate higher unemployment in order to reduce inflation was, it seems, being driven by a desire to send a signal to the currency markets as much as by domestic concerns.[52] It could be that the exchange-rate question merely provided Thorneycroft with one more stick with which to belabour his colleagues into accepting his deflationary strategy. Yet, in August 1957 Macmillan had noted, after a long private discussion with Thorneycroft, that 'He must be bold; caution is no good',[53] and in mid-September Macmillan felt it necessary to remind Thorneycroft that, although pressures on sterling were indeed a significant problem, it was essential that the government prioritize the battle against inflation on the basis that 'what will happen to the exchange is another matter'.[54] That Macmillan felt obliged to ask his supposedly 'inflation obsessed' Chancellor to concentrate on the internal situation is surely an indication that Thorneycroft *was* influenced by external policy issues.

[49] Thorneycroft, Memorandum to Cabinet, 'The Economic Situation', 7 Sept. 1957, CAB 129/88, C (57) 195, and see also n. 20 for his explicit rejection of 'full-blooded deflation' on the 1930 level.

[50] Thorneycroft in Parliament (Budget Speech), 9 Apr. 1957, *PD*, c. 966.

[51] Thorneycroft, Memorandum to the Cabinet, 'The Economic Situation', 14 Oct. 1957, CAB 129/89.

[52] See ibid. for Thorneycroft's emphasis on signalling the currency markets.

[53] Macmillan, Diary, 24 Aug. 1957, MP, MS Macmillan dep. d 29.

[54] Macmillan to Thorneycroft, 15 Sept. 1957, T233/1370.

But if Thorneycroft's goals in late 1957 were in some respects 'traditional', were his methods similarly unexceptional? Here it is necessary in the first instance to draw a distinction between the Chancellor and his Treasury colleagues. It is clear that Nigel Birch and Enoch Powell had, at least by 1957 if not earlier, imbibed monetarist arguments. Both felt that inflation was a monetary phenomenon, principally driven by public expenditure and/or borrowing, and they regarded the exchange-rate 'constraint' as a product of the government's 'misguided' adherence to Bretton Woods and its concomitant refusal to countenance a floating exchange rate. They had no time for 'wage push' inflation, and agreed with Lionel Robbins that: 'It is not the duty of governments to make the maintenance of employment the be-all and end-all of policy regardless of what happens to the value of money. It is their duty rather to maintain conditions which will make a high level of employment compatible with a stable value of money.'[55] In Birch and Powell's view the government's role was simply to guarantee a level playing-field for economic actors, the key element of which was a stable value of money. Thorneycroft, as noted above, had moved some way towards this outlook by September 1957,[56] but his continued emphasis on keeping unemployment levels at an acceptably low level, and his desire to avoid floating sterling, unless *force majeure* intervened, distanced him from Birch and Powell and their closest academic supporter, Robbins. If Thorneycroft was a monetarist, then he was of the corned beef rather than the fully roasted kind. Certainly there was no indication that he regarded the employment level as something that should be determined merely by a market adjustment to stable monetary conditions. Rather, he wished to revise the notion of what constituted full employment upwards to the 3 per cent level. This was below the level Keynes had thought realistic in 1944–5, and was in keeping with the definition announced by Gaitskell in 1951. Moreover, Robert Hall, hardly sympathetic to monetarist thinking, stated in August 1957 that there was 'a good deal to be said for interpreting full employment in this way'.[57] Thorneycroft did not embrace monetarism *tout court*, but instead appeared to be more of an 'old-fashioned' deflationist in terms of his primary concerns. Here, somewhat ironically, he was actually quite close to Macmillan. The Prime Minister, after all, had not only endorsed the battle against inflation, but also the use of a reduced money supply in pursuit of that goal: if Thorneycroft is to be labelled a 'monetarist' then Macmillan must be as well. In some respects, however, it is more

55 L. Robbins, Three Banks Review, Apr. 1958, quoted in Hutchison, *Economics*, 136.
56 For Powell's influence see Heffer, *Like the Roman*, 216–40.
57 Hall to R. Makins, 16 Aug. 1957, T233/1369.

accurate to see both the Chancellor and Prime Minister as 'new-fangled' deflationists, in that they sought to apply the braking mechanisms provided by the techniques of post-war demand managment to the particular circumstances the government faced.[58] The difference between them was that Thorneycroft wished to tread firmly on the brakes to dampen economic activity, whereas Macmillan was concerned that too hard a pressure on the brake would make it more difficult to push the accelerator in time for the next election, and, ultimately, he wished to temper the braking effect by maintaining or at least not over-curtailing the government's input into the economy. In fact *both* men were basing their positions on the same blend of Keynesian and Hawtreyan economic paradigms that were the essence of 1950s demand management—or what some have called 'bastardized Keynesianism'.[59] In terms of the *principles* of economic managment, it is very difficult to see the debates of late 1957 as being anything but peripherally informed by the kinds of dispute that were to emerge in the 1970s.

Indeed, if one examines Thorneycroft's (and Macmillan's) concerns about the role of money as a contributor to inflationary pressures, it becomes evident that there was a substantial gulf between them and later advocates and practitioners of monetarist policy. The fact that Thorneycroft and his team resigned on the issue of public expenditure has disguised his chief concern in 1957. In July Macmillan had told Thorneycroft that if the government was to obtain fuller control over the level of economic activity, then this would require greater control over the banking and credit system.[60] Thorneycroft concurred. His internal Treasury memorandum of August, which emphasized control of the money supply as a key anti-inflation device, stressed that *private* as well as public expenditure and borrowing had to be curbed,[61] and in September he complained to Enoch Powell that 'we are not in control of the credit base'.[62] This was not an original complaint. The Treasury had been concerned about this issue from at least 1955, and in April 1957 a committee had been set up under the chairmanship of Lord Radcliffe to enquire into the workings of the British monetary system in order to find more effective controls. The Radcliffe Committee was hearing evidence throughout and beyond the summer and autumn

[58] For another account of the debate that also emphasizes the similarities of approach adopted by Macmillan and Thorneycroft see N. Rollings, 'Butskellism, the Post-War Consensus and the Managed Economy', in H. Jones and M. Kandiah (eds.), *The Myth of Consensus* (Basingstoke ,1996), 106–7.
[59] For the blend of Hawtrey and Keynes in post-war economic management see Clarke, *Keynesian Revolution*, 313–30.
[60] Macmillan to Thorneycroft, 19 July 1957, T233/1369.
[61] Thorneycroft, 'Inflation', 7 Aug. 1957, Ibid.
[62] Thorneycroft to Powell, n.d. (20? Sept. 1957), T233/1370.

'crisis', and was to produce its report in 1959. But Thorneycroft, faced as he was by immediate difficulties, sought more rapid action and conclusions, and even set up his own working party in September 1957.

For Thorneycroft, the crucial problem was how to limit the amount of credit that Britain's banks were making available.[63] Hire-purchase restrictions were available to deal with the lower-grade elements of consumer credit, but bank advances were a more difficult question. Short-term interest-rate changes were one obvious and well-established means of acting on the level of private borrowing, but by the mid- to late 1950s they were increasingly regarded as a clumsy instrument, and a further drawback was that they increased the cost of government borrowing.[64] Thus, the Chancellor and his Treasury officials looked to establish other, more direct methods of curbing bank lending, with Edmund Compton bluntly stating, in early August 1957, that 'if the objective is to limit the money supply created by the banks, it is necessary to operate directly on their advances'.[65] But how was this to be done? Since 1945 informal government approaches to the banks, pursued through the medium of the Bank of England, had been the preferred option. However, Thorneycroft felt that this approach was inadequate, and that the severity of the inflationary problem he faced was clear evidence of this. He thus began to explore the possibility of issuing direct orders to the clearing and other banks to limit their advances, but soon discovered that there were limitations to this approach which he had not expected.

Like his predecessors, Thorneycroft sought to use the Bank of England as the institutional route to dealing with the banking system. This was problematic to begin with, for the Bank was far from enthusiastic about acting as the government's monetary catspaw. As early as April 1955, Robert Hall had noted that:

the Bank of England haven't been as co-operative on monetary policy as they might have been. They have been none too keen on being tough with the Banks. Now the Governor tells the Chancellor that he *is* being tough with them, but Oliver Franks (now Chairman of Lloyds) tells us that this is not so, and E[dwin] P[lowden] got the same story from the Chairman of Westminster [Lord Aldenham] and T. L. R[owan] from the Chairman at Barclays [A. W. Tuke] . . . we are working-up to some sort of *eclairissement* with the Governor, but whether the Chancellor [R. A. Butler] will

[63] On this point Macmillan and Thorneycroft were, once again, in agreement. For Macmillan's emphasis on limiting private as well as public contributions to the volume of money see Macmillan to Thorneycroft, 1 Sept. 1957, T233/1369.

[64] For the Treasury's concerns on this point see S. Howson, 'Money and Monetary Policy in Britain, 1945–90', in R. Floud and D. McCloskey (eds.), *The Economic History of Britain Since 1700*, 3 vols. (2nd edn., Cambridge, 1994), iii, 239–40.

[65] E. G. Compton, 'Limiting the Money Supply', 7 Aug. 1957, T233/1369.

support us I don't know—he has always felt that the Governor is in the saddle and that it is a very serious thing to disagree with him.[66]

Although in May 1955 Hall felt the Bank had 'been tougher', in December he was recording that he had 'told Oliver [Franks] that I thought the Bank of England and the Clearing Banks were on trial as well as the Government and the Treasury', as a result of rising inflation and the apparent inability of the 'credit squeeze' to bite effectively.[67] Writing to Thorneycroft in October 1957, Macmillan recalled that during his period at the Exchequer (in succession to Butler), 'the question arose as to the powers of the Treasury and the Bank of England vis-a-vis the Clearing Banks and other creators of credit', and he added, 'I hope the question is being vigorously pursued'.[68] Thorneycroft certainly did pursue this question vigorously, but it was to become clear that the basic situation remained unchanged.

Thoneycroft's aim in the late summer and autumn of 1957 was to get the banks to reduce their advances by 5 per cent. This he felt would do as much, if not more, to dampen economic activity than even his proposed public expenditure economies. Moreover, as Robert Hall argued, the international currency markets were almost certain to be impressed by such ruthless attempts to control the money supply, which could only benefit sterling.[69] However, in late August 1957 Edmund Compton noted that the Governor of the Bank, Lord Cobbold, was opposed to this course of action, and had told him that if the Chancellor was to proceed it 'would require compulsion' which he deemed 'not appropriate'.[70] Cobbold himself informed Roger Makins, the Head of the Treasury, that an 'attack' on bank credit was unwise and would prove ineffective, insofar as the only thing it would effect would be 'the financing of H[er] M[ajesty's] G[overnment]'s seasonal autumn deficit and the November maturity [of Treasury bills]'.[71] As an alternative Cobbold advocated raising interest rates, cutting local-government expenditure, and ensuring budgetary surpluses for the next two years.[72] Discussions between the Chancellor, Treasury officials, and the Bank in the first week of September produced a statement that the 'City' was

---

[66] R. Hall, diary entry, 19 Apr. 1955, in Cairncross (ed.), *Hall Diaries*, ii. 33.
[67] R. Hall, diary entries, 26 May, 21 Dec., 1955, in ibid. 37, 55.
[68] Macmillan to Thorneycroft, 28 Oct. 1957, PREM 11/4199.
[69] R. Hall, diary entry, 29 Oct. 1957, in Cairncross (ed.), *Hall Diaries*, ii. 126.
[70] E. G. Compton, Note of meeting with Lord Cobbold and L. O'Brien, 22, 23 Aug. 1957, T233/1369.
[71] Cobbold to Makins, 22 Aug. 1957, ibid.—whether the last could be interpreted as a veiled threat is unclear.
[72] Ibid.

'willing to co-operate',[73] but further meetings with the Committee of London Clearing Banks (CLCB) seemed to indicate that the Bank may have been indulging in wishful thinking, for the banks made it clear that limitations on their advances would damage their business.[74] All of these discussions confirmed Cobbold's initial view that a limit had been reached in terms of what could be achieved by *talking* to the banks about limiting advances,[75] but that left the question of what *action* could be taken. Unfortunately for Thorneycroft, the answer was very little. The Bank of England Act of 1946 stated that the Treasury did not have the power to direct the banks, and that if it wished to do so then they had to request the Bank to issue directives for them. But the Bank was only obliged to comply if the Court of Directors agreed that such directions were necessary in the public interest.[76] The Court's attitude, Treasury officials concluded, would probably be determined by 'the "look" of the Government's policy as a whole',[77] which implied that if the government seemed 'serious' about inflation in other policy directions then they might be sympathetic. However, Makins told Thorneycroft that any attempt to limit bank advances would run into 'the teeth of the opposition of the Court'.[78] This in turn raised the question of whether the Treasury had the powers to compel the Bank's Governor and Court to follow its instructions, and if they failed to do so to replace them, but detailed examinations of the 1946 Act by the Treasury Solicitor concluded that no such powers existed.[79] All of this apparently came as somewhat of a surprise to Thorneycroft, who, according to Robert Hall, had grown so frustrated with the Bank's (and the banks') non-cooperation on limiting advances that he had contemplated sacking Cobbold.[80] Instead he was left searching for ways '(a) . . . to control bank credit, (b) . . . to amend the law to give the Treasury the powers it thought it had already'.[81]

Given that new legislation either to amend the 1946 Act, or otherwise to redefine the relationship between the Treasury and the Bank, would have required time, which was precisely what Thorneycroft did not have in his 'crisis', there was little the Chancellor could do other than exhort

[73] Record Notes of a meeting between the Deputy Governor of the Bank of England (H. Mynors), the Chancellor, Sir T. Padmore, and J. Maude, 4 Sept. 1957, T233/1369.
[74] See Notes of Meetings with the CLCB, and with the Chairman of the CLCB, 9, 17 Sept. 1957, T233/1369, 1370.
[75] Cobbold to Makins, 22 Aug. 1957, T233/1369.
[76] See the summary in W. Armstrong to Sir T. Padmore, 3 Sept. 1957, ibid.
[77] Memorandum to the Chancellor by Treasury Officers, 20 Aug. 1957, ibid.
[78] Makins to Thorneycroft, 23 Aug. 1957, ibid.
[79] R. J. B. Anderson to W. Armstrong, 5 Sept. 1957, T233/1664.
[80] R. Hall, diary entry, 29 Oct. 1957, in Cairncross (ed.), *Hall Diaries*, ii. 126.
[81] Ibid. 127.

and hope in his efforts to control private bank credit. Consequently the problems which Thorneycroft's Chancellorship had focused attention upon did not go away, and Macmillan's government continued to be exercised about bank credit provision. In February 1958 Macmillan enquired of his new Chancellor, Derick Heathcoat-Amory, as to what steps were being taken to reconstitute Treasury–Bank relations, as it was 'very important that we should have adequate techniques when the need for re-inflation comes', a point he had also made to Thorneycroft in October 1957.[82] In replying, Heathcoat-Amory complained that:

It seems clear that our present controls over the provision of credit by the Banks and other agencies are inadequate to deal with severe inflationary pressure. Requests to the Banks to co-operate on a voluntary basis—which means asking them to act against their own commercial and financial interests—may succeed within limits . . . But by themselves they are not desirable as a long continuing arrangement.[83]

When the Radcliffe Committee finally reported in 1959, it recommended a new relationship between the Treasury and the Bank, with greater authority for the former, and also suggested giving the Bank powers to request 'Special (non-interest bearing) Deposits' from the clearing banks which would reduce their liquidity and thereby their advances if the government felt the economy was overheating. Both of these recommendations were acted upon, but, as seen in the previous chapter, these measures did not stem either concern or criticism.[84]

In terms of assessing the immediate and longer-term significance of the 1958 Treasury resignations, the ongoing debate over control of the 'credit base' is important. To begin with, it poses some interesting questions about Thorneycroft's position. That Thorneycroft saw the containment of inflation as a critical problem is as evident as it is well known. Furthermore, his emphasis on controlling bank credit provision confirms that he *did* see the money supply as a major cause of inflationary pressures.[85] However, his failure to find an effective means of curbing bank advances perhaps helps to explain why, in the end, he became so committed to reducing public expenditure. Unlike Birch and Powell, he was not wedded to the idea that governments create inflation. He was of the view that the banking system was at least equally culpable. It may be that Thorneycroft was persuaded that there was a link between public expenditure and/or borrowing and bank advances. In many ways this was the case, insofar as the banks' purchases and

---

[82] Macmillan to Heathcoat-Amory, 20 Feb. 1958, PREM 11/4199. For his earlier remarks see Macmillan to Thorneycroft, 28 Oct. 1957, ibid.
[83] Heathcoat-Amory to Macmillan, 26 Feb. 1958, ibid.
[84] See pp. 176–9.
[85] See n. 60 for Macmillan's agreement with his Chancellor on this point.

sales of Treasury bills in particular did provide them with a means of replenishing their reserves and thereby their liquidity. But Thorneycroft's stance indicated that he felt this was a contingent rather than a necessary relationship, in that the banks *should* not boost the money supply in this way if the government wished it otherwise. In short, he felt this was an *institutional* rather than a technical economic issue. But given that he could not, without recourse to time-consuming legislation, find a new institutional structure for limiting the banking system's 'inflationary' activities, then the *only* thing he could act upon in the short to medium term was public expenditure, particularly as he also felt the need to send a prompt anti-inflationary signal to the currency markets to reduce pressure on sterling.

Thorneycroft was clearly not alone in his concerns about the inadequate level of control over the credit base, given that both his predecessor and successor at the Exchequer expressed similar frustration. This raises the question as to why little or nothing was done to provide the government with more adequate credit-control mechanisms. In the course of the summer-to-autumn 'crisis' of 1957 Macmillan told Thorneycroft that 'it might be a very good and useful thing if we found that legislation [to control credit] *is* necessary', as this would 'circumvent the only kind of criticism which I feel is dangerous—that is Boothby etc. representing the natural instincts of those who believe in expansion'. The Prime Minister's reasoning was that '[m]any people will suspect the Treasury and Bank of England of gladly accepting the need for deflation at the moment, and of being less likely to respond to the need for re-inflation if it comes',[86] but if a *mechanism* of control was in place then the predilections of the Treasury and the Bank would be of little import. Given his remarks to Heathcoat-Amory in February of 1958, cited above, Macmillan was perhaps disingenuous in casting Boothby as the representative of 'instinctive expansionists', for the Prime Minister himself was not unfavourable to 'expansionism' and almost certainly viewed the idea of creating a new mechanism with some relish—no longer would his adversaries of the inter-war years, the Treasury and the Bank, be able to thwart him. And yet Macmillan and his government did not bring such a mechanism into being. In part this can be explained by the fact that ultimately they accepted the Radcliffe Committee's recommendations as adequate. That the Bank had regarded Special Deposits as the most unobtrusive proposal might have alerted the government to the fact that the 'City' had successfully defended its autonomy,[87] but there

---

[86] Macmillan to Thorneycroft, 28 Oct. 1957, PREM 11/4199.
[87] See Green, 'Influence of the City', for a discussion of the debate on Special Deposits and other proposals.

were other reasons for the Conservative government's reluctance to act.

The focus of efforts to control private credit was on bank advances. This was logical, in that the clearing banks were the largest providers of credit. But by the late 1950s they were not the *only* providers. The growth of the so-called 'secondary banks' and other credit institutions, which were, of course, in competition with the clearing banks, complicated the credit picture. The clearing banks' reluctance to co-operate with the government on limiting advances in part stemmed from their quite reasonable fears that if they curtailed their activities then the newer institutions would simply step into the gap in the market.[88] Likewise, this helps to explain their resistance to the government's proposals to impose controls on bank advances. By 1961 government awareness of this problem was made explicit by the then Chancellor, Selwyn Lloyd, who told Macmillan in the summer of that year that he was against using increased Special Deposits and further pressure on the banks to deflate, as 'there would be some embarassment about picking yet again upon the banks when we are still unable to produce any viable means of comparable restraint upon the finance houses'.[89] The implication of Lloyd's remarks was, in effect, that the increasingly complex structure of the private credit market made it too difficult to construct adequate and equitable techniques of control.

But there were political as well as technical concerns which restrained the Conservative government in addressing the issue of credit control. In 1955 Robert Hall had warned Oliver Franks that unless his bank (Lloyds) and others co-operated with the government more fully, 'there would be no arguments against the Labour party's return to controls, and none against nationalizing the banks'.[90] This concern was very much extant in Conservative circles in 1960, for when David Eccles, the President of the Board of Trade, discussed the pros and cons of giving the Treasury greater control over the Bank, and therefore the City, he suggested that there was a danger that

closer relations between the Bank and a Conservative Government [might] open the way to a disastrous control over the banking system by the next Labour Government . . . the weaker the Bank was, the more it was distrusted by the City and elsewhere [and] at the time the Socialists won an election, the easier it would be for such a Government to lay its hands on the City.[91]

---

[88] This concern was at the root of the CLCB's position in Sept. 1957, see T233/1370.
[89] Lloyd to Macmillan, 15 June 1961, PREM 11/3291.
[90] R. Hall, diary entry, 21 Dec. 1955, in Cairncross (ed.), *Hall Diaries*, ii. 55.
[91] D. Eccles, 'The Organization and Status of the Bank of England', 3 Aug. 1960, enclosed with Eccles to Macmillan, 4 Aug. 1960, PREM 11/3756.

Whether these technical and political concerns, or a combination of the two, were the key limitation on the Conservative government's action (or rather inaction) is uncertain. What is certain is that governments through the 1960s found that the Special Deposits scheme was not an effective constraint on bank lending, and continued to look for alternative methods of control.[92] Likewise, the Heath government's introduction of Competition and Credit Control in 1971 'continued the old practice of trying to control bank lending without controlling bank reserves', and led them to attempt to impose a lending 'corset' to supplement Special Deposits.[93] But the Heath government was not able to avert a large growth in speculative borrowing in the early 1970s, fuelled in large part by the newer credit institutions. Nor did it avoid the consequences, namely, the 'Secondary Banking' crash of 1973–4. The ghost of Thorneycroft's attempt to rein back private credit continued to haunt government approaches to monetary policy long after he had departed from the Exchequer.

Thorneycroft's emphasis on the need to control *private* contributions to the volume of money, and his search for an effective institutional means of achieving this, is the element in his outlook that most seriously undermines attempts to cast him as a forerunner of Thatcherite monetarism. From the mid-1970s until the mid-1980s the emphasis of Thatcherite economic policy was the centrality of the *Public* Sector Borrowing Requirement—enshrined in the Medium Term Financial Strategy of 1980 and based squarely on the notion that governments caused inflation. The abandonment of the 'corset', and comprehensive financial deregulation in the 1980s, left the government with only short-term interest rates to control credit. That the Thatcher administration in the early 1980s constantly failed to hit their targets for money growth, and presided over an exponential rise in bank and personal credit, was precisely the situation Thorneycroft had sought to avert.[94] The problems that Thorneycroft had wrestled with in terms of the government's control of the British monetary system were still evident in the 1980s, but his approach to dealing with them had been comprehensively rejected.

---

[92] See Howson, 'Money and Monetary Policy', 241.

[93] Ibid. 243, 245.

[94] It is interesting to note that both Milton Friedman and Brian Griffiths wanted to act on money growth by acting on the banking system, but that the Treasury and Bank rejected this idea. See P. Riddell, *The Thatcher Legacy* (1992), 18–19.

III

To see a *direct* link in terms of underlying economic ideas and policy between the Treasury resignations of 1958 and developments in the 1970s and 1980s is an error. But that does not mean that there are no instructive historical parallels to be drawn. Writing to Macmillan in September 1957, David Eccles argued that the inflationary problem the government faced was

in some ways new . . . the real change is that this is not an experts or Whitehall problem—as it was before—it is now a social problem. People are saying 'we do not want to be told that industry here can pass on the rising costs, or that inflation is as bad overseas. What is happening to British prices is undermining British society: all fixed incomes are a swindle; no sensible person saves except to make a capital profit; people in responsible positions are steadily being overhauled by those whose qualifications and contribution to society are inferior'. Our Publicity on inflation must change from its primarily economic to its social evils.[95]

Much the same point, albeit with a different twist, had been made earlier in the year by Harold Watkinson, who, in pointing out to Macmillan the problems of the '£500–£5000' per annum income group in the inflationary climate, argued that the Conservatives had to 'give back incentive and a sense of purpose to this section of *our people*'.[96] A number of points emerge from these late-1950s discussions of inflation that have a resonance in terms of 1970s and 1980s Conservatism. The empasis on inflation as a 'social problem' found an echo in Thatcherite formulations. Sir Keith Joseph's speech at Preston in September 1974, a key moment in his 'conversion' to 'true' (that is liberal market) Conservatism, was clear that '[i]nflation is threatening our *society*'.[97] For Joseph, Thatcher, and their close supporters inflation was a social scourge because its effect on the value of money undermined both the rationality and, more important, the values of thrift, hard work, saving, and aspiration that they felt characterized the best aspects of individual behaviour. These values were associated in the Thatcherite schema with small entrepreneurs, the self-employed, thrifty pensioners with fixed-income 'nest-eggs', home-owners, professionals, and those who aspired to join their ranks. These people, whom Thatcher herself was particularly prone to refer to as 'our people' (echoing Harold Watkinson), were deemed victims of 'Socialist' policies and economics which had, in effect, used inflation as a veiled form of social warfare. Conservative administrations from 1945 to the 1970s were seen to have conspired, or

[95] Eccles to Macmillan, 18 Sept. 1957, T233/1369.
[96] Watkinson to Macmillan, 11 Jan. 1957, PREM 11/1816.
[97] Joseph at Preston, 5 Sept. 1974, in *Reversing the Trend* (1975), 19 (my emphasis).

at any rate aquiesced, in letting 'our people' down—quislings, in effect, in the war against inflation. The 'inefficient' mixed economy and the 'over-generous' Welfare State, both funded by incentive-barring levels of personal taxation, were important aspects of 'our people's' ongoing troubles. However, equally—perhaps more—important was the ability of organized labour to pass on inflationary problems to those who were not organized, whilst using their power to 'proof' themselves against the consequences of rising prices. If inflation was removed, the chances for 'our people' would necessarily improve and the likelihood that others would then seek to join them would increase. Curbing inflation in a way that did not impact upon 'our people' had emerged as the lodestone of Conservative policy. Monetarism was in this sense always a means to an end for Thatcherism. Hence it was possible for the then Chancellor, Nigel Lawson, the author of the MTFS, to announce the end of the monetarist approach in 1985 but still to inist that the inflation rate was 'the judge and jury' of the government's economic policy.[98] The legacy of the Thorneycroft *era* had survived, but any real interest in Thorneycroft's own prescription for inflation had long since perished.

[98] N. Lawson in his Mansion House Speech, Oct. 1985, quoted in P. Riddell, *The Thatcher Legacy* (1991).

CHAPTER 8

Thatcherism: A Historical Perspective

MARGARET THATCHER resigned as Prime Minister and leader of the Conservative party in November 1990, but both she and the political ideology to which her name has been appended[1] continue to fascinate pundits and scholars. Indeed, since Thatcher's resignation in November 1990, curiosity about her political legacy has if anything increased, fuelled in part by the memoirs produced by the ex-premier herself and a large number of her one-time Cabinet colleagues. Since the early 1980s the bulk of work that has appeared on Thatcherism has been dominated either by what one might describe as the 'higher journalism' or by political-science scholarship,[2] both of which have been most exercised by the questions of what Thatcherism was and where it took British politics and society. In this essay I want to look at Thatcherism from a historical perspective and thus ask a different question, namely, where did Thatcherism, and in particular the political economy of Thatcherism, come from?

Given that Margaret Thatcher became leader of the Conservative party in 1975, this might seem a logical starting-point from which to track Thatcherism's origins. Some have argued, however, that Thatcher's election in itself was of little importance, in that the Conservative party's leadership contest in 1975 was a competition not to be Edward Heath, and that Thatcher won because she was more obviously not Edward Heath than anyone else.[3] This emphasis on the *personal* aspects of the leadership issue necessarily plays down any

---

[1] Robert Skidelsky, amongst others, has argued that 'Mrs Thatcher is the only Prime Minister whose name has given rise to an "ism" ', 'Introduction' to id. (ed.), *Thatcherism* (1988), 2. This is a commonly repeated, but inaccurate remark. Gladstonianism was a much-used term in the late 19th Century, see Clarke, *Question of Leadership*, 28–32, 318. Furthermore, Beaconsfieldism was used, as a political pejorative, by Disraeli's Liberal opponents.

[2] In the former category see in particular P. Jenkins, *Mrs Thatcher's Revolution* (1985); P. Riddell, *The Thatcher Government* (1989); H. Young, *One of Us* (1990). For the latter see e.g. A. Gamble, *The Free Economy and the Strong State* (2nd edn., 1994); K. Minogue and M. Biddiss (eds.), *Thatcherism: Personality and Politics* (1987); R. Skidelsky (ed.), *Thatcherism* (1988); K. Hoover and R. Plant, *Conservative Capitalism in Britain and America* (1989); T. Hames and A. Adonis (eds), *A Conservative Revolution* (Manchester, 1994).

[3] See Riddell, *Thatcher Government*, 21.

ideological significance of Thatcher's victory, a point often reinforced by reference to the fact that key elements of the policy agenda that came to be associated with Thatcherism, notably privatization, were by no means clearly articulated in the late 1970s and did not appear in the Conservative Election Manifesto of 1979.[4] On this basis Thatcherism had its ideological origins post 1975, and arguably post 1979—it was simply what Thatcher's party did after it came to government.

But there are problems with the notion that the events of 1975 were ideologically innocent. Margaret Thatcher was the candidate of the Conservative Right in 1975. She only stood after the Right's main standard-bearer, Sir Keith Joseph, had ruled himself out with a clumsy, eugenics-sounding speech at Birmingham in the autumn of 1974. But, since the summer of 1974, Thatcher had developed a close relationship with Joseph, and their alliance was well established by the time of the leadership contest. Moreover, between 1975 and 1979 both Thatcher and Joseph outlined in keynote speeches many of the broad policy objectives of what came to be known as Thatcherism, and in the same period the think-tank that Joseph established in 1974, the Centre for Policy Studies, produced a series of policy papers that foreshadowed the legislative developments of the Thatcher administrations.[5] There *was* more than contingency to Thatcher's gaining the Conservative leadership in 1975, and from 1975 to 1979 this became quite evident.[6]

Even if one admits an underlying ideological element to Thatcher's success in 1975, it could still be the case that it was a product of the 1970s. Thatcher's election could be viewed as a reaction to the failures of the Heath government of 1970–4. Arguably, this created within the party a desire for a change of approach as well as a change of leader, and this Thatcher, well tutored by Joseph and his acolytes at the CPS, seemed to offer. On a more general level, the ending of the post-war boom in the early 1970s triggered a combination of economic difficulties which it had been assumed were impossible to combine—in particular rising unemployment and rapid inflation. This posed problems for the supposedly dominant Keynesian paradigm of economic policy-making, insofar as (after Phillips) unemployment and inflation were supposed to enjoy an inverse relationship. This led to a questioning at various levels of the adequacy of Keynesianism, and especially to a renaissance of liberal market and monetarist economics—ideas suppos-

---

[4] See, e.g. Michael Biddiss's remark that in 1975 'Thatch*erism* . . . was . . . still only quite imperfectly formed', 'Thatcherism: Concept and Interpretations', in Minogue and Biddiss (eds.), *Thatcherism*, 6.

[5] See R. Cockett, *Thinking the Unthinkable* (1993), 254–74.

[6] See M. Wickham-Jones, 'Right Turn: A Revisionist Account of the 1975 Conservative Party Leadership Election', *TCBH* 8 (1997).

edly discarded in the boom years of the 1950s and 1960s. The political economy of Thatcherism could thus be viewed as a product of the economic context of the 1970s, and part of a larger, international rebirth of interest in liberal market and monetarist economics.[7] Undoubtedly such an analysis of Conservative party politics in the early 1970s, and the changing climate of both economic performance and debate, carries some explanatory weight. But this essay would suggest that one needs to go back a lot further than the 1970s to establish the pedigree of Thatcherite political economy.

A definition of terms is perhaps appropriate at this juncture—what do I mean when I speak of Thatcherite political economy? I will define it in terms of the self-professed intentions of Margaret Thatcher and her administrations. They saw their main aim as being to 'roll back the frontiers of the State'. This was to be achieved by replacing the mixed economy with a private-sector dominated market economy. This in turn was to be complemented by a reform and reduction of the Welfare State, by a lowering of direct personal taxation, and the encouragement of wider property ownership. Institutions which hampered the operation of the market, in particular trade unions, were to have their powers and legal privileges curbed. Finally, low inflation rather than full employment was to be the central goal of economic policy. In short, Thatcherism saw its task as being to challenge and ultimately dismantle the institutions, practices, and assumptions which underpinned what had come to be known by the mid-1970s as 'the post-war consensus', or what Thatcher herself referred to (without meaning to be complimentary) as 'the progressive consensus'.[8]

In terms of understanding Thatcherism *historically*, the explicit assault on the 'post-war consensus' is important. To begin with, it stemmed from Thatcherism's own historical interpretation of what had gone wrong with the British economy. Thatcherite interest in and use of history is best known in the context of eulogies about 'Victorian values',[9] but there is strong evidence to support the view that 'the values she [Thatcher] admired were the values of the inter-war years'.[10] Certainly the 1930s and the immediate post-war period played as important a role as the Victorian era in Thatcherism's construction of the past. Speaking to the CPS in January 1975, Keith Joseph argued that Britain needed to embrace *embourgeoisement*, 'which went so far in Victorian times *and even in the much-maligned "thirties"* '.[11] The importance of the 'thirties' to the Thatcherite schema was underscored by Thatcher herself in her second volume of memoirs. Commenting on 'thirties' life in her father's grocery in Grantham, she noted that the experience gave her

A sympathetic insight into what I would later come to think of as 'capitalism' or the 'free enterprise system'. Whereas for my . . . political contemporaries it was the *alleged* failure of that system in the Great Depression that convinced them that something better had to be found, for me the reality of business in our shop and the bustling centre of Grantham demonstrated the opposite . . . what I learned in Grantham ensured that abstract criticisms I would hear of capitalism came up against the reality of my own experience: I was thus inoculated against the conventional economic wisdom of post-war Britain.[12]

For Thatcher, like Joseph, the 'thirties' were a period to be praised, not condemned, and post-war acceptance of a 'pessimistic', Keynesian analysis of the period was seen to have informed a mistaken rejection of the liberal market orthodoxies of the inter-war years and, therefore, an equally erroneous adoption of Statist, Keynesian forms of economic management after 1945. On this basis, the reforms of the 1945–51 Attlee government, and more particularly the Conservative party's adaptation to them, had been a mistake based on a misinterpretation of the inter-war period and of the 1945 general election as a verdict on the 1930s. Sir Keith Joseph's speeches of 1974–5 were very precise in seeing the 'the past *thirty* years' as one long error of judgement.[13] Likewise, one of Thatcher's closest colleagues, Nicholas Ridley, noted that he had entered politics to reverse the Attlee governments' reforms,[14] whilst Thatcher's favourite party Chairman argued that 'the failure of the Conservative governments of 1951–64 to reverse the Attlee experiment was deplorable'.[15] More formal Thatcherite history was equally clear on this point, with Andrew Roberts noting that, 'Instead of treating it as the freak result it was, an entire generation of Tory politicians was emasculated by the 1945 election result, especially over the issues of nationalization, the growth of the State and trade union reform'.[16] Thatcherite history saw both the country and the Conservative party as

---

[11] Sir Keith Joseph, 1 Jan. 1975, repr. in id., *Reversing the Trend* (1975), 57 (my emphasis).
[12] M. Thatcher, *The Path to Power* (1994), 566.
[13] See e.g. Sir Keith Joseph at Upminster, 22 June 1974, in id., *Reversing the Trend*, 7 (my emphasis).
[14] N. Ridley, *My Style of Government: The Thatcher Years* (1991), 2.
[15] C. Parkinson, *Right at the Centre* (1991),191.
[16] A. Roberts, *Eminent Churchillians* (1994),253.

having taken a wrong turning in and after 1945 as a consequence of misreading the 'thirties'.

To rely upon memoirs and assessments from the 1970s and 1990s to demonstrate a point could be regarded as a dangerous valorization of *post hoc* judgements. But whether Thatcherite memoirs and commentaries are 'accurate' is not the real issue here. The fact that they all construct the past in similar fashion underscores the *political* essence of their historical judgement. More important still is the fact that Thatcherite 'history' represented the culmination of a long-standing Conservative critique, extant since at least 1945, of developments in national and Conservative party economic policy. In this respect this essay will seek to establish that the first step in understanding the vehemence of Thatcherism's assault on the 'post-war settlement' is to grasp that the Conservative party never fully accepted that anything had been settled.

At present the history of post-war Conservative politics suggests that, although the Conservatives were slow to appreciate the significance of the Beveridge Report's proposals and the 1944 White Paper on Employment, they rapidly made up ground after 1945. The shock of the general election defeat, it has been argued, demonstrated the popularity of Labour's commitment to reform and thereby strengthened the hand of 'progressive' opinion in the Conservative ranks. As a consequence of the related pressures of, on the one hand, electoral necessity, and on the other, internal reformers, the Conservative party, it has been suggested, shifted its position on issues of economic and social State intervention. The growing authority of 'progressive' figures such as R. A. Butler, Lord Hailsham, and Harold Macmillan have been seen as evidence of the Conservatives' determination to discard their hard-faced inter-war image.[17] Likewise, Conservative deeds seemed to speak as loudly as the words of their 'progressives'. Apart from returning the steel and road-haulage industries to private ownership, successive Conservative administrations after 1951 made no great attempt to roll back the Attlee governments' reforms. Indeed, as was seen in the previous chapter, in 1958 the Conservative premier, Harold Macmillan, proved willing to accept the resignation of his entire Treasury team in order, it seems, to defend and publicly demonstrate his government's commitment to full employment. The actions of Conservative governments in the 1950s appear to confirm a process which saw the party accommodate itself to the mixed economy and the Welfare State.

[17] For this interpretation see K. O. Morgan, *The People's Peace* (Oxford, 1991), 31–2. For a different analysis see H. Jones, 'The Conservative Party and the Welfare State, 1942–55', unpublished London University Ph.D thesis (1992).

As far as it goes, this story of Conservative accommodation to the Attlee governments' reforms is accurate, insofar as the Conservative *leadership* after 1945 assumed that it would be impolitic to launch an assault on either the Welfare State, full employment, or the mixed economy. But to see Conservative politics in the 1950s in terms of a triumph of 'progressive' Conservatism is to tell, at best, only part of the story. From the publication of the Beveridge Report in 1942, through the post-war Labour reform legislation, and on into the 1950s and 1960s there is evidence of deep-seated Conservative hostiltity, especially in the middle and lower ranks of the party, to the development and impact of State intervention in the economic and social spheres. Moreover, the intensity of this hostility, which was firmly grounded in a liberal-market critique of Labour's post-war reforms, increased rather than decreased as time went by.

When the Beveridge Report appeared in 1942 the Conservative response was at best lukewarm.[18] Popular interest in and approval of the Report forced the Conservatives to take it seriously, and a committee, chaired by Ralph Assheton, was set up to examine its proposals. Although there were aspects of Beveridge which this committee accepted, it made two fundamental criticisms. The first was voiced by Assheton personally, when he told R. A. Butler in December 1942 that, 'one of the chief troubles about the *Beveridge Report* is that whereas his diagnosis relates to Want, his proposals are very largely devoted to giving money to people who are not in want'.[19] In effect this was a critique of 'universality', a principle at the heart of Beveridge's proposals and which represented his attempt to remove Poor Law stigmatization from the post-war welfare structure. The second criticism was the level of taxation that would be required for Beveridge's scheme. Here Assheton's committee reported that, if the economy was to flourish after the war, this would require 'a substantial reduction of taxation, especially in the rate of income tax'.[20] The argument was clear and (to a 1990s audience) familiar: a successful economy requires incentives, and a welfare system based on universality hampers incentives, first by offering 'a sofa rather than a springboard' of benefits, and second, by requiring a level of taxation that reduced the rewards of productive enterprise.

In 1945 this liberal market opposition to plans for extensive social reform set the tone for the Conservative election campaign. The previous

---

[18] See K. Jeffreys, 'British Politics and Social Policy During the Second World War', *HJ* 30 (1987) and Jones, 'Conservative Party', *passim.*

[19] R. Assheton to R. A. Butler, 21 Dec. 1942, Butler papers, Trinity College Library, Cambridge, MS RAB, H77, fo. 70.

[20] Report on the Beveridge Proposals, 19 Jan. 1943, Conservative Party Archive [hereafter CPA], Bodleian Library, Oxford, CRD 2/28/6.

year had seen the publication of F. A. Hayek's *The Road to Serfdom*, with its warnings about the loss of liberty, choice, and efficiency that interventionist economies entailed. Mention of Hayek here is important: not simply because his oeuvre, and *The Road to Serfdom* in particular, became essential referents for Thatcherism, but because *The Road to Serfdom* played a major role in the Conservatives' 1945 campaign. Ralph Assheton, by then party Chairman, read Hayek's work soon after it was published, and was so impressed by it that he immediately advised Conservative election agents and candidates to read it, and wanted 12,000 copies of an abridged version to be distributed as campaign literature, which entailed promising the publishers one-and-a-half tons of the party's paper ration for the election. Moreover, it was Assheton who wrote the outline notes for Churchill's 'Gestapo' speech of the 1945 campaign. This speech, which claimed that Labour's proposed reforms would have to be enforced by State police, expressed, albeit crudely, basic Hayekian themes.[21]

The Conservative defeat in 1945 weakened the liberal market position within the party: that Assheton was replaced as party Chairman by the emollient figure of Lord Woolton in 1946, and that R. A. Butler took over the Conservative Research Department (CRD), marked the increased strength of the 'progressive' Conservative cause. But two points need to made here about Conservative politics and the Conservative electoral revival from 1945 to 1951. First, although the liberal market position was weakened it did not disappear, and such views played a major role in the Conservatives' ongoing criticisms of the Attlee governments' reforms, particularly in the realms of the creation of the National Health Service (NHS), nationalization, and housing.[22] Second, the Conservatives' effort to revive their electoral fortunes saw them target middle-class floating voters, especially in the South and South-East of England, by presenting themselves as the party that would reduce government expenditure and taxation, remove controls, especially building controls, and rationing, and thereby free the private sector to provide for expanded consumer demand and aspirant home-owners.[23] Thus, although the liberal market tone of the 1945 had been quietened by 1951, it is essential to remember that the Conservative leitmotif in 1950–1 was 'Set the People Free', not the welfare estate and the mixed economy are safe in our hands.

[21] For this information I am indebted to Jones, 'Conservative Party', 107–8.

[22] For the Conservative critique of Labour's health policy see in particular C. Webster, 'Conflict and Consensus: Explaining the British Health Service', *TCBH* 1 (1990). On housing see Jones, 'Conservative Party', 127–46. *Parliamentary Debates* remain the best source for the conflicts over nationalization.

[23] I. Zweiniger-Bargielowska, 'Rationing, Austerity and the Conservative Party Recovery After 1945', *HJ* 36 (1993).

It is worth dwelling briefly on the Conservative electoral revival of the late 1940s and early 1950s, and in particular on the Conservatives' underlying strategy, for this in itself brings home the importance Conservatives attached to opposing the Labour government's position. The basic Conservative aim was to target floating voters, particularly those antagonized by the rationing, austerity, and government controls associated with Labour's period in office.[24] According to internal party research, the profile and outlook of these floating voters was very similar to that of Liberal supporters,[25] and the Conservatives thus made every effort to attract Liberal voters. This included constructing an official pact with the National Liberal grouping, and, equally important, seeking to appeal to Liberal supporters 'where no [Liberal] organisation exists'—a large number of local Conservative associations even went so far as to rename themselves 'Conservative and Liberal'.[26] The *raison d'être* of this strategy was to construct an 'anti-Socialist' bloc such as Baldwin had built in the inter-war years. In this context it is significant that the supposedly 'progressive' Industrial Charter was welcomed by at least one local Conservative association on the grounds that there was 'nothing in it with which a Liberal would disagree'.[27] In 1951 this strategy paid dividends when the Conservatives gathered in the lion's share of the collapsing Liberal vote—not on the grounds of endorsing the Attlee government's reforms, but on the basis that they would at least ensure that there were no further extensions of State intervention.

The Conservative electoral revival by no means put an end to liberal market activism. In 1950 Richard Law, the overlooked son of the unknown Prime Minister, published *Return From Utopia*, a sustained critique of Labour's post-war reforms from a liberal market perspective. In particular, Law attacked the high levels of taxation required to fund the Welfare State, and argued that inflation was bound to exact a serious toll in an economy committed to full employment.[28] Law did not confine his criticism to publications. At the Conservative party conference in 1952 he was one of the principal speakers to a motion that

[24] See ibid. and also id., 'Consensus and Consumption: Rationing, Austerity and Controls after the War', in H. Jones and M. Kandiah (eds.), *The Myth of Consensus* (Basingstoke, 1996), 78–96.

[25] 'The Floating Vote', 6 Dec. 1949, CRD 2/21/1, and M. Kandiah, 'Conservative Leaders' Strategy—and Consensus, 1945–64', in Jones and Kandiah (eds.), *Myth*, 63.

[26] Lord Woolton to Conservative Constituency Agents, 8 May 1947, Woolton papers, Bodleian Library, Oxford, MS WLTN fos. 66–7. For the Conservatives' view of the Liberals as subaltern anti-Socialists see E. H. H. Green, 'The Conservative Party, the State and the Electorate, 1945–64', in M. Taylor and J, Lawrence (eds.), *Party, State and Society in Modern Britain* (Aldershot, 1996).

[27] Sheffield Conservative Party Agent, quoted in J. Ramsden, *The Age of Churchill and Eden* (1996), 150.

[28] R. Law, *Return From Utopia* (1950).

'public expenditure has increased, is increasing and ought to be diminished'[29]—a motion that was carried by an overwhelming majority. In 1952 most Conservative demands for 'economy' were directed at a 'bloated' Civil Service. However, by the 1955 party conference speakers were arguing that the Welfare State was 'admirable, *so long as you can afford it*', and that full employment was only being sustained by the profligate spending of government departments and nationalized industries.[30] Given the stringent administrative processes designed to filter out hostile comment at conference, the fact that such criticisms were being voiced was indicative of significant rank-and-file displeasure. Furthermore, the language of these criticisms was informed by clear liberal market imperatives.

Nor was it only the rank and file who expressed disquiet. As early as 1950 the backbench 1922 Committee was of the view that 'no more money can be spent on the welfare state', and they were keen to establish a Conservative approach to social policy that was not 'me-tooing Socialist solutions'. It was against this backdrop that the 'One Nation' group of Conservative MPs began to produce a series of publications which sought to define a distinctive Conservative approach to the economy and social policy. An interesting example of their thinking was provided by two young MPs, Iain Macleod and Enoch Powell, in a 1952 publication *The Social Services: Needs And Means*, which asserted that 'the question . . . which poses itself is not "should a means test be applied to a social service?" but "why should any social service be provided without a real test of need?" '[31] Once again, the universality of the Beveridge system was being challenged. The One Nation group, in the pamphlet *Change is Our Ally* (written by Enoch Powell and Angus Maude), also attacked Statist incursions into economic management. In spite of their Disraelian moniker, the One Nation group sought to bring liberal market thinking to the centre of Conservative debate on social and economic policy.

The 1951 Conservative government did not embrace any significant liberal market proposals.[32] The steel industry was denationalized, rationing and controls were removed, and Butler at the Exchequer was able to reduce personal taxation. Systematic means tests for benefits were, however, resisted and there was no major attempt to reduce the scale of the public sector or to reform the Welfare State. That the

---

[29] National Union, Conference Report, 1952, CPA, Microfilm Cards 8–9.
[30] Ibid.
[31] I. Macleod and E. Powell, *The Social Services: Needs And Means* (1952).
[32] Although the fact that the 'Robot' scheme to float the pound was so heavily canvassed is a significant indication that 'Keynesian' thinking was by no means entrenched in the party. See N. Rollings, 'Poor Mr. Butskell: A Short Life Wrecked by Schizophrenia', *TCBH* 5 (1994).

government was able to adopt this approach and still gain an increased majority in 1955 seemed to indicate that they were able to ignore liberal market opinion in the party. But after 1955 there were signs that the Conservatives could not ignore these voices with impunity.

Significant problems began to emerge for the Conservatives in and after 1956. Although they sustained only one loss before 1958 the Conservative government experienced greatly reduced majorities in a number of by-elections. At the same time two protest organizations emerged, the Middle Class Alliance (MCA) and the People's League for the Defence of Freedom (PLDF), both of which were highly critical of post-war economic and social reform. I have dealt at length with these organizations elsewhere and I will not discuss their activities and the Conservative response to them in detail here.[33] Suffice it to say that the MCA had a shopping-list of liberal market demands whilst the PLDF campaigned on the single issue of trade-union reform, and that both groups were considered to have a membership made up of people who would normally have been considered 'natural' Conservative voters. What made these organizations particularly worrying for the Conservative leadership was that they were seen as symptomatic of a wave of dissatisfaction with Conservative policy amongst, in particular, the British middle class—the social group regarded as the core Conservative constituency. The MCA and PLDF were seen as an extreme, institutional manifestation of grievances voiced by the party rank and file at the disagreeable party conferences of 1955–8 and of the 'middle-class revolt' which brought about the drop in the Conservative vote in Tunbridge Wells in 1956, at Torquay, Edinburgh, and Ipswich, and the lost seat of Lewisham North in 1957, and the loss of Torrington in 1958. Harold Macmillan, as usual, sought to conceal any anxiety behind an appearance of *sang froid*, telling the party's chief research officer: 'I am always hearing about the middle classes. What is it they really want? Can you put it on a sheet of notepaper, and then I will see if I can give it to them.'[34] But the fact that he and others in the party hierarchy *were* always hearing about the middle classes was the point. From mid-1956 on Butler was constantly being warned that the 'oppressed middle classes' would cause the party problems. In early 1957 some constituency parties were reporting difficulties of recruitment and subscription renewal, and in the autumn of 1957 both Oliver Poole and Lord Hailsham, the Conservative Chairman and Vice-Chairman, referred to 'Poujadist' tendencies amongst the party's middle-class voters and rank and file.[35]

[33] See Green, 'Conservative party', in Taylor and Lawrence (eds.), *Party, State and Society*.
[34] Macmillan to M. Fraser, 17 Feb. 1957, Public Record Office, PREM 11/1816.
[35] See J. Ramsden, *Winds of Change: The Age of Macmillan and Heath* (1996), 19, 29.

From the protests of the MCA and PLDF, and from party conference debates and constituency reports, it is possible to distil four main inter-related grievances behind the 'middle-class revolt'. First, inflation. Second, the growing power and abuses of trade unions in general, and in particular their ability under full-employment conditions to achieve inflationary wage settlements. Third, the level of taxation required to fund an 'over-generous' Welfare State and inefficient nationalized industries. Fourth, and perhaps most important, the apparent inability or unwillingness of the Conservative party to adopt 'real' Conservative policies to combat these problems and, as a corollary, the apparent tendency of successive Conservative governments to 'hang on to Socialist policies and legislation that should have been swept away long ago'.[36]

It was this pressure from the party rank and file and disaffected voters that explains Harold Macmillan's comments about the centrality of stable prices which he added as a rider to his 'never had it so good speech' at Bedford in 1957. It was also this pressure that provided the context for Peter Thorneycroft's attempt to prioritize the fight against inflation later in that year, which was to culminate in his and his Treasury team's resignation in January 1958.[37] Less publicly dramatic, but equally important, the Conservative hierarchy's establishment of a Policy Studies Group (PSG) in the summer of 1957, to examine possible changes of policy direction, the deliberations of the Party Commitee on the Nationalized Industries (PCNI), and the setting up of the Policy Committee on the Future of the Social Services (PCFSS) in 1959, were informed by a desire to find a means of quelling the concerns of the party's core constituents.[38]

None of the above-mentioned party committees produced proposals for sweeping changes of the kind advocated by the party rank and file, but their deliberations are indicative of an important debate on the merits of post-war economic and social policy that was taking place in the party in the late 1950s and early 1960s. The PSG's sessions saw much deliberation over inflation, with Macmillan acknowledging at its ninth meeting that, 'on the domestic front the reconciliation of full employment with a stable cost of living was the key problem', and he was prompted to ask, 'could either aim be said to be electorally more important?'[39] The Prime Minster's response to his Treasury team's resignation

---

[36] T. Constantine to O. Poole, 10 June 1956, CPA, CCO 120/3/4.

[37] See Green, 'Conservative party' and Ch. 7, above.

[38] For a discussion of the PSG's work see Green, 'Conservative party', and for the PCFSS see R. Lowe, 'the Failure to Reform the Welfare State', in I. Zweiniger-Bargielowska and M. Francis (eds.) *The Conservatives and British Society 1880–1990* (Cardiff, 1997). For the deliberations of the PCNI see CRD 2/6/2,3 in the CPA.

[39] PSG, Minutes of the 4th Meeting, 15 July 1957, CPA, CRD 2/53/28.

seemed to indicate that, in the short term at any rate, he saw full employment as more significant,[40] but the PSG's discussions indicated that there was significant and growing pressure for a prioritization of inflation.

With regard to the nationalized industries, both the PCNI and the PSG saw much critical comment of the performance of public corporations. It is worth noting that the PCNI's initial remit was 'to examine and make recommendations regarding the position of the nationalized industries . . . with particular reference to the possibility of introducing any element of competitive enterprise',[41] and that its chairman felt that one purpose its deliberations served was 'to bridge the gulf that existed on the subject between the Ministers and the Backbench'.[42] The very acknowledgement of such a gulf is in itself interesting, as is the fact that, when the party's Advisory Committee on Policy (ACP) discussed nationalized concerns, the idea of a half-way house between public and private ownership, referred to as 'the BP model',[43] was floated. Equally interesting, the chairman of the 1922 Committee greeted this suggestion with approval, and added that such a 'hiving off would receive support from the party as the first step to later more ambitious proposals'.[44] The PCNI, PSG, and ACP were loath (partly for fear of treading on particular ministers' toes) to endorse ideas of denationalization, but their discussions revealed an awareness of a body of opinion in the party that favoured such a radical move.

On trade unions, Macmillan's Minister of Labour, Iain Macleod, constantly stressed at PSG meetings that the legal and political problems involved in legislating on strike action, picketing, and the closed shop were too great to warrant action. Macleod was probably tired of having to make this point, given that he, like his predecessor Walter Monckton,[45] had been repeatedly forced to make it to hostile party audiences after taking on his office.[46] But other members of the PSG were supporters of legal curbs on trade unions.[47] In April 1957

[40] Through much of 1957 Macmillan offered a great deal of support to Thorneycroft and his team, which in part explains the legacy of bitterness which his 'back-pedalling' in the winter of 1957–8 engendered. See Green, 'Treasury Resignations.

[41] PCNI, Terms of Reference, CRD 2/6/2, CPA.

[42] PCNI, Chairman's notes at the 17th Meeting, record by J. Douglas CRD, 16 Dec. 1957, CPA, CRD 2/6/3.

[43] Minutes of the ACP, 25 Jan. 1957, CPA, ACP 2/1.

[44] J. G. Morrison, ibid.

[45] For rank-and-file criticisms of Conservative trade-union policy in the early 1950s see Roberts, *Eminent Churchillians*, 259–71.

[46] For a particularly uncomfortable conference for Macleod on this issue, see the debate at the party conference at Llandudno in 1956.

[47] The most powerful advocates were the MP John Simon and Peter Goldman from the party's Research Department.

Reginald Maudling and John Simon 'reported strong feeling in the party against Trade Unions',[48] and in autumn that year James Douglas of CRD noted that, 'since the 1955 election . . . there seems to have been a slight move to the right on trade unions issues, nothing so definite as a People's League attitude, but the political centre of gravity . . . seeems to have shifted appreciably'.[49] In 1958 the Conservative barristers' organization, the Inns of Court Society, published *A Giant's Strength*, which advocated the removal of many of the legal immunities given to trade-union activities under the 1906 Trades Disputes Act.[50] In 1959 even Macleod felt that the pressure to do something had reached such a level that he included a promise to introduce legal reforms in the first draft of the Conservative election manifesto, only to have Macmillan intervene personally to remove it.[51] Conservative opinion on the trade-union question was clearly hardening.

On the question of public expenditure on the Welfare State, the PSG's discussions also saw strong sentiments in favour of reform. Enoch Powell argued that 'the whole machinery of social security has to be overhauled', that 'Lloyd George, Chamberlain and Beveridge have had their day', and that 'their theories and their system . . . was simply the delayed reaction to Victorian poverty'.[52] Powell had two major criticisms to make. First—and here he restated earlier objections—he attacked the principle of universality—that the welfare structure was not needs driven. Second, he pointed to the practical problem of finance, arguing that, for example, the National Insurance scheme was only solvent because of constant post-war inflation and that, with the population ageing and other demands increasing, targets and priorities had to be established. The PSG concurred with the idea of 'switching the emphasis of state expenditure away from services which, in a fully employed community, people ought to be able to provide at least in part for themselves',[53] but, in spite of this sympathy for Powell's views, the government produced no major action in 1957–8. However, even after the Conservatives' handsome success at the 1959 election, the party's Advisory Committee on Policy established that a key long-term issue was 'the future financing of the social services as a whole and to what extent we should break away . . . from the principle of universality',[54]

---

[48] PSG, Minutes of the 4th Meeting, 12 Apr. 1957, CPA, CRD 2/53/28.
[49] J. Douglas to J. Rodgers, 8 Aug. 1957, CPA, CRD 2/9/38.
[50] It is perhaps worth noting that one member of the Society who took part in the discussions leading to the publication of this document was Geoffrey Howe.
[51] See R. Shepherd, *Iain Macleod* (1994), 149.
[52] E. Powell to J. Pain, n.d. (Mar. 1957), CPA, CRD 2/53/26.
[53] PSG, 13th Meeting, 24 Feb. 1958, CPA, CRD 2/53/28.
[54] Chairman's notes of the Meeting of the ACP, 9 Dec. 1959, CPA, ACP 1/10.

and it was precisely this issue that the PCFSS was set up to examine, with a remit that echoed the concerns Powell had expressed at the PSG.

As the 1950s drew to a close the liberal market critics of the supposed post-war settlement were on the march. The PSG's attempt in 1957–8 to frame the basis of what was referred to as 'the opportunity state'—an obvious attempt at differentiating Conservative thinking from the Welfare State—laid emphasis on 'the opportunity to make money and get on' through a regime that would facilitate spending opportunities, encourage wider property- and share-ownership, and introduce lower personal taxation.[55] Such a regime, Lord Home argued, would serve to quell 'the restlessness amongst the middle class voters who fear that the standards which they have so painfully gained by work and thrift are going to be lost',[56] and also allow the party to identify itself more broadly with social mobility and aspirational consumerdom. Important question-marks were being placed against the political and electoral viability of sustaining a system of social and economic policy that, in the eyes of many in the party, reflected 'Socialist' rather then Conservative values.

In September 1961 Harold Macmillan, after a Cabinet meeting about the economic situation, noted in his diary that there was a division of opinion between those who favoured 'old Whig, liberal, laissez faire traditions' and those who were 'not afraid of a little *dirigisme*'.[57] Not surprisingly, the author of *The Middle Way* sided with the *dirigistes*, and from 1961 to 1963 Macmillan sought to establish the institutional structure of a 'developmental state' through the creation of the National Economic Development Council (NEDC), a National Incomes Commission (NIC), and related actions such as the application to join the EEC and the abolition of Resale Price Maintenance.[58] But this served neither to quieten discontent in the lower echelons of the party nor to cement the Conservatives' electoral position, with the twin developments of a Liberal revival and adverse by-election reversals, most notably at Orpington in 1962, signalling a recurrence of the problems that had troubled the Conservatives in the mid- to late 1950s.

After Macmillan's resignation and the Conservative defeat at the 1964 general election, calls for a change in policy direction gathered pace, and the election of Edward Heath as leader in 1965 seemed to many in the party to presage such a change. Heath inherited a party whose backbenches and grass roots were very restive.[59] At this juncture

---

[55] P. Goldman, at PSG 2nd Meeting, 15 Mar. 1957, CPA, CRD 2/53/28.

[56] Home to R. A. Butler, 4 Mar. 1958, CPA, CRD 2/53/29.

[57] H. Macmillan, diary entry, 21 Sept. 1961, in id., *At the End of the Day* (1973), 37.

[58] For the most detailed description of these initiatives see K. Middlemass, *Power Competition and the State*, 3 vols (1986–91), ii. 28–58.

[59] See Ramsden, *Winds of Change*, 245–53.

one senior Conservative politician, Enoch Powell, emerged as the most articulate spokesman of this unease and an eloquent critic of post-war economic policy. Although he was to be dismissed from the Shadow Cabinet in 1968 after his Birmingham speech on immigration, Powell's main contributions to Conservative intra-party debate from 1964 to 1970 were focused on the economy. Powell's basic message, condensed in his 1965 collection of speeches, *A Nation Not Afraid*, was that the Conservative party had to stop apologizing for being a 'capitalist' party and embrace true, that is liberal market, capitalist policies. The grievances expressed by the party rank and file in the 1950s—inflation, high levels of public expenditure, and high taxation—were all highlighted by Powell as the incubi of the post-war economy.[60] After the Conservatives' 1966 general election defeat, Powell intensified his assault on post-war economic management with a further series of speeches in the autumn of that year criticizing State intervention and calling for a return to a liberal market approach.[61] One novelty of Powell's critique, and one that was to become central to liberal market thought in the 1970s, was an emphasis on government monetary policy as the chief cause of inflation. At the time, however, it was the general tenor of his economic liberalism rather than specifics that attracted attention.

Given that Powell had stood for the party leadership in 1965 and gained only fifteen votes, his ideas could easily be dismissed as the public musings of a maverick. But it would be wrong to measure his significance in these formal, 'high political' terms. Powell's poor showing in the leadership election owed more to his lack of interest in the politics of the Commons' tea-room than to indifference to his ideas. His old One Nation colleague Iain Macleod noted, in a review of *A Nation Not Afraid* in the *Spectator*, that 'Powellism is gaining converts every day' and that 'much of our programme when the general election comes will be based on ideas in this book'.[62] To see the Conservatives in 1966 as espousing 'Powellite' economics would overstate the case, but the party's 1965 document, *Putting Britain Right Ahead*, had seen a shift to a more liberal market agenda as the Conservatives sought to put—to use a 1990s expression—'clear blue water' between Conservative and Labour approaches to economic management.[63] Moreover, Powell was

---

[60] J. Wood (ed.), *A Nation Not Afraid: The Thinking of Enoch Powell* (1965).

[61] See J. E. Powell, *Freedom and Reality* (1969), where extracts from these speeches are collected.

[62] I. Macleod in the *Spectator*, quoted in D. E. Schoen, *Powell and the Powellites* (1977), 15.

[63] For example *Putting Britain Right Ahead* called for tax reductions, stimulation of competition, trade-union reform, and selectivity in the social services.

not, as some of his biographers suggest, a lone voice crying in the wilderness. Through the 1960s a complex, often overlapping, set of liberal market groups and intellectuals were establishing an influential voice in Conservative politics.[64] At an individual level people like Keith Joseph were identified as increasingly close to Powell, but the purchase of liberal market ideas was also reflected in the policy groups Edward Heath established as part of his 'government in exile' strategy. For example, Frederick Corfield, a member of the Industrial Policy committee, told Edward Boyle in December 1967 that there was 'a somewhat bigger split in our ranks than we had anticipated between those who would give top priority to region, and those who would give the priority to ensuring that there are no obstacles to growth in the "natural growth areas" '.[65] This would have come as no surprise to Boyle, who had warned the Shadow Cabinet in the summer about a group within the party trying to build an 'anti-planning orthodoxy'.[66] Nor would it have shocked Arthur Seldon of the Institute for Economic Affairs, who argued in the *Swinton Journal* in 1968 that 'the outsider has some difficulty in reconciling the views of Reginald Maudling, John Boyd-Carpenter and Edward Boyle ... with those of Powell, Joseph ... Thatcher, Maude, Maurice Macmillan, Home, Biffen, Bernard Braine, Patrick Jenkin and others'. Seldon concluded that, on economic policy, 'Conservatives speak with two voices',[67] one of those voices being decidedly liberal market in its accent. The *Sunday Times*'s comment of June 1965 that Powell had 'driven the true concept of market forces back into Tory thinking'[68] seemed, by 1967–8, no longer hyperbolic. But Powell was articulating, rather than leading, an important body of Conservative opinion.

That liberal market views were moving towards a more prominent position in the Conservative party during the 1960s is confirmed by the outlook of the rank and file, by party-policy deliberations, and the reaction to the Selsdon Park conference of early 1970. With regard to grass-roots opinion, John Ramsden's study of the 1960s party has shown that local party opinion was insistent on establishing a distinctive Conservative approach to the economy. Hence, the London Area conference of 1965 insisted on 'an assurance that the next Conservative Government will govern by true Conservative principles, not seeking electoral popularity by the adoption of quasi-Socialist measures', whilst the North Cornwall Conservatives demanded, in February 1966, that

[64] See R. Cockett, *Thinking the Unthinkable* (1994), 159–99.
[65] F. Corfield to E. Boyle, 7 Dec. 1967, quoted in Ramsden, *Winds of Change*, 230.
[66] Boyle, Memorandum to Shadow Cabinet, 25 July 1967, ibid.
[67] A. Seldon, *Swinton Journal*, quoted in ibid. 280.
[68] *Sunday Times*, 25 June 1965, quoted in Schoen, *Powell*, 15.

there should be 'a return to Conservative principles with a greater emphasis on individual freedom and less control from government'.[69] The language and underlying message of these statements is strikingly similar to the arguments of the 1950s, namely, that 'real' Conservatism meant a rejection of Statist economic and social policy and a return to liberal market governance. What made the 1960s different, however, was that the party hierarchy was more responsive to grass-roots opinion.

In this last context, party policy with regard to trade unions was particularly significant. In the 1960s grass-roots pressure on this issue continued unabated. In 1963 Edward Martell, whose PLDF had caused the Conservative leadership some anxiety in the 1950s, reappeared as chairman of the Hastings Conservative association, and his journal, the *New Daily*, still campaigning for trade-union reform, gained a circulation of 100,000.[70] Likewise, in November 1963 279 constituency associations supported a Monday Club proposal for making trade unions liable for losses incurred by employers during strikes, and a large majority of local Conservative discussion groups were pressing for compulsory ballots before strikes.[71] After 1964 such arguments went from being local party pipe-dreams to central party policy, and Edward Martell could have been forgiven for thinking that his PLDF campaign had finally borne fruit. After 1964, and especially with the publication of the party's *Fair Deal At Work* in 1968, legal reform of trade-union law became a central feature of Conservative policy, and provided a basis for the Heath government's industrial relations initiatives of the early 1970s.

Nor was the trade-union question the only one which saw movement. With regard to the nationalized industries, a Policy Group on the Nationalized Industries (PGNI), chaired by Nicholas Ridley, produced some ambitious statements. The PGNI's final report argued that 'the public sector is a millstone round our necks', that 'we have a built-in system of misallocation of capital in our economy', and that there was 'a very strong case for embarking on a course of gradually dismantling the public sector'.[72] The benefits of this course of action were to be increased efficiency, lower government costs, and wider share-ownership.[73] Candidate industries for denationalization were steel, BEA, BOAC, BAA, and Thomas Cook, and it was suggested that, at some stage, other sectors could be put on a sound financial basis and then sold off, notably coal, buses, electricity, gas, telephones, and Cable and Wireless.[74] As an interim measure, the 'BP model', as floated in the late

[69] Ramsden, *Winds of Change*, 219, 255.   [70] Ibid. 146–8.
[71] Ibid, 218.   [72] Report of the PGNI, CRD 3/17/12, CPA.
[73] Ibid.   [74] Ibid.

1950s, was put forward as a first step. Edward Heath was unenthusiastic about this Report, and even Keith Joseph baulked at its radicalism.[75] The 1970 Conservative manifesto was to reflect their caution rather than the PGNI's ambition, but, as the chief of CRD noted, the wording of the Manifesto's industrial section was 'sufficiently broad to give a mandate for as much of the Ridley–Eden policy as a Conservative government might wish to implement'.[76] Moreover, if one leaves aside the issue of direct policy influence, and compares the PGNI position to that of the 1957 PCNI, it is very apparent that liberal market thinking on the question of nationalization had become both more advanced and enjoyed greater latitude.

But it was the Selsdon Park conference of late January and early February 1970 that fully convinced liberal market Conservatives that their time had come. This meeting of the Shadow Cabinet was convened by Heath as a 'brainstorming' weekend of discussion to focus attention on the policy ideas that would form the basis of the Conservatives' next election campaign. As such, it was not very different from other so-called 'Chequers weekends' that Heath was wont to organize from time to time, but its impact was far greater than either Heath or his shadow team could have anticipated. The meeting enjoyed widespread publicity, partly because of the Labour government's response to the Conservatives' deliberations. Harold Wilson's reference to the emergence of 'Selsdon Man' ensured that the conference took on almost instant mythic status: the notion of 'Selsdon Man' being that the Conservatives had revealed themselves to be advocates of stone-age economics, and were bent on clubbing the economy with laissez-faire, market economics and dragging Britain back to a Conservative cave.

The prevailing historiographical orthodoxy on Selsdon Park suggests that the conference by no means represented an explicit Conservative endorsement of liberal market ideas, and that 'Selsdon Man', like Piltdown Man, was a fraud.[77] Certainly, those seeking evidence for such a development in Conservative thinking can find very little succour in the minutes of the conference discussions. There was minimal debate on the principles of economic policy, and there were few statements that could be regarded as unequivocally 'market' orientated.[78] There was talk, for example, of restoring a 'competitive framework' for the steel

---

[75] For Heath's attitude see Ramsden, *Winds of Change*, 283, for Joseph's see R. Taylor, 'The Heath Government, Industrial Policy and the "New Capitalism" ', in A. Seldon and S. Ball (eds.), *The Heath Government, 1970–74: A Reappraisal* (1996), 145.

[76] M. Fraser to J. Douglas, 18 May 1970, quoted in ibid. 146.

[77] J. Campbell, *Edward Heath* (1993), 265–7.

[78] The only exception was the discussion of trade unions. See Shadow Cabinet Conference, Selsdon Park, 7th Session, 1 Feb. 1970, CRD 3/9/93, CPA.

industry,[79] but it was also argued that the idea of denationalization was 'of no great interest to the general public'.[80] On the question of combating inflation through incomes policy, an area where the Conservatives had been very critical of Labour, the conference's briefing documents simply advised avoiding the use of the phrase,[81] and Reginald Maudling conceded that there was a gap in Conservative policy on this issue that could not easily be filled.[82] There was general agreement that inflation and the level of direct personal taxation had the most direct electoral relevance, but as to methods of addressing these questions, the conference was at best ambivalent. It is true that even the vague liberal market sentiments that were expressed were treated with respect, but then so were most arguments. There was no clear, underlying philosophy in the discussions that would enable an historian to say that Selsdon Park saw a 'proto-Thatcherite' agenda in the making.

So why did the Selsdon conference gain the reputation it achieved within the party? The answer lies with the context of its reception. After 1964, and especially after 1966, the Conservative rank and file had been hoping for a Conservative move against the 'post-war settlement'. The Conservative Opposition's statements on trade unions, its denunciations of the Labour government's economic management, particularly in the realms of inflation and prices and incomes policy, and its stress on the need for greater freedom for enterprise and personal incentives, had all served to create a climate of expectation. The response of the press and, paradoxically, of the Labour leadership to Selsdon Park only served to heighten this expectation. As Ramsden has suggested, this response gave the Conservative position in 1970 a free-market coherence that went beyond the intentions of Edward Heath and many of his Shadow Cabinet.[83] But the party leadership's response to their own publicity also played a part here. It may well be that the depiction of Selsdon Park at the time gave the Conservatives an unsought-for identity as a liberal market party, but it was an identity the leadership did not seek to repudiate. Indeed, their behaviour and statements during the 1970 election campaign and after the Conservative victory further heightened the sense that there had been a pronounced, liberal market shift in Conservative thinking.[84] Edward Heath's speech to the Conservative

---

[79] CRD document, 'Other Issues Requiring Policy Decisions', n.d. (Jan. 1970), CRD 3/9/92, CPA.

[80] CRD document, 'Publication of Policy During 1970, n.d (Jan. 1970), CRD 3/9/92, CPA.

[81] CRD document, 'Controlling Prices', 21 Jan. 1970, CRD 3/9/92, CPA.

[82] Selsdon Park Shadow Cabinet Conference, 7th Session, 1 Feb. 1970, CRD 3/9/93, CPA.

[83] See Ramsden, *Winds of Change*, 302–3.

[84] That the IEA, always quick to be critical of the Conservatives, greeted Heath's election with optimism is significant here. See Cockett, *Thinking*, 200, for the IEA's reaction.

conference in October 1970, which stood as both a victory celebration and statement of intent, declared that the government's aim was 'to change the course of history of this nation', which modest task was to be achieved by policies designed to:

reorganize the function of government, to leave more to individual or corporate effort, to make savings in government expenditure, to provide room for greater incentives for men and women and to firms and businesses . . . to encourage them more and more to take their own decisions, to stand firm on their own feet, to accept responsibility for themselves and their families.

Furthermore the government's actions in its first year of office appeared to confirm a bold start to this new approach. That Heath chose John Davies, the former Director-General of the CBI, to run the new Department of Trade and Industry, and appointed as his deputies Nicholas Ridley, John Eden, and Frederick Corfield, all known liberal market enthusiasts, could only be seen as a statement about the direction of industrial policy. In 1970–1 this team lived up to its reputation. The Industrial Reorganization Corporation was abolished, the Industrial Expansion Act was repealed, seven of the regional Economic Development Councils ('little Neddies') were scrapped, the Mersey Docks and Harbour Board was allowed to go into liquidation, the Land Commission was abolished, and the Prices and Incomes Board was wound up. All of these were regarded as key elements of 'Socialist' economic management, and their removal was greeted with enthusiasm by the Conservative press and the party rank and file. With regard to prices and taxation, the government was also making all the right noises and gestures. Heath's promise to cut prices 'at a stroke' was to prove a dangerous hostage to fortune, but a rhetorically tough stance on prices was precisely what the party faithful had been looking for. On taxation too, the government's first Budget saw a 6d (2.5p) cut in the basic rate of income tax, a 25 per cent reduction in corporation tax, and the phasing out of the Regional Employment Premium and Selective Employment Tax. The promise of new trade-union legislation was also rapidly fulfilled, with the publication in December 1970 of the Industrial Relations Bill. On all fronts the government seemed to be marching in its first year to the beat of a liberal market drum.

However, by 1972–3 the government was engaged in what famously became known as an economic 'U-turn'. The notion that there was any such dramatic reversal of policy has been played down in some studies of the Heath government.[85] There is a logic to this argument if one

---

[85] See Seldon and Ball, Introduction to id. (eds.), *The Heath Government*, and Campbell, *Heath*, 451–6, 468–83.

accepts that 'Selsdon Man' was a myth and that the government did not have a coherent liberal market strategy to start with. If that was the case then of course there could be no 'U-turn', and the argument that there was a change of direction becomes another piece of 'mythology', particularly attractive to Thatcherites. But this, once again, is to miss the point about historical myth. Without exception Thatcherite memoirs highlight the experience of 1970–4 as formative. For example, Lord Young comments that, 'when Ted Heath paraded Selsdon Man I perked up. Here at long last was the realization that the wealth of a nation has to be created by its citizens and not by its government', and that 'the 1970 election seemed to bring a ray of hope to us all'.[86] Likewise, Norman Tebbit notes that the 'Selsdon declaration . . . marked the Tory party's first repudiation of the post-war Butskellite consensus' and that 'the 1970 manifesto . . . was music to the ears of radical Conservatives like myself'.[87] It could be that Young, Tebbit, and others like them were just 'deceived' by the 'myth' of Selsdon, but two points are salient here. The first is that, in terms of understanding Thatcherism, it is important that this period, like the thirties and the immediate post-war era, is singled out by Thatcherite protagonists. In terms of how Thatcherites understood (understand) each other, a shared sense of the 'betrayal' of Selsdon and the promise of 1970 is a crucial point of contact. The second is that, whilst 'Selsdon Man' and the 'liberal market manifesto of 1970' may both have been 'myths', they became, because of the contemporary response to them, some of those 'myths we live by'—just as 'real' as any 'objective' assessment of the events of 1970. Why else should those Conservative MPs who dissented from the government's policies in 1973 have formed themselves into the 'Selsdon Group', if the name in itself did not conjure up a particular political message? Why also should Edward Heath have been so keen to tell the party conference in 1973 that the promises of Selsdon Park had been fulfilled, unless he too understood its resonance?

For those in the party, in both the upper and lower echelons, who had had their hopes and expectations raised in 1970, the disappointment of 1972–4 was all too palpable. Without acknowledging this sense of 'betrayal' one cannot fully understand why Sir Keith Joseph should have felt able to say that 'It was only in April 1974 that I was converted to Conservatism', meaning that he had finally understood that the liberal market approach *was* Conservatism. But equally, one cannot understand the depth of the sense of betrayal unless one acknowledges that 1970 was itself seen by a powerful body of Conservative opinion as the

---

[86] Lord Young, *The Enterprise Years* (1991), 16.
[87] N. Tebbit, *Upwardly Mobile* (1988), 94.

climax of a twenty-five-year battle against not only the Labour party's Socialism, but the 'quasi-Socialism' represented by their own party's failure to dismantle the 'post-war settlement'. Small wonder that in 1975 the party equipped itself with a leader who would commit herself to this battle with more vigour and 'conviction'. Thatcher herself instinctively recognized this, and constructed her appeal in these terms. Speaking at Finchley in January 1975, she declared: 'I am trying to represent the deep feelings of those many thousands of rank-and-file Tories in the country—and potential Conservative voters too—who feel let down by our party and find themselves unrepresented in a political vacuum.'[88] To address the concerns of these people, Thatcher argued, it was necessary only for the party to raise the banners of what she, like the party rank-and-file, deemed 'true' Conservative values, for then, she argued, 'we shall not have to convert people to our principles. They will simply rally to those that are truly their own.'[89] Nigel Lawson has commented that, whereas 'Harold Macmillan had a contempt for the party, Alec Home tolerated it, [and] Ted Heath loathed it, Margaret genuinely liked it. She felt a communion with it.'[90] Harold Macmillan, albeit from a different perspective, expressed a similar view. After seeing Thatcher at a party conference, he remarked on the contrast to his own period as leader, noting that: 'we [his cabinet] used to sit there listening to these extraordinary speeches urging us to birch or hang them all or other such strange things. We used to sit quietly nodding our heads and when we came to make our speeches we did not refer to what had been said at all . . . But watching her . . . I think she agrees with them.'[91] It is difficult fully to grasp Thatcher's special hold over the party rank and file unless one appreciates that, from 1975 to 1990 (and beyond), the Conservatives' middle and lower ranks felt they had a leader who shared their preferences and prejudices.

The Irish revolutionary James Connolly once remarked that any event, no matter how seemingly improbable, could be made by historians to appear to have been inevitable. This essay is content merely to argue that the triumph of Thatcherite political economy in the late 1970s and 1980s was unsurprising. From the very outset Conservative voices had been raised against the 'post-war settlement', and through the 1950s and 1960s elements of the Conservative party leadership, a substantial section of the backbenches, and probably a majority of the middle and lower ranks of the party, were predisposed to accept a

---

[88] M. Thatcher at Finchley, 31 Jan. 1975, *Margaret Thatcher: Complete Public Statements, 1945–1990 on CD-ROM*, ed. C. Collins (Oxford, 1999).
[89] Id. at Harrogate, 15 Mar. 1975, ibid.
[90] N. Lawson, *The View from No. 11* (1994), 14.
[91] Macmillan's comments are recorded in P. Walker, *Staying Power* (1991), 138.

liberal market diagnosis of and prescription for their own and the nation's economic troubles. That the Churchill, Eden, and Macmillan governments chose not to respond positively to liberal market opinion is explicable for two reasons. The first is that the generation of Conservative leaders that was dominant into the 1960s was heavily influenced by the trauma of the 1945 defeat and accepted the view that it was a 'delayed punishment' for the 'hungry thirties'. As a consequence, they were reluctant to take risks, particularly in the realm of unemployment. Equally important, the post-war boom that began in 1952 meant that for the most part Conservative governments were able to square the circle of high public expenditure and full employment with occasional tax-cuts and relatively stable prices. Indeed, in the context of the 1950s, when inflation was reasonably low (albeit historically high), the economy was growing, and living standards rising, the remarkable thing is the amount of discontent there was in the Conservative ranks. In this sense there was an indication in the disgruntled voices of the 1950s of how powerful the reaction might be if the post-war boom came to an end, inflation became more pressing, and the dilemma of the power of organized labour in a full-employment economy was more graphically exposed. In short, there was almost a ready-made Conservative audience for the Thatcherite agenda.

This may seem to lead back to the argument that it was the economic troubles of the 1970s that were crucial to Thatcherism's success. To a degree the 1970s *were* important, but whilst the immediate circumstances of that decade can help to explain the emergence of greater political space for Thatcherite political economy, they cannot explain why Thatcherism was chosen as opposed to any other potential strategy. History is perhaps a factor here, insofar as in the 'crisis' of the early 1960s the Conservative leadership had opted for Macmillan's *dirigiste* approach and Statist strategies had thereby become discredited. But there were other, broader factors at work.

Staying with the Conservatives themselves, changes were taking place in the parliamentary party in and after the 1960s that had important implications for the party's outlook. After the 1966 election only 60 per cent of Conservative MPs had sat continuously since 1959, and only eleven MPs had been in Parliament before 1945. This generational change understandably continued, and by February 1974 only 50 per cent of MPs had been in Parliament before 1964, and the bulk of them were of the 1959 vintage. For historians of Conservative politics in the 1950s and early 1960s the 'class of 1950' has had particular significance in terms of its contribution to Cabinet personnel and the influence it exercised. Arguably the 'class of 1959' should have equal importance for scholars of Thatcherism.[92] The 'class of 1950' had come into politics with the memory of the 1945 defeat still strong and with the 'myth' of the 'hungry thirties' seen as the explanation. The 'class of 1959' came into politics in a climate dominated by the questions of 'slow growth', the grumblings of grass-roots discontent, and a querying of the social and economic achievements of the 'post-war settlement'. At the same time, the social and geographical base of the 'class of 1959' was markedly different from that of their predecessors. The presence of the 'knights of the shires', military, and other public servants declined, and they were replaced by representatives of the salaried, professional middle classes. In short, the new generation of Conservative MPs were closer socially to the kind of people who had expressed discontent with the 'post-war settlement'—'Orpington Man' (or woman, for that matter) had arrived in the Conservative ranks in strength by the mid-1960s.

Furthermore, the new generation of MPs were increasingly returned from constituencies south of Birmingham. The changing, and narrowing, base of the Conservative parliamentary party thus reflected general economic and demographic shifts in the country, as employment and population trends followed the decline of Britain's old industrial heartlands. From 1951 to the 1970s, and accelerating through the 1980s, demographic and economic change saw the population and, through redistribution, the representation of the South and South-East of Britain growing inexorably. This growth was fuelled by, in particular, a massive surge in service-sector activity or what would once have been termed white-collar and black-coated employment. Many of these occupations were non-unionized, and, even if they were, employees showed a greater degree of 'economic instrumentalism' in their voting allegiance than workers in the older industrial communities.[93] The possibility that a Conservative, liberal market appeal could be made to this social and regional constituency had been mooted in the late 1950s, when the idea of the 'opportunity state' had been in vogue. Although this concept had been designed to meet the needs of the self-professed 'beleaguered middle class', it was also seen as appealing to the aspirational lower-middle- and working-class voter, on the basis that, as one Conservative minister put it, 'potentially the foreman class is ours'.[94] Likewise, the Conservative Lord Chancellor of the late 1950s hinted at a potential regional appeal of the 'opportunity state', noting that tax-cuts, wider

---

[92] The emphasis here is on the broad, generational, and prosopographical nature of the 'Class of '59' rather than the impact of particular individuals.

[93] A. Heath *et al.*, *Understanding Political Change* (Oxford, 1991), 102–19, 136–55.

[94] C. Hill to R. A. Butler, 11 Feb. 1958, CPA, CRD 2/53/29.

property ownership, and lower inflation were 'an acute political problem from the standpoint of Conservative workers South of the Trent, in the north they are much more concerned with their council houses, factories, schools and hospitals'. In the 1980s this constituency was to be labelled 'Essex Man', and was seen, rightly, as an electoral vanguard of Thatcherism.

Thatcherism did not emerge simply from a 'battle of ideas' within the Conservative party. Nor was it a product of 'high political' manoeuvre in the leadership contest of 1975. Thatcher*ism* existed long before Margaret Thatcher became leader of the Conservative party, and 1975 was as much the occasion as the cause of the 'Thatcherite Revolution'. In the mid-1970s the Conservative party, at both the parliamentary and grass-roots level, was looking for and found a leader in tune with their long-held aspirations, and one who was fortunate enough to reap the benefit of social and economic change that gave 'Thatcherite' political economy an opportunity to flourish. This is not to present a reductionist argument that simply collapses Thatcherite political economy into the liberal market ideas of the 1950s and 1960s. In the 1970s and 1980s monetarism was a new, and powerful, ingredient that had been largely (although not wholly) absent in earlier decades. But important though monetarist theory was to Thatcherite political economy, it is crucial to realize that it was *one* ingredient. The title of Sir Keith Joseph's 1976 Stockton lecture was, after all, 'Monetarism Is Not Enough', and he made it plain that reducing the size of the State, reducing public expenditure, curbing inflation, and providing tax incentives for individuals and businesses were essential in their own right.[95] In this respect monetarism may have given a new theoretical cutting edge to liberal market ideas, but the broader aims and desires of 1970s liberal economics were remarkably similar to earlier Conservative protests against the 'post-war settlement'.

The prefiguring of Thatcherite political economy in long-standing debates within the Conservative party has significance not only in the history of Conservatism. It also has relevance in terms of the notion of a 'post-war consensus'. In recent years a number of historians have questioned the historical veracity and helpfulness of the idea of 'consensus', and one of the implications of this essay is that they have been right to do so. One writer has recently argued that 'there was a certain amount of agreement at the elite level of British politics, but the extent and depth of this agreement is by no means clear'.[96] In terms of the issue of depth, this essay would conclude that the Conservative party's reaction to the

---

[95] K. Joseph, *Monetarism is Not Enough* (1976), 17–19.
[96] J. D. Marlow, *Questioning the Post-War Consensus Thesis* (Aldershot, 1996), 13.

Beveridge Report, the tenor of its election campaign in 1945, and the attitude of the party's rank and file through the 1950s and 1960s, indicates a very shallow level of 'commitment' to a 'consensual' framework, and that the party's attitude generally indicates, with some individual exceptions, a 'pragmatic' or 'instrumental' acquiesence rather than a 'normative agreement' with the policy framework associated with the 'post-war settlement'.[97] But although one can seriously question the 'reality' of consensus, that does not mean the notion is robbed of historical importance. *The Myth of Consensus*, to use the title of a recent publication,[98] has been as politically and historically significant as the 'myth' of Selsdon Man. The idea of consensus, as constructed by Thatcherism, was crucial to the whole Thatcherite project. Likewise, Thatcherism's opponents, whether Labour left or Social Democratic, deployed the idea as, respectively, either a justification for a radical Socialist departure from the policies of post-war Labour governments, or for a return to a similar set of goals. Hence, Tony Benn argued in 1981 that the SDP was not a new political force, because Britain had been governed by a centre party since 1945, and in 1982 a leading intellectual in the SDP, tongue firmly in cheek, informed this author that 'We want the policies that failed before'.[99] Perhaps the historical-politics of the idea of consensus have as much, if not more, importance to historians than the actual existence of such a shared approach.

[97] The terminology deployed here is that of Marlow, ibid. 24–5.
[98] Jones and Kandiah (eds.), *Myth*.
[99] Professor Peter Clarke, personal remark to the author, c.May 1982.

CHAPTER 9

Conservatism, the State, and Civil Society in the Twentieth Century

DEFINING THE role of the State was a leitmotif of twentieth-century Conservative politics. At the first meeting of the Unionist Social Reform Committee (USRC) in February 1911 the Conservative economist W. A. S. Hewins argued that 'there was a definite Conservative theory of the State . . . and that the soundest economic reforms can be deduced from this theory'.[1] This was an optimistic remark, not only for the period in which it was uttered but for all subsequent periods. At no point in 'the Conservative century' was there *a* definite Conservative theory of the State: there were many which overlapped, competed, and often conflicted. In particular, the Conservative position on State intervention in the social and economic sphere underwent periodic re-examination, with significant shifts and variations taking place both over and within different periods. In the same year that Hewins and his fellow members of the USRC produced their outline for a positive role for State intervention Lord Hugh Cecil was writing *Conservatism*, which took a very different stance. Indeed, in the decade before the Great War there was an extraordinary range of contrasting Conservative opinions on the role of the State which found eloquent individual and institutional expression. Strong interventionists like Hewins, W. J. Ashley, Arthur Steel-Maitland, J. W. Hills, and the USRC found themselve opposed by Lords Hugh and Robert Cecil, Lord Cromer, Sir Frederick Banbury, and the British Constitutional Association, who were either sceptical about or hostile to State action. And there were others, like Arthur Balfour and Andrew Bonar Law, who occupied an intermediate position.

The range of opinion on the role of State shown by the Edwardian Conservative party was, as this chapter will show, characteristic of Conservative ideas over the course of the twentieth century. In examining this gamut of ideas it is important to avoid an oversimplification of the categories of opinion that emerged. It is tempting to slip into using a framework of 'Statist' and 'anti-Statist', but this would draw an overly

---

[1] Minutes of USRC meeting, 28 Feb. 1911, SMP, GD 193/108/1/359.

straightforward divide in Conservative thought and leave too little room for nuance. For example, Margaret Thatcher could easily and understandably be characterized as an 'anti-Statist' Conservative, but her position required, to deploy the title of a well-known study of Thatcherite politics, 'the free economy and the strong State'.[2] Thatcher herself underscored this point in 1978, when she declared: 'We are not anti-State. On the contrary we seek a proper balance between State and society.'[3] To address this problem, this chapter will deploy the vocabulary used by W. H. Greenleaf, who drew a distinction between 'paternalist' and 'libertarian' Conservatives.[4] Greenleaf's *vocabulary* is helpful insofar as it implies predispositions and tendencies towards, respectively, 'Statist' and 'anti-Statist' positions rather than absolute demarcations. However, his underlying analysis of the Conservative ideological tradition is flawed. A particular problem for Greenleaf's binary model of Conservative ideas is that, throughout the twentieth century, individuals and groups within the party have, as will be shown below, held and expressed libertarian and paternalist views on different questions *at the same time*.[5] At first glance this might be regarded as cause for dispensing with the model and the vocabulary altogether, but this chapter will suggest that the apparent inconsistencies in Conservative thought can be explained by adopting a different analytical framework. Greenleaf's model suggests that attitudes to the *State itself* determined whether Conservatives adopted a libertarian or paternalist stance, but this chapter will argue that this emphasis on the State is mistaken, and that the primary focus should instead be on Conservative views of the effectiveness of agencies of civil society. If Conservatives have seen these agencies as socially effective they have wished the State to play a minimal role, but if they have seen them as ineffective or failing then they have regarded State intervention as necessary. At any given point some agencies have been viewed as functioning well whilst others have not, with the result that in some cases State action has been deemed appropriate and in others not. To explore the nuances of the Conservative position on this subject, this chapter will at first examine the development of aspects of Conservative thought on the State over the twentieth century and will then move to a more detailed discussion of the analytical framework outlined above.

[2] A. Gamble, *The Free Economy and the Strong State* (Basingstoke, 1994 edn.).

[3] M. Thatcher, Speech to the Bow Group on 'The Ideals of an Open Society', London 6 May 1978, in *Thatcher CD-ROM*.

[4] W. H. Greenleaf, *The British Political Tradition*, vol. 2, *The Ideological Heritage* (1983), 189–358.

[5] For a discussion which illustrates this apparent inconsistency see M. Francis, ' "Set the People Free"? The Conservative Party and the State, 1920–60', in Francis and Zweiniger-Bargielowska (eds.), *Conservatives*.

I

In the inter-war years Conservatives, like their Edwardian predecessors, adopted a range of positions. Harold Macmillan, Robert Boothby, John Loder, and those Conservatives associated with publications like *Industry and the State*, the movement for the 'self-government of industry',[6] and organizations like Next Five Years were advocates of a strong role for the State, and their supporters' views could, according to CCO, be 'summed up in the words "laissez faire is dead" '.[7] Most of the inter-war party, including the leadership, did not accept the need for the scale of State action demanded by Macmillan and his collaborators, and one Conservative Minister of Labour in the 1930s, Oliver Stanley, argued that their proposals for industrial intervention 'cut right across Conservative principles'.[8] But Stanley's views were not widely shared, and when he voiced them it was noted that 'he did not appear to be surprised at questions from the Chancellor of the Exchequer [Neville Chamberlain] and others as to what were the Conservative principles to which he referred'.[9] Indeed, Neville Chamberlain stated at a meeting of the party leadership 'that it was generally recognised that laissez faire was completely dead',[10] and the Conservative Research Department (CRD) subcommittee which examined relations between the State and industry was keen to establish that 'the frequently heard suggestion that any interference with industry whatever is contrary to Conservative principles has no foundation'.[11] Had there been a clear Conservative position on the role of the State there would have been no need for Chamberlain to ask CRD to address relations between the State and industry and 'draw up a series of conclusions as to what the State should try to do, and what it should try to avoid'.[12] Likewise, there would not have have been such concern to counter *frequently heard* assertions as to the un-Conservative nature of State intervention. There was, in effect, an ongoing debate within the party as to what constituted a definite Conservative theory of the State.

[6] See D. Ritschel, 'A Corporatist Economy in Britain? Capitalist Planning for Industrial Self-Government in the 1930s', *EHR* 56 (1991), id., *The Politics of Planning* (Oxford, 1997), 20–49, 183–231.

[7] S. G. 'Note', 18 June 1934, CPA, CRD 1/65/2. The summary is attributed to the Chief Whip, Margesson.

[8] CCO, Meeting of Sub-Committee A, 25 Oct. 1934, ibid. Paradoxically, Stanley was one of the authors of the interventionist *Industry and the State* (1927).   [9] Ibid.

[10] Minutes of a Conference at CRD, 2 Mar. 1934, CPA, CRD 1/64/2.

[11] Discussion document, 'The Relations Between the State and Industry', Dec. 1934, CPA, CRD 1/64/5.

[12] Unsigned CRD note, 'The Future Relations Between the State and Industry', 11 May 1934, CPA 1/65/2.

This debate continued during and after the Second World War as the Conservatives sought to address issues raised by wartime reconstruction plans and the programme of the Attlee government. The State loomed large in discussions of Conservative wartime committees on reconstruction,[13] and clear differences of opinion in the party loomed equally large. Whereas members of the Tory Reform Group saw the wartime role of the State as providing examples of intervention that could be carried over to peacetime,[14] others saw the State's extended role as purely for 'the duration'. The Conservative wartime Health Minister, Henry Willink, summed up the views of many who held the latter position when he noted that, for him, 'it was an article of faith that our fight was *against* Hitler . . . not "for" social reform'.[15] Positive, ambivalent, and hostile attitudes to State intervention were all to be found at play in wartime Conservatism, which helps to account for the difficulties the party faced in constructing a response to developments such as the Beveridge Report.[16] Labour's landslide victory on a Statist platform in 1945 served to intensify Conservative debate: Anthony Eden declared in 1946 that 'the fundamental political problem that faces us is that of the relation of the individual to the State',[17] and Quentin Hogg called for a new Tamworth Manifesto to provide the party with a clear strategy on social reform.[18] The State was a crucial part of Conservative discussions in the immediate post-war period as, in the words of R. A. Butler: 'We were shaken out of our lethargy and impelled to re-think our philosophy.'[19] The 'thinking machine',[20] or perhaps more accurately 'rethinking machine', of the CRD and the newly created Conservative Political Centre (CPC) produced the now famous documents *The Industrial Charter* and *The Worker's Charter*, plus a number of other papers which addressed and took a positive stance on the issue of State intervention. At the same time single authored works, some produced from within

[13] See in particular the final report of the 'Beveridge Report Committee', Dec. 1942, CPA, CRD 600/01.

[14] Members of the Reform Group included Quentin Hogg, Viscount Hinchingbrooke, and Hugh Molson.

[15] H. Willink, unpublished autobiography, 74 in Willink Papers, Churchill College, Cambridge, in J. Ramsden, *The Age of Churchill and Eden, 1940–57* (Harlow, 1995), 46. Interestingly, Willink himself was in favour of some reforms, notably in the realm of health policy.

[16] For discussions of wartime Conservatism see in particular Ramsden, *Churchill and Eden*, 38–49 and K. Jeffreys, *The Churchill Coalition and Wartime Politics, 1940–45* (Manchester, 1991), 112–38.

[17] Anthony Eden at Hull, 7 Mar. 1946, in Conservative Political Centre, *The New Conservatism: An Anthology of Post-War Thought* (1955), 71.

[18] Hogg's remark is noted in R. A. Butler, *The Art of the Possible* (1971), 133.

[19] R. A. Butler, Introduction to *The New Conservatism*.

[20] Ibid.

and some from outside the organizational machine, sought to construct more formal statements of Conservative philosophy of the State: Quentin Hogg contended that there was a distinctive Conservative stance which could be differentiated from that of the Society of Individualists on the one hand and from Socialism on the other,[21] and David Clarke emphasized the 'organic' nature of the Conservative view of the State.[22] The quest to define a Conservative position on the role of the State was intrinsic to the party's effort after 1945 to rebuild its damaged morale and secure its electoral revival.

Conservative discussion of the role of the State did not cease with the party's electoral successes of 1950–1; thirteen years of Conservative government in 1951–64 saw intense discussion of the subject. There were no large-scale attempts to dismantle the Attlee government's reforms, but it would be a mistake to see Conservative governments as enthusiastic *dirigistes*. Although major legislative reductions of State activity were eschewed, *administrative* action was used to hold the frontiers of the State in check and, in some instances, to reduce the scope of State responsibilities.[23] Moreover, there were many Conservatives who criticized or sought to amend significantly the party's position on State intervention.[24] Party Conferences, in spite of careful management of motions for debate, saw frequent outbursts of criticism of the government's unwillingness to reduce the level of State activity, or as a motion to the 1956 Conference described it, 'the Government's apparent inability to reverse trends resulting from Socialist maladministration'.[25] This rank-and-file criticism helped stimulate further debate amongst the party hierarchy and policy-makers. The Policy Committee on the Nationalized Industries (PCNI) and the Policy Study Group (PSG) which met between 1956 and 1959, and the Policy Committee on the Future of the Social Services (PCFSS), which was set up in January 1960 and sat until the late summer of 1963, all saw libertarian arguments aired in their discussions, partly because the leadership wished to reassure backbenchers and the rank-and-file that they were responsive to such views, [26] and partly because the prevalence of such views in the

[21] Q. Hogg, *The Case for Conservatism* (1947), 29.

[22] D. Clarke, *The Conservative Faith in a Modern Age* (1947). Clarke was a senior figure in the CRD and his book was published by the CPC.

[23] See C. Webster, 'Conservatives and Consensus: the Politics of the National Health Service, 1951–64', in A. Oakley (ed.), *The Politics of the Welfare State* (1994).

[24] Green, 'Conservative Party', in Taylor and Lawrence (eds.), *Party, State and Society*.

[25] B. G. Raine to NUCA Conference, Llandudno, 11 Oct. 1956, NUCA Conference Minutes, Microfilm Card 15.

[26] R. A. Butler commented that a principal reason for setting up the PCNI was to keep certain members of the party in particular 'quiet' on the question of the nationalized industries. See the minutes of the 9th meeting of the party's Steering Committee, 27 Jan. 1959, CPA, CRD 2/53/34.

middle and lower ranks of the party strengthened the hand of libertarians in the party hierarchy.

With regard to the nationalized industries, the terms of reference of the PCNI were to examine them 'both collectively and individually with particular reference to', in the first instance, 'the possibility of introducing any element of competitive enterprise'.[27] The setting up of the PCNI had been announced at the party conference at Llandudno in 1956, one of the most uncomfortable conferences the leadership endured in the 1950s. Its secretary noted in May 1957 that it had to avoid 'the temptation to blackguard all forms of nationalisation', but that a more subtle approach would 'not be easy to get accepted by the Party',[28] and its chairman, R. A. Butler, noted at the end of the year that, although the PCNI had 'done an awful lot to bridge the gap between . . . Ministers and the Backbench . . . there is still . . . a gulf between this Committee and the Ministers'.[29] Similar divisions of opinion were evident in the PSG. At a PSG meeting in August 1957, Enoch Powell argued that public ownership had to be reduced, contending that 'the idea of a free economy was irreconcilable with this great block of capital investment which was unrelated to the general economic situation . . . [and that] the group should consider the possibility of another wave of denationalization'.[30] The PSG divided four to three in Powell's favour on this issue, indicating that libertarian thought had gained strength by the late 1950s but that diversity of opinion was stronger still. This was confirmed at a PSG meeting shortly before the 1959 election, when Iain Macleod expressed disquiet at the possibility that the Conservative manifesto would leave open 'the possibility of further denationalization', whilst others voiced the concern 'that a positive statement in favour of the status quo would be undesirable, both because of the likely reactions to it within the Parliamentary party, and because of its effect on future policy'.[31] Doubtless this explains why Reginald Maudling concluded about the PCNI, 'I understand it to be the view of the Committee that our general policy should be to denationalise and restore competition where this is practicable', and at the same time to note that 'the Committee has so far felt that there is no case for complete denationalisation of any of the nationalised industries'.[32] The range of views on nationalization, in the PCNI, the PSG, and within the party more generally, made defining 'practicability' a theoretical issue,

---

[27] Note of PCNI terms of reference, n.d. (Nov.? 1956), CPA, CRD 2/6/2.
[28] J. Douglas to P. Dear, 27 May 1957, ibid.
[29] Chairman's notes of the 17th meeting of the PCNI, 16 Dec. 1957, CPA. CRD 2/6/3.
[30] Policy Study Group, Minutes of 10th meeting, 1 Aug. 1957, CPA, CRD 2/53/24.
[31] PSG, Minutes of 21st meeting, 9 Feb. 1959, CPA, CRD 2/53/24.
[32] PCNI, note by Mr Maudling, 25 Mar. 1957, CPA, CRD 2/6/3.

and provided extensive scope for debate on the relationship between the principles and practice of State ownership.

State welfare generated a similar range of opinions, with positive, negative, and ambivalent positions all finding expression. Hostility to the scale and scope of the Welfare State, as with the nationalized industries, was most pronounced in, but not confined to, the middle and lower ranks of the party. Again as with the nationalized industries, intra-party debate on welfare grew more intense towards the end of the 1950s, and prompted high-level policy discussion. In 1957 the CPC held a summer school at Oxford, which heard calls for 'a major shift in the nature, direction and emphasis of social spending', and in particular for a reduction of the scope of State provision.[33] In 1960 the PCFSS was set up, with a remit to examine the scope for economies in the provision of State welfare—a further example of the desire on the part of the Conservative hierarchy to address and even appease libertarian opinion in the ranks. But the PCFSS found it as difficult as the PCNI to agree upon, let alone construct, a radical strategy for reform of the Welfare State. In December 1960 the PCFSS noted after its nineteenth meeting that 'it was clear that there was a divergence of view among various members of the Committee as to the direction in which a number at least of the social services should develop',[34] and in March 1961, at its thirty-first meeting, it was still discussing 'the philosophy of the social services'.[35] A paper on this very subject had been prepared by James Douglas, a CRD official who was a member of the PCFSS, and it argued that 'we must get back to fundamentals', by which Douglas meant that the notions of rights and duties, and the relationship of the individual citizen to the State, implicit in the structure of the Welfare State, required re-examination.[36] But neither the PCFSS's interim reports nor its final report of 1963[37] provided the unequivocal 'clarification of Conservative philosophy with regard to the social services' envisaged in its initial terms of reference.[38] That the PCFSS produced no radical legislative proposals or results is of course politically significant, but of equal importance is the fact that across the spectrum of economic and social policy its 'first instinct . . . was to roll back the state in order to reduce taxation, release initiative and encourage

---

[33] P. Goldman, Preface to *The Future of the Welfare State: Seven Oxford Lectures* (1958), 10. This CPC pamphlet was the published version of the lectures to the 1957 summer school.

[34] Minutes of the 19th meeting of the PCFSS, 8 Dec. 1960, CPA, CRD 2/29/6.

[35] Minutes of the 31st meeting of the PCFSS, 8 Mar. 1961, CPA, CRD 2/29/8.

[36] J. Douglas, 'Philosophy of the Social Services', 3 Feb. 1961, ibid.

[37] See Second Report of the PCFSS, Aug. 1963, Butler papers, H50/81.

[38] The PCFSS terms of reference were stated in M. Fraser to J. Boyd-Carpenter, 10 May 1960, CPA, CRD 2/29/6.

personal responsibility'.[39] The very existence of the PCFSS, the PCNI, and the PSG, and the content of their discussion, showed that the Conservatives' intra-party debate on the State was still very much alive.

Outright hostility to the State was not uncommon in Conservative circles in the 1950s, but there was another powerful position that developed in that decade, namely, that advanced by the One Nation group. In a series of publications through the 1950s—*One Nation* (1950), *The Social Services: Needs and Means* (1952), *Change Is Our Ally* (1954), and *The Responsible Society* (1959)—the One Nation group[40] sought to construct a distinctive Conservative position on the role of the State which avoided 'me-tooing Socialist solutions'.[41] *One Nation* praised the nineteenth-century critics of laissez faire and trumpeted the Conservative contribution to the evolution of welfare legislation, but suggested that the pendulum had swung too far in favour of State intervention.[42] *Change Is Our Ally* pressed home this argument in relation to industrial policy, making a strong case for a reduction of State activity, but insisting that this was 'not an argument for a pure *laissez-faire* economy'.[43] *The Social Services* was critical of the universalism of the Welfare State, and looked to a system that targeted those in need and encouraged self-reliance. The title as well as the contents of the last major One Nation publication of the 1950s, *The Responsible Society*, summed up much of the One Nation project. The State, it argued, had taken on responsibilities better exercised by the citizenry, and it urged a shift towards an economic and social system that encouraged individual effort and achievement and decreased reliance upon State intervention and provision. In spite of their Disraelian moniker, which carried the historical baggage of the nineteenth-century Tory critique of laissez faire, One Nation sought to blend judicious Statism with strong inflections of liberal market, laissez-faire ideas. Here they were consciously echoing, but also developing, Quentin Hogg's argument that Conservatism should eschew both ultra laissez-faire Individualism and ultra-Statist Socialism.[44] The CCO press release announcing the publication of *The*

---

[39] Lowe, 'Replanning the Welfare State', in Francis and Zweiniger-Bargielowska (eds.), *Conservatives*, 256.

[40] One Nation did not have a fixed membership, but its *raison d'être* remained constant..

[41] I. Macleod to R. A. Butler, 6 Aug. 1950, R. A. Butler papers, Trinity College Cambridge, H36, fos. 24–5.

[42] A Group of MPs, *One Nation* (1950), 12–14, 19.

[43] J. E. Powell and A. Maude, *Change is Our Ally* (1954), 97.

[44] See The One Nation Group, *The Responsible Society* (1959), 7, for reference to Hogg's *Case*. Shortly after the publication of *The Responsible Society* Hogg, who had become Viscount Hailsham, published a second edition of his own book in which he cited and praised *One Nation* for its discussion of this theme. See Viscount Hailsham, *The Conservative Case* (1959), 113.

Responsible Society argued that One Nation were 'concerned with the political process of restoring a proper balance between the power of the State and the rights and initiative of the individual'.[45] This was not an easy task, even for a group like One Nation which presented an ostensibly collective identity. As the debates on nationalization between Iain Macleod and Enoch Powell demonstrated, members of the group were not always in accord with each other.[46] Nevertheless, these problems do not diminish the historical significance of the One Nation project, which led them to produce some of the most carefully prepared and wide-ranging contributions to the Conservative debate on the role of the State.

In the 1960s the centre ground that One Nation sought to extend shrank markedly. In 1961 Harold Macmillan noted a clear division in his Cabinet between *dirigistes* such as himself and those he classified as 'Whig' adherents of laissez faire.[47] That the Conservatives lost power in 1964 after pursuing Macmillan's *dirigiste* economic strategy weakened the purchase of paternalist arguments in the party, whilst, for the same reason, the libertarian line gained strength. Over the course of the decade, and especially after Edward Heath became leader of the party, the political culture of the Conservative party became suffused with libertarian ideas. The most prominent individual spokesman of anti-Statism was Enoch Powell, whose speeches from 1965 to 1968 called for the party to embrace the 'genuine' capitalism of the free-market economy.[48] 'Powellism' came to be (and remains) associated with the question of immigration, but before 1968 it referred to his free-market economics. As Powell himself put it in the autumn of 1968, ' "Powellism" has rather changed its connotations, much to my regret. It used to represent an almost unlimited faith in the ability of people to get what they want through price, capital, profit and a competitive market.'[49] For Powell the free market was economically, morally, and politically preferable to paternalist economic and social intervention. Planning for economic growth he deemed both wrong-headed and plain wrong, and his view of State welfare was that 'the current remedies for poverty, as it [*sic*] appears in the specific examples of housing, health, education and social security, have in common the elimination of self-expression and a system which is centralized and authoritarian'.[50] By

---

[45] Typescript of CCO press release, 24 Mar. 1959, CPA, CCO 150/4/2/5.

[46] The personnel of One Nation changed over the years, but it did not seem to alter the group's fundamental objective. That, for example, Powell and Macleod, who had written *The Social Services* together, could be so far apart on nationalized industries was indicative of the way the ideas of some individuals in the original group shifted over the 1950s.

[47] See p. 227.

[48] Wood (ed.), *A Nation Not Afraid* and J. E. Powell, *Freedom and Reality* (1969).

[49] J. E. Powell, 'Conservatism and Social Problems', *Swinton Journal*, 14:3 (Autumn 1968), 15.   [50] Ibid.

the late 1960s Powell was by no means alone in espousing this faith. Numerous individuals, think-tanks, and groups shared his libertarian vision, as did much of the party rank and file.[51] Moreover, many of the committees set up by Edward Heath as part of his 'Government in Exile' policy strategy also embraced free market anti-Statism.[52] This is not to say that libertarian views became utterly dominant. Senior party figures like Reginald Maudling, John Boyd-Carpenter, and Edward Boyle continued to see a positive role for State intervention, and they were not without backbench or rank-and-file support, but the libertarians' position in the party was much stronger, both institutionally and ideologically, by the late 1960s than it had been a decade before.

An important summary of libertarian ideas was presented in Margaret Thatcher's 1968 CPC lecture 'What's Wrong With Politics?' Thatcher stated that 'the great mistake of the last few years has been for the government to provide or to legislate for almost everything'. The root of the problem, she felt, lay 'in the plans for reconstruction in the post-war period when governments assumed all kinds of new obligations'. She accepted that these policies 'may have been warranted at the time', but argued that 'they have gone far further than was intended or is advisable'. The Conservative governments of the 1950s were, in Thatcher's view, 'concerned to set the framework in which people could achieve their own standards for themselves, subject to a basic standard. But . . . from the early 1960s the emphasis in politics shifted'. Here Thatcher saw the emphasis on 'growth' as having (mis)led first the Macmillan government and then, even more damagingly, the Wilson governments to adopt State planning mechanisms which had infringed personal liberties and produced 'an increasing authoritarianism'. This trend, Thatcher declared, had to be reversed—'What we need now is a far greater degree of personal responsibility and decision, far more independence from the government, and a comparative reduction in the role of government.'[53] Apart from its authorship, which in many respects only has retrospective significance, Thatcher's libertarian argument provides a window onto the libertarian case as it had developed by the late 1960s. Thatcher's periodization of the problem of 'too much government', with its focus on post-war reconstruction and the 1960s, indicated an emerging Conservative analysis of the 'ratchet effect', whereby Conservative administrations had failed to reverse and, in the case of Macmillan's government, anticipated and extended

---

[51] See pp. 227–9.   [52] See pp. 230–1.
[53] Margaret Thatcher, 'What's Wrong With Politics', CPC Lecture, London, 11 Oct. 1968, *Thatcher CD-ROM*.

Socialist Statism.[54] In addition, Thatcher's concern about the creeping authoritarianism that necessarily accompanied extensions of State action carried distinctly Hayekian inflections. In 1945 Hayek's equation of Statism with 'serfdom' had played a significant role in the Conservative election campaign,[55] but his ideas had been somewhat marginalized during the 1950s. The One Nation group's *The Responsible Society* noted, rightly, that Hayek had been the 'inspiration' for Churchill's 'Gestapo' speech of 1945, but argued that he had inspired 'very little else at the time' or since, because arguments for 'self-help' were not in vogue. But they felt that, as the 1950s drew to a close, opinion was moving in a more Hayekian direction.[56] By 1968 Hayekian assumptions had come once again to provide inspiration for libertarian arguments in the Conservative ranks, and in many ways Hayek's renewed kudos in Conservative circles was symptomatic of this.

The increasing strength and ultimate ascendancy of libertarian ideas within the Conservative party from 1970 to 2000 is a well-documented phenomenon, and will not be discussed here. Suffice it to say that, although the last quarter of the twentieth century saw libertarian arguments enjoy an unusual dominance, they were by no means uncontested. In this respect the 'Thatcherite era', like those that preceded it, saw debate within the Conservative party as to the proper realm of State action. The essential libertarian contentions were that the period since 1945 had witnessed a socially, economically, and politically damaging extension of State activity, that Conservative governments had contributed to this, and that it was essential to 'roll back the frontiers of the State'. The idea of a 'middle ground' between 'Statism' and 'laissez faire', 'Socialism' and 'Capitalism', was discarded. Keith Joseph's pamphlet, *Stranded On the Middle Ground*, summed up the argument here, indicating that any concessions to Statism were in effect concessions to Socialism.[57] That Joseph, who had been one of the authors of the One Nation group's *The Responsible Society*, explicitly rejected this centre-piece of One Nation argument was eloquent testimony to the shrinkage of the middle ground. The ambiguous legacy of One Nation Conservatism in this context is underlined by the fact that other members of the group, notably Ian Gilmour, emerged as some of the most vocal critics of the libertarian position in the 1980s and 1990s. For such critics, the historical 'failures' of Conservative Statism in particular, and State intervention more generally, were being overdrawn by Thatcherites, and the stability and peace of British society were threatened by the

[54] For a similar argument, also presented in 1968, see J. Jewkes, *The New Ordeal By Planning* (1968), 1–41.   [55] See pp. 219–20.
[56] One Nation, *Responsible Society*, 6.
[57] K. Joseph, *Stranded on the Middle Ground* (1976), *passim*.

State's retreat from the social and economic sphere.[58] The apparent tension within the Conservative party between paternalists and libertarians that had been a feature of the party's history throughout the twentieth century was still there, albeit with the paternalists increasingly marginalized, as the century ended.

The history of twentieth-century Conservative political thought seems to indicate a basic polarity in the party's ideological make-up: a divide between paternalists and libertarians. On the face of it, this divide is indicative of fundamental differences in social, economic, and political philosophy—a point which both paternalist and libertarian 'schools' have themselves frequently made. The question emerges as to how these differences can be accommodated within the same ideological framework. One answer is that they cannot. The strongest statements to this effect have been made by Conservative paternalists, many of whom argued, over the course of the century, that the libertarian position was not part of the Conservative tradition but was an alien, and more specifically a Liberal, philosophical incursion. In the Edwardian period the USRC buttressed its case by arguing:

We have in this country now outlived that curious philosophic conception of the relations between the State and the individual which finds its origin in Rousseau and its most powerful exponents on this side of the channel in Bentham, the two Mills, Herbert Spencer and Cobden . . . [and that] the old Cobdenite and laissez faire view that the conditions of wages, health, housing and labour among the vast majority of the population of this country was the concern of private individuals and of private contract has long since been abandoned.[59]

Nor was it only thoroughgoing paternalists in the Edwardian party who presented Victorian Liberalism as the ideological enemy, for Arthur Balfour was equally clear that 'laissez faire and individualism' were Cobdenite articles of faith.[60] In the inter-war years the authors of *Industry and the State* asserted that 'The policy of laissez faire never formed an integral part of Tory or Conservative policy',[61] and the CRD committee which examined relations between the State and industry declared that those who saw State intervention as 'contrary to Conservative principles . . . are confusing Conservative with Liberal principles'.[62] During the Second World War this point was pressed

---

[58] See in particular I. Gilmour, *Britain Can Work* (1983), 1–50, 158–221; id., *Dancing With Dogma* (1992), 105–76; F. Pym, *The Politics of Consent* (1984), 111–30.

[59] J. W. Hills *et al.*, *Industrial Unrest* (1914), 3.

[60] A. J. Balfour to Devonshire, 27 Aug. 1903, in J. L. Garvin and J. Amery, *The Life of Joseph Chamberlain*, 6 vols. (1932–69), v. 376–7.

[61] R. Boothby *et al.*, *Industry and the State*, 19.

[62] Draft Report of subcommittee 'A' to the Chairman's Committee, 28 Nov. 1934, CPA, CRD 1/65/2.

home with even greater vigour by Viscount Hinchingbrooke of the Tory Reform Group, who declared that:

True Conservative opinion is horrified at the damage done to this country since the last war by 'individualist' business men, financiers, and speculators ranging freely in a *laissez faire* economy and creeping unnoticed into the fold of Conservatism to insult the Party with their votes at elections, to cast a slur over responsible Government through influence exerted on Parliament, and to injure the character of our people ... these men should collect their baggage and depart. True Conservatism has nothing whatever to do with them and their obnoxious policies.[63]

Lord Beaverbrook did not match Hinchingbrooke's splenetic language, but he also described a head-on collision within the party when he told one correspondent in the autumn of 1945 that 'The battle within the party is a fight between the Tory individualists who follow ironically enough the creed of nineteenth century Liberalism, and the Tory Reformers who raise the banner ... of Disraeli's Young England'.[64] Quentin Hogg appeared to be in fundamental agreement with this view, for in *The Case for Conservatism* he stated that '*Laissez-faire* has never been good Conservative doctrine'.[65] This contention continued to be a refrain of Conservative critics of the libertarian position throughout the last half of the century, reaching a new peak of intensity in the 1990s. Ian Gilmour provided the most forthright restatement of the argument that '*laissez faire* was never ... the doctrine of the Conservative party',[66] and denounced Margaret Thatcher's 'devotion to Manchester Liberalism'.[67] Gilmour's stance was shared by other Conservatives who saw Thatcher as a devotee of laissez faire. As one remarked, 'We fought the Liberals in the nineteenth century *because* we disagreed with *laissez faire*. We [Conservatives] believed in intervention.'[68]

It was not just Conservative critics of the libertarian position who saw it as drawing on or embracing a Liberal ideological inheritance. Writing in 1949, Nigel Birch noted that although Conservatives had opposed nineteenth-century Liberalism at the time, it was right that, after 1945, they should espouse laissez-faire ideas because 'to-day they are seeking to preserve what was of lasting value in nineteenth-century Liberalism against the ever-increasing aggression of an authoritarian State'.[69] Ten years later Lord Hailsham echoed this point, and marked something of a departure from his own position in 1947, when he

[63] Viscount Hinchingbrooke, *Full Speed Ahead: Essays in Tory Reform* (1944), 21.
[64] Beaverbrook to E. J. Flynn, 11 Oct. 1945, in A. J. P. Taylor, *Beaverbrook* (1972), 728–9.
[65] Hogg, *Case for Conservatism*, 229.
[66] Gilmour, *Britain Can Work*, 49, and also *Dancing With Dogma*, 10.
[67] *Dancing with Dogma*, 269.
[68] P. Walker, *Staying Power* (1991), 236 (my emphasis).
[69] N. Birch, *The Conservative Party* (1949), 34.

argued that 'Laissez-faire economics were never orthodox Conservative teaching and Conservatives have only begun to defend them when there appears to be a danger of society swinging too far to the other extreme'.[70] The argument here was straightforward. In the nineteenth century Conservatives had supported State intervention in order to rectify the social, economic, and political imbalances caused by extreme laissez-faire Liberalism. In the twentieth century, and especially after 1945, the threat of imbalance was coming from the other direction in the shape of Socialist Statism, and hence laissez-faire Liberalism was acceptable as a counter-balancing philosophy. The trick, as Harold Macmillan argued in 1938 and reiterated in 1958,[71] as Quentin Hogg stated in 1947, and which the One Nation group sought to achieve in their publications, was to find a 'middle way' between 'State worship' and laissez faire.

If Liberal ideas were seen as useful in the battle against Socialism, the same thing was true of Liberal voters. In the inter-war years the Conservative party had made strenuous and successful efforts to construct an 'anti-Socialist front' by appealing to Liberal values and by building alliances with elements of the disintegrating Liberal party. After 1945 the Conservatives were keen to construct a similar social and political coalition of anti-Socialist forces. The Conservatives' relationship with the National Liberals, first established in 1931, was cemented and strengthened, and the circular sent to Conservative and National Liberal constituency associations after the discussions between Lord Woolton and Lord Teviot in 1947, which had resulted in the so-called 'Woolton–Teviot' pact, was simply entitled 'The United Front Against Socialism'.[72] By the time of the 1950 general election sixty-one Conservative constituency associations, either through fusion with local National Liberals or through unilateral action, had incorporated the term 'Liberal' in some form in their title, a trend that was to continue into the 1950s.[73] At the general election of 1951 the Liberal vote collapsed, and the bulk of former Liberal voters transferred their allegiance to the Conservatives. This was vital to the Conservative victory, and seemed to underscore the political and electoral importance of the ambivalent Conservative stance on State intervention. The work done by Butler's new 'thinking machine' had seen the Conservatives accept an

[70] Hailsham, *Conservative Case*, 133.

[71] H. Macmillan, *The Middle Way* (1938); id., *The Middle Way: 20 Years After* (1958); Hogg, *Case for Conservatism*, 110, uses the term 'middle way'. For the One Nation group's position, see above, pp. 247–8.

[72] See Woolton, Circular Letter to Conservative Agents re The United Front Against Socialism, 8 May 1947, CPA, CCO 500/12/1.

[73] For these developments see Ramsden, *Churchill and Eden*, 200.

extended role for the State, but it was a deliberately qualified acceptance. John Boyd-Carpenter described the *Industrial Charter* as occupy-
ing 'a central position betweeen Manchester and Moscow',[74] and part
of the positive local party response to the document was perhaps due to
the fact that, as the party's chief agent for Sheffield said, 'there was little
in it with which a Liberal could disagree'.[75] Harold Macmillan, who
had been flattered by the description of the *Industrial Charter* as a
'second edition of *The Middle Way*', was concerned in the run-up to the
1950 general election that Conservative economic policy still contained
too much 'Manchesterism'.[76] Certainly the emphasis in the
Conservative campaigns of both 1950 and 1951 was on the need for
loosening government controls on the economy and reducing the role of
the State—themes which were designed to appeal to a general popular
resentment of austerity and government controls, but to a Liberal audience in particular.[77] Both implicitly and explicitly the Conservatives had
acknowledged that their target constituency and their own party
membership contained 'many hundreds of thousands of Liberals who
see that in the present age it is the Tories who are the guardians and
preservers of the nineteenth century gains of Liberalism which the
Socialist party is bent on destroying'.[78] The underlying principles and
the *Realpolitik* of the 'anti-Socialist front' required Conservatives to
embrace, or at least display sensitivity towards, old Liberal values.

Both the need and space for a pragmatic assimilation of Liberal ideas
was evident in post-war Conservative politics, but the question remains
as to whether there was also a normative internalization of Liberal
tenets which led to a fundamental shift in the ideological make-up of the
Conservative party. A window is opened onto this by Conservative
responses to 'the recurrent post-war Conservative nightmare'[79]—the
possibility of Liberal revival. One aspect of the response in the 1950s
was for Conservatives to present themselves as the new home of traditional Liberalism. In June 1958, three months after the loss of the
Torrington by-election to the Liberals, the draft notes for a speech by
R. A. Butler took up this point, arguing that:

[74] In H. Jones, 'The Conservative Party and Social Policy, 1942–55', unpublished University
of London Ph.D thesis (1992), 30.
[75] Minutes of Sheffield Central Women's Advisory Committee, 4 July 1947 in Ramsden,
Churchill and Eden, 156.
[76] Ibid. 160. Macmillan, as noted on pp. 169–71 above, had been involved in drawing up
the Industrial Charter.
[77] See I. Zweiniger-Bargielowska, 'Rationing, Austerity and the Conservative Electoral
Recovery After 1945', *HJ* 37 (1993), Green, 'Conservative Party'.
[78] Birch, *Conservative Party*, 36.
[79] I. Gilmour, *Whatever Happened to the Tories* (1997), 279.

If the Liberals had a distinctive policy and something new to bring to politics, there would be a strong case for launching a third party. Yet all that is best in the Liberal tradition has long been absorbed into Tory philosophy: belief in personal liberty, in the importance of the individual, in the virtue of property-owning, in free enterprise, in fair competition and in national unity.[80]

The complementary aspect of this argument was to present the Liberal party as having shifted to the Left to the point where they had become subaltern Socialists. In 1961 CCO issued a circular to party agents on how to deal with Liberals which stressed that 'we must label them as left wingers',[81] and in 1962 the Liberals were described as 'increasingly advocating policies put forward at one time or another by the Socialists'[82] and, as in 1924 and 1929, voting with Labour in parliament.[83] Labelling the Liberals as, in the words of one Conservative Cabinet Minister of the 1980s, 'pink herrings—Enid-Blyton Socialists',[84] served to reinforce the argument that the Conservative party was the home of 'true' Liberalism. Margaret Thatcher was clear on this, arguing in her 1996 Keith Joseph Memorial Lecture that '[t]he kind of Conservatism which he [Joseph] and I . . . favoured would be best described as "liberal", in the old-fashioned sense. And I mean the liberalism of Mr. Gladstone not of the latter day collectivists.'[85] Statements such as these help to explain why it was possible for one 'Thatcherite' Cabinet Minister to say in 1982 that 'I am a nineteenth-century Liberal. So is Mrs Thatcher. That's what this [Conservative] Government is all about.'[86] Whether this was a wholly accurate description of the ideological base of Thatcherite Conservatism is open to question. However, that a Conservative Prime Minister could speak of her 'pride' in the fact that her Conservatism was closely related to 'old-fashioned Liberalism' indicates that the questions of the link between Conservatism and 'old' Liberalism and their respective positions on the role of the State are more than worthy of attention.

One possible interpretation of the trajectory of Conservative political ideas on the State in the twentieth century is to describe them in terms of the incremental absorption and ultimate ascendancy of Liberalism within the Conservative party. This is not an unproblematic argument, but the evidence supporting it is by no means insubstantial. Economic

[80] B. Sewill, notes for R. A. Butler's speech at Luton Hoo, 21 June 1958, CPA, CRD 2/9/39.

[81] C. F. R. Bagnall to Party Agents, 22 Mar. 1961, CPA, CCO 500/25/3.

[82] P. Dean, 'The Liberal Party', 26 Oct. 1962, Butler papers, H49, fos. 1–43.

[83] Briefing Document, 'The Liberal Party', 26 Oct. 1962, CPA, CCO 500/25/4.

[84] N. Tebbit, *Upwardly Mobile*, 164.

[85] M. Thatcher, 'Liberty and Limited Government', Keith Joseph Memorial Lecture, London, 11 Jan. 1996, *Thatcher CD-ROM*.

[86] J. Nott, *Guardian*, 13 Sept. 1982.

tenets such as free trade, free markets, minimal State intervention, and low public expenditure and taxation have been strongly associated with nineteenth-century Liberalism. Obviously there was much more to nineteenth-century Liberalism than 'free market economics',[87] but the two were intertwined. Moreover, throughout the twentieth century it is this vulgarized conception of Liberalism which has been used, notably by many Conservatives, to describe the nineteenth-century Liberal credo—laissez faire and Liberalism have frequently appeared as interchangeable. Margaret Thatcher, unlike others, was always very careful when she talked about 'Victorian values', but she identified Gladstonian Liberalism with placing 'greater confidence in individuals, families, businesses and neighbourhoods than in the State'.[88] Likewise, as noted above, Conservative critics of Thatcherism, and earlier forms of Conservative libertarianism, tended to see laissez-faire economics as synonymous with nineteenth-century Liberalism or 'Manchesterism'. Conservative critics and supporters of libertarian views offered simplistic, even jejune, views of nineteenth-century Liberalism, but it is difficult to construct libertarian economics as unequivocally Conservative.

It was not just in the realm of economic ideas that there was an imbrication of Conservatism and Liberalism. Individualist philosophy began to play an increasingly significant role in Conservative politics in the late nineteenth and early twentieth centuries. Although there were Conservative individualists before the 1880s, they were few in number and their ideas lacked significant purchase in the party. Attempts to categorize Burke as a founder of individualist Conservatism founder on the fact that he was too much of an 'organicist' to place the individual at the heart of his political philosophy, and that the vocabulary of his social and political Conservatism was based on a completely different set of terms and concerns from those of individualism.[89] It is equally difficult to present the 'Liberal Toryism' of the 1820s or Sir Robert Peel's economic liberalism as precursers of later individualist trends in the Conservative party. Lord Liverpool was many things, but he was not a clear-cut individualist, and the meaning of his view of 'limited government' was very period-specific. Peel's stance seems at first glance more promising, but in terms of his relationship to the Conservative canon two things are worthy of note: first, Peel's espousal of the 'individualist' economics of free trade resulted in the bulk of the Conservative party deserting him; second, reappraisals of Peel's career have concluded that 'Peel was not the founder of the

---

[87] See e.g. E. Biagini (ed.), *Citizenship and Community* (Cambridge, 1997).
[88] Thatcher, 'Liberty and Limited Government'.
[89] See J. G. A. Pocock, 'The Political Economy of Burke's *Reflections on the Revolution in France*', *HJ* 25 (1982).

Conservative party but was the progenitor of Gladstonian Liberalism'.[90] Locating individualism within the Conservative fold before the 1880s is problematic. Indeed, it is in many respects pointless to try. The meaning of terms and the language used to represent their meanings depends upon the political and intellectual context within which they are deployed. It was only in the last quarter of the nineteenth century that 'individualism' and 'collectivism', and the idea of conflict between them as a fulcrum of political debate, took on recognizably modern connotations. This is a question which will be looked at further below. Suffice it here to say that from 1880 onwards it becomes easier and more meaningful to identify Conservative individualists. Organizations such as the Liberty and Property Defence League (LPDL) and the British Constitutional Association (BCA), and individuals like Lord Wemyss, Herbert Spencer, A. V. Dicey, Auberon Herbert, and Ernest Benn, all explicitly espoused individualist ideas and were supporters or members of the Conservative party.[91] Yet, in spite of their party-political affiliation, the political *philosophy* to which these 'men versus the State' were self-consciously closest to was nineteenth-century Liberalism. Dicey, Herbert, and many others associated with the LPDL and BCA had no great love for Conservatism,[92] but, when faced with the development of a Collectivist New Liberalism, saw the Conservative party as the best chance for preserving old Liberal individualism. This is not to say that *all* individualist sympathizers in the Conservative ranks were former Liberals—Lords Wemyss, Hugh Cecil, and Robert Cecil stand out as Conservatives of long standing—but there is a marked coincidence between the rise of Conservative individualist thought and the arrival in the Conservative party, at all levels, of Liberal defectors.

The case for seeing a Conservative absorption of Liberal ideas is further strengthened by developments in Conservatism in the last quarter of the twentieth century. As noted above, both internal party critics and supporters of Thatcherism described its economic strategy as nineteenth-century Liberalism, and its social philosophy was also frequently seen as driven by a nineteenth-century Liberal individualism. It has been suggested that it is wrong to describe Thatcherism as a derivative of Liberalism, because, unlike in Liberalism, individualism was 'an adjacent concept' rather than a core element in Thatcherite ideology.[93]

[90] B. Hilton, 'Peel: A Reappraisal', *HJ* 22 (1979).

[91] For the fullest discussion of this individualist position see M. W. Taylor, *Men Versus the State* (Oxford, 1992).

[92] The 'guru' of the LPDL, Herbert Spencer, referred to Socialism as 'the New Toryism' on the grounds that Conservatism had always been antipathetic to Liberal economics and in favour of State intervention.

[93] M. Freeden, *Ideologies and Political Theory* (Oxford 1996), 385–93.

However, in her Nicholas Ridley Memorial Lecture of November 1996 Margaret Thatcher praised her late colleague as 'one of a long line of British individualists', and noted that individualist was 'a term which is often used disparagingly, but which should be rehabilitated'.[94] When she was challenged about her individualism she was forthright in defence of her philosophy. She demanded of the BBC's James Naughtie, 'How can you make up a community except of individuals?', and when asked to comment on her supposed 'ruthless individualism' she replied, 'it is the State's job to serve the freedom of the individual'. Likewise, she told the annual meeting of the Centre for Policy Studies that those who described her individualism as 'selfish' were talking 'nonsense', because wishing to do well for oneself and family was admirable and that she wished 'more people would in fact take responsibility for looking after their own families instead of expecting others to look after them'.[95] These comments were not made by a politician who saw individualism as an 'adjacent concept'. Rather, they imply a philosophy that emphasized a polity that was an aggregate of individual citizens and in which individual rights and duties were the fulcrum of social and political life. In short, they imply a philosophy which, like nineteenth-century Liberalism, regarded the individual as the primary locus of politics.

Nor is classical nineteenth-century Liberalism the only form of Liberalism that had an influence on late twentieth-century Conservatism. A similarly important role can be ascribed to Neo-Liberal ideas, in the shape of the monetarist and public-choice schools of economic thought, but above all in the philosophy of Friedrich Hayek. Hayek's *The Road to Serfdom*, which was written specifically to counter the growing influence of interventionist social and economic thought during the Second World War, identified individual freedom with political freedom, and political freedom with economic market freedom under the civil equality of the rule of law.[96] For Thatcherite Conservatives, and indeed for Thatcher herself, Hayek was a key reference point.[97] Leaving aside the story of Thatcher banging the table at a meeting with a copy of Hayek's *The Constitution of Liberty* and declaring 'this is what we believe', she stated in her Keith Joseph Memorial Lecture that *The Road to Serfdom* 'had such a great effect upon me when I first read it' and that it had 'a greater effect still when Keith

---

[94] M. Thatcher, Nicholas Ridley Memorial Lecture, London, 22 Nov. 1996, *Thatcher CD-ROM*. She went on to praise J. S. Mill as offering the best defence of this philosophy.

[95] M. Thatcher, Interview with James Naughtie, BBC Radio 4, 16 May 1990; Interview with Jimmy Young, BBC Radio 2, 22 July 1988; Speech to CPS, 28 Apr. 1988, *Thatcher CD-ROM*.

[96] F. Hayek, *The Road to Serfdom* (1943), *passim*, esp. 54–75.

[97] See Cockett, *Thinking the Unthinkable* and A. Gamble, *Hayek* (Cambridge, 1996), 100–25, 166–8.

[Joseph] suggested that I go deeper into Hayek's other writings'.[98] Thatcher also claimed in 1985 that Hayek 'has been one of my staunchest supporters', and stated that 'the conservatism which I follow does have some things in common with what Professor Hayek was preaching'.[99] The more formal statements of her political beliefs appear to confirm that this was the case, for they were redolent with Hayekian language and precepts, particularly those relating to liberty, markets, and the rule of law.[100] Whether or not one accepts that Thatcher was an avid reader of Hayek's work is in some respects not the point. The mere fact that she, and many of her close colleagues and supporters, chose to identify Hayek as an influence is in itself important. And it is particularly important insofar as the title of the last chapter in Hayek's *The Constitution of Liberty* was 'Why I Am Not a Conservative', and late in life he said of himself 'I am becoming a Burkean Whig'.[101] The marked and acknowledged influence of Neo-Liberal ideas serves to reinforce the argument that the late twentieth-century Conservative party had embraced a libertarian philosophy that was not intrinsic to the Conservative ideological tradition.

II

The case for Conservatism having been 'invaded' by libertarian Liberalism is strong, but it is not the only construction that can be placed on this development in Conservative thought. An alternative construction is made by W. H. Greenleaf, who sees Conservatism as, like Goethe's Faust, able to declare 'Zwei Seelen wohnen nach in meine Brust' ('Two souls together live in my breast')—one soul being 'libertarian' and the other 'paternalist'. This influential model of Conservatism, echoed by other scholars, allows space for late twentieth-century Conservative political thought on the grounds that it can be accommodated within the 'libertarian' strand of Conservative ideas, and also that the Thatcherite emphasis on the need for 'the framework of a strong State' is consistent with a traditional Conservative emphasis on order and authority.[102] As noted above, the centrality of the individual in

[98] For *The Constitution of Liberty* story see J. Ranelagh, *Thatcher's People* (1991), p. ix. Thatcher, 'Joseph Memorial Lecture'; id., 'The Ideals of an Open Society'.

[99] Thatcher, Interview with BBC Radio 3, 17 Dec. 1985, *Thatcher CD-ROM*.

[100] The 'Joseph Memorial Lecture' and 'The Ideals of An Open Society' are particularly good examples.

[101] F. A. Hayek, *The Constitution of Liberty* (1960; 1976 edn.), 397; id., 'Hayek on Hayek', in Gamble, *Hayek*, 100.

[102] R. Eccleshall, *English Conservatism Since the Reformation* (1990), 9–18; Freeden, *Ideologies*, 388–90.

twentieth-century Conservative thought places a question-mark against this interpretation, and points more in the Liberal direction. Nor is this the only query that can be raised. It is difficult to draw an absolute division in the Conservative ranks between 'libertarians' and 'paternalists'. The same individuals could hold both libertarian and paternalist views at the same time, with their outlook depending less on clearly stated principles than on the particular issue or realm of activity that was being addressed.[103] Lord Hailsham described his own position at the end of the Second World War in these somewhat contradictory terms. His memoirs state that,

in the main, for innovation, salesmanship and exports I was as firmly wedded to private enterprise as the most right wing of my fellow Conservatives. On social policy, however, as soon as the Beveridge Report was published, I believed that it would be in the interest of the Conservative party to support the main thrust of the Beveridge approach ... At the time my formula was 'Publicly organised social services, privately-owned industries'.[104]

Nor was Hailsham alone in this. From 1945 to 1951 the heaviest Conservative fire was brought to bear on the Attlee government's nationalization programme, and when the Conservatives were returned to office the only Labour reforms that were reversed were the nationalization of iron and steel and road-haulage. This could be taken to indicate that Conservatives preferred to be paternalist with regard to social services and libertarian with regard to the economy,[105] but this argument is difficult to sustain. In 1958, in the context of the Conservative effort to construct the idea of the 'Opportunity State',[106] R. A. Butler suggested that the two basic themes of future Conservative policy should be 'Opportunity' and 'Responsibility', and declared that 'the main aim of social policy from now on should be to switch the emphasis of State expenditure away from the services which, in a fully employed community, people ought to be able to provide for themselves'.[107] Butler's reference to full employment was crucial, for it was indicative of the way in which State management of the economy was seen as, in effect, a prerequisite for reducing the scope of State welfare. This was a notion that was built into much of the One Nation group's thought. For example, *The Responsible Society* envisaged that State pensions would be replaced by private, occupational pensions as the

---

[103] For an interesting discussion of this see M. Grimley, 'Conservatism and the Church of England in the Twentieth Century', unpublished MS.

[104] Lord Hailsham, *A Sparrow's Flight* (1990), 210.

[105] For this argument see Greenleaf, *Ideological Heritage*, 196–308.

[106] See Green, 'Conservative Party'. CPA, CRD 2/53/28 contains much discussion of the 'Opportunity State'.

[107] R. A. Butler to H. Macmillan 25 Feb. 1958, CPA, CRD 2/53/30.

main source of provision for the aged, and that a more targeted welfare system was the tale of the future.[108] But it also stated that a 'high and stable level of employment' was a 'basic requirement' for a stable society and for 'the freedom of the citizen'.[109] It seems that Conservatives were capable of accepting degrees of libertarianism and paternalism in both the economic and social spheres, and that any consistent pattern is difficult to establish using this straightforward binary model.

What this study suggests is that the problems outlined above can be best addressed by adopting an alternative model to explain Conservative ideas about the role of the State. At the heart of both the interpretation based on the Conservative absorption of Liberal ideas, and the libertarian-versus-paternalist model is the assumption that the primary fulcrum of analysis must be Conservative views of the State. This chapter argues that this is mistaken, and that the *primary* focus should instead be on Conservative views of the effectiveness of agencies of civil society. By agencies of civil society this essay means forms of social association which are not part of the apparatus of the State and are not directly sponsored or organized by the State. In 1947 Quentin Hogg provided a helpful outline of the kind of structures that can be included in this category. Speaking of the 'rich profusion of social forms' which made up 'a healthy society', Hogg argued that:

Such forms are seldom politically inspired, and form the natural barrier of defence between the individual and the State . . . societies and organisations which are at once the condition and the result, at once the glory and the cause, of a free society — trade unions, limited companies, co-operatives, literary and cultural societies, speaking clubs, associations of neighbours, societies of hobby lovers, social centres, political and social groups.[110]

For Conservatives, the key thing about these forms of associational life was that they had emerged spontaneously from the *voluntary* association of individuals and groups. Such associations were, in Conservative eyes, the essence of society. In 1950 R. J. White stated that 'society is not a collection of "universalized individuals", nor the sum of individuals statistically aggregated, but the product of a system of real relationships *between* individuals, classes and groups'.[111] Twelve years later the Young Conservatives' pamphlet *Society and the Individual* argued that the idea that society was 'just a collection of individuals' was a

---

[108] One Nation, *Responsible Society*, 36–7. See also the published lectures of the 1957 CPC Oxford Summer School, *The Future of the Welfare State* (1958), for a discussion of these themes.
[109] *Responsible Society*, 34.
[110] Hogg, *Case*, 29, and, for a further list, 84.
[111] R. J. White, *The Conservative Tradition* (1950).

product of the French Revolution, which, as a result of this erroneous assumption, had made the mistake of sweeping away all the old institutions between individuals and the State. Quoting Ernest Barker, the pamphlet declared that society was 'the whole sum of voluntary bodies and associations contained in the nation ... with all their various purposes and with all their institutions', ranging from folk-dance groups to giant trade unions.[112] These agencies represented twentieth-century versions of Burke's 'little platoons',[113] and were regarded by *all* Conservatives as valuable, indeed essential, social structures. However, the question which greatly exercised the minds of Conservatives in the twentieth century was whether these 'little platoons' were fit for duty.

The realm of the economy was the first to witness a major intra-party debate on the fitness of a platoon—the platoon in question being British industry. The tariff debate of the first decade of the twentieth century has been exhaustively studied, and this essay will not enter into a detailed survey here. Suffice it to say that many Conservatives saw British industry to be suffering from severe problems, even experiencing decline. This they attributed to the loss of overseas markets, import penetration into the domestic market, and the superior organizational structure of foreign industrial concerns. The remedies proposed were imperial tariff preference to increase the export trade, and protective tariffs to defend British industry in the home market and provide it with an opportunity to reorganize its structure to match that of its competitors.[114] Conservative (and Liberal) adherents of free trade argued that tariffs would simply protect inefficient industries from healthy competition and encourage the development of monopolies and trusts.[115] The tariff case rested on the premiss that industry required State assistance to combat problems that were beyond its control and to rectify flaws in its organizational structure. The free-trade argument was that such State intervention was unnecessary, in that British business as a whole was prospering and that 'decline' had affected only a few sectors. The call for tariff protection was, on this basis, simply special pleading by industries which sought to avoid making necessary adjustments to changed market conditions, and giving in to this would weaken British industry

[112] Young Conservative Policy Group, 'Society and the Individual', June 1962 CPA, CRD 2/50/9.
[113] This phrase became something of a favourite with Conservatives discussing the merits of voluntary associations: see White, *Conservative Tradition*, 32, Thatcher, Interview with BBC Radio 4, 16 May 1990, and D. Willetts, *Civic Conservatism* (1994), ch. 7.
[114] The literature is extensive, but see A. Marrison, *British Business and Protection, 1903–1932* (Oxford 1992) and Green, *Crisis*, 223–41.
[115] The Conservative free-traders are curiously under-studied, but see A. J. Ll. Morris, 'St. Loe Strachey and the Spectator', unpublished Cambridge University Ph.D thesis (1984) and R. Rempel, *Unionists Divided* (Newton Abbot, 1972).

rather than strengthen it. Whereas tariff-reformers saw industry as failing and requiring State aid, the free-traders argued that it was robust
and should be left to its own devices.

Conservative debate over the strength or weakness of British industry recurred in the inter-war years. Tariffs and currency questions were
areas in which State policy had important implications for industry, but
a central issue in the 1920s and 1930s was the structure of industry. The
Victorian staple industries suffered particularly severe difficulties, and
with large-scale unemployment a constant feature of British economic
life after 1921, there was general agreement in the inter-war
Conservative party on the need for industrial restructuring for both
economic and social reasons. But how to achieve this was another
matter. For men like Arthur Steel-Maitland, Harold Macmillan, Robert
Boothby, and their fellow 'capitalist planners',[116] the State had a key
role to play in industrial reorganization. The reason for this was that the
existing economic institutions—firms and industries and the banking
system—had proved to be incapable of bringing about the necessary
changes themselves. The authors of *Industry and the State* noted that

Captains of industry demand that industrial policy and industrial research should
be left in their hands alone, and the arguments they advance are undoubtedly
cogent. Few people nowadays seriously suggest that the State should conduct the
industries of the nation. But it is the duty of the State to create and sustain conditions under which it is possible for other people to conduct them.[117]

This established the basic parameters of capitalist planning. State
control of industry, and State-run schemes of industrial reorganization,
were ruled out: the State's role was to facilitate the process whereby
industry reorganized itself through rationalization, amalgamation, and
the adoption of the most up-to-date techniques of production and
marketing. Underpinning the capitalist planners' arguments was a view
that industrial institutions, and other economic agencies in Britain, had
failed to adapt to changes in the nature of the capitalist economy, and,
as a result, British industry was operating with structures and acting on
assumptions that had been overtaken by events. In 1934 Macmillan
noted that '*In modern conditions* the system of supply and demand
regulated by the price indicator alone ... is inadequate',[118] those
modern conditions being an economic world of corporate, large-scale
enterprise, and new product markets and marketing techniques. British
enterprise, in Macmillan's view, had failed to respond to these new
conditions, and he argued that 'the failure of enterprise to meet the new

---

[116] The phrase is taken from Ritschel, *Planning*.
[117] Boothby *et al.*, *Industry and the State*, 38.
[118] Macmillan, *Reconstruction*, 16–17.

demands of a developing society makes it essential for public authorities to step in and insist on bringing about the organization necessary to ensure that these needs are served'.[119] But this did not imply that the State was to control or own industries. In the industrial sphere, the State was to enable others to act, not act itself. This approach found its clearest expression in the Self-Government of Industry Bill brought before Parliament in 1934. The central goal of this Bill was to provide industrial associations which had drawn up a plan for the reorganization of their sector of industry with statutory powers to compel recalcitrant firms to co-operate with the plan. For each individual industry this process was to be overseen by a National Industrial Council (NIC), the membership of which would be made up of leading members of each respective industry. At the heart of the system was to be a Central Economic Council (CEC), which would have a membership drawn from each NIC and representatives of government.[120] The CEC's role, however, was not to be directive. It was to provide statistical information gathered by government departments and help co-ordinate the self-regulatory activities of each industry. The reorganization of industries was, according to Harold Macmillan, unwise for the State to attempt— 'it is a task', he said, 'which can only be performed by Industry itself'.[121] Macmillan's position, in spite of the fact that he was regarded with suspicion by the Conservative hierarchy, was echoed in CRD discussions, with one office simply noting that: 'It is better that the industry should recast its own organisation spontaneously, but where it fails to do so, it may become the duty of Parliament to act.'[122]

State assistance for industrial reorganization was also deemed necessary because other economic agencies were failing to take the initiative. Here the banking system was seen to be at fault. In *Industry and the State* it was noted that 'There is a marked divergence of outlook and opinion between finance and industry, involving a considerable amount of friction'.[123] This was seen to be a major problem, insofar as 'credit is the life-blood of an industrial community; and our banking system, in the opinion of some critics, has been insufficiently elastic to play a substantial part in the vital process of industrial reorganization'.[124] This criticism of the banking system's conservatism, as was seen in Chapter 3, lay

---

[119] Id., *Middle Way*, 127.
[120] For contemporary Conservative statements of this plan see Macmillan, *Reconstruction* and id., *The Middle Way*. For an excellent recent analysis see Ritschel, *Planning*, 183–231.
[121] Macmillan, *Reconstruction*, 32.
[122] H. S., 'The Future Relations Between the State and Industry', 17 May. 1934, CPA, CRD 1/65/2.
[123] Boothby *et al.*, *Industry and the State*, 55.
[124] Ibid. 64.

at the root of Arthur Steel-Maitland's plan for establishing a govern-ment-loan-funded industrial reorganization committee of businessmen and industrial experts.[125] It also provided a further rationale for the 'self-government of industry' and the setting up of NICs. If industry, with government assistance, demonstrated its willingness to reorganize, Harold Macmillan argued, 'the link between finance and industry and the direction of the flow of investments as advocated by the Macmillan Committee and the F[ederation of] B[ritish] I[ndustry] would be brought within the sphere of practical politics'.[126] State action would help break down the institutional rigidities of both industry and finance and, equally important, bring an end to their institutional separation.

A consistent theme that ran through the paternalist arguments outlined above was the need to avoid State *control* of either industry or the economy in general. These advocates of State intervention were concerned, not without reason, that 'every Conservative who suggests industrial changes or supports industrial legislation runs the risk of being dubbed a Socialist by his friends'.[127] Their answer to this not-infrequent accusation was that Socialists advocated State ownership and State control, whereas their schemes were designed to keep State action to a minimum. Steel-Maitland insisted that there would be no political control of his proposed industrial reorganization committee—its deci-sions were to be taken by businessmen for business reasons.[128] Likewise, Harold Macmillan stated that under the schemes advocated by him and other 'capitalist planners', 'industrial self-government could be reconciled with national economic efficiency and *political action restricted to its proper sphere* in the confident expectation that the prob-lems of production and employment would be adequately dealt with by those familiar with the daily questions which arise'.[129] The State was to act as an enabling body, acting where necessary to correct failings in the economic system, but, more important, providing opportunities for existing economic agencies to bring about corrections that were essen-tial to their own and the nation's prosperity. Here they were at odds with libertarian Conservatives, who indeed regarded any State interven-tion as Socialist, and who saw State 'assistance' as undermining the creative potential of the economic agencies themselves which was the best source of national prosperity.[130]

In the second half of the twentieth century Conservative debate on the economy saw similar patterns of ideas emerge. In the 1950s

---

[125] See above, pp. 96–8.   [126] Macmillan, *Reconstruction*, 9.
[127] Boothby *et al.*, *Industry and the State*, 36.   [128] See above, pp. 95–9.
[129] Macmillan, *Reconstruction*, 9 (my emphasis).
[130] For a clear statement of the inter-war libertarian case see E. Benn, *Account Rendered* (1930).

Conservative governments largely accepted State ownership of the nationalized industries as a *fait accompli*, and also adopted demand-management economics. However, in the 1950 and 1951 elections the Conservatives campaigned for the removal of direct State controls over the economy, and pursued this strategy of decontrol when in office. In this context the Conservatives' acceptance of so-called 'Keynesian' demand management to maintain a 'high and stable level of employment' is important, in large part because it called for minimal direct State intervention in the economy. Demand management set the macro-economic environment, but allowed economic agencies in the private sector freedom to pursue their own paths at the microeconomic level.[131] The aim, as described by the One Nation group in *Change Is Our Ally*, was for the State to create 'the atmosphere and conditions for continuous and *spontaneous* economic change'.[132] Lord Hailsham summed up much of the attraction of this approach to Conservatives very well in 1959 when he argued that:

Conservative planning implies that Government should advertise and prescribe certain general economic objectives, and impose certain general standards of quality, should use its immense influence and power to encourage industry to co-operate to those ends, should interfere only where it has become obvious that a serious breakdown in a commonly accepted objective has taken place.[133]

In the 1950s, full employment and widespread affluence seemed to indicate that Britain's economic condition was good, and that indirect management of the economy had allowed British business to flourish. But at the beginning of the 1960s the picture seemed less positive, and newly available international growth tables indicated that British economic performance, and in particular industrial performance, was comparatively weak.[134] Harold Macmillan and many of his Cabinet came to the conclusion that indirect management of the economy was no longer adequate. The details of the Macmillan government's economic planning initiatives have been discussed elsewhere.[135] However, a key point which requires emphasis here is that State control and management were eschewed. The State was not to be the instrument of change itself. Rather, the NEDC and other planning instruments were mechanisms for 'the new role of the State as "the catalyst of

---

[131] See N. Rollings, 'Poor Mr Butskell: A Short Life Wrecked by Schizophrenia', *TCBH* 5 (1994).

[132] One Nation, *Change*, 104 (my emphasis).

[133] Hailsham, *Conservative Case*, 133. The similarity with Macmillan's position in 1950 is striking. See above.

[134] See J. Tomlinson, 'Inventing Decline: The Falling Behind of the British Economy in the Post-War Years', *EcHR* 49 (1996).

[135] See pp. 180–6.

change" '[136]—Britain's economic agencies could not be relied upon to achieve 'commonly accepted objectives' through 'spontaneous economic change', hence assistance from the State was necessary.

Macmillan's Cabinet contained, as the Prime Minister himself noted, a number of libertarian critics of his government's paternalist *dirigisme*, and from the mid-1960s on libertarian ideas and strategies became increasingly powerful in the Conservative party.[137] In many respects their arguments were the exact reverse of those made by paternalists. In the spring of 1963, when the Macmillan government's 'modernization' plan was under way, Enoch Powell declared that:

in conditions of free enterprise and competition, one does not have to contrive modernisation or introduce it by government decree. It happens, and keeps on happening, of its own accord . . . Our motor undustry, our chemical industry, yes, our steel industry, do not have to be told to modernise themselves. They keep on doing it because they have to . . . in order to meet the challenge of a fiercely competitive and rapidly changing world.[138]

Two years later Powell further inveighed against State intervention, arguing that:

The politician's duty . . . is not to rush around trying to supplant the profit motive, either by coaxing others or by trying to do the job himself . . . It is to find out . . . what it is that is stopping the profit motive from working . . . [and] Quite often the blockage will turn out to be some interference or series of interferences for which he himself or his predecessor are responsible.[139]

The libertarian argument was that the notion that 'weaknesses in ordinary market operations' could 'be avoided by the intervention of planners' was completely wrong, and that the experience of all planning initiatives revealed that 'shortsighted and precipitate interference by public bodies can block the spontaneous adjustments of the market and magnify economic dislocations'.[140] The consequence of this, Margaret Thatcher argued in 1976, was that

State activity has cast a political blight on the capacity to make commercial decisions in this country. And yet our very prosperity depends upon taking the right decisions in world markets. The mixed economy has become a mixed-up economy where the Government . . . has become hopelessly entangled in . . . everyday business and personal decisions . . . [and] genuine economic expansion and social change [is] . . . squeezed by . . . the increasingly political character of the business world.[141]

---

[136] J. Douglas *et al.*, 'Briefing 5', n.d. (June 1963?), CPA, CRD 2/8/29.
[137] See above, pp. 227–33.   [138] Wood (ed.), *Nation Not Afraid*, 13.
[139] Ibid. 82.   [140] Jewkes, *New Ordeal*, 25.
[141] M. Thatcher to the Institute of Directors, London, 11 Nov. 1976, *Thatcher CD-ROM*.

Economic agencies, in the view of Thatcher and her libertarian supporters, had to be allowed to 'flourish and expand in response to the choice
of the consumer',[142] and attempts by the State to influence this process
were unwarranted and could only have a deleterious effect.

   This divergence of opinion between libertarians and paternalists over
the functioning of agencies of civil society was also evident in the
spheres of industrial relations and social policy. Conditions of work and
wages were singled out as of particular relevance in this area. The Trade
Boards Act of 1909 was a social reform introduced by the Liberal
government which was strongly supported by paternalist
Conservatives.[143] The measure was designed to regulate wages and
conditions of work in the 'sweated' trades, which provided a perfect
example of the failure of economic agencies. Employers in these trades
lacked either the incentive or, notoriously, the moral scruple to provide
good conditions and wages for their workers, and the workers themselves were unable to organize themselves into trade unions to secure
improvements. State intervention was thus necessary to address the
problem of the 'sweated' trades. Paternalist Conservatives were also
prepared to countenance State intervention in other trades and industries, and some accepted the principle of the minimum wage, on the
basis that other employers were also *de facto* 'sweaters', and that
although 'Parliamentary interference in rates of wages is attended by
dangers and disadvantages . . . [the] appalling results arising from
sweated wages . . . had got to be dealt with'.[144] The libertarian position
was that such general State interference with wage rates was socially
counter-productive. Lord Hugh Cecil argued that it would be 'oppres-
sive' for the State to enforce upon adults 'perfectly able to judge their
own interests, a particular way of following their occupation'. He added
that although it was 'sometimes true that poor men cannot protect
themselves in making bargains with rich men, it must not be assumed
without careful reflection that no voluntary way of protecting themselves exists'. Here he referred to trade unions, and argued that 'by
combination or otherwise workmen may find their own way out of an
inequality in bargaining, and may be able to do without the help of the
State'. Cecil saw this latter scenario as a better option for both working
men and society. The educative process of forming a union and negotiating with employers would, he argued, strengthen the 'character' of the
men and therefore society, and voluntarily-formed trade unions would

   [142] IM. Thatcher to the Institute of Directors, London, 11 Nov. 1976, *Thatcher CD-ROM*.
   [143] See above, pp. 86–7.
   [144] R. A. Cooper in Parliament, 13 May 1914, *PD* ccxlii, c. 1134. See also J. W. Hills *et al.*,
Industrial Unrest, 5.

be under the control of the membership and thus more adaptable to circumstance. The 'voluntary action of trade unions', he concluded, 'has served the working class better than any exertion of the powers of the State . . . Trade Unions have acted with an ease and adaptability which the State cannot imitate, and have at the same time given training to their members of high value in self control, in patience, in resolution and in capacity for leadership'.[145] The fundamental differences between libertarians and paternalists on the issue of wages legislation were between conflicting positions on the social value and effectiveness of existing agencies and whether State action was either a necessary supplement or potential danger to the ability of such bodies to bring about industrial harmony.

The management of industrial conflict itself further illustrates that the strength or weakness of civil agencies was the key to Conservative arguments for or against State intervention. The arbitration of industrial disputes was an issue that had been in the background of late-Victorian politics, but which was very much to the fore during the wave of industrial unrest in the years immediately prior to the Great War.[146] In 1914 the USRC advocated the establishment of government-administered arbitration councils to provide forums for employers and trade unions to settle disputes.[147] After the war, which had seen a substantial growth of trade-union membership, industrial conflict became a still greater concern, with the General Strike of 1926 marking the high-point. The full details of the inter-war Conservative governments' industrial relations policies are not the concern of this study, but two points are worth noting. The first is that Baldwinian Conservatism sought to stress the role of the government as an 'honest broker' in industrial conflict, with the onus being on employers and employees to settle disputes.[148] The second is that those within the party who called for State action did so for, at first glance paradoxically, libertarian and paternalist reasons. Supporters of the MacQuisten Bill of 1926 and the Trade Disputes Act of 1927 sought to deploy State intervention to curb what they regarded as the inappropriate 'political' activity of trade unions. Trade unions, in

---

[145] H. Cecil, *Conservatism* (1912), 188–90.

[146] See A. Fox, *History and Heritage* (1985).

[147] Hills *et al.*, *Industrial Unrest*. The USRC did not wish the State wholly to supplant voluntary action but to intervene when necessary. It took a similar position on public health, where its document 'The Theory of Public Health' noted that 'The boundary between the private and the official sphere is constantly changing and sometimes eludes precise definition . . . [it is] true that the voluntary association of individuals here and there intercepts the necessity for public action . . . that does not affect the general proposition that the care and improvement of its subjects' health must occupy a large place in the outlook of every modern and civilised government', USRC, 'The Theory of Public Health', n.d. (1913?), Astor papers, University of Reading Library, MS1066/1/813.

[148] See Williamson, *Baldwin*, 167–202.

their view, should have confined their actions to economic matters alone, and the General Strike represented the most obvious example of trade-union 'politicization'. In this context, Conservatives of both libertarian and paternalist persuasions adhered to a quite strict definition of what the behaviour of agencies of civil society should be, that is to say 'un-political'. This was very clear in both the MacQuisten Bill's and Trade Disputes Act's hostility to the trade-union political levy, but even those Conservatives less instinctively hostile to trade unions had points of intersection with the underlying rationale. In a memorandum to Stanley Baldwin in late 1926 designed to forestall the Trade Disputes Act, Arthur Steel-Maitland noted that 'relations between employers and employed were difficult enough before the [general] strike. Each side was suspicious of the other, and not without reason'. Having indicated that both groups had 'failed' before the General Strike, Steel-Maitland argued that

we have reached a stage at which it is possible for a concordat to be reached between the two sides in industry. But the initiative will not come from within, if only it would so come, it would be a much healthier development. The more that the alignment of political parties is economic, the more suspect the intervention of politicians in an industrial question. But failing initiatives from within, there should be an attempt from without, and it is probably only the Government that can make the endeavour.[149]

Steel-Maitland also wished to keep industrial and economic questions 'un-political', and would have preferred the governemt to have remained on the sidelines. But as a result of the unwillingness of employers and employees voluntarily to move towards concordat, the government had to act. Hence Steel-Maitland initiated the process which culminated with the Mond–Turner negotiations. The State was to provide a framework for the conciliation process, but was itself to remain at arm's length, giving employer and employee agencies the oppportunity to redeem their 'failures'.

There are parallels between the inter-war libertarian and paternalist Conservative responses to problems of industrial relations and their positions on the 'trade-union question' in the latter half of the twentieth century. The Attlee government repealed the 1927 Trade Disputes Act, allowing for a 're-politicization' of the unions, and conditions of full employment from 1945 to 1972 strengthened the bargaining power of organized labour. In the 1950s there was much hostility to trade unions amongst the Conservative rank and file, and calls for reform of

---

[149] A. Steel-Maitland to S. Baldwin, 'Memorandum on the Industrial Situation and Its Bearing on Trade Union Legislation', 11 Oct. 1926, Baldwin papers, Trinity College, Cambridge, vol. 11.

trade-union law. Successive Conservative Ministers of Labour acknowledged the strength of this opinion—the often uncomfortable debates they faced at party conferences made this unavoidable.[150] But the Conservative governments were reluctant to engage in State regulation of the existing industrial-relations structure. Iain Macleod stated in September 1959 that he was 'convinced there is no case at all for legislation aimed at strikes and restrictive labour practices',[151] and he described the proposals of the Conservative Inns of Court Society for trade-union reform as overly legalistic. His view was that the best approach to the 'trade-union problem' was to encourage the National Joint Advisory Committee—a body made up of trade unionists, employers, and civil servants—to examine each industry's industrial relations and working practices on a case-by-case basis.[152] Macleod's position, like that of the party hierarchy in general, was informed by a concern that 'anti-union' legislation would lead to a loss of the party's support amongst trade unionists, but it also reflected the view that trade unions and employers could and should solve their own problems. However, the establishment of the National Economic Development Council (NEDC) in 1961 indicated that faith in the ability of the economic agencies to achieve industrial concordat without government assistance had broken down, and increasing interest in the possibility of a statutory incomes policy within the Cabinet provided further evidence of this.[153]

The pressure within the Conservative party to embrace proposals for reform of industrial-relations law increased from the mid-1960s on, and the publication of *Fair Deal At Work* in 1968 indicated that the 'reformers' were gaining ascendancy.[154] The failure of the Industrial Relations Act, the defeat of the Heath government following the miners' strike of 1973–4, and the Conservatives in victory in 1979 in the wake of the industrial unrest of the 'winter of discontent', saw the introduction of major legislative reforms from 1980 to 1984. The trade-union legislation of the Thatcher governments can easily be presented as the product of a visceral loathing of organized labour, and certainly the Conservative party's desire to 'avenge' the downfall of the Heath government cannot be ignored in assessing the motives for reform. But to see the 1980–4 legislation solely in these terms would be to ignore its more profound meanings. One of the most important political features

[150] Green, 'Conservative Party'.
[151] I. Macleod, 'Trade Union Legislation', 24 Sept. 1959, CPA, CRD 2/53/31.
[152] Id., 'Trade Union Legislation', 2 July 1958, ibid.
[153] See pp. 182–5.
[154] See R. Taylor, *The Trade Union Question in British Politics* (Oxford, 1993), 181–3; L. Johnmann, 'The Conservative Party in Opposition, 1964–70', in R. Coopey, S. Fielding, and N. Tiratsoo (eds.), *The Wilson Governments, 1964–70* (1993).

of the trade-union reforms of the 1980s is that, unlike many Thatcherite policies, they had the support of the Conservative party as a whole.[155] This is explicable not simply in terms of the party being united in the face of a common enemy, but in terms of a common perception of the proper role of trade unions as an agency of civil society. In the late 1950s Lord Hailsham, Lord Chancellor in the early 1980s, had expressed scepticism about the both the need for and possibility of introducing trade-union reform, but had also stated that certain aspects of trade-union behaviour, such as closed shops, sympathy strikes, and political strikes, were unacceptable.[156] By the early 1980s, however, he had come to the conclusion that trade-union behaviour had become characterized by 'selfishness and . . . repeated attempts at domination'.[157] This view was widely shared in the Conservative party, and State action was deemed necessary to address the problem. In 1980 Thatcher outlined the case for trade-union legislation, stating that 'We don't want to stop proper Trade Unionism from operating, we need it. We need it to operate well, we need it to operate in the interest of its members.' The basic problem, she contended, was that trade unions were acting for political, not economic, ends and placing themselves above the rule of law.[158] In short, they were breaching all the essential norms for the behaviour of a civil agency—ignoring the rule of law, failing to stay outside the political sphere, and not acting in accord with their memberships' interests or even their wishes. Legislation was essential to force trade unions into fulfilling their proper functions, which required that their actions be disengaged from the political sphere and limited to the area of economic interest in which individual unions were involved.

The question of the adequacy and proper functioning of agencies of civil society was central to Conservative discussion of social policy in the twentieth century. In the Edwardian period the USRC, as noted above, saw State action as a means of supplementing or, if necessary, superseding the role of civil agencies in the economic and social spheres. Libertarian Conservatives, like Hugh Cecil, conceded that some State action 'to give assistance to those that suffer' was acceptable as an act of 'national charity',[159] but their preference was to look to voluntary acts of social beneficence.[160] The Conservative position on social policy

---

[155] The one chapter which has positive things to say about the Thatcher governments in Ian Gilmour's otherwise sustained philippic against the then Prime Minister is that which discusses trade-union legislation. See Gilmour, *Dogma*, 76–104.

[156] Minutes of the 6th Meeting of the Steering Committee, 24 Sept. 1958, CPA, CRD 2/53/31.

[157] Hailsham, *Sparrow's Flight*, 407.

[158] Thatcher, Interview with Brian Walden, 6 Jan. 1980, *Thatcher CD-ROM*.

[159] Cecil, *Conservatism*, 179.   [160] Ibid. 159–98.

until the Second World War in large part embodied an endorsement of a 'mixed economy of welfare'.[161] Even those Conservative politicians who were most active in the sphere of State social reform, like Neville Chamberlain, remained strong advocates of the need for extensive voluntary contributions to social policy.[162] The basic test for determining the need for State action, for both paternalists and libertarians, was the effectiveness of voluntary action. Harold Macmillan summed up the kind of considerations that were involved in this calculation when, discussing the possibility of minimum wage legislation, he argued that:

One might expect . . . that the vigilance of the consumer would be reinforced by that of other producers and that the weight of this social condemnation would be enough to compel a worthier sense of social responsibility on the part of the offending industrial or commercial undertakings. [But] If that did not suffice then it would be the duty of the Government to devise other means of ensuring that the minimum wage should be regarded as the first charge upon industry.[163]

In the first instance it was society itself, acting through employers with a sense of social responsibility or other groups capable of bringing pressure to bear, which could persuade exploitative employers to pay their workers a living wage. But if such pressure was either too weak or disregarded, then the State could and should act. A balance of such calculation underpinned the mixed economy of welfare.

The Second World War, and plans for post-war reconstruction, saw the Conservatives confront the issue of whether a mixed economy of welfare could be sustained. This presented them with some problems. Divisions within the Conservative Committee that examined the Beveridge Report over the issue of National Insurance are illustrative of the difficulties that emerged. From the time of the introduction of National Insurance in 1911 the scheme, although a State structure, had incorporated Friendly Societies as integral, quasi-autonomous elements of the administrative mechanism. Beveridge's plan was to bring the entire scheme under State control, and it was this that provoked the divide on the Conservative committee. One element accepted Beveridge's proposal, arguing that a unified scheme would be more efficient and that the 'approved societies' no longer served any useful purpose. The other element felt that, 'during their thirty years existence the Approved Societies have proved their capacity for beneficial and economical admninistration', and that although, alongside basic national insurance, different societies offered different benefits to their

---

[161] The term is drawn from J. Lewis, *The Voluntary Sector, the State and Social Work in Britain* (Aldershot, 1995).
[162] Greenleaf, *Ideological Heritage*, 236–7.
[163] Macmillan, *Middle Way*, 310.

members, this anomaly could be overcome and the societies retained
within the system.[164] If the voluntary societies within the National
Insurance scheme were one source of concern, the voluntary hospitals
were another, and their absorption into the National Health Service in
1948 was greeted with protest. In Parliament the Conservatives,
whether libertarian or paternalist, strongly opposed the Attlee government's health reforms, largely on the grounds that there was much in the
pre-war health system, principally the local and voluntary aspects,
which had functioned well.[165] In 1947 Quentin Hogg summed up this
Conservative sense of loss when he asked: 'Where are the Friendly
Societies since the Labour Party came to power? Where are the voluntary hospitals, or the municipal hospitals?'[166] All Conservatives
accepted that health and welfare were national concerns, but they felt
there should still be room for agencies other than the State to be
involved in the provision and administration of these services.

In 1952 Enoch Powell noted that all British political parties had, at
various times, 'added to that fabric of law and administration which
provides us with our social services', but he stressed that it was wrong
to assume that 'because . . . parties concur in certain practical measures
therefore they view them in the same light and their policies lead in the
same direction'. In particular he argued that for Liberals social policy
was focused on individuals, whereas for Conservatives and Socialists it
was socially based.[167] However, Powell contended that Socialists and
Conservatives defined what was 'social' in different ways. Socialism, he
said, tended to equate society with the State, whereas Conservatives
looked instead towards groups and organizations that had emerged
spontaneously from everyday social interaction. 'The "community" ',
Powell declared 'is not necessarily the State. It may be for the State to
co-ordinate, to complete, or even to do the lion's share, but wherever
possible the continuation of local responsibility and initiative is jeal-
ously guarded and individual beneficence is not regarded as having
played out its role.'[168] This emphasis on the importance of non-State
action in the context of social services was an important theme in
Conservative discussion of health and welfare in the last half of the
twentieth century. In 1950 the One Nation group stated that, in the
general provision of social welfare, 'we have no hesitation in saying that

[164] Beveridge Report Committee, 'Report on the Beveridge Proposals', 19 Jan. 1943, CPA,
CRD 600/01.
[165] C. Webster, 'Conflict and Consensus: Explaining the British Health Service', *TCBH* 1
(1990).
[166] Hogg, *Case for Conservatism*, 67.
[167] J. E. Powell, 'The Social Services: Theory and Practice', *Listener*, 17 Apr. 1952.
[168] Id., 'Conservatives and Social Services', *Political Quarterly*, 24 (1953).

voluntary effort must provide much the greatest part of the services needed'.[169] At the same time they acknowledged that there was much for the State to do in terms of establishing minimum standards for social provision and social need and ensuring that other agencies met these standards: 'it is perfectly true', One Nation argued, 'that a bad employer or landlord may fall, in the short run below the average standards of the State, and we fully support State intervention to force upon them acceptable standards of behaviour.'[170] Finding a balance between State and non-State provision, and recovering the social value of a mixed economy of welfare, lay at the core of much Conservative intra-party debate on social welfare, and this required careful assessment of the effectiveness of non-governmental agencies.

In the 1950s housing was the area in which Conservatives explored most fully the boundaries of State and non-State provision. Here there was ample scope to compare and contrast the Labour party's emphasis on municipal housing with Conservative efforts to match and surpass public provision through providing a stimulus for private building and the private rented sector. Hence, the Conservative governments removed the requirements for building licences, relaxed planning restrictions, and abolished rent control. 'Freeing' the housing market completely was an option strongly canvassed by libertarian voices in the party, but although legislation moved in this direction it was not embraced wholeheartedly. The reason for this was that private housing agencies, and in particular private landlords, were seen to have 'failed'. In 1953 Harold Macmillan stated in Cabinet that 'Property has rights only proportionate to the extent it carries out its obligation',[171] and in the late 1950s, especially following the abolition of rent controls, private landlords were deemed to have raised rents to unreasonable levels, failed to repair or improve their properties, and in the worst cases exploited and maltreated their tenants without scruple. Leaving aside the notorious 'slum landlords', it was accepted that in many cases private landlords did not have the means to maintain their properties, but this in itself indicated that the institutional structure of the agency of private housing was inadequate. In *The Responsible Society* the One Nation group proposed that this problem could be solved if landlords sold the freehold of their properties to housing associations and received loan stock in the association in exchange. The housing associations could then raise loans using the freeholds as collateral and carry out repairs and improvements. Echoing Macmillan's 1953 remark, *The Responsible*

---

[169] *One Nation*, 70.
[170] Ibid. 19.
[171] H. Macmillan, 'Houses Old and New', 22 Jan. 1953, CAB 129/58.

Society stated that: 'Ownership of rented property carries with it obligations. In the second half of the twentieth century these obligations most
certainly include basic amenities. If all these obligations were fulfilled by
private landlords we should be secure against municipalization.'[172] In
1961 the Conservative Housing Act provided government funds for
housing associations and introduced legislation which allowed landlords
only to raise rents after they had improved their properties.[173] By 1963
stricter State controls were planned, and Keith Joseph, the Parliamentary
Secretary to Housing and Local Government, and one of the authors of
The Responsible Society, argued that 'ownership of rented houses
requires responsible management . . . [but] Not all landlords . . . have the
capacity to supply this'. The consequence, he contended, was that the
Socialist argument for municipalization of rented property was strengthened, and that as 'We believe . . . ever-increasing municipalization is a
bad thing . . . we must provide an alternative'.[174] There was strong libertarian opposition to these new controls over the housing market,[175] but
the paternalist case was that the market and its agencies had failed.

The question of whether the State was doing too much and other
agencies too little did not disappear from the Conservative agenda. In
the 1960s Conservatives continued to press the case not only for *less*
State action but for *more* from the private and voluntary sector. In 1966
Margaret Thatcher, for one, proposed an amendment to the Budget to
allow friendly societies to engage more fully in life insurance and
endowment services. 'Friendly Societies', she argued' 'form part of the
group of voluntary and thrift societies which, in the past, have served
this country extremely well and have provided much relief from poverty
when no other relief was available. . .[but] Their sphere of activity has
decreased . . . as State provision has increased.' In order to rectify this
situation, Thatcher proposed that individuals be given the same tax
exemptions on their life and endowment policies with friendly societies
as they gained from National Savings.[176] In this way State and voluntary agencies were to be placed on a level playing-field. Enoch Powell
presented the case still more forcefully in 1968, when he declared that
'the current remedies for poverty, as it appears in the specific examples
of housing, health, education and social security, have in common the
elimination of self-expression and a system which is centralized and
authoritarian'.[177] By the late 1960s the Conservatives had turned in a

[172] One Nation, *Responsible Society*, 45.
[173] See P. Weiler, 'The Rise and Fall of the Conservative "Grand Design" for Housing,
1951–64', *CBH* 14(2000).
[174] K. Joseph in Cabinet, 10 May 1963, in ibid.   [175] Ibid.
[176] M. Thatcher in Parliament, 22 June 1966, *Thatcher CD-ROM*.
[177] J. E. Powell, 'Social Problems', 11.

more libertarian direction, and the paternalist-leaning Edward Boyle noted that:

There is today a relationship of 'mutual involvement' between the State and many outside bodies such as teachers' organisations, local authority associations, trade associations, consumer groups etc. In other words a greater range of functions of the State does not necessarily mean a corresponding increase in direct State control. One of our most important tasks on returning to power will be to find the right degree to which Government should call on other bodies for this type of assistance.[178]

The Heath government's inability to 'roll back the frontiers of the State' in the economic sphere was a particular focus of attention for internal party critics, but freeing the economy was only one aspect of the libertarian philosophy of Thatcherism. Thatcher herself consistently argued that an essential part of the general shift from a 'dependency' to an 'enterprise' culture was not only to reduce both the cost and scope of State welfare, but to acknowledge and enhance the contribution of the voluntary sector. Significantly, *her own* homilies to 'Victorian Values' were invariably accompanied by references to the charitable and philanthropic activities that characterized the nineteenth century: in Thatcher's view, entrepreneurship and benevolence went hand in hand.[179] To a certain extent an economic, and especially fiscal, rationale underpinned this argument, but there was a broader aspect to the case. In her 1977 Iain Macleod Memorial Lecture, Thatcher drew a contrast between State welfare and charitable action. 'In a market economy', she contended,

people are free to give their money and their home for good causes. They exercise their altruism on their own initiative and at their own expense, whether they give directly and personally through institutions, charities, universities, churches, hospitals. When the State steps in generosity is increasingly restricted from all sides. From the one side, the idea is propagated that whatever needs doing is best done by the State. Since the State knows best, causes it does not support must be of questionable worth. On the other side since the State takes more and more of people's earnings, they have less inclination to give . . . when the money is taken away and spent by government, the blessing goes out of giving and out of the effort of earning to give.[180]

Reducing State welfare, and therefore taxation, would provide both the means and the scope for 'genuine', voluntary giving. The point of Thatcher's political strategy was, as she explained in 1980, 'to re-invig-

[178] E. Boyle, 'Government and Society', *Swinton Journal* 15:1 (1969), 10–1.
[179] See e.g. Thatcher, Interview with BBC1, 24 May 1983, Interview with Brian Walden, 16 Jan. 1983, Interview with *Svenske Dagblat*, 16 May 1988, etc. *Thatcher CD-ROM*.
[180] Id., Iain Macleod Memorial Lecture, 4 July 1977, ibid.

orate not just the economy and industry, but the whole body of voluntary associations, loyalties and activities which gives society its richness and diversity, and hence its real strength'.[181] According to the Conservative MP and former member of Thatcher's Policy Unit, David Willetts, 'the free market' may have been 'the cutting edge of modern Conservatism', but there was a broader civic goal. 'Civic Conservatism', he argued, 'places the free market in the context of institutions and values which makes up civil society.'[182] And the institutions and values which were the perfect exemplars of this civil society were the 'great and proud institutions such as voluntary hospitals . . . [and the] network of voluntary organisations . . . created by working-class self-help: friendly societies, mechanics institutes, local guilds', all of which had been 'weakened if not destroyed by the advance of the State'.[183]

Thatcherism's goal of reinvigorating civil society enables one to recast the problem of situating Thatcherism in the Conservative ideological tradition. Rather than seeing it in terms of an attempt to blend the 'free economy and the strong State', or as a strong manifestation of 'libertarian' Conservatism, Thatcherism can be viewed as perhaps the ultimate expression of Conservative belief in agencies of civil society as the fulcrum of social life. For Thatcherism, the fundamental problem with State intervention was that it 'politicized' areas of social life which should have remained simply 'social'. Economic decisions taken by government were political decisions, not business decisions, and businesses were forced to conform to or anticipate political priorities and problems rather than economic ones. Similarly, consumer choice in the purchase and utilization of everyday goods and services had been constrained by State involvement in the economy. Trade unions engaged in political action to the detriment of others in society, because their leaders had forsaken their proper function as a consequence of looking to the State rather than to their own actions and their membership's interests in economic matters. Private life had been politicized by campaigning groups such as feminists and gay activists, and religious life had been politicized by a radical clergy who focused on social and economic rather than spiritual issues. Withdrawing the State meant, in effect, withdrawing 'politics' from aspects and walks of life it should never have entered. This, in turn, was to create space for agencies of civil society to flourish.

For Conservatives and Conservatism throughout the twentieth century, the relationship of the individual to the State and the nature of

---

[181] Id., Airey Neave Memorial Lecture, 3 Mar. 1980, ibid.
[182] Willetts, *Civic Conservatism*, 15, 18.
[183] Ibid. 16.

the State itself have been important issues, but this essay would conclude that they were neither in principle or in practice the unmediated fulcrum of intra-party debate. Libertarianism and paternalism remain as a useful shorthand for describing basic positions with regard to State intervention, but they cannot explain why one position is taken at any given moment or in a given sphere of activity; nor can they explain why both positions could be held by the same individual or group within the party simultaneously. This essay's basic contention is that if one switches the focus of analysis from attitudes to the State to agencies of civil society, a more subtle and plausible picture emerges. Essentially, if agencies of civil society have been seen to be fulfilling a valuable and effective social role, then the Conservative predisposition has been to keep the State from intervening in their sphere of activity; but if they have been seen as failing, then Conservatives have supported State intervention either to support or supplant them. Similarly, if the State has been seen to be intervening to the point where valuable agencies of civil association and action have been unnecessarily undermined, then demands for the State's withdrawal have been made. Clearly, the political and electoral context has shaped the reception and purchase of the arguments deployed, but this does not affect this essay's fundamental concern, which is to explain the *nature* and *content* of the arguments rather than their effectiveness as political or electoral strategies. In many respects the model presented by this essay is simple, but it is not simplistic, and possesses an intrinsic flexibility that enables it to encompass both the complexities and nuances of the historical development of Conservative ideas.

CHAPTER 10

Conclusion

IN 1930 THE Conservative historian Keith Feiling wrote a pamphlet
which posed the question *What Is Conservatism?*[1] In 1997 the
Conservative MP David Willetts co-authored a publication which asked
another question, namely, *Is Conservatism Dead?*[2] An answer to the last
question clearly requires an answer to the first, but the essays in this
book have shown that it is not easy to provide that answer. Scholars of
Socialism and Liberalism in Britain and continental Europe have shown
that the political ideologies of the Left and Centre are very complex
structures in terms of both theory and practice, and that it is in many
respects more accurate to speak about Socialisms and Liberalisms rather
than to use the singular. The same thing is true of Conservatism.

To observe that an ideology is complex and nuanced is not to deny
its existence as a constant or consistent political and historical entity,
but simply to acknowledge that any given ideology can take a variety of
forms. This, however, raises the question of why the different forms of
an ideology are not viewed and discussed as discrete systems of thought
rather than as subsets of another. Here the distinction made by Martin
Seliger between the 'fundamental' and 'operative' elements of an ideology is helpful.[3] The fundamental aspects of an ideology are a set of core
principles which are regarded by an ideology's adherents as offering an
approach to politics which has a trans-historical applicability and
verisimilitude. They form the underlying presuppositions and assumptions around which statements, arguments, and actions relevant to a
specific historical situation are formed and against which they are
tested. The operative aspects are those which express the particular
form or forms an ideology takes in a particular situation and in the face
of particular problems. Hence, operative expressions of an ideology
must all express its fundamental principles. There are thus limits to an
ideology's flexibility—certain parameters must remain constant. This is
as true for Conservatism as it is for any ideology. The notion that
Conservatism is simply a 'swivel-mirror', which shifts in reactive

---

[1] K. Feiling, *What Is Conservatism?* (1930).
[2] D. Willetts and J. Gray, *Is Conservatism Dead?* (1997).
[3] See Seliger, *Ideology and Politics, passim.*

response to the challenge presented by pro-active 'progressive' ideologies, overlooks the fact that the mirror can only swivel so far before it slips from its base.[4] When confronted by particular problems and challenges Conservatives may indeed produce multiple, differing responses, but these must all appear to be, and be acknowledged as, recognizably Conservative, especially by those who identify themselves most strongly as Conservatives.

The essays in this book underline the complexity and flexibility of Conservative thought over the twentieth century, but they also indicate that there have been leitmotifs which enable one to construct an answer to Keith Feiling's question; an answer which in large part confirms and builds upon arguments developed in the work of two Conservative political philosophers, Anthony Quinton and Michael Oakeshott. Quinton suggests, in his study *The Politics of Imperfection*, that four closely related principles make up the fundamental elements of Conservatism.[5] The first is the notion of *intellectual imperfection*. Related to, but distinct from the idea of original sin, the concept of intellectual imperfection rests on the premiss that human rational faculties are necessarily inadequate to the task of comprehending the complexities of social development, and that abstract reasoning cannot be trusted as a guide for social and political behaviour.[6] Quinton derives from this three other fundamental tenets of Conservatism. The first of these is *political scepticism*, or 'the belief that political wisdom . . . is not to be found in the theoretical speculations of isolated thinkers, but in the historically accumulated social experience of the community as a whole'.[7] The second is *traditionalism*, by which is meant that Conservatives have an attachment to established customs and institutions, and a hostility to 'sudden, precipitate and revolutionary change'.[8] The third is *organicism*, that is to say, Conservatives regard society as 'a unitary, natural growth, an organized living whole not a mechanical aggregate', composed of 'social beings, related to one another within a texture of inherited customs and institutions which endow them with their specific social nature'.[9]

At first glance Quinton seems to differ from one of the Conservative thinkers he studied, Michael Oakeshott, who argued that 'being Conservative' expressed 'not a creed or a doctrine, but a disposition'.[10] But Oakeshott's stance in fact conforms to Quinton's model very well.

---

[4] For Conservatism as a 'swivel-mirror' see M. Freeden, *Ideologies and Political Theory* (Oxford, 1996), 317–414.
[5] A. Quinton, *The Politics of Imperfection* (1978).   [6] Ibid. 12–13.
[7] Ibid. 17.   [8] Ibid.16.   [9] Ibid.
[10] M. Oakeshott, 'On Being Conservative', in id., *Rationalism in Politics and Other Essays* (1962; Indianapolis 1991 edn.), 407.

For Oakeshott, the Conservative 'disposition' was a 'propensity to use and enjoy what is available rather than to wish for or to look for something else', and a preference for the familiar which militated against change, especially rapid change, and the 'impulse to sail uncharted seas'.[11] In terms of specifically political matters, Oakeshott felt that being Conservative was not 'necessarily connected with any particular beliefs about the universe, about the world in general or about human conduct in general. What it is tied to is certain beliefs about the activity of governing and the instruments of government.'[12] He insisted that politics in general, and the work of government in particular, were and should be limited to the discussion and regulation of the 'collisions' which unavoidably occurred when people exercised their life choices.[13] Oakeshott rejected what he referred to as the 'jump to glory style of politics', and argued that 'the office of government is merely to rule'.[14] As a consequence, he stated that 'The intimations of government are to be found in ritual, not in religion or philosophy; in the enjoyment of orderly and peaceable behaviour, not in the search for truth or perfection'.[15] This view of the limits to politics and government was informed by Oakeshott's position on the limited role of rationalism in politics. For Oakeshott, people's rational faculties were necessarily inadequate to grasp the complexities of social development and, as a consequence, he felt that it was both wrong and dangerous to attempt to use abstract reasoning as a guide to political and governmental behaviour. Here he closely fits Quinton's description of Conservative thought, in that his intellectual imperfectionism leads him to a political scepticism which prefers established, familiar 'rituals' that have emerged from organic social interaction to abstract ideas as a guide to political behaviour and governance. But this did not mean that Oakeshott thought that being Conservative meant being irrationalist and atheoretical. He drew a distinction between two forms of human knowledge: 'technique', by which he meant skills which can be taught or acquired from manuals, and 'practical', by which he meant things like judgement and artistry.[16] For Oakeshott the 'rationalist' error was that it equated reason with technique, and in this respect the problem that could and often did arise was not the use of reason in politics as such, but the misidentification of what constituted reason. Conservatives, however, avoided this error, because their predisposition to prefer the known, the familiar, and the tested to 'what may be',[17] and to value the real above the ideal, ensured

---

[11] Oakeshott, 'On Being Conservative', 408–12.   [12] Ibid. 423.
[13] Ibid. 428.   [14] Ibid. 426–7.   [15] Ibid. 428.
[16] See M. Oakeshott, 'Rationalism in Politics', in idem, *Rationalism*, and see also P. Franco, *The Political Philosophy of Michael Oakeshott* (New Haven, 1990).
[17] Oakeshott, 'Being Conservative', 408.

that they grasped, either instinctively or through reflection, that one had to be wary of 'reason'.

To have introduced the work of Quinton and Oakeshott here may seem to be at variance with the overall structure and contents of this book, which has largely and quite deliberately avoided discussion of the most formal, 'highbrow' constructions of Conservative thought. But in fact their work serves to underline one of the main themes of this study. In his essay 'On Being Conservative', Oakeshott spoke of the 'common belief that it is impossible . . . [or] not worth while attempting to elicit explanatory general principles from what is recognized to be conservative conduct'.[18] In many respects this statement pointed to the depiction of Conservatism as 'non-ideological' or 'atheoretical', but the essay then demonstrated how these positions were themselves indicative of a particular view of the world, in which being 'non-ideological', 'atheoretical', or even 'apolitical' were intrinsic parts of adhering to Conservatism. Indeed, Oakeshott's reference to 'recognized . . . conservative conduct' is important here, for how could conduct be recognized as conservative unless there were clear conservative recognition signals which were given out, received, and understood as such? The essays in this book have shown that at all levels of political debate and political action throughout the twentieth century Conservatives articulated, in explicit and implicit statements and assumptions, a range of positions, norms, and beliefs that were designed to identify the nature and meaning of Conservatism. Moreover, these varied, complex, and often competing constructions, with one important exception,[19] fitted the patterns discerned by Quinton and Oakeshott.

Twentieth-century Conservatives demonstrated a marked adherence to the closely related tenets of intellectual imperfection and political scepticism, whether in the shape of, for example, the economics of the tariff-reform campaign being based on inductive rather than deductive economic thought, the Conservative dislike and disdain for bookish intellect over most of the century, the party's suspicion of wholly State-controlled and directed initiatives in the social and economic spheres, and their refusal to accept that 'the man in Whitehall knows best'. Clearly these positions had particular resonance at particular times, and were often directed at specific political opponents and problems, but they also reflected a more general approach. Conservative suspicion of abstract logic and reason (in the Oakeshottian technical sense) found expression in party criticisms of its own members, like Iain Macleod and Enoch Powell, who were, respectively, described as 'too clever by

---

[18] Ibid. 407.   [19] For this exception see below.

half'[20] and possessing an 'over-logical mind',[21] but also in a more general Conservative desire to trust instinct and experience over intellect and reason in the discussion and shaping of their response to political issues.

There was a link in Conservative thought between intellectual imperfection, political scepticism, and traditionalism, and that was a Conservative approach to history. For the Conservatives, as for any political party, viewing and interpreting the past was crucial to their identity, and part of their attachment to established institutions and customs and their preference for gradual change stemmed from their particular historical perspective. R. A. Butler was clear on this point when he drafted a chapter on 'Principles of Conservatism' for a book he was preparing to write in 1961, for he stated that, 'To a Conservative mind the future is not the abstract expression of some entirely new and self-contained existence . . . The cause of future events flows inexorably from what has happened in the past.'[22] This did not, however, mean that Conservatives had a 'theory of history' which allowed them to predict or anticipate the course of future events. Oakeshott is again helpful here in outlining the essence of the Conservative position. His criticism of 'jump to glory' politics rested in large part on his view that life was about people making sporadic, spontaneous, even chaotic decisions and choices, and that those who trusted to plans based on technical reason sought to impose an artificial, necessarily unworkable order on this chaos.[23] He had a similar view of the practice of history. The 'historical past', by which he meant the past seen on its own terms rather than in relation to the present, Oakeshott described as 'a complicated world, without unity of feeling or clear outline', in which 'events have no overall pattern, lead nowhere, point to no favoured condition of the world and support no practical conclusions . . . a world composed wholly of contingencies'.[24] With the past as with the present, however, there were those who sought to impose order on the past's contingencies in their search either for the 'origins of the present' or for 'laws' of historical development,[25] with the result that they misunderstood the past as like-minded

---

[20] As well as being a particularly Conservative insult this is also particularly *English*. There is, for example no equivalent phrase in, French or German. For this point I am grateful to Dr. Cecile Fabre and Professor Richard Sheppard.

[21] The comment on Macleod was made by Lord Salisbury in the House of Lords on 7 Mar. 1961, quoted in Shepherd, *Macleod*, 225. For the description of Powell see M. Fraser to R. A. Butler, 3 May 1954, Butler papers, H36, fos. 24–5.

[22] R. A. Butler, draft of chapter 2 of a proposed work 'People and Politics', Butler papers, H27 fos. 39–48.

[23] Oakeshott, 'Being Conservative', 425–8.

[24] Id., 'The Activity of Being An Historian', in id., *Rationalism*, 182.

[25] Ibid. 161–71.

rationalists did the present. For Oakeshott, history was not devoid of meaning inasmuch as events in the past could but have influenced the present, as the present would influence the future, but he felt that it was crucial to avoid reading the past simply in terms of the present. On this point Keith Feiling was aligned with Oakeshott, for he argued in 1930 that if Conservatism wished to find 'the principles of action which alone can enable it to survive . . . We shall not find them in abstract propositions and theoretical rights . . . Conservatism must . . . rest on history, the interpretation of the past, but [only] if we go to history in order to learn, and not to inflict upon her our own petty prejudices, the last thing that we shall find is a fixed programme.'[26] For Conservative historians like Feiling, Arthur Bryant, Herbert Butterfield, and others there was a 'Tory' interpretation of history[27] which, unlike its Whig counterpart, did not seek to discover and describe 'progress' towards the present, but which provided a narrative of events that demonstrated 'a continuing spirit'[28] in the English and then British ability to confront the challenges that providence produced. The only pattern in this history, with its focus very much on the British Isles, was the *absence* of pattern, and the primacy of contingency. Hence, the British Empire had emerged as Britain 'conquered and peopled half the world in a fit of absence of mind', rather than as a consequence of systemic economic imperatives or the demands of strategic planning.[29] Likewise, the 'English Saga', which had seen the largely peaceful transition from monarchical rule to parliamentary democracy, and witnessed the nation's endurance and triumph in the Napoleonic and two world wars, was in effect a *story* in which events had produced spontaneously, often unexpectedly, brilliant and heroic responses from the nation's leaders and its people.[30] In this story's unfolding, customs, institutions, laws, and values were generated which represented the process of learning through and from experience, which in turn embodied the kind of wisdom that Conservatives valued most. In the same vein, the history of other countries, notably those which had endured internal turmoil and revolutionary upheaval,

---

[26] Feiling, *Conservatism*, 8.

[27] For Tory history see R. N. Soffer, 'Commitment and Catastrophe: Twentieth Century Conservative History in Britain and America', in F. M. Leventhal and R. Quinault (eds.), *Anglo-American Attitudes: From Revolution to Partnership* (Aldershot, 2000); id., 'British Conservative Historiography and the Second World War', in B. Stuchley and P. Wende (eds.), *British and German Historiography, 1750–1950* (Oxford, 2000); E. H. H. Green, *The Tory Interpretation of History* (forthcoming).

[28] Feiling, *Conservatism*, 8.

[29] J. R. Seeley, *The Expansion of England* (1883; 1897 edn.), 10. See A. Bryant, *Freedom's Own Island: Britain's Oceanic* Expansion (1987).

[30] Bryant's work was the best expression of this. See his *English Saga, 1840–1940* (1940), *The Years of Endurance, 1793–1802* (1942), *The Years of Victory, 1802–12* (1944), and *Set in A Silver Sea* (1985).

provided examples of the danger of falling prey to the related errors of a reliance on abstract reasoning, ignoring the wisdom of tradition and experience, and believing that 'the laws of history' were on one's side. As a consequence, these countries had abandoned the familiar and appropriate rules of civil conduct and governance in pursuit of a chimerical ideal, and having experienced periods of extreme incivility and arbitrary government, had been forced to attempt to reconstruct and reacquire institutions and practices that had been destroyed. For Conservatives, history was not philosophy teaching by example, but the lessons it taught were important nonetheless.

Built into the Conservative view of the complex and contingent nature of the past was Conservatism's organicist conception of social structure. This notion of society as a living whole rather than a 'mechanical aggregate' was held up most specifically in antagonism to, on the one hand, individualist philosophies and, on the other hand, Socialism with its class-based precepts. This did not mean that Conservatives denied the existence or importance of either the individual or class; rather, they argued that neither could nor should be abstracted from their existence within a larger whole. The USRC's hostility to the individualism of Rousseau, the Mills, Cobden, and Spencer[31] was matched by David Clarke's statement in 1947 that 'society is an organic whole in which the social atoms react in all their movements upon one another'.[32] In July 1952 Clarke's colleague at CRD, Michael Fraser, stressed that, 'It is a feature of Conservatism . . . not to consider society as merely a haphazard aggregation of individuals in isolation . . . We believe man to be a social animal, happiest when he is free to take part in the life of a variety of groups and communities within the nation',[33] and this was underlined by the Young Conservatives' 1962 pamphlet *Society and the Individual*, which denounced the notion of society as an aggregate of individuals as one of the most misleading and damaging ideas promulgated by the French Revolution,[34] and further underscored by Enoch Powell, who argued in 1965 that 'society is much more than a collection of individuals acting together, even through the complex and subtle mechanisms of the free economy, for material advantage. It has an existence of its own; it thinks and feels; it looks inward, as a community, to its members; it looks outward as a nation.'[35] For Conservatives, the relationship between

[31] See p. 251.
[32] D. Clarke, *The Conservative Faith in a Modern Age* (1947), 13.
[33] M. Fraser, 'The Ownership of Property', a lecture given in Oxford, 8 July 1952, enclosed with id. to R. A. Butler, 18 July 1952, Butler papers, H34 fos. 173–90.
[34] Young Conservatives, *Society and the Individual*, 1.
[35] J. E. Powell at Bromley, 24 Oct. 1963 in Wood, *Not Afraid*, 4–5.

individuals and society was necessarily symbiotic and the notion that one had primacy over the other was a misconception, in that it was only as a consequence of familiar rules and customs that had developed through social interaction and which were regulated and enforced by laws and social norms that individuality could be expressed.[36] Similarly, classes were an important aspect of society, but they were not the only, nor the most important, form of social grouping, and conflict between classes was not, as Socialists contended, a necessary result of their existence, nor did it demand that they should be 'abolished'. Keith Feiling argued in 1930 that society was 'composed of many groups . . . families, churches, localities, professions and races, lives interpenetrated, interdependent, but yet each integral. At their back are deep spontaneous affections and persistent impulses, finding expression in variable ways.'[37] Classes were just one expression of this social interdependence, but members of a given class would have many other expressions, often in the form of associations and activities which they engaged in with members of other classes. Moreover, in many important social activities, for example, in the actual process of production and in competition, whether economic, imperial, or military, with other nations, classes would share common bonds. The organicist conception of society served to provide Conservatives with a distinctive social philosophy that differentiated it in crucial ways from classical Liberalism and Socialism.

It is in relation to the organicist tenet that the question most clearly arises as to whether the Conservative party in the last quarter of the twentieth century abandoned Conservatism. As was noted earlier in this study, a number of Conservative politicians, and other commentators, suggested that the 1980s and 1990s had witnessed such an abandonment. Clearly this argument was frequently driven by specific political agendas, many of which were the product of the Conservatives' intra-party battles in those decades. Nevertheless, the question of whether the late twentieth century witnessed a 'strange death of Tory England' is one that needs to be addressed.

For some, notably Lord Gilmour, the key departure of the Thatcherite Conservative party from Conservatism was in the economic and social spheres, where the desire to 'roll back the frontiers of the State' saw the party embrace a free-market antagonism to State intervention that was characteristic of either classical nineteenth-century liberalism or late twentieth-century neo-liberalism. This argument in turn implied, although it was rarely stated explicitly, that Thatcherite

---

[36] Oakeshott, 'Being Conservative', 432–3.
[37] Feiling, *Conservatism*, 14.

Conservatives had also embraced a political economy that was intellectually 'perfectionist', insofar as it rested on the scientific/technical certainties of monetarist and neoclassical economics. But there are problems with seeing the adoption of liberal market economics as indicative of a Conservative 'conversion' to neo-liberalism. To begin with, although the Conservative party and governments engaged with neo-liberalism they did not fully embrace, and on occasion explicitly rejected, neo-liberal economics in its purest forms.[38] Furthermore, the period after 1975 was not the first occasion when the Conservative party adopted aspects of liberal market economics, and these doctrines have been and can be defended on Conservative rather than neo-liberal grounds. Hugh Cecil was clear, in *Conservatism*, that 'a policy of State interference is not, as such, alien from Conservatism',[39] but he supported free trade and wished to limit State action in the sphere of social policy. His grounds for this were that the decisions of the market were wholly impersonal, were thus free of ethical content, and that the State, as an ethical entity, had no part to play in them.[40] In Cecil's formulation, State action to deal with the social ills that market outcomes produced, such as poverty or hardship in old age, could only be deemed acts of national philanthropy rather than acts of social justice.[41] For Cecil and later Conservative advocates of the free market, notably Enoch Powell, liberal market economics were also justifiable in terms of intellectual imperfectionism and political scepticism, in that market transactions and outcomes were natural, spontaneous products of the 'invisible hand', and attempts to regulate them through State intervention were necessarily based on the (erroneous) assumption that those who implemented them had a complete grasp of human material wants and needs and how to satisfy them.

But if a case for liberal market economics can be made on Conservative grounds, it is not unproblematic. To begin with, liberal market economics can be deemed guilty of intellectual perfectionism, insofar as its attempts to establish models of supply, demand, and propensity to save, invest, or consume in terms of rational expectation can be, and have been, criticized as dependent upon abstract, deductive reasoning which makes assumptions that are as flawed as those made by advocates of State intervention and regulation of the market.[42] In

[38] A notable example is the proposal for the privatization of health care put forward by the Adam Smith Institute.

[39] Cecil, *Conservatism*, 195.

[40] For a discussion of Cecil's position see Meadowcroft, *State*, 90–106.

[41] Cecil, *Conservatism*, 176–80.

[42] See e.g. the critique of the Conservative historical economists, which is discussed in Green, *Crisis*, 159–83. For a late 20th-century critique see P. Ormerod, *The Death of Economics* (1994).

addition, market relations may be deemed spontaneous, but, as Oakeshott argued, they are different from other actions of social association, such as friendship, in that a *result* is expected from them. This in turn raises two further problems for Conservatism. The first is that if market relations assume a result—an outcome that will see a distribution of gains and losses—it is difficult to sustain the notion that market relations are free of ethical content. Gunnar Myrdal argued that in the study of economic theory the perpetual game of hide-and-seek was to find the norm hidden in the concept,[43] and this underlines the problem of harmonizing liberal market economics with the political scepticism of Conservative thought. The second objection, again identified by Oakeshott, is that those of a conservative disposition wish to defend and preserve the freedom of activities which bring enjoyment without producing 'a reward, a prize or a result in addition to the experience itself',[44] and market relations and activities are difficult to describe in these terms. Indeed, this last point leads to the most difficult aspect of reconciling Thatcherism with Conservatism.

The problems that liberal market economics produces for Conservatism stem from their broad socio-political implications as much as from their political-economic logic. In September 1987 Margaret Thatcher stated that people had developed a tendency to cast 'their problems on society and who is society? There is no such thing!'[45] As well as being one of the best-known statements of the 1980s, this is also one of the most misquoted and misunderstood. In the same statement she argued that instead of society there were 'individual men and women and there are families and . . . It is our duty to look after ourselves and then also to help look after our neighbour . . . life is a reciprocal business'.[46] Thatcher did not deny the existence of society, but objected to the use of the term as an abstract concept. This is confirmed by an exchange she had with George Urban at a meeting of the Centre for Policy Studies shortly after her resignation. Urban suggested that a major problem in Eastern and Central Europe under Communist rule had been the collapse of civil society, which prompted Thatcher to demand 'What on earth is civil society?' Urban explained that he meant 'all those customs and assumptions among individuals which are not regulated by law but upon which civilized living depends. They are distinct from the State; they are spontaneous', and having provided examples, such as the assumption that policemen help children cross the street, employees of charities do not embezzle donations, and voluntary

---

[43] G. Myrdal, *The Political Element in the Development of Economic Thought* (1953), 192.
[44] Oakeshott, 'Conservative', 415.
[45] M. Thatcher, Interview for *Woman's Own*, 23 Sept. 1987, *Thatcher CD-ROM*.
[46] Ibid.

were indeed voluntary and did good works, he noted that
r was 'mollified'.[47] Thatcher's stance was in accord with the
.......s, discussed in this study, that she and her closest political asso-
ciates placed on rolling back the State to allow room for spontaneous,
voluntary, civic associations to flourish.[48] But whether as a consequence
of a mismatch between intention and outcome, or as a result of a failure to anticipate where a liberal market strategy could lead,
Thatcherism stretched organicism to breaking-point. In *Is Conservatism
Dead?*, John Gray noted that the emphasis in late twentieth-century
Conservatism on market relations as a basis for social relations more
generally had acted as a solvent of social bonds, which had existed in
the shape of varied and complex webs of associational activity.[49] The
individualist logic of the liberal market, often explicitly embraced by
Thatcher and her party,[50] carried the intrinsic possibility of a tendency
not only to *political* individualism but also to social *individuation*, both
of which placed question-marks, in terms of theory and practice, against
the importance of social action and social capital. That the emphasis on
market relations which had informed much of the political, economic,
and social agenda of the 1980s and 1990s appeared to have brought
about the possibility of such a fracturing of social cohesion was a matter
of concern across the political spectrum, and it was a concern that was
not confined to Britain.[51] But it presented particular problems for
British Conservatives,[52] in that its implications were wholly at odds
with the organicist emphasis on social association that had been such a
marked feature of Conservative thought. As the Conservative Century
came to and end, it seemed that even if the Conservative party had
survived, Conservatism had not.

[47] G. Urban, *Diplomacy and Disillusion at the Court of Margaret Thatcher: An Insider's View* (1996), 170–1.

[48] See Ch. 8.

[49] Gray and Willetts, *Is Conservatism Dead?*, 3–65.

[50] For Thatcher's individualist outlook, and her praise for colleagues who adhered to indi-vidualist positions, see in particular her Keith Joseph Memorial Lecture, 11 Jan. 1996, and her Nicholas Ridley Memorial Lecture, 22 Nov. 1996, *Thatcher CD-ROM*.

[51] For a study of this phenomenon in the US context see R. D. Putnam, *Bowling Alone: The Collapse and Revival of American Community* (New York, 2000). For Britain see P. A. Hall, 'Social Capital in Britain', *British Journal of Political Science*, 29 (1999).

[52] One association which showed a marked decline in participation was, of course, the Conservative party, the membership of which decreased significantly over the 1980s and 1990s. See P. Whiteley, P. Seyd, and J. Richardson, *True Blues: The Politics of Conservative Party Membership* (Oxford 1994), esp. 219–38.

Bibliography

Place of publication is London, unless otherwise shown.

MANUSCRIPT SOURCES

Astor papers, Reading University Library.
Baldwin papers, Cambridge University Library.
Balfour papers, British Library, London.
Boutwood papers, Corpus Christi College Library, Cambridge.
Bryant papers, King's College, London.
Butler papers, Trinity College Library, Cambridge.
Cecil of Chelwood papers, British Library.
A. Chamberlain papers, Birmingham University Library.
J. Chamberlain papers, Birmingham University Library.
N. Chamberlain papers, Birmingham University Library.
Conservative party archive, Bodleian Library, Oxford.
Croft papers, Churchill College Library, Cambridge.
Cromer papers, Public Record Office, London.
Crookshank papers, Bodleian Library, Oxford.
Gwynne papers, Bodleian Library, Oxford.
Hailes papers, Churchill College Library, Cambridge.
Hamilton papers, British Library, London.
Hewins papers, Sheffield University Library.
Law papers, House of Lords Record Office, London.
Lloyd papers, Churchill College Library, Cambridge.
Macmillan papers, Bodleian Library, Oxford.
Maxse papers, West Sussex Record Office, Chichester.
Milner papers, Bodleian Library, Oxford.
Monckton papers, Bodleian Library, Oxford.
Steel-Maitland papers, National Archives of Scotland, Edinburgh.
Strachey papers, House of Lords Record Office, London.
Wargrave papers, House of Lords Record Office, London.
Willoughby de Broke papers, House of Lords Record Office, London.
Winterton papers, Bodleian Library, Oxford.
Woolton papers, Bodleian Library, Oxford.

PRINTED PRIMARY SOURCES (Books only; for essays see footnotes)

ASHLEY, W. J., *The Tariff Problem* (1903).
—— *The Economic Organization of England* (1914).

BALDWIN, S., *On England and Other Addresses* (1926).
BALFOUR, A. J., *Essays and Addresses* (Edinburgh, 1893).
—— *Economic Notes on Insular Free Trade* (1903).
—— *Fiscal Reform* (1906).
BALL, S. (ed.), *Parliament and Politics in the Age of Baldwin and MacDonald: The Headlam Diaries, 1923–35* (1992).
—— (ed.), *Parliament and Politics in the Age of Churchill and Attlee: The Headlam Diaries, 1935–51* (Cambridge 1999).
BARNES, J. and D. NICHOLSON, *The Leo Amery Diaries, I, 1896–1914* (1980).
—— —— (eds.), *The Empire at Bay: The Leo Amery Diaries, 1929–45* (1983).
BENN, E., *Account Rendered* (1930).
BIRCH, N., *The Conservative Party* (1949).
BOYD, C. (ed.), *Speeches of the Right Honourable Joseph Chamberlain*, 2 vols. (1914).
BRYANT, A., *The Spirit of Conservatism* (1929).
—— *English Saga, 1840–1940* (1940).
—— *The Years of Endurance, 1793–1802* (1942).
—— *The Years of Victory, 1802–12* (1944).
—— *Set in A Silver Sea* (1985).
—— *Freedom's Own Island: Britain's Oceanic Expansion* (1987).
CAIRNCROSS, A. (ed.), *The Robert Hall Diaries*, 2 vols. (1991).
CECIL, H., *Conservatism* (1912).
CHAMBERLAIN, A. *Politics From Inside* (1936).
CLARKE, D., *The Conservative Faith in a Modern Age* (1947).
Compatriots' Club Lectures (1905).
Conservative Central Office, *The Industrial Charter* (1947).
Conservative Political Centre, *Conservatism 1945–50* (1950).
—— *The New Conservatism: An Anthology of Post-War Thought* (1955).
Conservative Political Centre Oxford Summer School, *The Future of the Welfare State* (1958).
COWIE, D., *An Empire Prepared*, Right Book Club (RCB) edn. (1939).
CUNNINGHAM, W., *Politics and Economics* (1885).
—— *The Alternative to Socialism in England* (Cambridge, 1885).
—— *Political Economy and Practical Life* (1893).
—— *The Rise and Decline of the Free Trade Movement* (1904).
—— *The Wisdom of the Wise* (1904).
—— *Christianity and Socialism* (1909).
—— *The Case Against Free Trade* (1911).
EGERTON, H. (A. Boutwood), *Patriotism* (1905).
—— *National Toryism* (1911).
—— *National Revival* (1914).
ELLIOT, W., *Toryism and the Twentieth Century* (1927).
FEILING, K., *What Is Conservatism?* (1930).
FOXWELL, H. S., *Papers on Current Finance* (1919).
FREEDEN, M. (ed.), *Minutes of the Rainbow Circle* (1988).
GIBBS, P., *Ordeal in England*, RBC edn. (1938).
GILMOUR, I., *Britain Can Work* (1983).

A Group of MPs, *One Nation* (1950).

HAILSHAM, Viscount (Q. Hogg), *The Conservative Case* (1959).

HAYEK, F., *The Road to Serfdom* (1943).

—— *The Constitution of Liberty* (1960, 1976 edn.).

HILLS, J. W., *Managed Money* (1937).

—— *et al., Industrial Unrest* (1914).

HINCHINGBROOKE, Viscount (ed.), *Full Speed Ahead: Essays in Tory Reform* (1944).

HOBHOUSE, L. T., *Democracy and Reaction* (1904; Brighton, 1974 edn.).

HOGG, Q., *The Case for Conservatism* (1947).

JERROLD, D., *Georgian Adventure: The Autobiography of Douglas Jerrold* (1937; RBC edn. 1938).

JEWKES, J., *Ordeal By Planning* (1948).

—— *The New Ordeal By Planning* (1968).

JOSEPH, K., *Reversing the Trend* (1975).

—— *Monetarism is Not Enough* (1976).

—— *Stranded on the Middle Ground* (1976).

KEYNES, J. M., *The Means to Prosperity* (1934).

—— *The General Theory of Employment, Interest and Money* (1936; 1973 edn.).

—— *The Collected Writings of John Maynard Keynes*, 30 Vols. (1973–82).

KIDD, B., *Individualism and After* (1908).

LAW, R., *Return From Utopia* (1950).

LUDOVICI, A., *A Defence of Conservatism: A Further Text-Book for Tories* (1927).

MALMESBURY, Lord (ed.), *The New Order* (1908).

MACMILLAN, H., *The Next Step* (1932).

—— *Reconstruction* (1933).

—— *The Middle Way* (1938).

—— *The Middle Way: Twenty Years After* (1958).

—— R. BOOTHBY, J. LODER, and O. STANLEY, *Industry and the State* (1927).

MACKENZIE, N. (ed.), *The Letters of Sidney and Beatrice Webb*, 3 vols. (Cambridge, 1976).

MACLEOD, I. and J. E. POWELL, *The Social Services: Needs and Means* (1952).

MILNER, A., *The Nation and the Empire* (1913).

The Next Five Years (1935).

NORTHAM, R., *Conservatism: The Only Way*, RBC edn. (1938).

The One Nation Group, *The Responsible Society* (1959).

PETRIE, C., *The Chamberlain Tradition* (1938).

POWELL, J. E., *Freedom and Reality* (1969).

—— *Still To Decide* (1971).

—— *No Easy Answers* (1973).

—— and A. MAUDE, *Change is Our Ally* (1954).

PYM, F., *The Politics of Consent* (1984).

SEELEY, J. R., *The Expansion of England* (1883; 1897 edn.).

SELF, R. C. (ed.), *The Austen Chamberlain Diary Letters* (Cambridge, 1995).

STEEL-MAITLAND, A., *Foreword to the Socialists' Bible: Karl Marx's Theory Discussed* (1920).
—— *The Trade Crisis and the Way Out* (1931).
—— *The New America* (1934).
TEELING, W., *Why Britain Prospers*, RBC edn. (1938).
THATCHER, M., *The Revival of Britain* (1989).
—— *Margaret Thatcher: Complete Public Statements, 1945–1990 on CD-ROM*, ed. C. Collins (Oxford, 1999).
URBAN, G., *Diplomacy and Disillusion at the Court of Margaret Thatcher: An Insider's View* (1996).
VINCENT, J. (ed.), *The Crawford Papers* (Manchester 1984).
WELLS, H. G., *The New Machiavelli* (1911).
WILLETTS, D., *Civic Conservatism* (1994).
—— and J. GRAY, *Is Conservatism Dead?* (1997).
WILLIAMSON, P. (ed.), *The Modernisation of Conservative Politics: The Diaries and Letters of William Bridgeman, 1904–1935* (1988).
WHITE, R. J., *The Conservative Tradition* (1950).
WILSON, A., *Thoughts and Talks*, RBC edn. (1938).
WOOD, J. (ed.), *A Nation Not Afraid: The Thinking of Enoch Powell* (1965).
WYNDHAM, G., *The Development of the State* (1904).
YEATS-BROWN, F., *The European Jungle*, RBC edn. (1938).
Young Conservatives, *Society and the Individual* (1962)

SECONDARY SOURCES (Books)

ADAMS, R. J. Q., *Bonar Law* (1999).
ALLETT, J., *New Liberalism: The Political Economy of J. A. Hobson* (Toronto, 1981).
AMERY, L. S., *My Political Life*, 3 vols. (1953–5).
ASHLEY, A., *William James Ashley: A Life* (1925).
BENTLEY, M. (ed.), *Public and Private Doctrine* (Cambridge, 1993).
BIAGINI, E. (ed.), *Citizenship and Community* (Cambridge, 1997).
BLAKE, R., *The Unknown Prime Minister* (1955).
—— *The Conservative Party From Peel to Thatcher* (1985).
BLEWETT, N., *The Peers, the Parties and the People: The General Elections of 1910* (1972).
BOYD-CARPENTER, J., *Way of Life* (1980).
BRACCO, R. M., *Merchants of Hope: British Middlebrow Writers and the First World War, 1919–39* (Oxford, 1993).
BURROW, J., S. COLLINI, and D. WINCH, *That Noble Science of Politics* (Cambridge 1985).
BUTLER, R. A., *The Art of the Possible* (1982).
CAIRNCROSS, A. and N. WATTS, *The Economic Section, 1939–61* (1989).
CASSIS, Y. (ed.), *Finance and Financiers in European History, 1880–1960* (Cambridge, 1992).
CECIL of Chelwood, Lord, *All the Way* (1949).

CHARMLEY, J., *Lord Lloyd and the Decline of the British Empire* (1987).
—— *A History of Conservative Politics, 1900–1996* (Basingstoke, 1996).
CLARK, A. *The Tories: Conservatives and the Nation State, 1922–1997* (1998).
CLARKE, P. *Lancashire and the New Liberalism* (Cambridge, 1971).
—— *Liberals and Social Democrats* (Cambridge, 1978).
—— *The Keynesian Revolution in the Making, 1924–1936* (Oxford, 1988).
—— *A Question of Leadership* (1991).
—— *The Keynesian Revolution and its Economic Consequence* (Cheltenham, 1998).
COCKETT, R., *Thinking the Unthinkable* (1993).
COETZEE, F., *For Party or Country: Nationalism and the Dilemmas of Popular Conservatism in Edwardian England* (Oxford, 1990).
COLLINI, S., *Liberalism and Sociology* (Cambridge, 1979).
COOPEY, R., S. FIELDING, and N. TIRATSOO (eds.), *The Wilson Governments, 1964–70* (1993).
COWLING, M., *The Impact of Labour* (Cambridge, 1971).
CROWSON, N. J., *Facing Fascism: The Conservative Party and the European Dictators, 1935–40* (1997).
CUNNINGHAM, A., *William Cunningham: Teacher and Priest* (1953).
DE GROOT, G., *Blighty: British Society in the Era of the Great War* (Harlow, 1996)
DEN OTTER, S., *British Idealism and Social Explanation* (Oxford, 1997).
DAVENPORT-HINES, R., *Dudley Docker: The Life and Times of a Trade Warrior* (Cambridge, 1984).
DUGDALE, B. E. C., *Arthur Janes Balfour*, 2 vols. (1939).
DUTTON, D., *Austen Chamberlain: Gentleman in Politics* (Bolton, 1985).
ECCLESHALL, R., *English Conservatism Since the Reformation* (1990).
ELLIOTT, J. H., *National and Comparative History: An Inaugural Lecture* (Oxford, 1991).
FFORDE, M., *Conservatism and Collectivism, 1880–1914* (Edinburgh, 1990).
FLOUD, R., and D. McCLOSKEY (eds.), *The Economic History of Britain Since 1700*, 3 vols. (2nd edn., Cambridge, 1994).
FOX, A., *History and Heritage* (1985).
FREEDEN, M., *The New Liberalism* (Oxford, 1977).
—— *Ideologies and Political Theory* (Oxford, 1996).
FRANCIS, M., and I. ZWEINIGER-BARGIELOWSKA (eds.), *The Conservatives and British Society, 1880–1990* (Cardiff, 1996).
FRANCO, P., *The Political Philosophy of Michael Oakeshott* (New Haven, 1990).
GARVIN, J. L., and J. AMERY, *The Life of Joseph Chamberlain*, 6 vols. (1932–69).
GAMBLE, A., *The Conservative Nation* (1974).
—— *The Free Economy and the Strong State* (1994, 2nd edn., 1994).
—— *Hayek* (Cambridge, 1996).
GARNETT, M., *Alport: A Study in Loyalty* (Teddington, 1999).
GILMOUR, I., *Inside Right* (1980 edn.).
—— *Dancing With Dogma* (1992).

GILMOUR, I., *Whatever Happened to the Tories?* (1997).

GREEN, E. H. H., *The Crisis of Conservatism: The Politics, Economics and Ideology of the British Conservative Party, 1880–1914* (1995).

—— (ed.), *An Age of Transition: British Politics, 1870–1914* (Edinburgh, 1997).

GREENGARTEN, I. M., *Thomas Hill Green and the Development of Liberal-Democratic Thought* (Toronto, 1981).

GREENLEAF, W. H., *The British Political Tradition*, 3 vols. (1983).

GOLLIN, A. M., *Balfour's Burden* (1965).

GORST, A. *et al.* (eds.), *Post-War Britain, 1945–64* (1989).

HAILSHAM, Lord (Q. Hogg), *A Sparrow's Flight* (1990).

HALCROW, M., *Keith Joseph: A Single Mind* (1989).

HALL, P., *Governing the Economy* (Cambridge, 1986).

HAMES, T., and A. ADONIS (eds.), *A Conservative Revolution* (Manchester, 1994).

HARTE, N. B., (ed.), *The Study of Economic History* (1971).

HEATH, A. *et al.*, *Understanding Political Change* (Oxford, 1991).

HEFFER, S., *Like the Roman: The Life of Enoch Powell* (1998).

HEWINS, W. A. S., *The Apologia of an Imperialist*, 2 vols. (1929).

HOFFMAN, J. D., *The Conservative Party in Opposition, 1945–51* (1964).

HOOVER, K., and R. PLANT, *Conservative Capitalism in Britain and America* (1989).

HONDERICH, T., *Conservatism* (1990).

HORNE, A., *Macmillan* 2 vols. (Basingstoke, 1989).

HOSKYNS, J., *Just In Time: Inside the Thatcher Revolution* (2000).

HUTCHISON, G., *The Last Edwardian at No. 10* (1980).

HUTCHISON, T. W., *Economics and Economic Policy in Britain, 1946–66* (1968).

JEFFREYS, K., *The Churchill Coalition and Wartime Politics, 1940–45* (Manchester, 1991).

—— *Retreat From New Jerusalem* (1997).

JENKINS, P., *Mrs Thatcher's Revolution* (1985).

JONES, H., and M. KANDIAH (eds.), *The Myth of Consensus* (Basingstoke, 1996).

JUDD, D., *Balfour and the British Empire* (1968).

KINNEAR, M., *The Fall of Lloyd George: The Political Crisis of 1922* (1973).

KOOT, G. M., *The English Historical Economists* (Cambridge, 1988).

LAMB, R., *The Macmillan Years: The Emerging Truth* (Basingstoke, 1997).

LAWSON, N., *The View from No. 11* (1992).

LEVENTHAL, F. M., and R. QUINAULT (eds.), *Anglo-American Attitudes: From Revolution to Partnership* (Aldershot, 2000).

LEWIS, J., *The Voluntary Sector, the State and Social Work in Britain* (Aldershot, 1995).

LIGHT, A., *Forever England: Femininity, Literature and Conservatism Between the Wars* (1991).

MACBRIAR, A., *An Edwardian Mixed Doubles* (Oxford, 1987).

MACKAY, R., *International Statesman: A Life of A. J. Balfour* (Oxford, 1985).

MACMILLAN, H., *Winds of Change, 1914–39* (1966).
—— *Tides of Fortune, 1945–55* (1969).
—— *Riding the Storm, 1956–9* (1971).
—— *Pointing the Way, 1959–61* (1972).
—— *At the End of the Day, 1961–63* (1973).
MARLOW, J. D., *Questioning the Post-War Consensus Thesis* (Aldershot, 1996).
MARRISON, A., *British Business and Protection, 1903–32* (Oxford, 1992).
MCCRILLIS, N., *The British Conservative Party in the Age of Universal Suffrage: Popular Conservatism, 1918–29* (Columbus, Ohio, 1998).
MCKIBBIN, R., *The Ideologies of Class* (Oxford, 1991).
—— *Classes and Cultures: England, 1918–1951* (Oxford, 1998).
MIDDLEMASS, K., *Power Competition and the State* 3 vols (1986–91).
MINOGUE, K., and M. BIDDISS (eds.), *Thatcherism: Personality and Politics* (1987).
MORGAN, K. O., *Consensus and Disunity: The Lloyd George Coalition Government, 1918–22* (Oxford, 1978).
—— *The People's Peace* (Oxford, 1991).
MOWAT, C. L., *The Charity Organization Society* (1961).
MURPHY, P., *Party Politics and Decolonization: The Conservative Party and British Colonial Policy in Tropical Africa, 1951–1964* (Oxford, 1995).
MYRDAL, G., *The Political Element in the Development of Economic Thought* (1953).
OAKLEY, A. (ed.), *The Politics of the Welfare State* (1994).
ORMEROD, P., *The Death of Economics* (1994).
O'SULLIVAN, N., *Conservatism* (1976).
PARKINSON, C., *Right at the Centre* (1991).
PEDEN, G. C., *The Treasury* (Oxford, 2000).
PLANT, R., and A. VINCENT, *Politics, Philosophy and Citizenship* (Oxford, 1984).
PUGH, M., *State and Society* (1994).
PUTNAM, R. D., *Bowling Alone: The Collapse and Revival of American Community* (New York, 2000).
QUINTON, A., *The Politics of Imperfection* (1975).
RAISON, T., *Tories and the Welfare State* (Basingstoke, 1990).
RAMSDEN, J., *The Age of Balfour and Baldwin, 1902–40* (1978).
—— *The Age of Churchill and Eden, 1940–57* (1995).
—— *Winds of Change: From Macmillan to Heath, 1957–75* (1996).
—— *An Appetitite For Power* (1998).
RANELAGH, J., *Thatcher's People* (1991).
REMPEL, R., *Unionists Divided* (Newton Abbot, 1972).
RICHTER, M., *The Politics of Conscience* (1964).
RIDDELL, P., *The Thatcher Government* (1989).
—— *The Thatcher Legacy* (1992).
RIDLEY, N., *My Style of Government: The Thatcher Years* (1991).
RITSCHEL, D., *The Politics of Planning* (Oxford, 1997).
ROBERTS, A., *Eminent Churchillians* (1994).
SCHOEN, D. E., *Powell and the Powellites* (1977).
SCRUTON, R., *The Meaning of Conservatism* (1980).

SEARLE, G. R., *The Quest For National Efficiency* (Oxford, 1971).
—— *Corruption in British Politics, 1895–1930* (Oxford 1987).
SELDON, A. (ed.), *How Tory Governments Fall* (1996).
—— and D. KAVANAGH (eds.), *The Thatcher Effect* (Oxford, 1989).
—— and S. BALL (eds.), *Conservative Century: The Conservative Party Since 1900* (Oxford, 1994).
—— —— (eds.), *The Heath Government, 1970–74: A Reappraisal* (1996).
SELIGER, M., *Ideology and Politics* (1976).
SHANNON, R., *The Age of Disraeli, 1868–81* (1992).
—— *The Age of Salisbury, 1882–1902* (1995).
SHEPHERD, R., *Iain Macleod* (1994).
—— *Enoch Powell* (1996).
SKIDELSKY, R. (ed.), *Thatcherism* (1988).
SMOUT, T. C. (ed.), *Victorian Values* (1992).
SUPPLE, B., and M. FURNER (eds.), *The State and Economic Knowledge* (Cambridge, 1992).
SYKES, S., *Tariff Reform in British Politics, 1903–13* (Oxford, 1979).
TAYLOR, A. J. P., *Beaverbrook* (1972).
—— (ed.), *Lloyd George: Twelve Essays* (1971).
TAYLOR, M., and J. LAWRENCE (eds.), *Party, State and Society: Electoral Behaviour in Modern Britain Since 1820* (Aldershot, 1996).
TAYLOR, M. W., *Men Versus the State* (Oxford, 1992).
TAYLOR, R., *The Trade Union Question in British Politics Since 1945* (Oxford, 1993).
TEBBIT, N., *Upwardly Mobile* (1988).
THATCHER, M., *The Path to Power* (1994).
THORPE, D. R., *Selwyn Lloyd* (1989).
—— *Alec Douglas-Home* (1996).
TOLLIDAY, S., *Business, Banking and Politics* (Cambridge, Mass., 1986).
TOMLINSON, J., *Employment Policy: The Crucial Years* (Oxford, 1988).
—— *Democratic Socialism and Economic Policy, 1945–51* (Cambridge, 1997).
TURNER, J., *Macmillan* (1994).
WAITES, B., *A Class Society at War* (Leamington Spa, 1987).
WALKER, P., *Staying Power* (1991).
WEBBER, G. C., *The Ideology of the British Right, 1918–39* (1986).
WHITELEY, P., P. SEYD and J. RICHARDSON, *True Blues: The Politics of Conservative Party Membership* (Oxford, 1994).
WIENER, M., *English Culture and the Decline of the Industrial Spirit* (Cambridge, 1981).
WILLIAMSON, P., *National Crisis and National Government: British Politics, the Economy and Empire, 1926–32* (Cambridge, 1992).
—— *Stanley Baldwin* (Cambridge, 1999).
WITHERELL, LARRY L., *Rebel on the Right: Henry Page Croft and the Crisis of British Conservatism, 1903–14* (1997).
YOUNG, Lord *The Enterprise Years* (1991).
YOUNG, H., *One of Us* (1990).
ZEBEL, S., *Balfour: A Political Biography* (Cambridge, 1973).

SECONDARY SOURCES (essays and articles)

BIDDISS, M., 'Thatcherism: Concept and Interpretations', in K. Minogue and M. Biddiss (eds.), *Thatcherism* (1987).

BOOTH, A., 'Inflation, Expectations, and the Political Economy of Conservative Britain, 1951–64', *HJ* 43 (2000).

CAIN, P., 'The Economic Philosophy of Constructive Imperialism', in C. Navari (ed.), *British Politics and the Spirit of the Age* (Keele, 1995).

CLARKE, P., 'Keynes, Buchanan and the Balanced Budget Doctrine' in id., *The Keynesian Revolution and Its Economic Consequences* (Cheltenham, 1998).

COCKETT, R., 'The Party, Publicity and the Media', in A. Seldon and S. Ball (eds.), *Conservative Century The Conservative Party Since 1900* (Oxford, 1994).

COETZEE, F., 'Villa Toryism Reconsidered: Conservatism and Suburban Sensibilities in Late-Victorian Croydon', in E. H. H. Green (ed.), *An Age of Transition: British Politics, 1880–1914* (Edinburgh, 1997).

COLLINI, S., 'Hobhouse, Bosanquet and the State: Philosophical Idealism and Political Argument in Britain, 1880–1914', *P&P* 72 (1976).

CORNFORD, J., 'The Transformation of Conservatism in the Late Nineteenth Century', *Victorian Studies*, 7 (1963).

DAUNTON, M. J., 'How to Pay for the War: State, Society and Taxation in Britain, 1917–24', *EHR* 110 (1996).

DEN OTTER, S., ' "Thinking in Communities": Late Nineteenth-Century Liberals, Idealists and the Retrieval of Community', in E. H. H. Green (ed.), *An Age of Transition: British Politics, 1880–1914* (Edinburgh, 1997).

FINDLEY, R., 'The Conservative Party and Defeat: The Significance of Resale Price Maintenance for the Election of 1964', *TCBH* (forthcoming).

FRANCIS, M., 'Set the People Free'? The Conservative Party and the State, 1920–60', in M. Francis and I. Zweiniger-Bargielowska (eds.), *The Conservatives and British Society 1880–1990* (Cardiff 1996).

FREEDEN, M., 'Biological and Evolutionary Roots in New Liberalism in England', *Political Theory*, 4 (1976).

GOULD, J., and D. ANDERSON, 'Thatcherism and British Society', in K. Minogue and M. Biddiss (eds.), *Thatcherism* (1987).

GREEN, E. H. H., 'Rentiers versus Producers? The Political Economy of the Bimetallic Controversy, 1890–98', *EHR* 102 (1988).

—— 'The Bimetallic Controversy: Empiricism Belimed or the Case for the Issues', *EHR* 104 (1990).

—— 'The Influence of the City Over British Economic Policy, 1880–1960', in Y. Cassis (ed.), *Finance and Financiers in European History, 1880–1960* (Cambridge, 1992).

—— 'The Conservative Party, the State and the Electorate, 1945–64', in M. Taylor and J. Lawrence (eds.), *Party, State and Society: Electoral Behaviour in Modern Britain Since 1820* (Aldershot 1996).

—— 'The Political Economy of Empire, 1880–1914', in A. Porter (ed.), *The Oxford History of the British Empire*, Vol. III, *The Nineteenth Century* (Oxford, 1999).

GREEN, E. H. H., 'No Longer the Farmer's Friend: The Conservative Party and Agricultural Protection, 1880–1914', in J. R. Wordie (ed.), *Agriculture and Politics in England, 1830–1914* (Basingstoke, 2000).

HALL, P. A., 'Social Capital in Britain', *British Journal of Political Science*, 29 (1999).

HARRIS, J., 'Political Thought and the Welfare State, 1870–1940: An Intellectual Framework for British Social Policy', *P&P* 135 (1992).

HOWSON, S., 'Money and Monetary Policy in Britain, 1945–90', in R. Floud and D. McCloskey (eds.), *The Economic History of Britain Since 1700*, 3 vols. (2nd edn., Cambridge, 1994).

HILTON, B., 'Peel: A Reappraisal', *HJ* 22 (1979).

JARVIS, D. A., 'Mrs. Maggs and Betty: The Conservative Appeal to Women Voters in the 1920s', *TCBH* 5 (1994).

—— 'British Conservatism and Class Politics in the 1920s', *EHR* 110 (1996).

—— 'The Shaping of the Conservative Electoral Hegemony, 1918–39', in J. Lawrence and M. Taylor (eds.), *Party, State and Society: Electoral Behaviour in Modern Britain Since 1820* (Aldershot, 1996).

JARVIS, M., 'The 1958 Treasury Dispute', *CBH* 12 (1998).

JEFFREYS, K., 'British Politics and Social Policy During the Second World War', *HJ* 30 (1987).

JOHNMANN, L., 'The Conservative Party in Opposition, 1964–70', in R. Coopey, S. Fielding, and N. Tiratsoo (eds.), *The Wilson Governments, 1964–70* (1993).

KANDIAH, M., 'Conservative Leaders' Strategy and Consensus, 1945–64', in H. Jones and M. Kandiah (eds.), *Myths of Consensus* (Basingstoke, 1996).

LOWE, R., 'Resignation at the Treasury: The Social Services Committee and the Failure to Reform the Welfare State', *Journal of Social Policy* 18 (1989).

—— 'The Replanning of the the Welfare State, 1957–64', in M. Francis and I. Zweiniger-Bargielowska (eds.), *The Conservatives and British Society 1880–1990* (Cardiff, 1996).

—— 'The Core Executive, Modernization and the Creation of PESC, 1960–4', *Public Administration*, 75 (1997).

—— 'The Plowden Committee: Milestone or Millstone?', *HJ* 40 (1997).

McDONALD, G. W., and H. F. GOSPEL, 'The Mond–Turner Talks, 1927–33: A Study in Industrial Co-operation', *HJ* 16 (1973).

MCKIBBIN, R., 'Class and Conventional Wisdom', in id., *The Ideologies of Class* (Oxford, 1991).

MIDDLETON, R., 'The Treasury in the 1930s: Political and Administrative Constraints to Acceptance of the "New" Economics', *Oxford Economic Papers*, 34 (1982).

—— 'Keynes's Legacy for Post-War Economic Management', in A. Gorst *et al.* (eds.), *Post-War Britain, 1945–64* (1989).

MINKIN, L., 'Radicalism and Reconstruction: the British Experience', *Europa*, 5 (1982).

MORGAN, K. O., 'Lloyd George's Stage Army: the Coalition Liberals, 1918–22', in A. J. P. Taylor (ed.), *Lloyd George: Twelve Essays* (1971).

MORROW, J., 'Liberalism and British Idealist Political Philosophy: A Reassessment', *History of Political Thought*, 5 (1984).

—— 'Ancestors, Legacies and Tradition: British Idealism', *HOPT* 6 (1985).

OAKESHOTT, M., 'The Activity of Being An Historian' and 'On Being Conservative', in id., *Rationalism in Politics and Other Essays* (1962, Indianapolis 1991 edn.).

PEDEN, G. C., 'Sir Richard Hopkins and the "Keynesian Revolution" in Employment Policy, 1929–45', *EcHR*, 36 (1983).

—— 'The "Treasury View" on Public Works and Employment in the Interwar Period', *EcHR*, 37 (1984).

—— 'Old Dogs and New Tricks', in B. Supple and M. Furner (eds.), *The State and Economic Knowledge* (Cambridge, 1992).

PHILLIPS, A. W., 'The Relation Between Unemployment and the Rate of Change of Money Wage Rates in the United Kingdom, 1861–1957', *Economica*, 25 (1958).

POCOCK, J. G. A., 'The Political Economy of Burke's *Reflections on the Revolution in France*', *HJ* 25 (1982).

POWELL, J. E., 'The Conservative Party', in A. Seldon and D. Kavanagh (eds.), *The Thatcher Effect* (Oxford, 1989).

RAMSDEN, J., 'Baldwin and Film', in N. Pronay and D. Spring (eds.), *Politics, Propaganda and Film, 1928–45* (Basingstoke, 1982).

—— 'A Party for Owners or a Party for Earners? How Far Did the British Conservative Party Really Change After 1945?', *TRHS* 37 (1987).

RIDLEY, J., 'The Unionist Social Reform Committee, 1911–14: Wets Before the Deluge', *HJ* 30 (1987).

RUBINSTEIN, W. D., 'Henry Page Croft and the National Party', *Journal of Contemporary History* (1975).

RINGE, A. (ed.), 'Witness Seminar: The National Economic Development Council, 1962–7', *CBH* 12 (1998).

RITSCHEL, D., 'A Corporatist Economy in Britain? Capitalist Planning for Industrial Self-Government in the 1930s', *EHR* 56 (1993).

ROLLINGS, N., 'Poor Mr. Butskell: A Short Life Wrecked by Schizophrenia', *TCBH* 4 (1994).

—— 'Butskellism, the Post-War Consensus and the Managed Economy', in H. Jones and M. Kandiah (eds.), *The Myth of Consensus* (Basingstoke, 1996).

SELDON, A., 'Conservative Century', in A. Seldon and S. Ball (eds.), *The Conservative Century: The Conservative Party Since 1900* (Oxford, 1994).

SOFFER, R. N., 'British Conservative Historiography and the Second World War', in B. Stuchley and P. Wende (eds.), *British and German Historiography, 1750–1950* (Oxford, 2000).

—— 'Commitment and Catastrophe: Twentieth Century Conservative History in Britain and America', in F. M. Leventhal and R. Quinault (eds.), *Anglo-American Attitudes: From Revolution to Partnership* (Aldershot, 2000).

—— 'The Long Nineteenth Century of Conservative Thought', in G. K. Behlmer and F. M. Leventhal (eds.), *Singular Continuities: Tradition, Nostalgia and Identity in Modern British Culture* (Stanford, 2000).

SYKES, A., 'The Confederacy and the Purge of the Unionist Free Traders, 1906–10', *HJ* 18 (1975).

TAYLOR, R., 'The Heath Government, Industrial Policy and the "New Capitalism" ', in A. Seldon and S. Ball (eds.), *The Heath Government, 1970–74: A Reappraisal* (1996).

TOMLINSON, J., 'Inventing Decline: The Falling Behind of the British Economy in the Post-War Years', *EcHR* 99, (1996).

—— 'Conservative Modernisation, 1960–64: Too Little, Too Late?', *CBH* 11 (1997).

TRENTMANN, F., 'The Strange Death of Free Trade', in E. Biagini (ed.), *Citizenship and Community* (Cambridge, 1996).

TURNER, J., 'The British Conservative Party in the Twentieth Century: From Beginning to End', *Contemporary European History*, 8 (1999).

WEBSTER, C., 'Conflict and Consensus: Explaining the British Health Service', *TCBH* 1 (1990).

—— 'Conservatives and Consensus: the Politics of the National Health Service, 1951–64', in A. Oakley (ed.), *The Politics of the Welfare State* (1994).

WEILER, P., 'The Rise and Fall of the Conservatives' "Grand Design" for Housing, 1951–1964', *CBH* (2000).

WHITING, R., 'Taxation and the Working Class, 1915–22', *HJ* 33 (1990).

WICKHAM-JONES, M., 'Right Turn: A Revisionist Account of the 1975 Conservative Party Leadership Election', *TCBH* 8 (1997).

WILLIAMSON, P., 'The Doctrinal Politics of Stanley Baldwin', in M. Bentley (ed.), *Public and Private Doctrine* (Cambridge, 1993).

WITHERELL, L., 'Political Cannibalism Amongst Edwardian Conservatives', *TCBH* 8 (1997).

ZWEINIGER-BARGIELOWSKA, I., 'Rationing, Austerity and the Conservative Electoral Recovery after 1945', *HJ* 37 (1993).

—— 'Consensus and Consumption: Rationing, Austerity and Controls after the War', in H. Jones and M. Kandiah (eds.), *The Myth of Consensus* (Basingstoke, 1996).

UNPUBLISHED THESES

BAMBERG, J. H., 'The Government, the Banks, and the Lancashire Cotton Industry', Cambridge University Ph.D thesis (1984).

BATES, J. W. B., 'The Conservative Party in the Constituencies, 1918–39', Oxford University D.Phil. thesis (1994).

DEWEY, R. F., 'British National Identity and the First Application to Europe', Oxford University D.Phil. thesis (2001).

JARVIS, D. A., 'Stanley Baldwin and the Ideology of the Conservative Response to Socialism, 1918–31', Lancaster University Ph.D thesis (1991).

JONES, H., 'The Conservative Party and the Welfare State, 1942–55', London University Ph.D thesis (1992).

MORRIS, A. J. LL., 'St Loe Strachey and the *Spectator*', Cambridge University Ph.D thesis (1984).

SHORT, M. E., 'The Politics of Personal Taxation: Budget Making in Britain, 1917–31', Cambridge University Ph.D thesis (1984).

Index

Adam Smith Institute 4
Addison, C. 121, 125
Aldenham, Lord 205
Aliens Act (1905) 18
Alport, C. (Lord) 11, 141, 155–6
All Souls College 44–5, 73, 75
Amery, L. C. M. S. 7, 11, 44, 65–6,
    69, 75, 108, 118, 120, 150, 154
Anti-Socialist Union 7
Anti-Waste League 122–5, 133
appeasement 148–50, 169
Ashley, W. J. 26, 45, 58, 62–3, 65, 77,
    239
Ashridge 9, 135–7, 139–40, 143,
    145–6, 150–1, 154–5
Asquith, H. H. 19, 35, 44, 52
Assheton, R. 12, 154, 219–20
Attlee Government 11, 169, 217–19

Baldwin, S. 9–10, 72, 94, 114, 132,
    141–2, 145, 147, 151–2, 269
Balfour, A. J. 5–6, 18–41, 81, 239,
    251
Ball, S. 44
Balliol College 43–5, 72, 93
Banbury, F. 239
banking sector 162–8, 178–80, 188,
    205–11
Bank of England 163, 171, 205–10
Barker, E. 152, 262
Beaverbrook, Lord 109, 189
Benn, A. 238
Benn, E. 257
Bentham, J. 251
Beveridge Report 10, 169–70, 218–19,
    222, 243
Beveridge, W. 75, 77, 169, 226, 273
Bevin, E. 100–1
Biffen, J. 229
Bigland, A. 6
bimetallism 24
Birch, N. 176, 192, 197, 203, 208,
    252
Birkenhead, Lord 7, 114, 128–9
Bledisloe, Viscount 125, 129
Bligh, T. 157
Bloomsbury Group 138
Blyton, W. J. 148
Bolshevism 120, 126, 136

Booth, C. 62, 77, 83
Boothby, R. 8, 191, 209, 242, 263
Bosanquet, B. 43, 54
Boutwood, A. 16, 46–56, 67, 70
Boyd-Carpenter, J., 196, 229, 249,
    254
Boyle, E. 229, 249, 277
Bradley, F. H. 43–4
Braine, B. 229
Bridgman, W. C. 130
British Constitutional Association
    (BCA) 7, 257
Brittain, H. 100
Brooke, H. 11
Broughton, U. 135–6
Bryant, A. 8–9, 136–8, 141–55
Buchan, J. 3, 129, 142, 153
Burke, E. 256, 259
Butler, R. A. 11, 144, 156, 198,
    205–6, 218–20, 243, 246,
    253–4, 260, 284
Butterfield, H. 285

Cairncross, A. 157
Carlton Club 114, 120, 129–30, 139
Cecil, Lord Hugh 7–8, 36, 55, 239,
    257, 268, 272, 288
Cecil, Lord Robert 20, 40, 124–5,
    128, 239, 257
Centre for Policy Studies (CPS) 4, 215,
    217, 258
Chalmers, R. 24
Chamberlain, A. 10, 73, 114, 118–19,
    121–2, 126–30
Chamberlain, J. 19, 32–40, 61, 65–6,
    81, 93, 90
Chamberlain, N. 9, 148, 226, 242,
    273
Chamberlain, Norman 73, 85
Chanak Crisis (1922) 116
Churchill, W. S. 99, 117, 172, 220,
    236
Clarke, D. 11, 244, 286
Clissett, W. 127
Cobbold, Lord 206
Cobden, R. 34, 251, 286
Coefficients' Club 66
Committee of London Clearing Banks
    (CLCB) 206–7

Compatriots' Club 6, 65, 67, 74, 82, 86
Comyn-Platt, T. 74
Confederacy 73
Confederation of British Industry (CBI) 233
Connolly, J. 235
Conservative Central Office (CCO) 12, 129, 139, 141–3, 155, 194, 242, 247, 255
Conservative Philosophy Group 4
Conservative Political Centre (CPC) 11–12, 156, 243, 246
Conservative Research Department (CRD) 9, 11, 14, 187, 197, 220, 226, 231, 242, 246, 252, 264, 286
Corfield, F. 229, 233
Council of Prices, Productivity and Income 198
Cowdray, Lord 124
Cowie, D. 139
Crawford and Balcarres, Earl 114, 129
Croft, H. Page 129
Cromer, 1st Earl 239
Cromer, 3rd Earl 178
Crooks, W. 91
Cunningham, W. 26, 45, 58–62, 65

Davidson, J. C. C. 99
Davies, J. 233
Davis, D. 127
Dawson, G. 9
Devonshire, 8th Duke 33
Dicey, A. V. 257
Diehards 55–6, 115–16, 129
Docker, D. 90
Douglas, J. 226, 246
Dyer, General 116

Eccles, D. 180, 210, 212
Eden, A. 236, 243
Eden, J. 231, 233
education 10, 18, 121
Elliot, W. 3, 8, 130–1
Ellis, G. 143–4
empire 5, 8, 30, 34, 37, 40, 66–70, 79–86, 94, 109, 115–16, 136, 189–90, 285
English Mistery 151
Europe (EEC, EU) 13, 155, 189–90, 227

Fabian Society 4, 11, 54, 66–7, 137, 156
Farrer, T. H. 24

Federation of British Industry (FBI) 163, 181, 183, 265
Feiling, K. 7, 140, 280, 285, 287
Fell, A. 6
Fisher, H. A. L. 121
Forester, Lord 123
Foster, H. S. 119, 126
Foxwell, H. S. 26, 61, 77
Foyle, C. 141, 145
Foyle, W. 141
Foyle, W. & G. 140, 145
Franks, O. 205, 210
Fraser, M. 187, 286
free trade 20–1, 28–41
friendly societies 86–7, 273, 276, 278

Garvin, J. L. 65, 82, 141–2
Geddes Axe 124
General Strike 99, 101, 158–9, 269–70
Gibbs, P. 139, 141, 148, 150–1
Gilmour, I. 3–4, 250, 252, 287
Gladstone, W. E. 18, 132, 157, 172, 255
Gold Standard 96, 106
Gollancz, V. 9, 139–40
Gray, J. 290
Green, T. H. 16, 42–6, 50, 93
Greenleaf, W. H. 241, 259

Hailsham, Lord 11, 191, 194, 197, 218, 223, 243–4, 247, 252, 260–1, 266, 271, 274
Halifax, Lord 9, 142, 150
Hall, R. 200, 203, 205–6, 210
Hamilton, E. 32
Hamilton, Lord G. 33
Harrod, R. 157, 176
Hatherton, Lord 123
Hawtrey, R. 77, 204
Hayek, F. A. 220, 250, 258–9
Hearnshaw, F. J. C. 140
Heath, E., 14, 192, 211, 214, 227, 229, 231–2, 234–5, 248–9, 271, 277
Heathcoat-Amory, D. 208–9
Hegel, G. W. F. 50, 63, 93
Henderson, H. 78
Herbert, A. 257
Hewins, W. A. S. 26, 45, 55, 61, 63, 65, 76, 78, 81–2, 93, 239
Hills, J. W. 45, 65, 86, 239
Hilton, J. 153
Hinchingbrooke, Viscount 189, 252
Hindlip, Lord 123
historical economists 26–31, 57–64
Hitler, A. 147–8

Hoare, S. 142
Hobhouse, L. T. 44, 66
Hobson, J. A. 44
Hogg, Q., *see* Hailsham
Home, Lord 227, 229, 235
Horne, R. 72, 114
Hoskins, General R. 154
Hughes, C. 127
Hunt, R. 21
Hutchinson, W. G. 142

Idealism 16, 42–71, 93–4
Imperial Maritime League 7
industrial relations 8, 99–103, 158,
    269–70
industrial reorganization 97–103, 110,
    158–63, 169, 181–2
industrial transference 102–3
inflation 12, 106, 134, 168, 175–9,
    192–213, 215, 224, 233
Inns of Court Society 226, 271
Institute for Economic Affairs (IEA)
    14, 229
Ireland 5, 18–19, 23, 69, 115–16, 120
Iwan-Muller, E. B. 22

Jefferies, J. M. N. 138
Jenkin, P. 224
Jerrold, D. 138–9, 141, 150
Jones, H. 43
Joseph, K. 4, 212, 215, 217, 234, 238,
    250, 255, 259, 276
Jowett, B. 43–4, 93
Joynson-Hicks, W. 10, 105

Kant, I. 93
Keynes, J. M. 16, 76–7, 95, 104–5,
    107, 110–11, 157, 163–9, 176,
    193, 197
Keynesianism 16, 104, 110–11,
    176–81, 192, 200, 204, 215,
    217
Kidd, B. 64–5, 67
Kilmuir, Lord 238

Labour party 3, 8–9, 94–5, 104, 118,
    120, 126, 135, 171–2, 221, 238,
    275
land reform 5, 87–90, 93
Laski, H. 139
Lawson, N. 213, 235
Law, A. B. 21, 61, 88, 114–15,
    118–19, 122, 127, 239
Law, R. 221
Left Book Club (LBC) 9, 139–40,
    142–3, 145–6, 149, 152, 156
Liberal Land Campaign 88–9

Liberal party 3, 9, 42, 45, 50, 88,
    114–15, 119–20, 130–2, 221,
    227, 252–5
Liberalism 42–3, 50, 53, 171–2, 189,
    221, 252–60, 262, 287; *see also*
    New Liberalism
Liberal Unionism 126, 129
Liberty and Property Defence League
    (LPDL) 257
List, F. 62–3, 76
Liverpool, Lord 256
Lloyd George, D. 16, 55, 88, 105–6,
    108, 114–15, 117–18, 120, 123,
    127–8, 130, 226
Lloyd, S. 179–80, 182–3
Loder, J. 8, 191, 242
London School of Economics (LSE)
    45, 73, 75–6, 78, 82, 93
Lonsdale, Earl 20
Ludovici, A. 141
Lyttelton, O. 154

Macdonald, J. R. 64
Mackinder, H. 66
Maclachlan, D. 157
Macleod, I. 152, 222, 225–6, 271,
    277, 284
Macmillan, H. 8, 13, 16, 157–99, 201,
    203–10, 212, 218, 223–4,
    226–7, 235–6, 242, 248–9,
    253–4, 263–7, 273, 275
MacQuisten Bill (1926) 269–70
Major, J. 2
Makins, R. 206
Malmesbury, Earl 73
Marconi Scandal 117
Martell, E. 230
Marx, K. 148
Maude, A. 222, 229
Maudling, R. 180, 183, 226, 229,
    232, 245
Maxse, L. J 21, 120
Medium Term Financial Strategy
    (MTFS) 211, 213
mercantilism 80–2
Middle Class Alliance (MCA) 12, 134,
    194, 223–4
Middle Class Defence League 7
middle classes 7, 12, 122–5, 132–4,
    139, 175, 187, 193–4, 220–1,
    223, 227, 237–8
Middle Class Union (MCU 122–5,
    133
Midland Bank 179, 188
Mill, J. 251, 286
Mill, J. S. 2, 3, 64, 251, 286
Milner, A. 7, 44, 65–7, 75, 84–5, 93

Monckton, W. 9, 179, 225
Mond–Turner talks 112
monetarism 16, 166, 176, 192, 200–1,
    203–4, 211, 213, 215, 238
Morgan, J. H. 136
Morpeth, Earl 20
Myrdal, G. 289

National Book Association (NBA) 4,
    141–56
National Economic Development
    Council (NEDC) 182–5, 190,
    266, 271
National Economic Development
    Office (NEDO) 182, 185, 227
National Incomes Commission (NIC)
    184–5, 190, 227
National Liberals 172, 221, 253
National Party 118
National Recovery Administration
    (NRA) 108
National Service League 7
National Union of Conservative and
    Unionist Associations (NUCA)
    11, 19, 21, 34, 94, 115, 119–20,
    122, 126–7, 131, 135, 193, 214
nationalization 170–1, 217, 224–7,
    230–1, 244–5
Navy League 7
New Deal 75, 108
New Liberalism 5, 42–3, 62, 64–6, 70,
    112, 117, 120, 172, 257
Next Five Years 163, 242
Norman, M. 78, 97–9
North Atlantic Treaty Organization
    (NATO) 189
Northam, R. 141, 150, 155
Northcote, S. 131–2

Oakeshott, M. 281–5, 289
Olivier, S. 44
One Nation 13, 155, 222, 247–8,
    250–1, 253, 266, 274–6
Organization for Economic
    Cooperation and Development
    (OECD) 181
Ormsby-Gore, W. 55
Ottawa Agreement 109
Oxford Extension Movement 45

Paish, G. 77
Parkinson, C. 217
Parliament Act (1911) 55
Paul, H. 9
Peacock, E. R. 78, 97–8, 107
Peel, R. 256
Penguin Books 144

People's Budget 52, 55, 91, 117
People's League for the Defence of
    Freedom (PLDF) 12, 34, 223–4,
    226–7, 230
People's Union for Economy 124
Petrie, C. 140–1, 150
Phillips, A. W. 198, 215
Plowden Committee 177, 196
Plowden, E. 205
Policy Committee on the Future of the
    Social Services (PCFSS) 196,
    224–6, 244–7
Policy Committee on the Nationalized
    Industries (PCNI) 224–7, 244–5
Policy Group on the Nationalized
    Industries (PGNI) 230
Policy Study Group (PSG) 198, 201,
    224–5, 227, 244
Poole, O. 184, 213
Powell, J. E. 14, 152, 176, 192, 197,
    203–4, 208, 222, 226, 228–9,
    246, 248–9, 267, 274, 276, 283,
    286, 288
Price, H. A. 194
Price, L. L. 26, 45, 61–2, 65
public works 110, 112, 164–5

Quinton, A. 281, 283

Radcliffe Committee 178–9, 204,
    208
Rainbow Circle 64
Resale Price Maintenance (RPM)
    184–5, 190, 227
Ridley, N. 217, 230–1, 233, 258
Right Book Club (RBC) 9, 140–3,
    145–6, 150, 152–5
Ritchie, C. T. 32–3, 73, 78–9
Ritchie, D. G. 43
Robbins, L. 200, 203
Roberts, A. 217
Roosevelt, F. D. 75, 108
Rousseau, J.-J. 141, 251, 286
Rowan, T. L. 205

Salisbury, 3rd Marquis 18, 22–3,
    131–2
Salisbury, 4th Marquis 89, 93, 125,
    127
Salvidge, A. 130
Samuel, H. 44, 99
Sanders, J. S. 22
Schmoller, G. 62, 76
Seeley, J. R. 67
Selborne, Earl 21, 55, 124
Seliger, M. 2
Selsdon Group 235–6

Selsdon Park/Selsdon Man 14, 231–2, 234, 238
Serge, V. 148
Shanks, M. 181
Short, W. S. 22
Sidgwick, H. 23
Simon, J. 226
Skelton, N. 8, 191
Smith, F. E., *see* Birkenhead
Smithers, W. 171
Snowden, P. 117
Social Democratic Party (SDP) 238–9
Socialism 5, 8–9, 12, 53, 61, 70, 89, 98–9, 109, 112, 114, 117–18, 120–2, 125–6, 129–32, 135–6, 138–40, 155, 172–3, 175, 212, 224, 253–5, 265, 287
social policy 75–83, 85–93, 160–1, 187, 212–13, 218–22, 272–3
Soviet Union 120
Spencer, H. 42, 65, 251, 257
Squire, R. 73, 85
Stanley, O. 9, 191, 242
Steel-Maitland, A. 9, 16, 45, 62, 68, 72–113, 118, 124–5, 128, 130–1, 239, 263, 265, 270
Stott College 135
Strakosch, H. 77
Street, C. 146
sweated trades 85–6, 268
Swinton College 13, 155

tariff reform 5–6, 19–41, 61–2, 72, 75, 78–89, 92, 94–6, 109, 160, 188, 262–3
Tariff Reform League 7
taxation 52, 55, 83–4, 120–5, 132, 216, 219, 224
Tebbit, N. 234, 255
Teeling, W. 140–1, 148–50
Teviot, Lord 253
Thatcherism 4–5, 16, 193, 211–28, 248, 250, 252–8, 271, 277–8, 287–8, 290
Thatcher, M. 4, 192–3, 211, 214–16, 249, 252, 255, 258, 267–8, 276–8, 289–90
Thorneycroft, P. 175–6, 192–211, 213, 224

Tory Reform Group 243, 252
Toynbee, A. 44
Toynbee Hall 44–5
Trade Boards Act (1909) 86, 268
Trade Disputes Act (1927) 269–70
trade unions 12, 62, 186–7, 216–17, 225–6, 268–72
Treasury View 105–6, 110
Trevelyan, G. M. 146
Tryon, G. C. 6
TUC 182, 184
Tuke, A. 205

unemployment 8, 18, 72, 77–9, 82–3, 94–6, 103–10, 158–60, 177, 187, 236
Unionist Social Reform Committee (USRC) 6, 45, 62, 67, 75, 86, 88–9, 95, 239, 251, 269, 272
Urban, G. 289
Uthwatt Report 10

Wagner, A. 62, 76
Walker-Smith, D. 141
Walpole, H. 153
Watkinson, H. 212
Webb, S. 66
Weir, Lord 100–1
Welfare State 12, 172, 176, 187, 212–13, 216, 218–22, 224, 226, 246, 272–3
Wemyss, Earl 257
White, R. J. 261
Willetts, D. 278, 280
Williams, H. 171
Willink, H. 243
Willoughby de Broke, Earl 52, 55
Wilson, A. 140–1, 149–50
Wilson, Harold 176, 249
Wilson, Henry 115
Wilson, L. 124, 129
Wood, E., *see* Halifax
Woolacott, W. J. 127
Woolf, V. 153
Woolton, Lord 220, 253
Wyndham, G. 70

Yeats-Brown, F. 138, 140–1, 149–50
Young, Lord 234